FUNDAMENTALS
OF PROGRAMMING
IN BASIC

FUNDAMENTALS OF PROGRAMMING IN BASIC

Robert C. Nickerson
San Francisco State University

Little, Brown and Company
Boston   Toronto

Library of Congress Cataloging in Publication Data

Nickerson, Robert C
  Fundamentals of programming in BASIC

  Includes index.
  1. BASIC (Computer program language) I. Title.
QA76.73.B3N52   001.64′24   82–15213
ISBN 0–316–60646–4   AACR2

Library of Congress Catalog Card No. 82–15213

ISBN 0-316-60646-4

9 8 7 6 5 4

HAM
Published simultaneously in Canada
by Little, Brown & Company (Canada) Limited

Printed in the United States of America

To Lisa

CONTENTS

*Sections marked with an asterisk describe only nonstandard features of BASIC.

PREFACE

The purpose of this book is to introduce the reader to computer programming and the BASIC language. Computer programming is the process of developing a computer-based procedure to solve a problem. BASIC is a computer language that is commonly used to implement the procedure. This book not only describes the characteristics of BASIC but also explains the process of program development. As a result the reader gains a *general* understanding of programming and a *detailed* knowledge of BASIC.

The features of BASIC covered in the book are those in ANS minimal BASIC along with common extensions found in other versions of the language. The text adheres strictly to the ANS version for the fundamental characteristics of the language. Virtually all of ANS minimal BASIC is described. Additional features that are not available in the ANS version are discussed where appropriate. These nonstandard items are drawn primarily from DEC BASIC-PLUS and Dartmouth BASIC 7. Any section or subsection that describes only such features is marked with an asterisk and may be skipped without loss of continuity. The table on the next page lists the nonstandard features and the sections in which they are discussed.

The language characteristics are covered in conjunction with the program development process. The emphasis is on structured programming. Basic program structure is discussed early with complete chapters on decision logic (Chapter 4) and loop control (Chapter 5). The programming process is covered in detail in Chapter 7 where program structure, style, refinement, testing, and documentation are examined. The use of subroutines in the top-down design and development of large programs is explained in Chapter 12. Upon completion of

Nonstandard Features Covered in the Text

Feature	Section
IF statement variations	4-3
Structured decision statements (IF/IFEND)	4-4
WHILE loops (DO WHILE/LOOP)	5-2
PRINT USING statement with numeric variables	6-4
PRINT USING statement with string variables	9-1[†]
String inequality	9-2[†]
String functions (substrings, concatenation)	9-3
One-dimensional string arrays	10-5
Two-dimensional string arrays	11-1[†]
Matrix operations	11-2
User-defined string functions	12-1[†]
Multiple line functions	12-2
ON-GOSUB statement	12-3[†]
Subprograms	12-4
Sequential file processing	13-2
Random access file processing	13-3
Chaining	13-4

[†]Feature is covered in a *subsection* within this section.

the book the reader should be able to systematically develop well-structured, understandable, and correct programs in BASIC.

No previous exposure to computers or programming is necessary to understand the book. All necessary background material is covered in the first chapter. Every effort has been made to minimize the need for a specialized mathematical background. All of the examples and most of the problems have been drawn from situations that the reader will readily recognize. A more than adequate prerequisite is a year of high school algebra.

The book is organized into three parts. The first part, consisting of Chapters 1 and 2, introduces the background material necessary to understand programming in BASIC. Chapters 3 through 7, comprising the second part, present the main elements of BASIC and develop fundamental programming methodology. Advanced BASIC features and programming are discussed in the third part, which consists of Chapters 8 through 13. With some exceptions, the material in these advanced chapters can be covered in any order.

Computer applications are emphasized throughout the book. Sample programs illustrate many common uses of computers. Programming problems provide additional examples of computer applications.

Since BASIC is designed for use on interactive computers, emphasis is placed on the design of interactive programs. Early examples demonstrate the characteristics of such programs. Interactive program design is described in detail in Chapter 6. The design of large "menu-driven" programs is covered in Chapter 12.

A number of features make the text especially useful for instruction. These include the following:

- The book is designed so that the reader can begin working with the computer as soon as possible. Computer exercises at the ends of Chapters 1 and 2 require the reader to become familiar with the available computer facilities. The first complete programs can be written after finishing Chapter 3.

- Many examples and illustrative programs are provided throughout the book. The examples are nonmathematical in nature and are oriented toward applications that the reader can readily understand.

- Each chapter contains questions to review the material covered in that chapter. The answers to many of the review questions are found in Appendix C.

- Chapters 3 through 13 each contain a substantial number of programming problems. Most of the problems require only a minimal mathematical background and emphasize nontechnical fields including business and the social sciences. In addition, a number of problems will be of interest to math, science, and engineering students. The programming problems range in difficulty from relatively easy to very difficult and challenging. Test data is provided with most problems.

- BASIC syntax is summarized in Appendix A. Both the language elements of ANS minimal BASIC and the extensions described in the text are covered.

- Flowcharting is described in Appendix B. This allows the instructor to discuss this material at the most appropriate time. All flowcharts are keyed to program examples in the book.

An instructor's manual is available that contains teaching suggestions, course schedules, chapter notes, answers to review questions, test questions and answers, and overhead transparency masters for a number of illustrations from the text.

The ideas in a book such as this always come from many sources. I am grateful to the many professors, writers, colleagues, and students who have contributed in some way to this book. My special appreciation goes to Jack Yuen who read the entire manuscript and to Arturo Salazar for his comments on some of the material.

Finally, I would like to thank my wife, Betsy. As always she played a significant role in the writing process, serving as editor, typist, critic, and companion.

R. C. N.

FUNDAMENTALS
OF PROGRAMMING
IN BASIC

1

COMPUTERS
AND PROGRAMS

Computers are devices used to solve problems. The process of preparing a computer to solve a problem is called programming. This book explains a particular type of computer programming. However, before we can understand the programming process in detail, we should become familiar with a few background ideas. In this chapter the basic concepts necessary to begin studying programming are discussed.

1-1. COMPUTERS

Any calculating device can be called a "computer". For example, adding machines, slide rules, and pocket calculators are all "computers" because each calculates or computes. However, normally the word "computer" is not used for these devices. Instead, we call something a *computer* if it has three distinguishing characteristics.

First, a computer is electronic, that is, it calculates by electrical means. We are not concerned here with how this is done, but an important consequence of this characteristic should be mentioned. Because a computer calculates by electrical means, it can perform its calculations at a very high speed. Thus, modern computers are able to do hundreds of thousands of operations (such as additions and subtractions) in a second.

The second distinguishing characteristic of a computer is that it has the ability to "remember" things. We call the things that a computer can remember *data*. Data†is facts, figures, numbers, and words that are

---

†The word "data" is most correctly used as a plural noun. The singular of data

1

important to the problem being solved. A computer can remember or, more correctly, *store* data for immediate or future use.

The final characteristic that distinguishes a computer from other calculating devices is its ability to remember and follow a set of instructions that tells it how to solve a problem. Such a set of instructions is called a *program*. The program is prepared by a person, called a *programmer*, who is familiar with the different things that a computer can do. Once the program is prepared, it is given to the computer in a form that the computer can understand and *stored* along with the data to be used by the program. Then the instructions in the program are performed, or *executed*, automatically by the computer.

The process of preparing computer programs is called *programming*, and this book explains one commonly used way of programming computers. However, before we can describe programming in detail, we must have an understanding of the physical organization of a computer.

1-2. THE ORGANIZATION OF A COMPUTER

As explained in the previous section, computers are distinguished from other calculating devices by their electronic, data storage, and stored program characteristics. The physical organization of a computer, however, is more complex than might appear from this discussion. One way of viewing the organization of a computer is shown in Fig. 1-1. In this diagram, boxes represent different components of the computer, and lines with arrowheads show the paths that data and instructions can take within the computer. In this section we describe each of the computer components shown in Fig. 1-1.

There are five basic components in most computers. These are the input device, the output device, the internal storage, the processor, and the auxiliary storage. Sometimes the internal storage and processor together are called the central processing unit, or CPU.

Input and Output Devices

An *input device* is a mechanism that accepts data from outside the computer and transforms the data into an electronic form understandable to the computer. The data that is accepted is called *input data*, or simply *input*. For example, one common way of entering input data into a computer is to type in the data using a typewriter-like *keyboard*. The keyboard in this case is an input device. Each time a key is pressed, the electronic form of the symbol on the key is sent to the computer. Figure 1-2 shows two examples of keyboard input devices.

---

is "datum." However, people commonly use the word data in a singular rather than plural sense. We will follow the usual practice in this book.

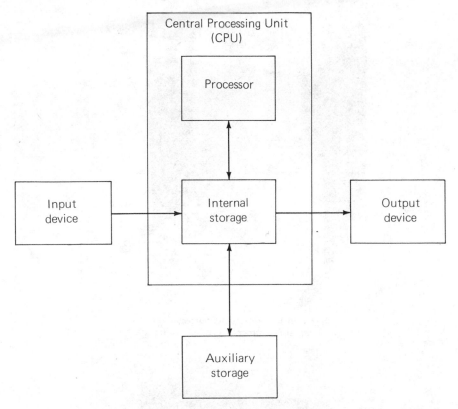

FIGURE 1-1.   The organization of a computer.

An *output device* performs the opposite function of an input device. An output device transforms data from its internal, electronic
form to a form that can be used outside the computer. The data that
results is called the *output data*, or simply the *output*, from the computer. For example, one of the most common forms of output is a
printed document or report. We often call this type of output computer
"print out". Such output is produced by a device called a *printer*. In the
printer, data from the computer is transformed into printed symbols
and a paper copy of the output is produced. Figure 1–2(a) shows an
example of a printer that prints one character at a time like a typewriter. This type of printer is called a *character printer*. Instead of being
printed on paper, output is sometimes displayed on a TV-like screen.
Such a video display unit is called a *CRT*, for *cathode ray tube* (another
name for a TV tube). Figure 1–2(b) shows an example of a CRT.

Usually a keyboard input device is combined with a character
printer or a CRT to form a combined input/output (or *I/O*) device.
Such a unit is often referred to as a *terminal*. Figure 1–2 shows two
types of terminals — a printing terminal and a video display terminal.

There are other types of I/O devices besides keyboards, character

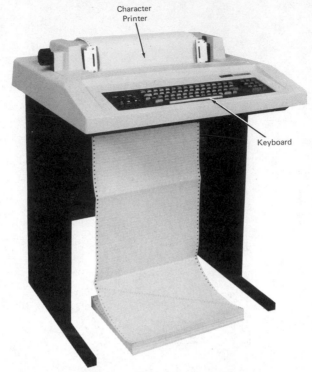

(a) A printing terminal. (Courtesy of
Digital Equipment Corp.)

(b) A video display terminal. (Courtesy of Lear Siegler, Inc.,
Data Products Division, Anaheim, CA)

FIGURE 1-2.   Computer terminals.

printers, and CRTs. For example, a common type of input device is one that reads the data punched into cards (i.e., "IBM" cards). This device is called a *card reader*. An example of a card reader is shown in Fig. 1-3. Also used are output printers that print one line at a time instead of just a character at a time. These are called *line printers* and they are much faster than character printers. Figure 1-4 shows a line printer.

Most computers have several input devices and several output devices attached at one time. For example, a typical medium-sized computer may have a card reader, a line printer, and a number of terminals for input and output. Some small computers, however, have only one input device and one output device (such as a terminal).

The Central Processing Unit

Between the input device and the output device is the component of the computer that does the actual computing or processing. This is the *central processing unit*, or *CPU* (refer to Fig. 1-1). Input data is transformed into an electronic form by the input device and sent to the central processing unit. In the CPU the input data is stored and used in calculations or other types of processing to produce the solution to the desired problem. After processing is completed, the results are sent to the output device, where the data is transformed into the final output.

The central processing unit contains two basic units that work to-

FIGURE 1-3.   A card reader. (Courtesy of IBM Corp.)

FIGURE 1-4.   A line printer. (Courtesy of IBM Corp.)

gether to perform the functions of the CPU—the internal storage and the processor.

The *internal storage* is the "memory" of the computer. It is in this device that data currently being processed is stored. Instructions in the program being executed are also stored in the internal storage. The internal storage of a computer is not the same as human memory. Like human memory, however, data and instructions can be put into the computer's internal storage and recalled at some time in the future.

The *processor* is the unit that executes instructions in the program. Among other things, the processor contains electronic circuits that do arithmetic and logical operations. A computer can do the basic arithmetic tasks that a human can do; that is, a computer can add, subtract, multiply, and divide. More complicated calculations, such as finding the square root of a number, are usually not built into the computer. Instead, such complex processing must be performed by an appropriate sequence of basic arithmetic operations. The logical operations that a computer can do are usually limited to comparing two numbers to determine whether they are equal or whether one is greater than or less than the other. Complex logical processing, such as that required to play a game like chess, is accomplished by long sequences of these simple operations.

The processor also contains electronic circuits that control the processing in the other parts of the computer. This is done by following the instructions in the program. As we have seen, the program is stored in the computer's internal storage. During processing, each instruction in the program is brought from the internal storage to the processor. The control circuits in the processor analyze the instruction and then send signals to the other units based on what the instruction tells the computer to do. The execution of one instruction may involve actions in any of the other parts of the computer. After executing an instruction, the next instruction in the programmed sequence is brought to the processor and executed. This continues until all the instructions in the program have been executed.

As an example of a simple computer program, assume that we wish to solve the problem of finding the sum of two numbers using a computer. To do this the computer must get the two numbers to be added from the input device, the numbers must then be added, and finally the sum must be sent to the output device so that we can see the result. Thus, a computer program to solve this problem would involve three instructions:

1. Get two input numbers.
2. Add the numbers.
3. Print the result.

The programmer would enter these instructions into the computer using the computer's input device; for example, the instructions could be keyed in using a terminal keyboard. The input device would then transfer the instructions to the computer's internal storage.

On a signal to start (perhaps from the person operating the computer) the first instruction in the program would be brought from the internal storage to the processor. Execution of the instructions would then proceed as follows:

1. Get two input numbers. The processor examines this instruction and sends a signal to the input device that causes the two numbers (input data) to be transferred to the internal storage. The second instruction is then brought to the processor.

2. Add the numbers. To execute this instruction the processor issues a signal to the internal storage that causes the two numbers to be sent to the arithmetic circuit in the processor. Then the numbers are added and the result is stored in the internal storage. The last instruction is then brought to the processor.

3. Print the result. The processor executes this instruction by sending a signal to the internal storage to transfer the result to the output device. Then the output device prints or displays the output data.

The central processing units of computers vary considerably in terms of the speed at which they can execute instructions, the size of their internal storage, and their cost. The smallest computers contain small, relatively slow processors that are called *microprocessors*. These computers have a small amount of memory and may cost only a few hundred dollars. Very large computers have high-speed processors and large internal storage capacity, and may cost millions of dollars.

Auxiliary Storage

The final component of a computer is the *auxiliary storage*, which stores data that is not currently being processed by the computer and programs that are not currently being executed. This is different from internal storage, which stores the data and instructions that are being processed at the time by the computer. Sometimes internal storage is called *primary storage* and auxiliary storage is called *secondary storage* or *mass storage*.

A common type of auxiliary storage is *magnetic disk*, which resembles a phonograph record. Information is recorded on the surface of the disk by using patterns of magnetic spots. Figure 1-5(a) shows an example of several magnetic disks stacked on top of each other to form a *disk pack*. The disks in this illustration are large, inflexible platters commonly called *hard disks*. Disks that are smaller and less rigid are called *floppy disks*. Figure 1-6(a) shows several floppy disks, each contained in a cardboard case. A *magnetic disk drive* is a device for recording data on magnetic disks and retrieving data from disks [see Figs. 1-5(b) and 1-6(b)].

Another type of auxiliary storage is *magnetic tape*, which is much like tape recorder tape [see Fig. 1-7(a)]. It comes in various size reels and even in the form of cassette tape. Data is recorded on the surface of the tape by patterns of magnetic spots. A *magnetic tape drive* is a device that records data on magnetic tape and also retrieves data from the tape [see Fig. 1-7(b)].

Most computers have several auxiliary storage devices attached at one time. For example, a computer may have four disk drives and two tape drives. Other types of auxiliary storage can also be used. However, magnetic disk and magnetic tape are the most common.

Computer Hardware and Software

Figures 1-8 and 1-9 illustrate typical computers described in this section. The computer in Fig. 1-8 has two terminals and several disk drives. (Actually, this size computer would probably have many more terminals.) Figure 1-9 shows a small computer with a keyboard, a CRT, a printer, and two floppy disk drives.

The physical equipment that makes up a computer system is called

(a) A magnetic disk pack.

(b) A magnetic disk storage unit with eight disk drives.

FIGURE 1-5. Magnetic disk storage. (Courtesy of IBM
Corp.)

hardware. Computer hardware consists of keyboards, printers, CRTs,
terminals, card readers, CPUs, disk drives, tape drives, and other pieces
of equipment. As we have seen, hardware is controlled through a set of
instructions called a program. In general, programs are referred to as
software. The software for a computer is any computer program used

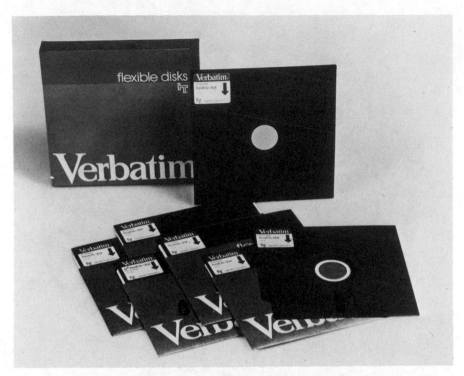

(a) Floppy disks. (Courtesy of Verbatim Corp.)

(b) Floppy disk drives. (Courtesy of Shugart Associates)

FIGURE 1-6.   Floppy disk storage.

(a) A magnetic tape reel.

(b) A magnetic tape drive.

FIGURE 1-7.　Magnetic tape storage. (Courtesy of IBM
Corp.)

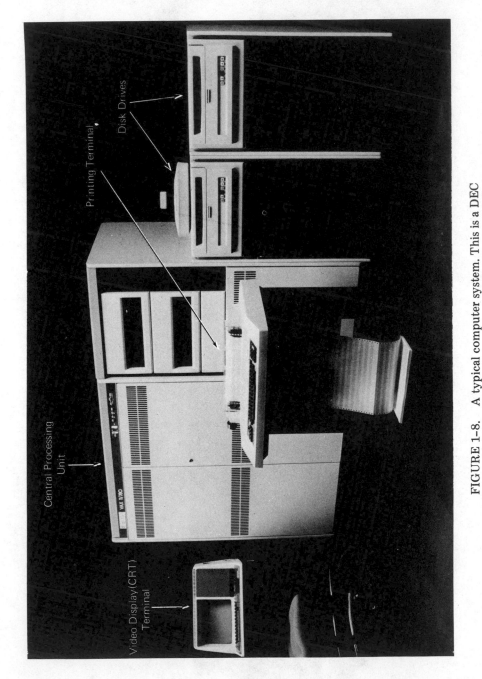

Central Processing Unit

Video Display (CRT) Terminal

Printing Terminal

Disk Drives

VAX 11/780

FIGURE 1-8. A typical computer system. This is a DEC VAX 11/780. (Courtesy of Digital Equipment Corp.)

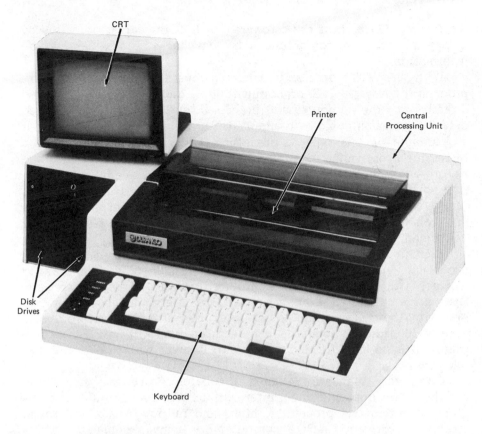

CRT

Printer

Central
Processing Unit

Disk
Drives

Keyboard

FIGURE 1–9.   A small computer system. This is a Durango
F-85. (Courtesy of Durango Systems, Inc.)

with the computer. A computer cannot operate without software. Thus, when we think of a computer system we must think of the hardware (equipment) *and* the software (programs).

1-3.   MODES OF PROCESSING

There are two basic ways, or *modes*, of processing data on a computer: batch processing and interactive processing. In *batch processing* all of the data that is to be processed is prepared in some form understandable to the computer prior to the actual processing. For example, all of the data may be punched into cards. Then the batch of data is processed by the computer and the resulting output is received in a batch. An example of batch processing is the preparation of the weekly payroll for a business. At the end of the week, each employee turns in a time sheet. The information from each sheet is punched into one or more cards. Once all of the cards are punched, the data is processed by a payroll program to produce the paychecks and other payroll information.

With *interactive processing* a human must interact with the computer at the time that the processing is done. Each set of data is entered directly into the computer and processed, and the output is received before the next input data is supplied. An airline reservation system is an example of this type of processing. When a customer requests a ticket for a particular flight, the reservation clerk enters the information directly into the computer using a terminal. The computer processing involves determining whether there is a seat available on the requested flight. The output comes back to the terminal almost immediately so that the customer knows whether or not the reservation is confirmed.

Sometimes the term *time-sharing* is heard instead of interactive processing. In fact, time-sharing is a mechanism used by a computer to interact with several different computer users at one time. With time-sharing the computer allows each user a small amount of time for data processing before going on to the next user. In effect, the computer "shares its time" among the people interacting with it. With time-sharing it is possible for many people to interact with the computer at one time.

Computers that are designed for batch processing often have punched-card input and line-printer output. When a computer is to be used for interactive processing, input and output is usually through terminals. Normally, such a computer has many terminals so that a number of people can interact with the computer. This usually requires time-sharing. Such is the case with the interactive computer system shown in Fig. 1-8. Some interactive systems have only one terminal and can interact with just one person at a time. In this case time-sharing is not needed. The computer in Fig. 1-9 is such a single-user, interactive system.

The type of programming discussed in this book is usually used with interactive computer systems. The examples emphasize interactive processing with terminal keyboard input and either printer or CRT output. However, most of the techniques and concepts are also applicable to batch processing.

1-4. COMPUTER LANGUAGES

In Section 1-2 we saw how a computer solves a problem by following the instructions in a program. The program must describe precisely everything that the computer has to do to solve the problem. The instructions in the program must be prepared in a form that the computer can understand and interpret. Every instruction must be prepared according to specific rules. If the rules are not followed, the computer will not be able to understand the instructions in the program.

When we program a computer, we are communicating with a machine. In general, when we want to communicate with someone or something we use a *language*. For human communication we use *natural languages* such as English and Spanish. When we want to communicate with a computer, we use a *computer language*.

To write a sentence in a natural human language, we form words and phrases from letters and other symbols. The way that we put together the sentence is determined by the grammar rules of the language. Depending on what words are used and how they are organized, the sentence has some meaning associated with it. With a computer language the rules that describe how to combine various symbols into recognizable patterns are called the *syntax* of the language. The meanings associated with different patterns of symbols are called the *semantics* of the language. For example, the *syntax* of a particular computer language may say that one type of instruction has the following form:

ln LET *variable = numeric expression*

That is, the instruction consists of a line number (abbreviated *ln*) followed by the word LET, then a *variable*, an equal sign, and a *numeric expression*. (Of course, we must know what a line number, a variable, and a numeric expression are in order to complete the instruction.) The *semantics* of the language tells us that this instruction means that the value of the expression on the right of the equal sign is to be assigned to the variable on the left. (In Chapter 3 we will study this instruction in detail.)

In this book we describe the syntax and semantics of the BASIC language. BASIC is just one of many computer languages. In fact, there are several groups of languages and many different languages in each group.

One group of languages is called *machine language*. Machine language is the language in which a computer actually does its processing. To a computer this type of language is a series of electronic impulses. A programmer expresses this language using binary numbers, that is, using a series of ones and zeros. Each type of computer has its own machine language, and since there are many different types of computers, there are many machine languages. However, the most important characteristic of machine language is that, for any particular computer, the machine language for that computer is the *only language that it can understand. Every program for that computer must be either written in its machine language, or written in another language and then translated into its machine language.*

We think of machine language as a low-level language because it is the basic language of a computer. Several higher levels of computer languages exist. These languages are called "high-level" because they are closer to natural human or mathematical language than to machine language. While there are many high-level languages, all high-level languages have one characteristic in common—any program that is written in a high-level language must first be translated into machine language before the program can take control of the computer. The translation process differs for each language, but fortunately for the programmer it is done automatically by the computer. (We will discuss the translation process in more detail in the next section.)

One of the most widely used high-level languages is called *BASIC*, which stands for Beginner's All-purpose Symbolic Instruction Code. Originally developed at Dartmouth College in the mid-1960s, BASIC was designed to make it easy for beginning students to learn programming. Its popularity and ease of use has resulted in its being applied to a wide variety of computer problem-solving situations. It is especially well suited for use on interactive computer systems and is probably the most commonly used language on small computers.

Since its original development, BASIC has undergone a number of modifications and improvements. Frequently a computer manufacturer would add features or make changes in the language with the result that BASIC on one computer would be slightly different from BASIC on another computer. As a consequence, many different "dialects" or *versions* of BASIC were developed. This created a problem since, in general, it was not possible to write a program in BASIC for one computer and then use it on a different computer without making some modifications.

In order to overcome this problem of incompatibility among different versions of BASIC, the American National Standards Institute (or ANSI) developed a standard version of BASIC in 1978. This version is known as *American National Standard* (or *ANS*) *minimal BASIC*. It contains the most commonly used elements of BASIC but not many of the advanced features that are available on a number of computers. Still, a program written in minimal BASIC should be able to be processed on a variety of computers without changes in the program.†

In this book we describe the characteristics of ANS minimal BASIC, as well as many features found in other versions of BASIC. When a particular characteristic of the language is not common to all versions of BASIC, this is noted in the text. Any section that describes only nonstandard features is marked with an asterisk. These variations may or may not apply to the computer being used. The appropriate computer reference manual must be consulted to determine the exact character-

---

†A complete description of minimal BASIC can be found in *American National Standard for Minimal BASIC*, X3.60–1978, published by the American National Standards Institute, Inc., New York.

istics of the language. Finally, Appendix A summarizes the fundamental elements of BASIC.

1-5. PROGRAM TRANSLATION AND EXECUTION

As we have seen, a program written in a high-level language must be translated into machine language before it can take control of the computer. For BASIC the translation process is called either *compilation* or *interpretation*, depending on how it is done. (The difference between these is not important here.) The translation is performed by a special translator program called a *compiler* or an *interpreter*. First a program is written in BASIC. Then the BASIC program is translated into an equivalent machine-language program using the translator program. Finally the machine-language program is executed by the computer.

As a simple analogy, assume that we have a business with one employee who speaks only Spanish and that we speak only English. Each day when the employee comes to work we must give him or her a list of what we want done during the day. Since we only speak English, we have to prepare the list in English and then have it translated into Spanish. For this purpose we hire an English-to-Spanish translator. This person speaks Spanish but also has an English-to-Spanish dictionary and a grammar book for English. With this information the translator is able to take our list of English-language instructions for the day's work and translate it into an equivalent list in Spanish. Then the Spanish-speaking employee can follow the instructions in the list, performing the tasks that we want done. This process is illustrated in Fig. 1-10.

Basically the same idea lies behind the translation and execution of a BASIC program. The steps are shown in Fig. 1-11. The BASIC program that is prepared by the programmer is called the *source program*. The programmer usually enters the source program into the computer by typing it on a terminal keyboard. Then the translator program (which is a machine-language program) translates the BASIC program into machine language. The resulting machine-language equivalent of the source program is called the *object program*. After translation, the object program is executed. This often involves getting input data, using the data in calculations and other types of processing, and producing output.

Although the translation of a BASIC program into an object program may seem complicated, to a large extent it is handled by the computer. Most programmers never need see their object programs. Instead, the programmer prepares the BASIC source program and the data, and the computer automatically does everything else. It is impor-

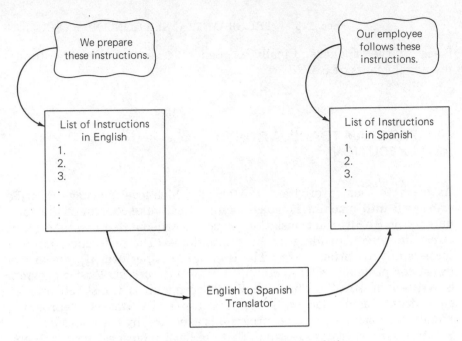

FIGURE 1-10. English-to-Spanish translation.

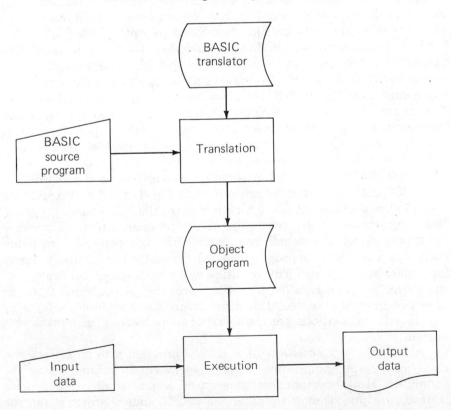

FIGURE 1-11. BASIC translation and execution.

tant to remember, however, that this translation process is required for every BASIC program that is run on a computer.

REVIEW QUESTIONS

1. What are three characteristics that distinguish computers from other calculating devices?

2. What is a computer program?

3. Data to be processed by a computer is called _____.

4. The result produced by a computer is called _____.

5. One of the most common output devices for a computer is a _____.

6. A video display terminal uses a _____ for input and a _____ for output.

7. The unit of a computer that does the actual computing or processing is the _____.

8. What units of the computer are found in the CPU?

9. What happens during the execution of a program? Explain in terms of the units in the CPU.

10. What is the difference in function between internal storage and auxiliary storage?

11. Name two common devices that can be used for auxiliary storage.

12. What is the difference between computer hardware and software?

13. Explain the difference between batch processing and interactive processing. Give an example of each.

14. What is meant by time-sharing?

15. The rules that describe how the instructions of a computer language are formed are called the _____ of the language.

16. The meanings of the patterns of symbols in a computer language are called the _____ of the language.

17. What is the difference between a machine-language program and a high-level language program?

18. Can a program that is written in BASIC be processed on different types of computers? Explain.

19. Translation of a program written in a high-level langauge into machine language is called _____.

20. What is the difference between a source program and an object program?

COMPUTER EXERCISE

Investigate the computer that will be used to process the programs you prepare. Who manufactured the computer and what model is it? What input and output devices are available? What type of auxiliary storage is available? Is it a batch-processing system or an interactive system? (Some computers process in both a batch mode and an interactive mode.) What version of BASIC will you be using? What computer languages other than BASIC are available on the computer?

2

INTRODUCTION TO BASIC

The background concepts discussed in Chapter 1 provide a foundation for understanding computer programming. Most of these concepts apply to all computer languages. In this chapter we present an overview of the BASIC language without giving detailed descriptions of how to prepare programs. In later chapters we will explain the specific requirements of BASIC.

2-1. FUNDAMENTALS OF BASIC

Figure 2–1 shows a sample BASIC program. This program performs a simple calculation to find the total and average of three numbers. In the next section we will explain how this program works, but for now we are interested only in the language concepts illustrated in this program.

BASIC Statements

Each instruction in a BASIC program is called a *statement*. A BASIC statement tells the computer something about the processing

```
10 INPUT X,Y,Z
20 LET T=X+Y+Z
30 LET A=T/3
40 PRINT X,Y,Z,T,A
50 GO TO 10
60 END
```

FIGURE 2-1.   A sample program.

that is to be done in the program. In the sample program in Fig. 2–1, each line is a statement. A BASIC *program* is a sequence of BASIC statements that describes some computing process. To prepare a BASIC program, the programmer must know how to form statements in the BASIC language and what each statement means.

One of the fundamental rules of BASIC is that every statement must begin with a number called a *line number*. A line number can be any number between 1 and 9999. (Some versions of BASIC allow larger line numbers.) No two statements, however, can have the same number, and the numbers must be in *increasing* numerical order.

Besides these rules, there are no restrictions on line numbers. Thus, we can number the statements in a program 1, 2, 3, 4, . . . , or 10, 20, 30, 40, . . . (as in the sample program in Fig. 2–1), or 18, 37, 108, 256, ... The usual practice, however, is to number the statements by tens as in the sample program. The reason for using this approach is that it makes it easy to add statements to the program. For example, if we wish to add a new statement between lines 30 and 40, we can number it 35 and not change any other numbers. If the statements had been numbered by ones, we would have to renumber all statements following the new statement.

Another good practice is to make the line numbers in a program the same length; that is, all line numbers are either two digits, three digits, or four digits. This makes the program easier to read. If the program has fewer than ten statements, we start the numbers at 10 (e.g., 10, 20, 30, . . .). For longer programs we start the line numbers at 100 or 1000 (e.g., 100, 110, 120, . . .). We will see examples of programs with longer line numbers in later chapters.

After the line number in a BASIC statement, there must be at least one blank space and then a special word called a *keyword*. (In some versions of BASIC the space is optional; however, extra spaces can always be included.) The keyword identifies the statement and indicates what type of processing is to take place. In the sample program in Fig. 2–1, the keywords are INPUT, LET, PRINT, GO TO, and END. Each has a special meaning in BASIC. There must be at least one space after the keyword. (Again, this space is optional in some versions of BASIC.)

Constants, Variables, and Expressions

In addition to a keyword, a BASIC statement often contains constants, variables, and expressions. A *constant* is simply a number in a program (other than a line number). For example, 3, 6.5, –37, .0012, and –78.36 are constants that might appear in a program. In the sample program in Fig. 2–1, the number 3 in the statement numbered 30 is a

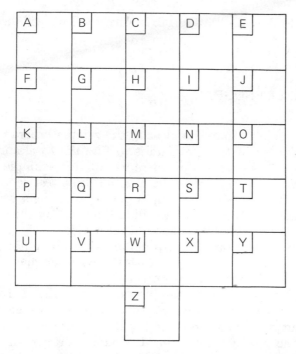

FIGURE 2-2.   Variables in BASIC.

constant. (The number 10 in statement 50 is *not* a constant, as we will see.)

A *variable* is a name that is used to refer to data in a program. For simplicity we might think of the internal storage of the computer as being composed of twenty-six boxes (see Fig. 2-2). Actually the boxes are called *storage locations*. Each storage location is identified by a letter of the alphabet, which is the variable, and each can store a single numeric value. By using the letter (i.e., the variable) for a storage location, we tell the computer to use the value in the location identified by the letter. Thus, if we tell the computer to add X and Y, we mean add the values found in the storage locations identified by X and Y. We can change the value in a location by using the letter (variable) for the location in such a way that the value is replaced. In the sample program in Fig. 2-1, the variables are X, Y, Z, T, and A.

We combine constants and variables with other symbols to form *expressions*. An expression is an instruction to the computer to perform some operation with data. Usually these are arithmetic operations such as addition, subtraction, multiplication, and division. In the sample program in Fig. 2-1, there are two expressions — X+Y+Z and T/3. The first expression tells the computer to add the values of the variables X, Y, and Z. The second expression tells the computer to divide the value of the variable T by the constant 3. In Chapter 3 we will discuss expressions in detail.

2-2. A SAMPLE PROGRAM

We can now begin to understand what the sample program in Fig. 2–1 does. The purpose of this program is to find the total and average of three numbers. The numbers might represent, for example, a student's scores on three tests. The input data is the three test scores. The program accepts the scores from an input device, adds the scores to get the total, calculates the average by dividing the total by three, and prints the results of the calculations on an output device.

The actual execution of the program on a computer is shown in Fig. 2–3. As we will see, the lines with the question marks contain the input data. The other lines are the output.

The first statement in the sample program in Fig. 2–1 is an INPUT statement. This statement instructs the computer to accept some data from an input device and to store the data in the computer's internal storage. By "accept" we mean that the data is brought from the input device to internal storage. The input device is a terminal keyboard. The input data is typed in and stored in the storage locations that are associated with the variables in the INPUT statement. These are the variables X, Y, and Z in the sample program.

The actual effect during execution of the INPUT statement is illustrated in the first line of Fig. 2–3. When the INPUT statement is encountered, a question mark is printed by the computer on the terminal printer or displayed on the CRT. After the question mark appears, the person at the terminal must type the input data—in this case, three numbers separated by commas. For example, in the first line of Fig. 2–3 the input data that is typed is the numbers 78, 95, and 82. The computer then stores these numbers in the storage locations in the computer's internal storage identified by the letters X, Y, and Z. Thus, after

```
? 78,95,82
   78              95          82          255           85
? 100,84,92
   100             84          92          276           92
? 78,65,72
   78              65          72          215           71.6667
? ^C
```

FIGURE 2–3.   The result of executing the sample
program.

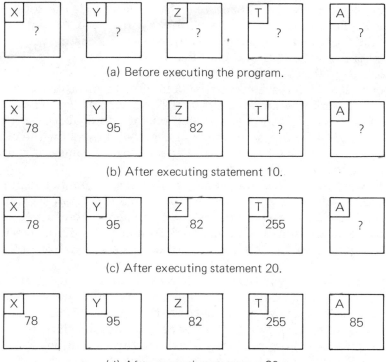

(a) Before executing the program.

(b) After executing statement 10.

(c) After executing statement 20.

(d) After executing statement 30.

FIGURE 2-4. Variables during the execution of the
sample program.

execution of the INPUT statement with the input data shown in Fig.
2-3, the value of the variable X is 78, the value of Y is 95, and Z is 82.

Following the INPUT statement in the sample program in Fig. 2-1
are two statements that perform calculations. These are called LET
statements. The first LET statement instructs the computer to add the
values of X, Y, and Z. The result of the calculation (i.e., the total)
is stored in the storage location identified by the letter T. The next
statement then tells the computer to divide the total just calculated by
three to obtain the average, which becomes the value of the variable
named A.

Figure 2-4 summarizes the execution sequence so far by showing
the values of the variables at different points in the program. Before the
program is executed, the values of the variables (X, Y, Z, T, and A) are
unknown. This is shown in Fig. 2-4(a). (Some versions of BASIC set
all variables to zero before executing the program.) After statement 10
(the INPUT statement) is executed with the data in the first line of
Fig. 2-3, the values of the variables are as shown in Fig. 2-4(b). Notice
that X, Y, and Z are equal to 78, 95, and 82, respectively (i.e., the
input data), but the values of T and A are unknown. After the first LET

25

statement (statement 20) is executed, the value of T is the total of X, Y, and Z. This is shown in Fig. 2–4(c). With the execution of the second LET statement (statement 30), the average is computed and stored in the storage location identified by the letter A [Fig. 2–4(d)].

Statement 40 in the sample program in Fig. 2–1 is called a PRINT statement. This statement causes the computer to print or display the values of all variables given in the PRINT statement. In this case the values of X, Y, Z, T, and A are printed on the terminal printer or displayed on the CRT. The second line in Fig. 2–3 shows how the output data is printed. Notice that the data is the current values of the variables shown in Fig. 2–4(d).

Following the PRINT statement is a GO TO statement. The number (10) in this statement is the line number of another statement in the program. The effect of execution of this statement is to cause the computer to go to the statement numbered 10 and to continue execution from that point. In this case, the program is repeated from the first statement.

Repeating the program causes the INPUT statement to be executed again. Thus, new input data must be supplied. This is shown in the third line of Fig. 2–3. The new input values are the numbers 100, 84, and 92. Prior to executing the INPUT statement for the second time, the values of all variables are those remaining from the first execution of the program [see Fig. 2–5(a)]. Then the new input data replaces the old values of X, Y, and Z as shown in Fig. 2–5(b). Notice that the values of T and A are as yet unchanged. Execution of statement 20 causes a new total to be calculated replacing the old value of T [Fig. 2–5(c)]. A new average is then calculated with statement 30, replacing the previous value of A [Fig. 2–5(d)]. Finally, the new results are printed as shown in the fourth line of Fig. 2–3.

The program is then repeated a third time with more input data. In fact, the program will continue as long as input data is supplied each time the INPUT statement is executed. The program stops only after a special control character is entered through the terminal. (This will be described in greater detail in the next section.)

There is one final statement in the sample program—the END statement. It contains only the keyword END. Every BASIC program must have an END statement as the last statement in the program; that is, the highest numbered statement in a program must be an END statement. The END statement indicates the end of the program to the computer. We will see later how it can be used to stop execution of a program.

These statements make up a complete BASIC program. The statements are performed in the order in which they are written. Thus, it is important that they be written in a logical order. For example, the order of the two LET statements cannot be reversed because the total is

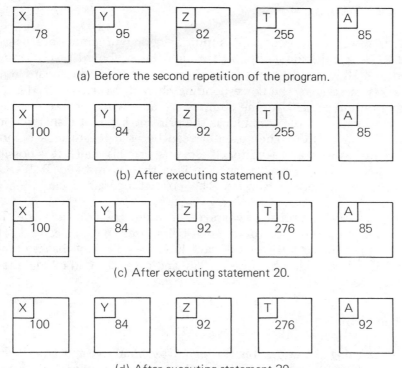

(a) Before the second repetition of the program.

(b) After executing statement 10.

(c) After executing statement 20.

(d) After executing statement 30.

FIGURE 2-5. Variables during the second repetition of
the sample program.

used in the calculation of the average and must therefore be calculated first.

Notice that most of the statements in the program are fairly easy to understand. This is especially true of the LET statements, which are written very much like mathematical formulas. Beginning with Chapter 3, we will explain in detail how to write different types of BASIC statements.

2-3. RUNNING A BASIC PROGRAM

The program in Fig. 2–1 is a complete BASIC program that can be executed by a computer. First the program is stored in the computer. Then the program is executed and input data is supplied. Finally, the output is produced. We often refer to this process as *running* the program. This section describes generally how a BASIC program is run on an interactive computer system. The details, however, will vary from one computer to another.

Using a Terminal

With interactive processing, input data and programs are usually typed directly into the computer through the keyboard of a terminal. Figure 2-6 shows a diagram of the keys on a typical keyboard. Each time a key is pressed, the corresponding character (i.e., letter, digit, or special symbol) is sent to the computer. Each keyed character is also printed on paper, if the terminal is the printing type, or displayed on a screen, if it is a CRT. The space bar can be used to advance without printing just as with a typewriter. If a typing error is made, it is possible to backspace by pressing a special key that is marked RUBOUT, DELETE, or something similar. The correct character can then be typed.

Only a certain number of characters can be typed on each line. The limit depends on the type of terminal being used, but typically it is 80 characters per line. At the end of each line, a special key that is usually marked RETURN *must* be pressed. This indicates the end of the line to the computer.

Logging In

Before using the computer through a terminal, we must perform a procedure called "logging in" or "signing on" to connect the terminal to the computer. The actual procedure that is used depends on the computer, but typically it involves pressing special keys on the keyboard or typing a certain word such as HELLO or LOGIN. Then an account number or user ID number is entered, followed by a special word called a password. (The account number and password are normally supplied by the computer center that operates the computer.) It is important to remember that after anything is typed into the computer, the RETURN key on the keyboard must be pressed. If the log-in procedure is followed correctly, the computer will usually respond by printing or displaying a message signifying that we can proceed. Sometimes just the word READY appears to indicate that the computer is ready for its next task.

After logging in, it is sometimes necessary to indicate that the BASIC language is going to be used. This is usually done by typing the word BASIC. Some computers automatically assume that BASIC will be used, in which case this step is not needed.

Various instructions can now be given to the computer. These instructions are called *system commands* and are different from BASIC statements. As we have seen, all BASIC statements begin with a line number. System commands, however, do not have line numbers. In addition, BASIC statements are executed only after all statements in

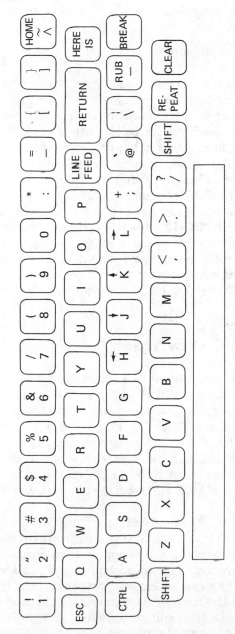

FIGURE 2-6. A terminal keyboard. (Courtesy of Lear Siegler, Inc., Data Products Division, Anaheim, CA)

the program have been entered, while system commands are executed immediately. There are a number of system commands, and the remainder of this section is devoted to explaining some of them.

Running an Existing Program

On occasion we may wish to execute an existing program. Perhaps another programmer has prepared a program that we want to use. Such a program would be stored in the auxiliary storage and given a name to identify it. However, a program can be executed only if it is in internal storage. Thus, we first have to bring the program into the internal storage of the computer. This is usually done by typing a system command such as OLD, GET, or LOAD followed by the name of the program. For example, assume that the program's name is PROGX. Then on one common computer we would use the command OLD PROGX to bring the old program marked PROGX into the computer's internal storage. We can now execute or run this program by typing the command RUN. During the execution of the program, we may have to supply input data. It is important to remember that input data should be separated by commas and that the RETURN key must be pressed after the data has been typed.

Entering and Running a New Program

If we wish to enter and run our own program, we begin by typing a command that clears out any old program in the internal storage and indicates that a new program is about to be entered. This command is usually the word NEW or SCRATCH. Following this we give the new program a name to identify it in the computer. Typically a program name can be no more than six or eight characters long. The name is sometimes typed after the word NEW (e.g., NEW PROGY), or a command such as the word NAME followed by the program name is used (e.g., NAME PROGY).

We can now begin to enter a BASIC program. Each line of the program is typed exactly as it is written. If typing mistakes are made, they can be corrected by backspacing and retyping. If an entire line is wrong, we can simply retype the line and the computer will replace the old line with the new one. A line can be erased completely just by typing the line number. Although the line numbers must be in increasing sequence, we can usually enter the lines out of sequence and the computer will rearrange the order. For example, we can first enter line 10, then line 30, and finally line 20. The computer will arrange the statements in the proper numerical sequence.

After we have entered part or all of the program, we can list the program on the printer or the CRT by using the system command LIST. Any errors that were corrected while the program was being entered will not appear in the listing.

To run the program we type the command RUN. This causes the computer to execute the statements in the program in sequence beginning with the first statement. While the program is running, we may have to supply input data (as in the sample program in Fig. 2-1). To stop the program from running (for example, when we do not want to enter any more input data), we use a special control character. On many computers this involves holding down a key marked CTRL (for control) and pressing the letter C (called a "control C"); this is shown in the last line of Fig. 2-3. With other computers we may press the BREAK or ESC (for escape) key to stop execution.

Saving a Program

If we wish to save a program for future use, we usually type the system command SAVE. This stores the program in auxiliary storage and identifies it by the name that we gave it earlier. (If a program is not saved, it will be lost when we disconnect the terminal from the computer or when we start another new program.) We can retrieve a saved program at some time in the future by using the OLD, GET, or LOAD command described above. If we want to destroy a previously saved program, we type a command such as UNSAVE, KILL, or PURGE followed by the name of the program.

Logging Out

After we have finished using the computer, we must disconnect the terminal. This is often called "logging out" or "signing off" and is usually done by typing the word BYE. After doing this, we must log in if we wish to use the computer again.

Summary of System Commands

Figure 2-7 shows an example of the printout that results from entering and running a program on a typical computer. In this figure, underlined parts are items that we enter; the other parts are typed by the computer. In the sequence shown in Fig. 2-7, we first log in with the required account number and password. Then we start a new program, giving it an appropriate name. While typing the program, we correct lines with errors by retyping the lines entirely (we will discuss error detection in the next section.) We then list the corrected version of the program. Next we run the program, supplying input data and getting output. Finally, we save the program for future use and log out.

```
HELLO

RSTS V06C-03
#12,34
Password: ABCD

Ready

NEW DEMO1

Ready


10 INPUT X,Y,Z
20 LET T=X+Y+Z
30 LET A=
?Syntax error at line 30

Ready


30 LET A=T/3
40 PRINT X,Y,Z,T,A
50 GO TO 10
60 END
LIST
DEMO1
10 INPUT X,Y,Z
20 LET T=X+Y+Z
30 LET A=T/3
40 PRINT X,Y,Z,T,A
50 GO TO 10
60 END

Ready

RUN
DEMO1
? 78,95,82
 78              95              82              255             85
? 76,39,84
 76              39              84              199             66.3333
? ^C

Ready

SAVE

Ready

BYE
```

FIGURE 2-7.   Entering and running a BASIC program.

The system commands that we have described here vary from one computer to another, although the basic functions performed are the same. In addition, there are usually many other commands that we have not discussed. The programmer will have to determine the exact form of each command for the computer being used.

2-4. ERROR DETECTION

In this description of the processing of a BASIC program, we have assumed that the program contains no errors. In fact, one of the greatest problems that a programmer faces is the detection and correction of errors. More often than not, the program does not complete its run successfully. It is the programmer's responsibility to locate and correct any errors in the program.

Errors can be detected in the processing of the program at three times — while entering the program, during execution, and after execution. The computer can detect errors that occur during the first two times, but only the programmer can detect errors after the program has executed.

Errors can be discovered by the computer while the program is being entered. These are usually errors that the programmer has made in the use of the language and are called *syntax errors*. For example, spelling a keyword incorrectly is a syntax error. When such an error is detected, a message that describes the errors is printed (see line 30 in Fig. 2–7). The message may appear immediately after the line that contains the error or it may come at the end of the program (after typing RUN). Even though an error has been detected, it usually cannot be corrected by the computer and the program will not be executed. The programmer must correct any syntax errors that are detected.

If the program has no syntax errors, it can be executed by the computer. During execution, other errors may appear. These are called *execution errors*. For example, attempting to divide a number by zero is an execution error. Detection of such an error causes the computer to print an error code or message and to stop executing the program.

The final type of error is detected only after the program has been run. If the output from the program does not agree with what is expected, there is a *logic error* in the program. For example, in the sample program in Fig. 2–1, if the first LET statement (statement 20) had been incorrectly written as

$$20 \text{ LET } T=X-Y-Z$$

then no syntax or execution error would be detected. However, the final output would be incorrect since the total of three numbers is found by adding the numbers, not subtracting them. This error is in the logic of the program. The computer cannot detect such an error since it cannot understand the logic of the program. It is the programmer's responsibility to check the results of processing and to correct any logic error that may be found.

An error in a computer program is called a *bug*. The process of locating and correcting bugs in a program is called *debugging*. Only after a program has been completely debugged can the programmer be reasonably certain that the program is correct.

2-5. A PREVIEW OF THE PROGRAMMING PROCESS

Although we have so far concentrated primarily on the BASIC language, an equally, if not more, important topic is the process of developing a computer program. As we stated at the beginning of Chapter 1, programming involves preparing a computer program to solve a problem. It is important to emphasize that programming is a problem-solving process; that is, given a particular problem, how do we develop a computer program that solves the problem? The process applies no matter which computer language is being used. In fact, many of the ideas apply to noncomputer problem solving. Thus, by studying the programming process we gain a better understanding of problem solving in general.

The first step in the programming process is to understand the problem to be solved. Understanding the problem involves determining the requirements of the problem and how these requirements can be met. The programmer must know what the program is required to do. This usually means understanding what output must be produced by the program and what computations must be performed. In addition, the programmer must determine what resources are available to meet these requirements. This includes determining the available input.

With an understanding of the problem, the programmer can begin to design a program to solve the problem. The sequence of steps that is necessary to solve the problem must be carefully planned. This program-designing activity does *not* involve writing the instructions in the program. Before this activity can start, the programmer must think through the solution procedure completely. The programmer sometimes writes down the solution procedure in rough notes in English or draws a diagram that represents the solution graphically. In Appendix B we discuss a tool that is sometimes used for program planning.

After the solution to the problem has been planned, the program can be written. This is called *coding* the program. The programmer uses his or her knowledge of the computer language, an understanding of the problem to be solved, and the program design determined previously.

With this background the programmer codes the program to solve the problem by writing the necessary computer language instructions on paper.

The next step is to test the program by running the program on the computer with some input data. The output produced by the program is then compared with the expected output and any discrepancy indicates an error. Testing the program in this manner will not necessarily find all the errors, but it will usually point out any serious problems with the program. The actual process of determining the correctness of a program involves much more than just testing the program on a computer. A program is correct because it makes sense logically. The programmer makes sure of this as he or she plans and codes the program.

Finally, the programming process is completed by bringing together all the material that describes the program. This is called *documenting* the program, and the result of this activity is the program's *documentation*. Included in the documentation is the program listing and a description of the input and output data. Documentation enables other programmers to understand how the program functions. Often it is necessary to return to the program after a period of time and to make corrections or changes. With adequate documentation it is much easier to understand a program's operation.

Throughout most of this book we describe the coding activity. We illustrate other activities in the programming process by discussing the development of sample programs. In Chapter 7 we examine the various aspects of program development in more detail.

REVIEW QUESTIONS

1. Each instruction in a BASIC program is called a _____.

2. Each statement in a BASIC program must begin with a _____.

3. What are keywords?

4. What is the difference between a constant and a variable?

5. What is the purpose of the LET statement?

6. The last statement in a BASIC program must be _____.

7. When a program is run on a computer, what must the computer have first, the program or the input data?

8. What is the function of system commands in an interactive processing system? Are they part of the BASIC language?

9. Explain the difference between syntax errors, execution errors, and logic errors.

10. Removing errors from a program is called _____.

11. What are the five steps in the programming process?

12. The process of writing on paper the instructions in a computer program is called ————————.

COMPUTER EXERCISES

1. Usually there are a number of games available on an interactive computer. For example, there are card and dice games, number and word guessing games, football, golf, and other sports games. A very popular game is called "Star Trek". In all of these games you "play" against the computer. Find out what games are available on the computer you are using. Log in and play one of the games for 15 to 30 minutes. Prepare a general outline of the steps that the *computer* must go through in playing the game.

2. The program shown in Fig. 2-1 is complete and can be run on a computer. In order to become familiar with the fundamental characteristics of BASIC along with the procedures for entering and running a program, this program should be processed on an actual computer. Log in and enter the sample program exactly as it is listed in Fig. 2-1. Any syntax errors that occur are the result of typing mistakes. Correct any lines that have errors. Then list the program. Next run the program with the input data given in Fig. 2-3. Be certain that the output is the same as that shown in Fig. 2-3. Finally, run the program with several additional sets of input.

3

ESSENTIAL ELEMENTS OF BASIC

When we write a computer program to solve a problem, we prepare a sequence of instructions for the computer to follow. There are many different sequences that can be used, depending on the problem to be solved. However, one *pattern* appears over and over again. This pattern is simply

$$input \longrightarrow process \longrightarrow output$$

That is, first the computer accepts some input data to be used in the problem solution. Then the processing and computation necessary to solve the problem using the input data is carried out. Finally, the output data that represents the results of the processing is produced.

For example, in Chapter 2 we saw a sample program that computes the total and average of three numbers. The first step in this program was to accept the three numbers (i.e., the input data). Then the processing involved calculating the total and average of the numbers. Finally, the results were printed out.

There are many other patterns that appear in computer programs, but this is one of the most common. In addition, the input, process, and output systems may each be quite complex, especially the process step.

In this chapter we describe the elements of BASIC that are essential for practically all programs. These elements include the statements necessary for data input and output, for numeric data processing, and for program repetition. In later chapters we will discuss various other types of processing that can be done in a BASIC program.

3-1. CONSTANTS AND VARIABLES

In Chapter 2 we introduced the ideas of constants and variables in a program. In this section we elaborate on these ideas and give detailed rules for constants and variables in BASIC.

Simple Constants

A *constant* is a number that is used in a program. A constant is formed from digits (0, 1, 2, . . . , 9) and may include a decimal point and possibly a plus or minus sign. For example, the following are valid constants in BASIC:

$$
\begin{array}{ll}
482.59 & 0.00056 \\
25 & +16 \\
-18 & 0.0 \\
+5.1083 & -128.9 \\
0 & 5280
\end{array}
$$

Note that a constant *cannot* contain a comma. Thus, the number 5,280 is not a valid constant in BASIC.

E-notation Constants

Sometimes it is necessary to write very large or very small constants. For example, we may wish to use the following constants in a program:

$$-128460000000000$$

$$0.000000000008203$$

While we can use constants such as these, it is tedious to write them. We therefore have a shorthand notation that can be used for such constants. It is called *E-notation.*

E-notation is similar to scientific notation. To write a number in scientific notation, we shift the decimal point until it is just after the first nonzero digit. We then multiply the number obtained by the power of ten necessary to shift the decimal point back to its correct place. For example, the two numbers above can be written in scientific notation as follows:

$$-1.2846 \times 10^{14}$$
$$8.203 \ \times 10^{-12}$$

Notice that the exponent (i.e., the power of ten) is the number of places that the decimal point is shifted. If the decimal point is shifted to the left, the exponent is positive; if it is shifted to the right, the exponent is negative.

In BASIC we write a constant in E-notation by substituting the letter E for the symbols "× 10". Then the exponent is written immediately after the E. For example, the two numbers above are written as follows in E-notation:

$$-1.2846E14$$

$$8.203E-12$$

The E means "times ten to the power". Thus, the first constant is −1.2846 times ten to the power 14.

In writing an E-notation constant, we can place the decimal point anywhere as long as we adjust the exponent appropriately. For example, the following are all equivalent to the first example above:

$$-0.12846E15$$

$$-128.46E12$$

$$-12846.0E10$$

$$-12846E10$$

In the last example, the decimal point is omitted, in which case it is assumed to be to the right of the last digit. Note also that the exponent must have a minus sign if it is negative (as in 8.203E−12), but that a plus sign is optional for a positive exponent. Thus, −12846E14 and −1.2846E+14 are equivalent.

As we will see, E-notation is important not only because it is used for constants in a program, but also because output is sometimes printed in E-notation. The programmer should be able to convert a number written in E-notation to its simple form and vice versa. This is easy to do if one remembers that the exponent indicates the number of places that the decimal point is shifted.

The following are additional examples of constants written with and without E-notation:

Simple Constant	E-notation Constant
48003600	4.80036E7
−.000003921	−3.921E−6
−5863.25	−.586325E+4
1000000000	1E9
+.0000087	+0.87E−5

Variables

As we saw in Chapter 2, a variable identifies a storage location in the computer's internal storage. Each storage location can store one number. Depending on how the variable for a particular storage location is used, we can retrieve the number that is stored in the location or change the value that is stored there.

In Chapter 2 we indicated that the twenty-six letters of the alphabet can be used for variables. In fact, for many programs we need more than twenty-six variables. To make this possible, BASIC allows variables consisting of not only a letter, but also a letter followed by a single digit (0, 1, 2, . . . , 9). Thus, the following are valid variables in BASIC:

A	H1
A0	J4
A3	M2
A7	S8
A9	Z5

Notice that a letter (e.g., A) and the same letter followed by a digit (e.g., A3) are *different* variables referring to *different* storage locations. Just because two variables begin with the same letter does not make them the same.

Variables cannot have more than one letter or more than one digit. In addition, other symbols are not allowed in a variable. Thus, the following are *not* valid variables in BASIC for the reasons given:

A27	(contains two digits)
XY	(more than one letter)
B.	(contains a period)
3Z	(does not begin with a letter)

(Some versions of BASIC allow variables to be composed of two letters; for example, AB or XX are valid variables in these versions. Other versions of BASIC allow variables that contain any number of symbols; for example, SUM, TOTAL, and X37Z are valid variables in some versions of BASIC.)

Limitations on Data Values

The BASIC language does not set a limit on the size of numbers that can be used for constants or that can be assigned to variables.

Since, however, a computer has a limited capacity, there are practical maximum and minimum values that can be used depending on the computer. We will illustrate these limitations with a typical computer, but the details will vary from one machine to another.

All numbers, no matter how they are written, are stored in a form similar to E-notation. In this form, known as *floating-point notation*, the number is converted to E-notation with the decimal point just to the left of the first nonzero digit. Thus, the number 28.35 would be converted to .2835E2 and the number .058 would be converted to .58E–1. The limitations on sizes of numbers are expressed in terms of the maximum number of digits between the decimal point and the E (called the *fraction*) and in terms of the maximum and minimum exponent.

On a typical computer there can be six digits at most in the fraction (i.e., between the decimal point and the E). If a number is written with more than six digits, it is rounded off to six digits and all other digits are converted to zeros. For example, the constant 123456789 would be rounded off to 123457000 and stored in E-notation as .123457E9.

The exponent on a typical computer can range between +38 and –38 (i.e., the number can have a magnitude between 10^{+38} and 10^{-38}). For example, the constant .987654E36 is acceptable as is the constant .234567E–37. If, however, an exponent is outside this range, the constant is usually not valid. For example, the constant .192837E45 is invalid and results in an error.

The limitations on data values apply to all numeric values used in a program. Thus, all constants, the values of all variables, and all input and output data must be within the limits for the particular computer being used.

3-2. NUMERIC DATA PROCESSING

Numeric data processing involves computations with numbers. For example, computing an employee's pay or calculating the trajectory of a rocket involves processing numeric data. In this section we describe the elements of BASIC that are essential for this type of computation. These elements include numeric expressions and the LET statement.

Numeric Expressions

A numeric expression is an instruction to the computer to perform arithmetic. Numeric expressions are formed from constants, variables, and numeric operators.

Numeric operators are symbols that indicate what form of arithmetic is to be performed. The symbols used in BASIC and their meanings are as follows:

+   addition
−   subtraction
*   multiplication
/   division
∧   exponentiation (i.e., raising to a power)

To form a simple numeric expression using these symbols, we write an unsigned constant or variable on each side of the operator. For example, the following are valid arithmetic expressions in BASIC:

A+B
X−Y
2*K
T/3
X∧2

[In some versions of BASIC, the symbol used for exponentiation is an up-arrow (↑). In other versions of BASIC, a double asterisk (**) may be used for exponentiation. Thus, the last example above is sometimes written X↑2 or X**2.]

Each of these expressions tells the computer to perform the indicated operation using the values of the variables and constants. For example, A+B means add the value of A and the value of B. If A is 8.3 and B is 5.2, then the value of A+B is 13.5. With subtraction, the value on the right of the subtraction operator is subtracted from the value on the left. Thus, X−Y means subtract the value of Y from the value of X. Notice that multiplication is indicated by the asterisk symbol. Hence, 2*K means multiply the value of K by the constant 2. With division, the value on the left of the division operator is divided by the value on the right. Thus, T/3 means divide the value of T by 3. Exponentiation means raise the value on the left of the operator to the power of the value on the right. Hence, X∧2 means raise the value of X to the second power (i.e., square the value of X).

Any variable and any type of constant can be used in a numeric expression. This includes variables composed of more than one symbol (such as X5) and E-notation constants. For example, the following are valid numeric expressions:

X5−Z3
A/3.7E15
B7*3E8

It is important not to confuse an E-notation constant with the exponentiation operator. For example, 3E8 is the constant 300000000, while 3∧8 means raise three to the eighth power (which is 6561).

The addition and subtraction symbols may be used alone in front of a single constant or variable to form a numeric expression. In fact, a variable or a constant by itself is considered to be a numeric expression. Hence, each of the following is a numeric expression:

```
3
J
+7.5
+P
-.0063
-A
```

In the last example, if the value of A is –6.2, then the value of the numeric expression is -(-6.2) or 6.2.

To form more complex numeric expressions, several numeric operators are used. For example, the following are valid numeric expressions:

```
E5/F3+2.5
8-I*J
A*X^2+B*X-C
3.14159*R**2
-B+B/2/A
```

With complex numeric expressions the order in which the operations are performed is very important. The order is as follows:

1. All exponentiation is performed.
2. All multiplication and division is performed left-to-right.
3. All addition and subtraction is performed left-to-right.

For example, consider the following expression:

```
3.7-A*2.5/C+D^2+E
```

This expression is evaluated in the following order:

1. D is raised to the second power.
2. A is multiplied by 2.5 and the result is divided by C.
3. The answer from step 2 is subtracted from 3.7; the result is

added to the result of step 1; and finally E is added to obtain the final value of the expression.

In algebraic notation, the expression appears as follows:

$$3.7 - \frac{A \times 2.5}{C} + D^2 + E$$

To change the order of evaluation, numeric expressions can be enclosed in parentheses and combined with other expressions. When this is done, expressions in parentheses are evaluated before operations outside the parentheses are performed. For example, consider the following modification of the previous expression:

$$3.7-A*2.5/(C+D^2)+E$$

The expression C+D^2 is enclosed in parentheses and is evaluated before any other operations are carried out. Thus, the computer first raises D to the second power and adds the result to C. Next, A is multiplied by 2.5, and the result is divided by the value of C+D^2. Finally, the other addition and subtraction is performed. The result in algebraic notation is as follows:

$$3.7 - \frac{A \times 2.5}{C + D^2} + E$$

Numeric expressions in parentheses may be imbedded in other parenthetic expressions. When this is done, the computer evaluates the expression in the innermost parentheses before continuing with the expression in the next level of parentheses. For example, consider the following:

$$3.7-A*(2.5/(C+D^2)+E)$$

First the computer evaluates C+D^2. The result is then divided into 2.5 and the value of E is added. The final multiplication by A and subtraction from 3.7 are then performed. In algebraic notation, this expression is as follows:

$$3.7 - A \times \left[\frac{2.5}{C + D^2} + E \right]$$

Notice that when using parentheses, as in these examples, each left parenthesis must have a matching right parenthesis. In addition, extra sets of parentheses that do not change the order of evaluation can always be used.

A common mistake when writing a numeric expression is to forget that certain operations are performed before others. For example, assume that the programmer must write a numeric expression in BASIC for the following algebraic expression:

$$\frac{A + B}{C + D}$$

In coding the expression, the programmer may hastily write the following:

$$A+B/C+D$$

This is incorrect since division is done before addition, and this numeric expression is therefore interpreted as follows:

$$A + \frac{B}{C} + D$$

To have the additions done before the division, the programmer must use parentheses. Hence, the correct numeric expression is as follows:

$$(A+B)/(C+D)$$

It is important to remember that when there is a series of multiplications and divisions, the order of evaluations is left-to-right. Thus, in the expression A/B*C the division is performed first and the result is multiplied by C. Hence, in algebraic notation the expression is

$$\frac{A}{B} \times C$$

If we wish to write the algebraic expression

$$\frac{A}{B \times C}$$

in BASIC, we must use parentheses to have the multiplication done before the division. Thus, the equivalent BASIC expression for this example is A/(B*C).

The left-to-right evaluation also applies to addition and subtraction. For example, in the expression J–K+L the subtraction is done first followed by the addition. If J is 3, K is 2, and L is 1, then the value of this expression is 2. Had we interpreted the expression incorrectly and assumed that the addition is done first, we would get zero as the result. But because of the left-to-right order of evaluation this is incorrect. To change the order we would have to use parentheses and write the expression as J-(K+L).

With a series of exponentiations, the order of evaluation is also left-to-right. Hence the expression $X^\wedge Y^\wedge Z$ is interpreted as $(X^\wedge Y)^\wedge Z$. If we want to have the computer evaluate the expression right-to-left, we must use parentheses and write the expression as $X^\wedge(Y^\wedge Z)$.

Unlike algebra, omitting a numeric operator does not mean multiplication. For example, 3K is invalid and must be written 3*K. Similarly, parentheses cannot be used to imply multiplication. For example, (A+B)(C+D) is invalid and must be written (A+B)*(C+D).

Two numeric operations may not appear adjacent to each other. For example, A/-B is invalid. (Although in some versions of BASIC this expression is valid.) However, -B by itself is a numeric expression and may therefore be enclosed in parentheses to give meaning to the expression. This example can be written correctly as A/(-B). The same does not hold true for the invalid expression A*/B; there is no way of making this expression meaningful.

The LET Statement

A numeric expression by itself is not a BASIC statement. Rather, a numeric expression is part of a statement that is then used in a program. The most common statement in which a numeric expression appears is the LET statement. This statement causes the computer to evaluate a numeric expression and then to assign the result to a variable.

The syntax of the LET statement is as follows:

ln LET *variable = numeric expression*

This form shows what must appear in the different parts of the statement. The abbreviation *ln* stands for *line number.* Thus, the first thing in the statement must be a line number (as is the case with all statements in BASIC). Following this is the keyword LET. (In some versions of BASIC the word LET is optional.) Then there must be a variable, followed by an equal sign, and finally a numeric expression. For example, the following are valid LET statements:

```
 20 LET T=X+Y+Z
 30 LET A=T/3
 90 LET Y=A*X^2+B*X+C
100 LET A=3.14159*(D/2)^2
150 LET X3=Z7-3.5E15/Y5
160 LET M9=.0083/A^2
```

In a LET statement, the computer uses the current values of the variable names to evaluate the numeric expression. The result is then stored at the storage location identified by the variable on the left of the equal sign. For example, in the statement

$$20 \ \text{LET} \ T=X+Y+Z$$

if the value of X is 78, Y is 95, and Z is 82, then after the execution of this statement the value of T is 255. This value replaces the previous value of T and is the value that is retrieved with any subsequent use of the variable T. Notice that the values of X, Y, and Z are unchanged by the execution of this statement; only the value of T is affected.

The equal sign in a LET statement does not mean equality; it means *assignment*. That is, the equal sign tells the computer that the value of the expression on the right is to be *assigned* to the left-hand variable (i.e., stored in the storage location identified by the variable). This is why there must be one variable on the left of the equal sign. For example, the statement

$$200 \ \text{LET} \ A+B=X+Y$$

is invalid because it would mean assign the value of X+Y to the expression A+B. Since the left-hand expression is not a single storage location, such assignment is meaningless and therefore not allowed. There must always be a single variable on the left.

A further consequence of this concept of assignment is that some algebraically invalid equations become valid statements in BASIC. For example, the following statement is valid and often useful:

$$70 \ \text{LET} \ K=K+1$$

The meaning of this statement is that 1 is added to the current value of K and the result is returned to the storage location reserved for K (see Fig. 3-1). Thus, the value of K is increased by 1. Similarly, the following statement causes the current value of A to be replaced by a value that is five times as large:

$$80 \ \text{LET} \ A=5*A$$

We can use the LET statement to assign a constant to a variable or to assign the value of one variable to another. For example, the statement

$$120 \ \text{LET} \ M=3$$

assigns the value of 3 to the variable M. Similarly, the statement

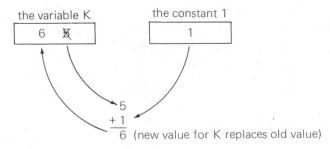

the variable K

6 ~~5~~

the constant 1

1

5
+ 1
—
6 (new value for K replaces old value)

FIGURE 3-1.   Evaluation of the statement LET K=K+1.

130 LET N=M

assigns the value of M to N. If M is equal to 3 before this statement is executed, N will be 3 afterwards. Notice also that this assignment does *not* change the value of M; it is still equal to 3 after statement 130 is executed.

The LET statement is the fundamental statement that is used in BASIC for numeric data processing. The sample program in Chapter 2 (see Fig. 2-1) illustrated its use in a program. In the next section we will see more examples of the use of the LET statement in a program.

3-3. WRITING COMPLETE PROGRAMS

We can now begin to write complete programs in BASIC. Using sequences of LET statements we can develop programs that perform numeric computations. We should, of course, remember that the last statement in a BASIC program must be an END statement, which is just a line number and the keyword END.

As an example, assume that we wish to compute the amount of interest that a bank deposit will earn in a year. Assume that we put $500 in a bank account at an interest rate of 6%. How much interest do we earn in a year and what is the total amount we have in the bank at the end of the year?

Figure 3-2 shows how a program to solve this problem can be written. In this program, B is the original bank balance ($500) and R is the interest rate expressed in decimal form (.06). These variables are assigned values in statements 10 and 20, respectively. Statement 30 then computes the interest, I, by multiplying B by R. Finally, in statement 40 we add the interest to the initial bank balance to obtain the balance at the end of the year (B1). The END statement stops the execution of the program.

Notice the sequential order of the execution of the statements in

```
10 LET B=500
20 LET R=.06
30 LET I=B*R
40 LET B1=B+I
50 END
```

FIGURE 3-2.   A simple interest calculation program.

the program. The statements are always executed in the order in which they are written, one statement after another. This order must be carefully planned when the program is designed so that it correctly solves the problem.

While this program is correct and can be run on a computer, it is not very useful because there is no way to determine the answer to the problem. What are the interest and end-of-year balance? To obtain this information we need to print the values of I and B1. This is accomplished with the PRINT statement.

The PRINT Statement

The syntax of the PRINT statement is as follows:

ln PRINT *list of variables separated by commas*

The statement begins with a line number (*ln*), followed by the keyword PRINT, and finally a list of variables separated by commas. For example, the following are valid PRINT statements:

```
75 PRINT A
85 PRINT P,Q,R
95 PRINT B5,X7,Z8,A9,C2
```

The effect of the PRINT statement is to cause the computer to print on the terminal typewriter or to display on the CRT the values of all variables listed in the statement. For example, statement 75 above causes the value of A to be printed; statement 85 causes the values of P, Q, and R to be printed; the last statement above prints the values of five variables. Whatever values are currently assigned to the variables in the computer's internal storage are printed.

Each PRINT statement causes a line to be printed. A print line has a fixed number of spaces for printing called *print positions*. The number of print positions in a line depends on the terminal, but typically the limit is between 72 and 80. The print positions are divided into areas called *print zones*. Each print zone contains a certain number of print positions. Usually there are five print zones, each fourteen or fif-

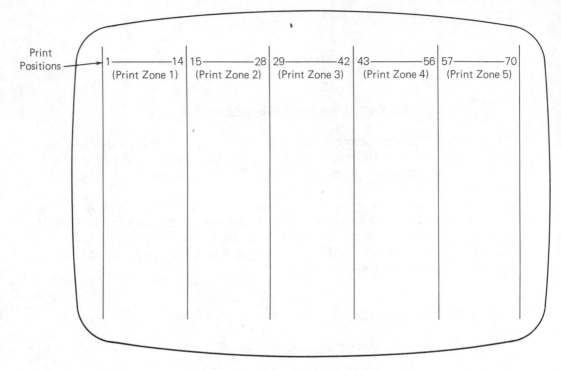

FIGURE 3-3. Print zones on a CRT.

teen print positions wide. The print zones on a typical CRT are shown in Fig. 3-3. Here we assume that each zone contains fourteen print positions.

When a PRINT statement is executed, the values of the variables are printed in successive zones. For example, assume that the value of X is 10, Y is -75.5, and Z is .003, and that the following PRINT statement is executed:

```
105 PRINT X,Y,Z
```

Then the output appears as follows:

```
|(Print Zone 1)|(Print Zone 2)|(Print Zone 3)|(Print Zone 4)|(Print Zone 5)|
 10             |-75.5          |.003
```

Since there are three variables in the PRINT statement, the values are printed in the first three print zones. The remaining print zones are left blank. (Of course, just the numbers appear in the output; the vertical lines and the words identifying the print zones are not printed.)

Each PRINT statement starts a new line. Thus, if there are three PRINT statements executed in sequence, each with five or fewer variables, three lines are printed.

50

If there are more than five variables in the PRINT statement, a new line is started after the first five values are printed. For example, consider the following statement:

```
115 PRINT A,B,C,D,E,F,G
```

When this statement is executed, the values of the first five variables are printed on one line. The values of the remaining two variables are then printed in the first two print zones of the next line.

The form of the output depends on the number to be printed. If the number is an integer (i.e., a whole number) such as 10 or –385, the number is printed without a decimal point. A negative sign is printed if the number is negative. A blank space is left if the number is positive. Most numbers with fractional parts are printed with a decimal point as we would normally write them. For example, the numbers 289.372 and .000461 would be printed in these forms. If the number is very large or very small, however, it is printed in E-notation. For example, assume that the value of A is 84023600000 and B is .0000000000296042 and that the following PRINT statement is executed:

```
125 PRINT A,B
```

The output appears as follows:

(Print Zone 1)	(Print Zone 2)	(Print Zone 3)	(Print Zone 4)	(Print Zone 5)
8.40236E 10	2.96042E-11			

We can now write a more complete version of the interest-calculation program discussed earlier. Assume that we want to print the original bank balance, the year's interest, and the end-of-year balance. The program in Fig. 3-4 accomplishes this. Notice that the PRINT statement contains the variables that we want printed. The output appears as follows:

(Print Zone 1)	(Print Zone 2)	(Print Zone 3)	(Print Zone 4)	(Print Zone 5)
500	30	530		

```
10 LET B=500
20 LET R=.06
30 LET I=B*R
40 LET B1=B+I
50 PRINT B,I,B1
60 END
```

FIGURE 3-4. The interest calculation program with a PRINT statement.

This program is still not very adequate. The difficulty is that it solves the problem for only one bank balance ($500) and one interest rate (6%). If we wish to change either of these, we must change the program. A better approach is to design the program so that the values of B and R can be supplied when the program is run without modifying the actual program. This is accomplished with the INPUT statement.

The INPUT Statement

The purpose of the INPUT statement is to accept input data from the terminal keyboard. The syntax of this statement is as follows:

ln INPUT *list of variables separated by commas*

As always, the statement begins with a line number. Then comes the keyword INPUT, followed by a list of variables separated by commas. For example, the following are valid INPUT statements:

```
15 INPUT A
25 INPUT P,Q,R
35 INPUT B5,X7,Z8,A9,C2
```

When an INPUT statement is encountered during the execution of a program, the computer prints a question mark on the terminal and waits for input data to be typed. The question mark is called a *prompt*. It indicates that input data must be entered. The person operating the terminal must type one number after the question mark for each variable in the INPUT statement. The numbers must be separated by commas. After typing the input data, the RETURN key must be pressed.

For example, assume that we are running a program that contains the following INPUT statement:

```
45 INPUT X,Y,Z
```

This statement requires three input values because there are three variables. When the statement is executed, a question mark prompt is printed and we then type three numbers separated by commas. For example, we might enter the data after the prompt as follows:

```
? 10,-75.5,.003
```

After the RETURN key is pressed, the computer accepts these numbers and assigns them in order to the variables in the INPUT statement. Thus, 10 would be assigned to X, -75.5 would be assigned to Y, and .003 would be assigned to Z.

The input data that is entered must follow the rules for constants in BASIC. The numbers can be positive or negative, contain decimal points or be whole numbers, or be written in E-notation. However, a comma cannot appear in an input value because commas are used to separate the data.

One value must be entered for each variable in the INPUT statement. If too little or too much data is entered, the computer prints a message indicating the error. All data must then be reentered. (With some computers, if too little data is entered, it is only necessary to type the additional data, while if too much data is entered, any excess data is ignored.)

With the addition of an INPUT statement, the interest-calculation program can be designed to compute the interest for any bank balance and any interest rate. The program is shown in Fig. 3–5. Notice that the program no longer assigns values to B and R; these variables appear in the INPUT statement. Whatever values are entered when the program is run are used in the calculation. Thus, if we type the data after the prompt as follows

? 500,.06

the program gives the same answer as before (i.e., the interest on $500 at 6%). However, if we type

? 2000,.075

the program computes the interest on $2000 at 7.5%.

It is important to recognize the general nature of the program in Fig. 3–5. The program solves the general problem of finding the interest on a bank deposit without knowing the actual values of B and R. These values are supplied when the program is run. At that time a specific instance of the problem is solved.

This program also illustrates the idea of interactive processing. The person operating the terminal interacts with the computer by supplying input data when a prompt is printed. Then the output is printed almost immediately.

```
10 INPUT B,R
20 LET I=B*R
30 LET B1=B+I
40 PRINT B,I,B1
50 END
```

FIGURE 3–5.   The interest calculation program with an INPUT statement.

Program Repetition

The program in Fig. 3–5 solves the interest-calculation problem for one set of input data. If we want to solve the problem for more data, we can run the program again. An easier approach, however, is to design the program so that it automatically repeats.

We accomplish this in BASIC by using a GO TO statement. The syntax of this statement is as follows:

$$ln \text{ GO TO } ln$$

The first line number is the number of the GO TO statement. The second line number, after the keyword GO TO, must be the number of another statement in the program. For example, the following is a valid GO TO statement:

```
75 GO TO 150
```

The effect of the GO TO statement is to cause the computer to interrupt the normal sequential execution of the program and to continue execution at the statement whose number is given in the GO TO statement. This process of breaking the execution of the program at a certain point and continuing elsewhere is called *branching* or *transfer of control*. For example, statement 75 above causes the computer to branch to statement 150. Execution then continues from that point.

It is possible to branch from a point in a program either in the direction of the end of the program (i.e., "down" the program) or toward the beginning of the program (i.e., "up" the program). In later chapters we will discuss examples of branching down the program. For now, however, we will concentrate on branching up.

A GO TO statement can cause the computer to branch up a program so that a series of statements is repeatedly executed. When this is done, the group of statements that is repeated is called a *loop* and the process is called *looping*.

We can include a GO TO statement in the interest-calculation program to create a loop. Figure 3–6 shows how this is done. Statement 50 is a GO TO statement that causes the computer to branch to statement 10. Because of this, statements 10 through 50 are repeatedly executed and thus form a loop.

The first time that the loop is executed, the INPUT statement accepts input data for B and R. The calculations are performed with this data and the PRINT statement prints the output. The GO TO statement then causes the computer to go back to the INPUT state-

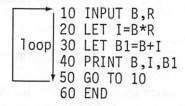

```
         10 INPUT B,R
         20 LET I=B*R
    loop 30 LET B1=B+I
         40 PRINT B,I,B1
         50 GO TO 10
         60 END
```

FIGURE 3-6.   The interest calculation program with a
              loop.


```
? 500,.06
  500              30             530
? 2000,.075
  2000            150            2150
? 1250,.055
  1250          68.75          1318.75
?
```

FIGURE 3-7.   Input and output for the interest calcula-
              tion program.

ment. This causes new input values to be accepted for B and R, replacing the previous values. This new data is then used in the calculations
and the output is printed. Then the GO TO statement causes the program to be repeated again. In fact, the program will continue to repeat
as long as we supply it with input data. Figure 3-7 shows the input and
output for this program for several repetitions.

The biggest problem with looping in a program is not how to create
a loop, but rather how to stop the computer from looping. In the program in Fig. 3-6, this is done by typing a special control character
(usually a "control C") following the input prompt. When the computer
senses that the control character has been entered, it branches to the
END statement. This causes the computer to stop execution of the
program. (In Chapter 5 we will discuss other ways of stopping a loop.)

The REM Statement

A statement that is not essential but often used in BASIC programs
is the REM, or remarks, statement. The syntax of the REM statement
is as follows:

ln REM *any comments or remarks*

The REM statement is simply a line number, followed by the keyword

REM, and then any comments or remarks that we wish to include. For example, the following is a valid REM statement:

```
10 REM - INTEREST CALCULATION PROGRAM
```

REM statements can go anywhere in the program before the END statement. During the execution of the program, the computer ignores all REM statements; that is, whenever it encounters a REM statement the computer passes over it and continues with the next statement in sequence.

The purpose of the REM statement is to allow the programmer to include explanatory comments or remarks in the program. Such remarks are often used to identify the program, to describe the processing that is done, or to otherwise elaborate upon the program. Remarks like these help other programmers to understand and use the program. In Chapter 7 we will discuss the use of remarks in more detail. Figure 3-8 shows the final version of the interest-calculation program with a REM statement.

An Illustrative Program

As another example of a BASIC program, assume that it is necessary to compute the gross pay, withholding tax, and net pay for an employee. Input to the program consists of the employee's identification number (I) and his or her hours worked (H). The gross pay (G) is to be computed at the rate of $6.50 per hour; the withholding tax (W) is 18% of the gross pay; the net pay (P) is the gross pay less the withholding tax. Output should list the employee's identification number, gross pay, withholding tax, and net pay.

The program in Fig. 3-9 satisfies these requirements. First the input data is accepted. Next the gross pay, withholding tax, and net pay are computed. Notice that the order of the three LET statements is important. The gross pay must be computed first since it is needed in the calculation of the withholding tax. In addition, the tax must be computed before the net pay can be found. After all calculations are completed, the output is printed.

```
10 REM - INTEREST CALCULATION PROGRAM
20 INPUT B,R
30 LET I=B*R
40 LET B1=B+I
50 PRINT B,I,B1
60 GO TO 20
70 END
```

FIGURE 3-8.   The interest calculation program.

```
10 REM - PAYROLL CALCULATION PROGRAM
20 INPUT I,H
30 LET G=6.50*H
40 LET W=.18*G
50 LET P=G-W
60 PRINT I,G,W,P
70 GO TO 20
80 END
```

FIGURE 3-9.   A payroll calculation program.

Notice that the program includes a loop. The loop consists of the INPUT statement through the GO TO statement. The first time the loop is executed, the first set of input data is accepted and assigned to I and H. This data is processed and one line is printed. The computer then executes the GO TO statement, returning to the INPUT statement. This causes the computer to get the second set of input data. The data is assigned to I and H, replacing the old values of these variables. The second time through the loop, the calculations use the second set of data; the second line printed gives the results for these calculations. Then the computer goes to the INPUT statement again, gets more input data, and proceeds as before. The program continues to loop until no more input data is supplied.

3-4.   PROGRAM STYLE

The most important objective during the programming process is to produce a program that correctly solves the required problem. The process of program testing, discussed briefly in Chapter 2, is designed to help locate errors in a program. We will describe program testing in more detail in a later chapter.

After correctness, the most important characteristic of a program is its understandability. By this we mean the qualities of the program that make it understandable or readable to others. Program understandability is important because programs are often reviewed by people other than the original programmer. For example, the programming manager may review a program to check for completeness and consistency with the problem definition. Other programmers may have to read the program to make corrections for errors that are not detected until after the program has been in use for a while. Often modifications are necessary in the program because of changing requirements. For example, payroll programs have to be modified regularly because of changing tax structures. Sometimes a program is enhanced to do more than was originally planned. In all of these situations, someone must look at the program months or even years after it was first coded. Even if the original programmer is given the task, he or she may have difficulty remembering the program's logic unless the program is easily understood.

Program style deals with those characteristics of a program that make it more understandable. Even though we have covered only a few features of the BASIC language, it is possible to begin incorporating good style in our programs. One basic rule is to use variables that symbolize the data to which they refer. For example, in the program in Fig. 3–9, we used I for the employee identification number and H for the hours worked. Similarly, G, W, and P symbolized the gross pay, withholding tax, and net pay.

Another good style rule is to use remarks to explain complex parts of the program. Although the examples so far have been relatively straightforward, many programs involve sophisticated processing. REM statements can be used to include explanations of the processing at different points in the program.

Sometimes long numeric expressions are difficult to understand because of the order in which the operations are performed. When this is the case, it is often useful to include extra sets of parentheses around parts of the expression. Although these parentheses may not change the way the expression is evaluated, they often make the expression easier to understand.

The rules discussed here are just a few of the ways that a program can be made more understandable. As we explain other features of the BASIC language, we will give more rules for program style.

REVIEW QUESTIONS

1. Indicate whether each of the following is a valid or invalid constant in BASIC:
   - (a) –.004352
   - (b) 83,250
   - (c) 8.213∧8
   - (d) 273.51E–12

2. Convert the following E-notation constants to simple constants:
   - (a) 4.23E5
   - (b) –8031E+2
   - (c) .1234E–6
   - (d) –5E–1

3. Convert the following constants to E-notation:
   - (a) –38204
   - (b) .0000456

(c) –10000000

(d) 7.8316

4. Indicate whether each of the following is a valid or invalid variable:
   (a) AMT
   (b) F
   (c) 4H
   (d) X7

5. What are the limitations on data values for the computer you are using?

6. What is the order of evaluation of the operations in a numeric expression?

7. Convert each of the following algebraic expressions to its equivalent numeric expression in BASIC:
   (a) $x^2 - 2x + 3$

   (b) $\dfrac{4x}{y} + \dfrac{a}{3}$

   (c) $\dfrac{a - b}{a + b}$

   (d) $\dfrac{\left(4 - \dfrac{x}{a + b}\right)^3}{(c - d)^2}$

8. Assume that the value of A is 2, B is 3, and C is 4. What is the value of each of the following numeric expressions?
   (a) A–B+C
   (b) C/A*B
   (c) C+B∧A
   (d) A–B*C/A+B/C

9. Write a BASIC statement to compute the miles per gallon that an automobile uses given the distance traveled and the gallons used.

10. The LET statement is sometimes called an assignment statement. Why?

11. What is the effect of the following statement?

$$50 \text{ LET } X=X/2$$

12. Write a BASIC statement to print the values of three variables.

13. How many lines of output are printed with the following statements and how many values are printed on each line?

```
80 PRINT X5,A3,Z7,P,Q,R5
```

14. Write a BASIC statement to accept five values from the terminal.

15. What happens when an INPUT statement is executed?

16. Write a BASIC statement to branch from statement 50 to statement 100.

17. A group of statements that is repeatedly executed is called a _____.

18. The _____ statement can be used to add comments or remarks to a program.

19. Consider the program shown in Fig. 3-9. If the input entered is the numbers 123 and 40, what output is printed?

20. Why is good program style important?

PROGRAMMING PROBLEMS

1. The annual depreciation of an asset by the straight-line method is calculated by the following formula:

$$\text{Depreciation} = \frac{\text{Cost} - \text{Salvage value}}{\text{Service life}}$$

Write a BASIC program that accepts the cost, salvage value, and service life, calculates the depreciation, and prints all input along with the calculated result. Test the program using $13,500 for the cost, $1,500 for the salvage value, and 7 years for the service life.

2. Fahrenheit temperature is converted to Celsius temperature by the following formula:

$$C = \frac{5}{9} \times (F-32)$$

In this formula F is the temperature in degrees Fahrenheit and C is the temperature in degrees Celsius. Write a BASIC program to convert a Fahrenheit temperature to its equivalent in Celsius. Input should be the value of F. Output should be the values of F and C. To test the program use the following Fahrenheit temperatures as input data:

78.4
-50
98.6
32
212
0

3. In economic theory, supply and demand curves can sometimes be represented by the following equations:

$$\text{Supply: } P = A \times Q - B$$

$$\text{Demand: } P = C \times Q - D$$

In these equations, P represents the price and Q is the quantity. The values of A, B, C, and D determine the actual curves. These equations can be solved for P and Q, giving the equilibrium price and quantity for the commodity. The formulas are as follows:

$$P = \frac{C \times B - A \times D}{C - A}$$

$$Q = \frac{D - B}{A - C}$$

Write a BASIC program to calculate the equilibrium price and quantity of a commodity. Input to the program should be the test number and the values of A, B, C, and D. Output should be the test number and the price and quantity at equilibrium. Test the program with the following data:

Test Number	A	B	C	D
1	.19	1.20	-.42	8.50
2	.5	0	.5	100
3	0.	25	1	20

4. The system of linear equations

$$ax + by = c$$

$$dx + ey = f$$

has the following solution:

$$x = \frac{ce - bf}{ae - bd}$$

$$y = \frac{af - cd}{ae - bd}$$

Write a BASIC program to solve the system and to print the values of x and y. Input consists of the values of a, b, c, d, e, and f. Use the following data to test the program:

a	b	c	d	e	f
1.0	2.0	3.0	4.0	5.0	6.0
5.2	8.9	13.2	-6.3	7.2	2.1
-83.82	42.61	-59.55	14.73	5.32	-39.99
.035	-.327	1.621	.243	.006	.592

5. Several calculations are important in analyzing the current position of a company. The formulas for the calculations are as follows:

$$\text{Working capital} = \text{Current assets} - \text{Current liabilities}$$

$$\text{Current ratio} = \frac{\text{Current assets}}{\text{Current liabilities}}$$

$$\text{Acid-test ratio} = \frac{\text{Cash} + \text{Accounts receivable}}{\text{Current liabilities}}$$

Write a BASIC program that accepts the cash, accounts receivable, current assets, and current liabilities; performs the above calculations; and prints the results. Use the following data to test the program:

Cash:	$10,620
Accounts receivable:	$ 5,850
Current assets:	$22,770
Current liabilities:	$14,680

6. The final score for a particular test is equal to the number of questions answered correctly minus one-fourth of the number answered incorrectly. Assume that test data available for input includes the student's identification number, number correct on the test, and number incorrect. Write a program to calculate the final score from this data and to print the results along with the input data. Use the following input data to test the program:

Student Number	Number Correct	Number Incorrect
1	90	10
2	75	20
3	84	0
4	57	35
5	10	50
6	95	5

7. The interest and maturity value of a promissory note can be calculated as follows:

$$\text{Interest} = \frac{\text{Principal} \times \text{Rate} \times \text{Time}}{360}$$

Maturity value = Principal + Interest

Write a BASIC program that accepts the loan number, principal, rate (percent), and time (days); performs the above calculations; and prints the loan number, rate, time, interest, and maturity value. Note that the rate is expressed as a percentage for input purposes but must be converted to decimal form for the calculation (e.g., 5% = .05). This conversion should be done within the program; the input and output of the rate should be in percentage form. Use the program to find the interest and maturity value of loan number 1875 which is a $450 note with a rate of 6% for 60 days.

8. The payroll in a particular business is calculated as follows:
   (a) Gross pay is the hours worked times the pay rate.
   (b) Withholding tax is found by subtracting thirteen times the number of exemptions from the gross pay and multiplying the result by the tax rate.
   (c) Social security tax is 6.05% of the gross pay.
   (d) Net pay is the gross pay less all taxes.

Write a BASIC program that accepts as input an employee's identification number, hours worked, pay rate, tax rate, and number of exemptions. Then calculate the employee's gross pay, withholding and social security taxes, and net pay. Print these results along with the employee's identification number.

Use the following input data to test the program:

Employee Number	Hours Worked	Pay Rate	Tax Rate	Number of Exemptions
1001	40	4.50	20%	3
1002	36	3.75	17.5%	4
1003	47	6.50	24%	0
1004	25	5.25	22.5%	2

9. Grade point average (GPA) is calculated by multiplying the units for each course that a student takes by the numeric grade that he or she receives in the course (A = 4.0, B = 3.0, C = 2.0, D = 1.0, F = 0.0), totaling for all courses, and dividing by the total number of units. For example, assume that a student received a C (2.0) in a four-unit course and a B (3.0) in a two-unit course. Then his or her GPA is calculated as follows:

$$\frac{4 \times 2 + 2 \times 3}{4 + 2} = 2.33$$

Write a BASIC program to calculate one student's GPA, given the units and grade in each of five courses that he or she took. Input for the program is the student's identification number and the units and numeric grade for each of the five courses. Output from the program should list the student's number, total units, and grade point average.

Test the program with data for student number 18357, who got an A in a two-unit course, a C in a three-unit course, a D in a one-unit course, a C in a four-unit course, and a B in a three-unit course.

10. The percent correct for each part of a three-part test needs to be calculated. The test is such that the number of questions in each part is different and not known in advance. Write a BASIC program to perform the necessary calculations. The first set of input for the program should be the number of questions in each of the three parts. Then input for a student is entered, giving the student's number and his or her scores for the three parts. The program should calculate the percent correct for each part and the percent correct for all three parts combined. Output should list the student number, the number and percent correct for each part, and the total number and percent correct.

To test the program assume that part I contains 50 questions, part II contains 90 questions, and part III contains 40 questions. The student's results are as follows:

Student Number	Part I Correct	Part II Correct	Part III Correct
18372	37	83	28
19204	25	30	30
20013	45	87	36
21563	0	53	40

4

PROGRAMMING FOR DECISIONS

When a program contains only a sequence of INPUT, LET, and PRINT statements, these statements are executed in the order in which they are written, as illustrated by the examples in the last chapter. Sometimes we wish to alter this normal sequential execution. For example, we may want the computer to select among several sequences of statements based on a particular condition or to repeat a group of statements until a condition occurs. These activities involve controlling the order of execution of the statements in a program. The BASIC statements that are used to accomplish this are called *control statements*. (The GO TO statement, discussed in the last chapter, is an example of a control statement.)

This chapter discusses control statements and program control for decision making. Decision making involves selecting among alternative sequences of statements based on a condition that occurs during the execution of the program. For example, assume that we need to write a program that calculates the tuition for a college student based on the number of units for which the student is enrolled. If the student is taking fewer than a certain number of units, the tuition is calculated one way; otherwise a different calculation is used. Thus, the computer must select between two calculations based on a particular condition.

In this chapter we describe the BASIC control statements necessary for decision making and discuss related program logic. Other aspects of program control are discussed in the next chapter.

4-1. THE IF STATEMENT

The fundamental decision-making statement in BASIC is the IF statement. The syntax of this statement is as follows:

ln IF *relational expression* THEN *ln*

Following the line number and keyword IF is a *relational expression*. Such an expression determines whether a particular relationship holds between two values. For example, A>B is a relational expression that determines whether A is greater than B. (We describe relational expressions in detail below.) Following the relational expression is the keyword THEN and the line number of another statement in the program. For example, the following is a valid IF statement:

```
50 IF A>B THEN 200
```

Execution of an IF statement causes the computer to evaluate the relational expression and determine whether it is true or false; that is, whether or not the relationship holds. If the expression is true, the computer branches to the statement whose number is given following the word THEN. If the condition is false, the computer does *not* branch; rather it continues with the next statement after the IF statement. In the previous example, if the value of A is greater than the value of B, the computer branches to statement 200. If A is *not* greater than B, the computer goes on to the next statement in sequence following the IF statement.

Relational Expressions

A relational expression compares the values of two numeric expressions. Values can be compared to determine whether one is greater than or less than the other, whether they are equal or not equal, or whether combinations of these conditions are true. The relational expression has a *truth value* of *true* or *false* depending on the result of the comparison.

The way in which the values of the numeric expressions are compared is given by a *relational operator*. The relational operators in BASIC and their meanings are as follows:

Relational Operator	Meaning
<	Less than
<=	Less than or equal to
>	Greater than
>=	Greater than or equal to
=	Equal to
<>	Not equal to

The simplest form of a relational expression is a constant or a variable, followed by a relational operator, and then another constant or variable. For example, the following are valid relational expressions:

$$J<K$$
$$6<=C$$
$$Q>5.6$$
$$K>=-5$$
$$A3=B4$$
$$7<>J$$

To evaluate each of these, the values of the variables and constants are compared according to the relational operator. For example, if J is 6 and K is 5, the first expression is *false*. Similarly, if both J and K are equal to 6, this expression is *false*. However, if J is 6 and K is 7, the expression is *true*.

Relational operators can be used to compare the values of complex numeric expressions. For example, the following relational expressions are valid:

$$Q>P-5.6$$
$$K+8>=-5-L$$
$$X+Y/(4.56-Z)=Z-M$$
$$(A7-I2)<>(K-5)$$

Notice that parentheses can be used to enclose part or all of either numeric expression in a relational expression.

In evaluating a relational expression containing numeric expressions, the current values of the variables are used to evaluate each numeric expression. The resulting values of the numeric expressions are then compared according to the relational operator to determine the truth value of the relational expression. If the condition specified by the relational operator is correct, the relational expression is *true*. If the condition is not correct, the relational expression is *false*. For example, consider the following relational expression:

$$N-3>=5$$

If the value of N is 10, then N-3 is 7. Since 7 is greater than 5, the relational expression is true. However, if N is 4, then N-3 is 1. Since 1 is not greater than or equal to 5, the expression is false. Finally, if N is 8, then N-3 is 5 and the relational expression is true.

An Illustrative Program

To illustrate the use of the IF statement and relational expressions in a program, assume that we need to write a program that calculates

the tuition for a college student. The input data is the student's identification number and the number of units for which the student is enrolled. The tuition is $350 if the student is taking twelve or fewer units.
However, if the student is taking more than twelve units, the tuition is
$350 plus $20 per unit for all units over twelve. The program must
print the student's identification number and tuition for any valid input.

The program to accomplish this requires decision making. First the
input data must be accepted. Then the computer must examine the
number of units to determine the tuition. This decision-making step can
be stated as follows: If the number of units is less than or equal to
twelve, the tuition is $350; otherwise the tuition is $350 plus $20 per
unit for all units over twelve. In other words, the computer must select
between two ways of calculating the tuition based on a comparison
between the number of units and twelve. After the tuition is calculated,
the output can be printed.

The program in Fig. 4-1(a) solves this problem. The INPUT statement accepts the student's identification number (I) and number of
units (U). The IF statement then compares the number of units with
twelve. If U is greater than twelve, the computer branches to statement
50. The tuition (T) is calculated at $350 plus $20 per unit for all units
over twelve. Then the output is printed. If U is less than or equal to
twelve, the computer does not branch. Instead, the computer goes on
to the next statement in sequence and the tuition is set equal to $350.
The purpose of the GO TO statement following statement 30 is to

```
10 INPUT I,U
20 IF U>12 THEN 50
30 LET T=350
40 GO TO 60
50 LET T=350+20*(U-12)
60 PRINT I,T
70 GO TO 10
80 END
```

(a) The program

```
? 123,15
  123           410
? 456,9
  456           350
? 789,12
  789           350
?
```

(b) Input and output

FIGURE 4-1.   The tuition calculation program.

branch around statement 50 to the PRINT statement so that the output can be printed. Figure 4–1(b) shows the results of running the program on a computer.

It is important to understand why the statement GO TO 60 (line 40) is necessary in this program. Recall that the statements in a program are executed in sequence unless the sequence is broken with a branch instruction. If this GO TO statement were omitted and the number of units were less than or equal to twelve, the result would be incorrect. In this case the computer would set T equal to $350. Then, since the GO TO statement would be missing, the next statement in sequence would be statement 50. Hence, the tuition would be calculated again, this time incorrectly. The second value for the tuition would replace the first value and would be the value printed. This situation is avoided by including the GO TO statement to branch around statement 50.

The program described has a loop in it so it will be repeated until no more input is supplied. If there is only one set of input data, so that a loop is not needed, the statement GO TO 10 (line 70) can be eliminated.

4-2. PROGRAM LOGIC FOR DECISION MAKING

The pattern of program logic in the example given at the end of the last section is used in many decision problems. The pattern is represented by the diagram in Fig. 4–2. Usually we want to test a logical condition.

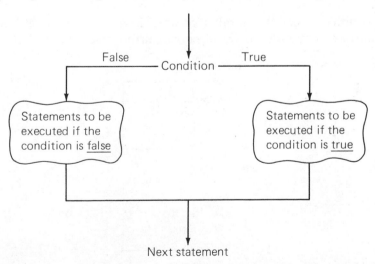

FIGURE 4–2.   Decision-making logic.

If the condition is true, one group of statements is executed, if the condition is false, another set of statements is performed. After executing either group of statements, we want the computer to continue with the next statement in sequence.

We can express this pattern of logic in the form shown in Fig. 4–3. We call the statements to be executed if the condition is true the *true part* of the decision, and the statements to be executed if the condition is false the *false part*. Figure 4–3 shows that if the condition is true, then the true part is executed; else the false part is executed.

While the form in Fig. 4–3 expresses very clearly the logic that we wish to use in decision making, it is not the pattern used by the IF statement. (In the next two sections, we will discuss variations of the IF statement that are available in some versions of BASIC and that do follow this pattern.) All that the IF statement can do is to branch to another statement or to continue with the next statement in sequence depending upon the truth or falsity of a relational expression. Hence, if we wish to obtain the same result as in the pattern shown in Fig. 4–3, *we must branch to the true part. The false part must follow the IF statement and end with a GO TO statement that branches around the true part.* This pattern is shown in Fig. 4–4.

The tuition-calculation program (Fig. 4–1) illustrates this approach. The decision-making step in this program is as follows:

```
20 IF U>12 THEN 50
30 LET T=350
40 GO TO 60
50 LET T=350+20*(U-12)
60 (next statement)
```

If the condition that the number of units is greater than twelve is true, the computer branches to the second tuition calculation. If the con-

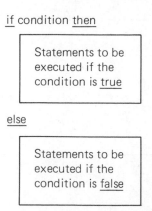

FIGURE 4–3.   A basic decision-making pattern.

IF condition THEN n1

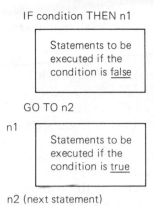

Statements to be
executed if the
condition is <u>false</u>

GO TO n2

n1

Statements to be
executed if the
condition is <u>true</u>

n2 (next statement)

FIGURE 4-4. The basic decision-making pattern using an
IF statement.

dition is false, the computer goes on (we say that it "falls through") to the next statement in sequence. The statement GO TO 60 is necessary to branch around the true part.

Sometimes the decision logic is easier to understand if we use the *complementary condition* in the IF statement. The complement of a condition is the condition that is true if the original condition is false and vice versa. For example, the complement of "less than" is "greater than or equal to". Similarly, the complement of "equal to" is "not equal to". As an example of the use of a complementary condition in a program, assume that if A is greater than B, we wish to print the value of A; otherwise we want to print B. We could write this section of the program as follows:

```
50 IF A>B THEN 80
60 PRINT B
70 GO TO 90
80 PRINT A
90 (next statement)
```

Alternatively, we could use the complement of the "greater than" condition which is the "less than or equal to" condition. Then the true and false parts can be exchanged and the program segment written as follows:

```
50 IF A<=B THEN 80
60 PRINT A
70 GO TO 90
80 PRINT B
90 (next statement)
```

Whether the programmer wishes to do this depends on what he or she finds easier to understand. If we use the complementary condition in

71

the tuition calculation, the decision-making step is as follows:

```
20 IF U<=12 THEN 50
30 LET T=350+20*(U-12)
40 GO TO 60
50 LET T=350
60 (next statement)
```

In the examples so far, there is only one statement to be executed if the condition is true and one if the condition is false. In fact, there may be any number of statements in the true and false parts. For example, assume that we wish to calculate employee pay. The gross pay is $4.50 per hour for the first forty hours worked and $6.75 per hour for all time over forty hours. In addition, the withholding tax is 18% of the gross pay if forty or fewer hours are worked and 20% of the pay if more than forty hours are recorded. The net pay is the gross pay less the withholding tax.

The program in Fig. 4–5 satisfies these requirements.[†] The program first accepts input data consisting of the employee's identification number (I) and the hours worked (H). Then the hours worked are compared with forty. If the hours are less than or equal to forty, the payroll calculations following the IF statement are performed and the computer branches to statement 170. However, if the hours are greater than forty, the computer branches to statement 150 and performs the payroll calculations beginning there. After the gross pay and withholding tax are computed by one of the two methods, the net pay is computed and the output is printed.

Program Style

To make the decision logic easier to understand in the program, many programmers indent the true and false parts. For example, the decision part of the previous payroll program could be coded as follows:

```
110 IF H>40 THEN 150
120    LET G=4.50*H
130    LET W=.18*G
140 GO TO 170
150    LET G=180.00+6.75*(H-40)
160    LET W=.20*G
170 LET P=G-W
```

[†]Notice that because this program is longer than previous examples, we have begun the line numbers at 100 rather than 10. This is done so that all line numbers are the same length.

```
100 INPUT I,H
110 IF H>40 THEN 150
120 LET G=4.50*H
130 LET W=.18*G
140 GO TO 170
150 LET G=180.00+6.75*(H-40)
160 LET W=.20*G
170 LET P=G-W
180 PRINT I,G,W,P
190 GO TO 100
200 END
```

FIGURE 4-5.   A payroll program.

The statements indented between the IF statement and the GO TO 170 statement are the false part of the decision. The indented statements after GO TO 170 are the true part. Whether a style such as this is used depends on whether the programmer thinks that it is helpful in understanding the program logic.

One-Sided Decisions

The decision-making pattern that we have described requires the computer to select between two alternative sequences of statements based on a logical condition. Sometimes it is only necessary either to select or to bypass a set of statements based on a condition. This "one-sided" decision logic can be represented by the diagram in Fig. 4-6 or in the form shown in Fig. 4-7. If the condition is true, the true

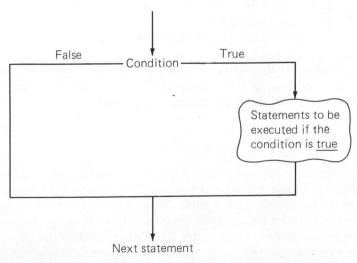

FIGURE 4-6.   One-sided decision-making logic.

if condition then

```
┌─────────────────────┐
│ Statements to be    │
│ executed if the     │
│ condition is true   │
└─────────────────────┘
```

FIGURE 4-7.   A one-sided decision-making pattern.

IF complement of condition THEN n

```
┌──────────────────────────────────┐
│ Statements to be                 │
│ executed if the                  │
│ condition is true                │
│ (i.e. if complement is false)    │
└──────────────────────────────────┘
```

n (next statement)

FIGURE 4-8.   The one-sided decision-making pattern
using an IF statement.

part is executed; otherwise the computer bypasses this part and goes on to the next statement in sequence. To implement this pattern with the IF statement, we must use the complementary condition and branch around the true part if this condition is true. The technique is shown in Fig. 4-8.

To illustrate the use of this technique, assume that if A is greater than B, we must not only calculate C=A-B but also print C. Then the necessary statements are as follows:

```
45 IF A<=B THEN 75
55 LET C=A-B
65 PRINT C
75 (next statement)
```

The complement of the "greater than" condition is "less than or equal to". If this condition is true, we branch around the LET and PRINT statements; otherwise these statements are executed.

Nested Decisions

Within the true or false parts of a decision-making structure may be any number or type of statements. In fact, there may be other IF statements in the true or false parts. When an IF statement is included within a set of statements that is executed depending on the condition in another IF statement, we say that there are *nested decisions*.

As an example of nested decisions, assume that the tuition charged a college student is not only based on the number of units for which

74

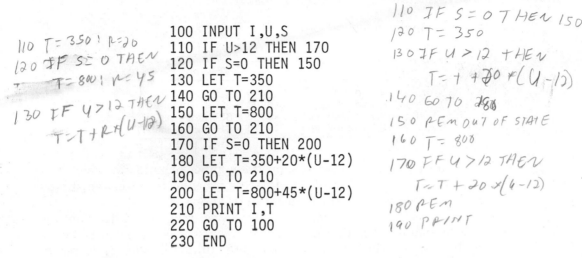

The handwritten annotations to the left of the program:

```
110 T=350 ! R=20
120 IF S=0 THEN
          T=800 ! R=45
130 IF U>12 THEN
          T=T+R*(U-12)
```

The program listing:

```
100 INPUT I,U,S
110 IF U>12 THEN 170
120 IF S=0 THEN 150
130 LET T=350
140 GO TO 210
150 LET T=800
160 GO TO 210
170 IF S=0 THEN 200
180 LET T=350+20*(U-12)
190 GO TO 210
200 LET T=800+45*(U-12)
210 PRINT I,T
220 GO TO 100
230 END
```

The handwritten annotations to the right of the program:

```
110 IF S=0 THEN 150
120 T=350
130 IF U>12 THEN
          T=T+20*(U-12)
140 GO TO 210
150 REM OUT OF STATE
160 T=800
170 FF U>12 THEN
          T=T+20*(U-12)
180 REM
190 PRINT
```

FIGURE 4-9. Tuition calculation with nested decisions.

the student is enrolled, but also on whether the student is a resident of the state. If the number of units is less than or equal to twelve and the student is a state resident, the tuition is $350. However, if the student is not a resident (and the units are less than or equal to twelve) the tuition is $800. If the number of units is greater than twelve and the student is a resident, the tuition is $350 plus $20 for all units over twelve. For a nonresident with more than twelve units, the tuition is $800 plus $45 for each excess unit.

This problem involves first deciding whether the number of units is or is not greater than twelve and then determining whether the student is or is not a state resident. Assume that the input data is the student's identification number (I), the number of units (U), and an in-state code (S) which is 1 if the student is a state resident and 0 otherwise. A program to accomplish this is shown in Fig. 4-9. After accepting the input data, the program compares U with twelve. If U is less than or equal to twelve, the computer falls through to the second IF statement. This statement checks S to determine whether the student is a state resident. If U is greater than twelve, the computer branches to statement 170 which also checks S. The actual tuition depends both on the number of units and on the in-state code.

Within a nested decision may be other nested decisions. In fact, there may be as many nested decisions as the programmer needs. Usually, however, nesting more than one or two decisions makes the program more difficult to understand.

Case Selection

A special type of nested decision involves selecting from among several cases. For example, assume that the tuition charge is based on the following schedule:

Units	Tuition
0.1 to 6.0	$200
6.1 to 12.0	$200 + $25/unit over 6
12.1 to 18.0	$350 + $20/unit over 12
18.1 and up	$470 + $15/unit over 18

There are four cases, depending on the number of units for which the student is enrolled. We wish to write the program to select the appropriate case and perform the required calculations.

The selection process can be accomplished using nested decisions by first determining whether the number of units is less than or equal to six. If it is, we select the first case and the tuition is $200. However, if the number of units is greater than six, we must check whether the number is less than or equal to twelve. If it is, we select the second case and the tuition can be calculated appropriately. However, if the number of units is greater than twelve, we compare the number with eighteen. If it is less than or equal to eighteen, we select the third case; otherwise we select the fourth.

Figure 4-10 shows the tuition-calculating program using this selection logic. The program selectes the appropriate case by comparing U with 6, 12, and 18. After the tuition is calculated, the output is printed. The three GO TO 210 statements are required to branch around the other cases to the PRINT statement when the first, second, or third case is selected.

For certain very specialized types of case selection, BASIC provides the ON-GO TO statement. We will discuss this statement in Section 4-5.

```
100 INPUT I,U
110 IF U>6 THEN 140
120 LET T=200
130 GO TO 210
140 IF U>12 THEN 170
150 LET T=200+25*(U-6)
160 GO TO 210
170 IF U>18 THEN 200
180 LET T=350+20*(U-12)
190 GO TO 210
200 LET T=470+15*(U-18)
210 PRINT I,T
220 GO TO 100
230 END
```

FIGURE 4-10.   Tuition calculation with case selection.

*4-3. VARIATIONS ON THE IF STATEMENT

All versions of BASIC allow the form of the IF statement described in Section 4-1. Some, however, permit alternate forms that may make programming easier. In this section we describe several of these variations on the IF statement. Another variation is described in the next section.

In some versions of BASIC, the words GO TO can replace the word THEN in the IF statement; that is, the syntax is as follows:

ln IF *relational expression* GO TO *ln*

For example, the following IF statement conforms to this syntax:

```
50 IF A>B GO TO 200
```

The effect is the same as the basic form of the IF statement. In this example, if A is greater than B, the computer branches to statement 200; otherwise the computer continues with the next statement in sequence.

Sometimes another BASIC statement can be used in place of a line number in the IF statement. The form is as follows:

ln IF *relational expression* THEN *statement*

For example, the following statement may be used:

```
50 IF A>B THEN PRINT A
```

The effect is that the computer executes the statement within the IF statement if the relational expression is true. If the expression is false, the statement is skipped. In the previous example, if A is greater than B, the computer prints the value of A. If A is not greater than B, the computer bypasses the PRINT statement and goes on to the next statement in sequence.

Most BASIC statements may be used in this form of the IF statement. For example, the following are valid:

```
75 IF X<Y THEN INPUT A,B,C
85 IF K=7 THEN LET K=K+1
98 IF U<=12 THEN GO TO 35
```

---

*Sections marked with an asterisk describe only nonstandard features of BASIC.

In each of these examples, the computer either executes the statement in the IF statement or skips it depending on whether the relational expression is true or false. If the condition is true, then after the statement in the IF statement is executed, the computer continues with the next statement in sequence unless a GO TO statement or other branching statement has been executed.

Another variation of the IF statement is known as the IF-THEN-ELSE statement. The syntax of this statement is as follows:

$$ln \text{ IF } relational \ expression \text{ THEN } \left\{ \begin{matrix} statement \\ ln \end{matrix} \right\} \text{ELSE} \left\{ \begin{matrix} statement \\ ln \end{matrix} \right\}$$

Following the word THEN must be either a statement or a line number, then the word ELSE, and another statement or line number. For example, the following are valid IF-THEN-ELSE statements:

```
60 IF A>B THEN 200 ELSE 100
70 IF X<=Y THEN PRINT X ELSE PRINT Y
80 IF P=Q THEN LET C=0 ELSE 150
```

The effect of the IF-THEN-ELSE statement is that if the relational expression is true, the computer does what is indicated after the word THEN. If a line number is given, the computer branches to the indicated line; if a statement appears after the word THEN, the statement is executed. On the other hand, if the relational expression is false, the computer bypasses the THEN part and does whatever is indicated after the word ELSE. This may involve branching if a line number is given or executing the statement following the word ELSE.

To illustrate, consider the first statement (numbered 60) above. The effect of this statement is that if A is greater than B, the computer branches to statement 200, but if A is not greater than B, the computer branches to statement 100. In the second example above (statement 70), if X is less than or equal to Y, the value of X is printed; otherwise the value of Y is printed. Notice that in this example, since no branching takes place, the computer goes on to the next statement in sequence after executing the appropriate PRINT statement. In the third example above (numbered 80), the computer either executes a LET statement or branches to statement 150 depending on whether P equals Q.

It is sometimes easier to read the IF-THEN-ELSE statement if the different parts of the statement are put on separate lines and indented. For example, we may wish to write statement 70 above as follows:

```
70 IF X>Y THEN
     PRINT X
   ELSE
     PRINT Y
```

```
10 INPUT I,U
20 IF U<=12 THEN
       LET T=350
   ELSE
       LET T=350+20*(U-12)
30 PRINT I,T
40 GO TO 10
50 END
```

FIGURE 4-11.   The tuition calculation program using
an IF-THEN-ELSE statement.

This is accomplished by pressing a special key (not the RETURN key) when we wish to continue the statement on the next line. Sometimes this is the LINE FEED key. In this example, we would type the first line and press LINE FEED, then type the second line followed by the LINE FEED key, then the third line and LINE FEED, and finally the fourth line followed by the RETURN key since this is the end of the statement. Notice that only the first line has a number; the other lines are part of the same statement and thus do not have separate numbers.

To illustrate the use of the IF-THEN-ELSE statement, consider the tuition-calculation program discussed in Section 4-1 (see Fig. 4-1). We can write this program using the IF-THEN-ELSE statement as shown in Fig. 4-11. Notice that if the number of units is less than or equal to twelve, T is set equal to $350; otherwise the value of T is computed by the second LET statement.

In some versions of BASIC, more than one statement can appear between the words THEN and ELSE or after the word ELSE. Such multiple statements must be separated by colons. For example, the following statement may be valid:

```
90 IF A>B THEN LET C=A-B: PRINT C:
          ELSE LET D=B-A: PRINT D
```

In this example, if A is greater than B, the value of C is computed and printed; otherwise the value of D is calculated and printed. Note that some versions of BASIC only allow multiple statements separated by colons after the ELSE (or THEN if there is not an ELSE) in the IF statement. If this were the case, the previous example would be invalid because two statements appear between the THEN and ELSE. The programmer will have to determine what is acceptable in the version of BASIC being used.

It is usually permissible to nest IF-THEN-ELSE statements. For example, the following statement may be acceptable:

```
100 IF X<Y THEN
        PRINT A
    ELSE
        IF X=Y THEN
            PRINT B
        ELSE
            PRINT C
```

While this example is fairly straightforward, the rules can become quite complex especially when an IF statement without the ELSE part is nested in an IF-THEN-ELSE statement. In general, nesting of these statements should be avoided until the programmer becomes very familiar with the language.

*4-4. STRUCTURED DECISION STATEMENTS

A few versions of BASIC provide special statements that simplify programming for decisions. These statements follow very closely the decision-making patterns shown in Figs. 4-3 and 4-7. We refer to these statements as *structured decision statements*. In this section we describe these statements and demonstrate their use in decision making.[†]

To form the basic decision-making pattern shown in Fig. 4-3, we use the structured decision statements in Fig. 4-12. Four statements are required. These are a special form of the IF statement, the THEN statement, the ELSE statement, and the IFEND statement. The IF statement contains only a relational expression following the keyword IF. The THEN statement must appear on the next line after the IF statement. Following the THEN statement must be one or more other BASIC statements and then the ELSE statement. Next come one or more additional BASIC statements and finally the IFEND statement. The statements must always appear in the order shown in Fig. 4-12.

When the computer executes this sequence of statements, it first determines whether the relational expression in the IF statement is true or false. If the expression is true, the computer executes the statements between the THEN statement and the ELSE statement (the true part). If the condition is false, the statements between the ELSE statement and the IFEND statement (the false part) are executed. After performing either the true part or the false part, the computer continues with the next statement following the IFEND statement (unless a branch statement has been executed).

[†]The statements described in this section are available in Dartmouth BASIC 7 and in related versions of BASIC.

ln IF relational expression
ln THEN
$$\vdots$$
statements
$$\vdots$$
ln ELSE
$$\vdots$$
statements
$$\vdots$$
ln IFEND

FIGURE 4-12. The IF/THEN/ELSE/IFEND statements.

```
10 INPUT I,U
20 IF U<=12
30 THEN
40    LET T=350
50 ELSE
60    LET T=350+20*(U-12)
70 IFEND
80 PRINT I,T
90 GO TO 10
99 END
```

FIGURE 4-13.   The tuition calculation program using
IF/THEN/ELSE/IFEND statements.

As an example, consider the simple tuition-calculation program in Fig. 4-1. Using the IF, THEN, ELSE, and IFEND statements, the program can be written as shown in Fig. 4-13. In this program, T is set equal to $350 if the number of units is less than or equal to twelve; otherwise the value of T is computed by the second LET statement. Notice that branching statements are not needed with the structured decision statements. The computer automatically goes to the true or false part and then to the statement following IFEND. In addition, it is not necessary to use the complementary condition in the IF statement. These features make these statements especially easy to use.

In this example we have indented the true and false parts, a common program style used with these statements. This style helps the programmer to see the structure of the decision logic.

There may be any number of statements between the THEN statement and the ELSE statement, and between the ELSE statement and the IFEND statement. The computer will execute all statements in the

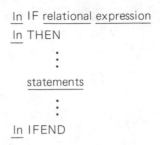

In IF relational expression
In THEN
⋮
statements
⋮
In IFEND

FIGURE 4-14. The IF/THEN/IFEND statements.

true or false part depending on the relational expression in the IF statement. However, the IFEND statement is essential. If it is omitted, the computer will not know where the end of the false part is.

The one-sided decision-making pattern in Fig. 4-7 is coded using the IF, THEN, and IFEND statements. The form is shown in Fig. 4-14. If the relational expression in the IF statement is true, the statements between the THEN statement and the IFEND statement are executed; otherwise these statements are skipped. For example, consider the following sequence of statements:

```
30 IF A>B
40 THEN
50    LET C=A-B
60    PRINT C
70 IFEND
```

If A is greater than B, the computer will execute the LET and PRINT statements and then continue with the next statement following IFEND; otherwise it will skip these statements and go directly to the next statement after the IFEND statement.

The statements shown in Figs. 4-12 and 4-14 can be used for nested decisions. The only restriction is that each IF statement must have a corresponding IFEND statement. For example, consider the tuition-calculation program in Fig. 4-9. The nested decisions in this program could be written as shown in the program in Fig. 4-15. In this program the first IFEND statement (line 180) corresponds to the second IF statement (line 130). The second IFEND statement (line 250) corresponds to the third IF statement (line 200). The last IFEND statement (line 260) is paired with the first IF statement (line 110). All of the IFEND statements are required for the nested decision to function properly. Other valid patterns of nested decisions are shown in Fig. 4-16. Brackets in this figure show the pairing of IF and IFEND statements.

82

```
100 INPUT I,U,S
110 IF U<=12
120 THEN
130    IF S=1
140    THEN
150      LET T=350
160    ELSE
170      LET T=800
180    IFEND
190 ELSE
200    IF S=1
210    THEN
220      LET T=350+20*(U-12)
230    ELSE
240      LET T=800+45*(U-12)
250    IFEND
250 IFEND
270 PRINT I,T
280 GO TO 100
290 END
```

FIGURE 4-15.　The tuition calculation using nested
IF/THEN/ELSE/IFEND statements.

Selecting from among several cases can be done using nested decisions. For example, consider the tuition-calculation program shown in Fig. 4-10. This program can be rewritten as in Fig. 4-17. In this program, if the first condition is true, T is assigned the value of 200 and the computer continues with the next statement following the last IFEND statement (line 260). If the first condition is false, the computer checks the condition in the second IF statement. If this condition is true, the tuition is calculated by the second LET statement; otherwise the condition in the third IF statement is checked. If none of the conditions is true, the LET statement following the last ELSE statement is executed. Notice that there must be a matching IFEND statement for each IF statement.[†]

The structured decision statements discussed in this section can make programming for decisions considerably easier than using the standard IF statement. While not currently available in all versions of BASIC, their availability is expected to increase in the future.

[†]Some versions of BASIC have a special group of statements called a SELECT structure that can be used for case selection in programs such as this.

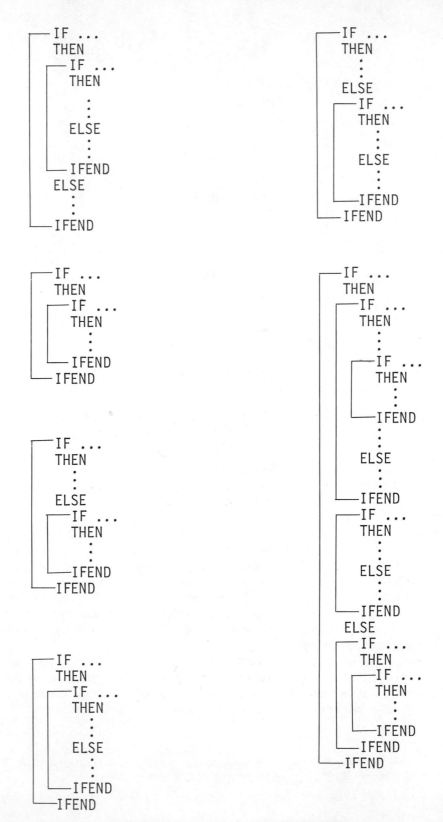

FIGURE 4-16. Some valid nested decisions.

```
100 INPUT I,U
110 IF U<=6
120 THEN
130    LET T=200
140 ELSE
150 IF U<=12
160 THEN
170    LET T=200+25*(U-6)
180 ELSE
190 IF U<=18
200 THEN
210    LET T=350+20*(U-12)
220 ELSE
230    LET T=470+15*(U-18)
240 IFEND
250 IFEND
260 IFEND
270 PRINT I,T
280 GO TO 100
290 END
```

FIGURE 4-17.   The tuition calculation using the IF/
THEN/ELSE/IFEND statements for
case selection.

4-5.   THE ON-GO TO STATEMENT

A statement that can be used for a special type of case selection is the
ON-GO TO statement. The syntax of this statement is as follows:

ln ON *numeric expression* GO TO *ln,ln,* . . .

Following the word ON must be a numeric expression, then the words
GO TO, and finally a list of line numbers separated by commas. For
example, the following is a valid ON-GO TO statement:

```
25 ON X-3 GO TO 45,55,35
```

The effect of the ON-GO TO statement is that the computer first
evaluates the numeric expression. For example, if X equals 4.7 in statement 25 above, X-3 is computed to obtain 1.7. The value of the expression is then rounded to the nearest integer (i.e., whole number). In
the example, the value of the expression (1.7) is rounded to the integer
2. (Some versions of BASIC do not round the value. Instead, the
fractional part is simply dropped. This is called *truncation*. If this were

the case in the example above, 1.7 would be truncated to get the integer 1.) Finally, the computer counts over the number of places in the list of line numbers indicated by the integer value and branches to the statement whose number appears in that place. In the example, the computer would count over two places and branch to statement 55.

As another example, consider the following statement:

$$65 \text{ ON N GO TO } 45,55,55,25,45,75,75$$

In this example, the numeric expression is just the variable N. The value of N would be rounded to the nearest integer. Then, if the integer value is 1 or 5, the computer branches to statement 45; if it is 2 or 3, the branch is to statement 55; if the value is 4, the computer branches to statement 25; and finally, if the integer value is 6 or 7, the branch is to statement 75.

The integer that results from rounding the value of the numeric expression must be between 1 and the number of line numbers in the list. For example, in the previous statement the value must be between 1 and 7. If the integer is less than 1 or greater than 7, an execution error occurs causing an error message to be printed and the program to stop. (In some versions of BASIC, an error does not occur in this situation. Instead, the computer continues with the next statement in sequence after the ON-GO TO statement.)

The ON-GO TO statement is usually used to select one of several cases based on the value of a variable with an integer value. For example, in the tuition-calculation problem, assume that the variable C is a code indicating the amount of the scholarship that a student is to receive. If the value of C is 1, the scholarship is $100. If C is 2 or 3, the scholarship is $150. A value of 4 indicates a $300 scholarship, while if C equals 5, the scholarship is $400. In this program, the following sequence of statements can be used to select the appropriate scholarship:

```
51 ON C GO TO 52,54,54,56,58
52 LET S=100
53 GO TO 59
54 LET S=150
55 GO TO 59
56 LET S=300
57 GO TO 59
58 LET S=400
59 (next statement)
```

The ON-GO TO statement branches to statement 52,54,56, or 58 based on the value of C. The variable S is then assigned the appropriate scholarship amount. Notice that after each LET statement (except the

```
100 INPUT I,H,S
110 ON S GO TO 120,140,160
120 LET G=4.50*H
130 GO TO 170
140 LET G=6.50*H
150 GO TO 170
160 LET G=9.00*H
170 PRINT I,G
180 GO TO 100
190 END
```

FIGURE 4-18.   A payroll program.

last, where it is not necessary), the statement GO TO 59 causes the computer to bypass the other cases and go on to the next part of the program.

As another example of the use of the ON-GO TO statement, assume that an employee's pay rate is based on the shift that the employee works. The input contains a code that indicates the shift. If the code is 1, the employee works the day shift at the rate of $4.50 per hour. A shift code equal to 2 indicates that the employee works the evening shift at $6.75 per hour. A night shift employee has a code equal to 3 and earns $9.00 per hour. Figure 4-18 shows the program that computes the employee's gross pay based on this schedule. Input consists of the employee's identification number (I), hours worked (H), and shift code (S). The ON-GO TO statement selects the appropriate calculation based on the value of S. Then the output is printed.

The ON-GO TO statement can be useful in certain case-selection situations. There are many times, however, when it cannot be used. At such times nested decisions using IF statements are required.

REVIEW QUESTIONS

1. What is the meaning of each of the following relational operators?
    (a) >
    (b) <=
    (c) <>
    (d) =

2. Write a statement that branches to statement 100 if the value of A is less than or equal to 7.5.

3. Write a single statement that branches to statement 200 if the value of X is greater than Y or the value of Y is greater than X.

4. If the value of A is 2, B is 3, and C is 4, what is the truth value of each of the following relational expressions?
   (a) A>B
   (b) C<=B+1
   (c) 12/A+3=B^2
   (d) A*B<>C+2

5. Assume that the value of X is 5, Y is 3, and Z is 1. What is the number of the next statement executed after each of the following statements is executed? (Assume that the statements are numbered by tens.)
   (a)   50 GO TO 80
   (b) 150 IF X<>Y THEN 180
   (c) 250 IF Z>=X-Y THEN 280
   (d) 350 ON Y GO TO 130,230,330,430,530

6. What is the complement of each of the following?
   (a) A=B
   (b) X<=Y
   (c) P>Q
   (d) S<>T

7. Consider the program shown in Fig. 4–5. What output is printed for each of the following sets of input?
   (a) 234, 40
   (b) 345, 44
   (c) 456, 32
   (d) 567, 0

8. Write a sequence of statements containing one IF statement that assigns the larger of X and Y to Z. Did you use a one-sided or two-sided decision? Write another sequence of statements using the other approach.

9. A program structure in which one decision is contained in another is called _____.

10. Consider the program shown in Fig. 4-9 or 4-15. What output is printed for each of the following sets of input?
    (a) 1001, 8, 1
    (b) 1002, 15, 0
    (c) 1003, 12, 0
    (d) 1004, 13, 1

11. Consider the program shown in Fig. 4-10 or 4-17. What output is printed for each of the following sets of input?
    (a) 123, 15

    (b) 234, 3

    (c) 345, 12

    (d) 456, 20

    (e) 567, 8

    (f) 678, 14

12. What variations on the IF statement are available in the version of BASIC you are using? Are the structured decision statements available?

13. Write a single statement that branches to statement 100 if the value of A is 1, 3, or 4; to statement 200 if A is 2 or 5; and to 300 if A is 6.

14. Rewrite the program in Fig. 4–18 without using the ON-GO TO statement.

PROGRAMMING PROBLEMS

1. Commission paid to a salesperson is often based on the amount sold by the person. Assume that the commission is 7½% if a person's sales total less than $10,000 and 9% if sales total $10,000 or more. Then the commission is calculated by multiplying the person's sales by the appropriate commission percentage.

    Write a BASIC program that accepts the salesperson's identification number and total sales, calculates the commission, and prints the result along with the identification number. Test the program with data for salesperson number 18735 with sales of $11,250; with data for salesperson number 27630 whose sales total $6,500; and with data for salesperson 31084 whose sales were $10,000.

2. The telephone company's charge for long-distance calls is based on distance and on the length of time of a call. Assume that between two cities the rate is $1.10 for the first three minutes or fraction thereof, and $.40 for each additional minute. Data for a number of customers who made calls between these two cities consist of the customer's number and length of call.

    Write a BASIC program to calculate the charge for each call. Print the customer number; the length of the call, and the charge. Use the following data to test the program:

Customer Number	Length of Call
9606	8
9735	3
2802	2
7921	5
1509	4
5371	1

3. Write a BASIC program to find the absolute value of a number. The absolute value of x is x if x is non-negative and $-x$ if x is negative. Input should be the number; output should give the original number and its absolute value. (Do *not* use the built-in absolute value function.) Use the following input data to test the program:

$$25.0$$
$$-25.0$$
$$0.0$$
$$-84.6$$
$$132.5$$

4. A real estate office employs several salespeople. At the end of each month, the total value of all property sold by each salesperson is used to calculate the person's commission. If total sales exceed $400,000, the commission is 3½% of the sales. If the sales are greater than $200,000 but not more than $400,000, the commission is 3% of sales. Otherwise the commission is 2½% of the sales.

Write a BASIC program that accepts the salesperson's number and total sales, performs the necessary commission calculation, and prints the result along with the salesperson's number and total sales.

Use the following data to test the program:

Salesperson's Number	Total Sales
1085	$452,350
1720	$142,500
2531	$ 95,000
3007	$255,500
3219	$173,250
4806	$482,950
6111	$310,000
7932	$218,000

5. An electric company charges its customers 5 cents per kilowatt-hour for electricity used up to the first 100 kilowatt-hours; 4 cents per hour for each of the next 200 kilowatt-hours (up to 300 kilowatt-hours); and 3 cents per hour for all electricity used over 300 kilowatt-hours. Write a BASIC program to calculate the total charge for each customer. Input to the program consists of the customer's number and kilowatt-hours used. Output from the program should give the customer number, the kilowatt-hours used, and the total charge. Use the following data to test the program:

Customer Number	Kilowatt-hours Used
1065	640
2837	85
3832	220
6721	300
8475	100

6. Write a BASIC program that finds the maximum of three numbers. Input consists of the three numbers; output should be the largest of the three. Use the following sets of input data to test the program:

$$10,25,16$$
$$17,38,41$$
$$100,52,77$$
$$-3,-8,-1$$
$$0,45,-6$$
$$-37,0,-42$$
$$39,39,39$$
$$14,14,8$$

7. Write a BASIC program to determine whether a student is a freshman, sophomore, junior, or senior based on the number of units that the student has completed. Input to the program consists of the student's number and the number of units completed.

A student's classification is based on his or her units completed according to the following schedule:

Units Completed	Classification	Code
Less than 30 units	freshman	1
30 units or more but less than 60 units	sophomore	2
60 units or more but less than 90 units	junior	3
90 units or more	senior	4

The output from the program should give the student's number, units completed, and the classification code (1, 2, 3, or 4). Use the following data to test the program:

Student Number	Units Completed
2352	38.0
3639	15.5
4007	29.5
4560	67.0
4915	103.5
8473	89.0

8. Write a BASIC program to evaluate the following function:

$$f(x) = \begin{cases} -x \text{ if } x < 0 \\ 1 \text{ if } x = 0 \\ 0 \text{ if } x > 0 \text{ and } x \leqslant 10 \\ 2x \text{ if } x > 10 \end{cases}$$

Input is the value of x; print the values of x and $f(x)$. Use the following data to test the program:

$$38.60$$
$$9.00$$
$$10.00$$
$$0.00$$
$$-45.60$$
$$0.01$$
$$-0.01$$
$$10.53$$

9. The basic charge for computer time is based on the number of hours of time used during a month. The schedule is as follows:

Hours Used	Basic Charge
0.00 to 5.00	$200
5.01 to 15.00	$200 plus $35 per hour for all time over 5 hours
15.01 and up	$550 plus $30 per hour for all time over 15 hours

In addition, there is a surcharge added to the basic charge depending on the priority used. The priority is indicated by a code. The surcharge is as follows:

Priority Code	Surcharge
0	0
1	$50
2	$150

Write a BASIC program that accepts a customer's account number, number of hours used, and priority code; calculates the total charge; and prints the account number and charge. Use the following data to test the program:

Account Number	Hours Used	Priority Code
11825	3.52	0
14063	17.06	1
17185	7.93	1
19111	12.00	2
20045	5.00	1
21352	5.84	0
22841	27.94	2
23051	1.55	2
29118	15.02	0

10. Write a BASIC program to analyze the results of a psychological experiment. Each subject in the experiment took from one to four tests. The first set of input is the subject's identification code and number of tests taken. The next set of input is the test scores. The program must calculate the average test score for each subject. The output should give the subject's identification code, the number of tests taken, the score on each test, and the average score. (*Hint:* After accepting the first set of input, use an ON-GO TO statement to select the appropriate routine based on the number of tests taken.)

Use the following data to test the program:

Identification Code	Number of Tests Taken	Test Scores
408	3	17, 16, 21
519	1	24
523	2	14, 18
584	4	22, 16, 17, 14
601	1	12
677	3	25, 23, 24
701	4	17, 18, 21, 15
713	2	13, 12

11. Write a BASIC program that computes the coordinates of the point of intersection of two straight lines. Assume that the lines are given by the following equations:

$$y = sx + a$$

$$y = tx + b$$

where s and t are the slopes, and a and b are the intercepts. In addition determine the number of the quadrant (1, 2, 3, or 4) of the point of intersection. (If the point of intersection falls on an axis, use the lower quadrant number of the quadrants separated by the axis.)

The program should accept the values of s, a, t, and b; perform the necessary computations; and print the coordinates of the point of intersection and the quadrant number. Use the following data to test the program:

s	a	t	b
18.0	6.0	30.0	6.0
2.0	8.0	-3.0	-2.0
1.0	8.0	-2.0	-22.0
3.0	-7.0	1.0	-1.0
-0.5	-3.0	2.0	-8.0

12. Input to a payroll program consists of the employee's number, year-to-date pay, base pay rate, shift code, and hours worked. Write a program to accept this data; compute the employee's gross pay, withholding tax, social security tax, and net pay; and print these results along with the employee's number.

The gross pay is found by multiplying the hours worked by the pay rate, where the pay rate is the product of the base pay rate and the shift factor. The shift factor comes from the following table:

Shift Code	Shift Factor
0	1.00
1	1.25
2	1.50

The withholding tax is the product of the gross pay and the tax rate. The tax rate is found from the following table:

Gross Pay	Tax Rate
Less than $100.00	0
$100.00 to $149.99	8%
$150.00 to $199.00	12%
$200.00 to $299.00	15%
$300.00 or more	17.5%

The social security tax (FICA tax) depends on the gross pay and the year-to-date pay. If the year-to-date pay is greater than $17,300, there is no social security tax. If the year-to-date pay plus the gross pay is less than or equal to $17,300, the social security tax is 6.05% of the gross pay. If the year-to-date pay is less than $17,300, but the sum of the year-to-date and gross pay is greater than $17,300, the tax is 6.05% of the difference between $17,300 and the year-to-date pay.

The net pay is computed by subtracting the withholding tax and social security tax from the gross pay.

Use the following input data to test the program:

Employee Number	Year-to-date Pay	Base Pay Rate	Shift Code	Hours Worked
1001	10,312.00	4.50	1	34.5
1002	3,888.75	3.25	0	25.0
1003	12,365.50	4.00	0	30.0
1004	15,284.25	5.25	2	38.5
1005	17,138.50	6.25	0	40.0
1006	18,465.00	8.95	2	48.0
1007	12,061.25	5.00	1	35.0
1008	17,225.00	6.00	1	40.0

5 | PROGRAMMING FOR REPETITION

As we have seen, a group of statements that is repeatedly executed is called a loop. In Chapter 3 we introduced the use of a loop to repeat the steps of a program so that more than one set of input data can be processed. We call such a loop an *input loop* since there is an input operation within the loop. Sometimes a loop does not contain an input operation but just processes data. We call this type of loop a *processing loop*. We will see several examples of processing loops in this chapter.

Whenever there is a loop in a program, one important question is how to *control* the loop. By this we mean how do we get the computer to *stop* looping? For example, consider the tuition-calculation program shown in Fig. 5-1. [This is the same program as that shown in Fig. 4-1(a).] The loop consists of statements 10 through 70. Notice that there is nothing in the program that stops the loop. The program will continue to loop as long as input data is supplied. When there is no

```
10 INPUT I,U
20 IF U>12 THEN 50
30 LET T=350
40 GO TO 60
50 LET T=350+20*(U-12)
60 PRINT I,T
70 GO TO 10
80 END
```

FIGURE 5-1.   The tuition calculation program.

more input data (i.e., when a control C is entered), the computer will stop the program.

The type of loop used in this program is called an *uncontrolled loop* because there is no mechanism within the program to stop the repetition. As another example of an uncontrolled loop, consider the following statements:

```
10 LET K=1
20 GO TO 10
```

If these statements were in a program, the computer would continue to loop until stopped by the computer operator. Again there is nothing within this group of statements that causes the computer to stop after a period of time. Hence, this is an uncontrolled loop.

In this chapter we discuss programming techniques for controlling loops. We also describe special BASIC statements that are used specifically for loop control.

5-1. CONTROLLING LOOPS

As we have seen, the GO TO statement can be used to create a loop by branching from the end of a group of statements to the beginning. To control such a loop, we normally use an IF statement to branch out of the loop when a particular condition occurs. The techniques discussed here illustrate this approach to loop control for input loops and processing loops.

Input Loops

The program in Fig. 5-1 contains an uncontrolled input loop. Each time the loop is executed, the computer accepts a new set of input data. A common technique for controlling such a loop is to use a special set of input data to indicate the end of the regular data. Each time that input data is accepted, the program checks whether the special end-of-data input has been entered. If not, the program continues with the normal execution of the statements in the loop. When the end-of-data input has been entered, the program branches out of the loop.

Usually the end-of-data input contains a value for one of the variables that is not used in any other set of input data. This is called a *trailer value* or a *sentinel*. For example, in the tuition-calculation program in Fig. 5-1, the input consists of the student's identification number and number of units. We could use a special identification number as a trailer value. The value would have to be one that is not used as an

```
10 INPUT I,U
20 IF I=9999 THEN 90
30 IF U>12 THEN 60
40 LET T=350
50 GO TO 70
60 LET T=350+20*(U-12)
70 PRINT I,T
80 GO TO 10
90 END
```

FIGURE 5-2.   The tuition calculation program with
input loop control.

actual student's identification number. Thus, each time that a set of
input data is accepted we can test for this value.

We will assume that the trailer value for the tuition data is the
identification number 9999. Figure 5-2 shows the program with this
form of loop control. First the program accepts the identification number (I) and number of units. Then it checks the value of I. If I is *not*
equal to 9999, the program continues with the next statement in
sequence. If the value of I equals 9999, the program branches out of
the loop to the END statement. This causes the computer to stop execution of the program. Notice that the end-of-data test comes immediately after the INPUT statement. We must check for the end of the
input at this time since we do not want to process the trailer value.

Notice that the program branches to the END statement when the
trailer value is detected. This causes the END statement to be executed,
which stops the program. While this is appropriate for the problem discussed, there are situations where additional processing is necessary
before the END statement is executed. We will see an example of this
later in the chapter.

When running the program in Fig. 5-2, it is important to enter the
trailer value correctly. Since the INPUT statement has two variables,
two values must be typed each time a question mark appears at the
terminal. This is required even with the trailer value. Thus, when the
9999 identification number is typed, we must also type a value for
the units even though this value will not be processed. The usual procedure is to enter zero for any additional variables, but any value will
do. Thus, the input line with the trailer value for the tuition-calculation
program would appear as follows:

? 9999,0

The program will stop execution after this line is typed.

Processing Loops

A processing loop is a loop that is controlled by a particular condition on the data that is processed in the loop, not by an input value. Usually computations take place within the loop that affect the value of some variable. Each time the loop is executed, the variable is used in a relational test to determine whether the loop should be terminated. If the loop is properly designed, the condition will eventually become true and the program will branch out of the loop.

For example, consider the problem of determining the amount of time that it takes for a bank deposit to double at a given interest rate. Assume that $1000 is put into a bank at 5% interest compounded annually. This means that at the end of the first year, the interest is 5% of $1000 or $50, which is added to the original deposit to give a balance of $1050. At the end of the second year, the interest is 5% of $1050 or $52.50. The balance is then $1102.50. Thus, the interest is added to the balance at the end of each year and used in the next year's interest calculation. Our problem is to write a program that prints a table of yearly interest and balance until the deposit has doubled to $2000.

Figure 5–3(a) shows a program that accomplishes this. Notice that there is no INPUT statement in the program; this program does not require any input data. The variable B is the bank balance; initially B is $1000. Y is a variable that counts the number of years; for the first year's calculation Y is 1. The loop consists of statements 30 through 80. The IF statement, numbered 30, stops the loop when B is greater than or equal to $2000. Within the loop, the current year's interest (I) is calculated by multiplying B by .05. The value of I is then added to B to give the new balance. (Recall from Chapter 3 that the statement LET B=B+I adds the value of I to the old value of B and assigns the result to B.) The output is then printed and Y is increased by 1 for the next year. The GO TO statement branches back to the beginning of the loop (which is *not* the first statement in the program). The processing is repeated as long as B is less than $2000. The output from the program is the table shown in Fig. 5-3(b). The first column is the year, the second column is the interest for the year, and the last column is the year-end balance.

Counting Loops

A special type of processing loop control that is often used involves counting the number of times that a loop is executed and branching out

```
10 LET B=1000
20 LET Y=1
30 IF B>=2000 THEN 90
40 LET I=.05*B
50 LET B=B+I
60 PRINT Y,I,B
70 LET Y=Y+1
80 GO TO 30
90 END
```

(a) The program

1	50	1050
2	52.5	1102.5
3	55.125	1157.63
4	57.8813	1215.51
5	60.7753	1276.28
6	63.8141	1340.1
7	67.0048	1407.1
8	70.355	1477.46
9	73.8728	1551.33
10	77.5664	1628.89
11	81.4447	1710.34
12	85.517	1795.86
13	89.7928	1885.65
14	94.2825	1979.93
15	98.9966	2078.93

(b) The output

FIGURE 5-3.   The interest calculation program.

of the loop when the count reaches some desired number. This approach uses a variable as a *counter*. Before entering the loop, the counter is *initialized* to some beginning value. Each time the loop is executed, the value of the counter is *tested* to determine whether its value has exceeded some final value; in addition, the counter is *modified*, usually by increasing or *incrementing* its value by 1.

For example, the following statements show the general form of a loop that is to be executed 100 times:

```
25 LET K=1              (initialize counter)
35 IF K>100 THEN 95     (test counter)
        .
        .
        .
(statements in loop)
```

.
.
.

```
75 LET K=K+1                    (modify counter)
85 GO TO 35
95 (next statement)
```

In this example, the counter is the variable K. Initially K is assigned the value 1. Then K is tested to see whether it exceeds 100. If this is the case, the computer branches out of the loop. However, if K is less than or equal to 100, the loop is executed. At the end of the loop, the value of K is increased by 1 and the loop is repeated.

Notice that the IF statement is such that the loop is terminated when K is *greater than* 100. This is necessary to insure that the loop is executed exactly 100 times. If the IF statement were coded so that the computer branched out of the loop when the counter *equaled* 100, the loop would be executed only 99 times.

We can use this technique in the interest-calculation program. Assume that we only wish to print a table of interest and balance for ten years. The variable Y may be used to count the number of years and, at the same time, the number of times that the loop is executed. The program is shown in Fig. 5-4. In this program, Y is initialized to 1 in statement 20. Each time through the loop, Y is incremented by 1 (statement 70). The loop is stopped when Y becomes greater than 10 (statement 30).

As another example of this form of loop control, consider the problem of finding the total and average of twenty test scores. Assume that the test scores are to be entered one at a time at the terminal and that there is no trailer value. The program must accept the data, calculate the total and average, and print the results.

One way to write the program is to use twenty variables, one for each test score. Such a program, however, would be tedious to code. A better approach is to accept and process the data within a loop. Al-

```
10 LET B=1000
20 LET Y=1
30 IF Y>10 THEN 90
40 LET I=.05*B
50 LET B=B+I
60 PRINT Y,I,B
70 LET Y=Y+1
80 GO TO 30
90 END
```

FIGURE 5-4.   The interest calculation program with a counting loop.

```
100 LET T=0
110 LET I=1
120 IF I>20 THEN 170
130 INPUT S
140 LET T=T+S
150 LET I=I+1
160 GO TO 120
170 LET A=T/20
180 PRINT T,A
190 END
```

FIGURE 5-5.   A program to total and average twenty
test scores.

though the loop in this case contains an INPUT statement, we cannot use an end-of-data check to terminate it because there is no trailer value. However, since we know that there are exactly twenty test scores, we can control the loop by counting the number of times that the loop is executed.

The program is shown in Fig. 5-5. The variable T is used to accumulate the total of the test scores. Each time through the loop, the INPUT statement accepts a test score (S). The value of S is then added to T and the result is assigned to T. Notice that initially T must be set equal to zero outside the loop so that with the first execution of the loop, the first test score is added to zero. (Some versions of BASIC automatically set all variables to zero before the program is executed.) Each successive time through the loop, T is increased by the value of another test score until all twenty scores have been entered and added.

The loop in this program is controlled by using the variable I as a counter. Initially I is set equal to 1. Each time through the loop, I is increased by 1 and tested to see whether it is greater than 20. When I exceeds 20, the program branches out of the loop and calculates the average by dividing T by 20. Then the output is printed and the program terminates.

This program processes exactly twenty test scores. A variation on the program is to accept the number of test scores to be processed as input ahead of the other data. Then the program is not limited to processing exactly twenty values.

The program with this modification is shown in Fig. 5-6. The first INPUT statement accepts the number of test scores and assigns the value to the variable N. The loop in this program is the same as in the previous program except for the IF statement. In the IF statement, the counter is compared with N and the loop is terminated if I is greater than the number of test scores. The average is computed by dividing T by the number of scores (N).

```
100  INPUT N
110  LET T=0
120  LET I=1
130  IF I>N THEN 180
140  INPUT S
150  LET T=T+S
160  LET I=I+1
170  GO TO 130
180  LET A=T/N
190  PRINT T,A
200  END
```

FIGURE 5-6.   A program to total and average a given
number of test scores.

In these examples the testing step is at the beginning of the loop.
However, this is not essential. We could put the testing step in the
middle or at the end of the loop depending on the requirements of the
problem. For example, the following statements execute a loop 100
times but with the counter test at the end of the loop:

```
25 LET K=1                       (initialize counter)
35 (first statement in loop)
     .
     .
     .
   (statements in loop)
     .
     .
     .
75 LET K=K+1                     (modify counter)
85 IF K<=100 THEN 35             (test counter)
95 (next statement)
```

Note that the loop is repeated as long as the value of the counter is
less than or equal to 100.

We can also vary the way in which counting is done. The initial
value of the counter does not have to be 1; it can be any value, depending on the problem. In addition, we need not count by ones. We can
modify the counter by adding or subtracting any reasonable value. The
test condition is determined by the initial value of the counter, how it
is modified each time through the loop, and the number of times we
wish to execute the loop.

To illustrate these variations, the following sequence counts from 0
to 10 by twos:

```
20 LET L=0
30 IF L>10 THEN 80
     .
     .
     .
60 LET L=L+2
70 GO TO 30
80 (next statement)
```

Another alternative is to count backwards, as in the following example that counts from 10 to 1:

```
130 LET M=10
140 IF M<1 THEN 200
     .
     .
     .
180 LET M=M-1
190 GO TO 140
200 (next statement)
```

Notice in this example that each time through the loop we decrease or *decrement* the counter by one. We can also modify the counter by a fractional amount. For example, the following statements count from 0 to 1 in increments of .05:

```
210 LET X=0
220 IF X>1 THEN 280
     .
     .
     .
260 LET X=X+.05
270 GO TO 220
280 (next statement)
```

Patterns of Loop Control

The discussion and examples in this section illustrate several different patterns of loop control. In all patterns the loop is repeated until some condition occurs that signals the end of the loop. However, the patterns vary in the placement of the end-of-loop test. Figure 5–7 summarizes the differences graphically.

Figure 5–7(a) shows the basic loop pattern with the termination test in the middle of the loop. In Fig. 5–7(b) the test is at the beginning

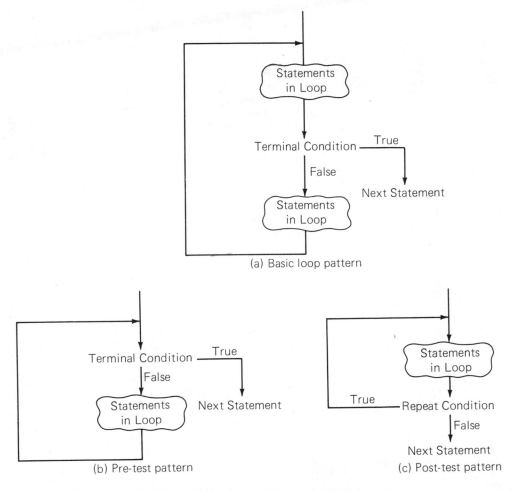

(a) Basic loop pattern

(b) Pre-test pattern

(c) Post-test pattern

FIGURE 5-7. Patterns of loop control.

of the loop. This pattern is called a *pre-test* loop. When the test is the last statement in the loop, as in Fig. 5-7(c), the pattern is called a *post-test* loop. All loops in programs fall into one of these patterns. The implementation of these patterns in BASIC using IF and GO TO statements is shown in Fig. 5-8.

Program Style

To make the loop structure easier to understand in the program, many programmers indent the statements within a loop. For example, the loop part of the interest-calculation program in Fig. 5-3 might be coded as follows:

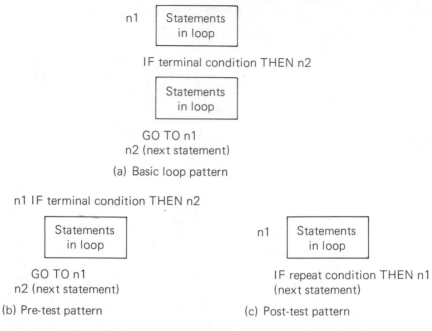

(a) Basic loop pattern

(b) Pre-test pattern

(c) Post-test pattern

FIGURE 5-8. Loop control patterns using IF and GO TO statements.

```
30 IF B>=2000 THEN 90
40    LET I=.05*B
50    LET B=B+I
60    PRINT Y,I,B
70    LET Y=Y+1
80 GO TO 30
```

The statements indented between the IF statement and the GO TO statement form the main part of the loop. Whether or not a style such as this is used depends on whether the programmer thinks it is helpful in understanding the program logic.

Nested Loops

Within a loop may be other loops. Such a combination is referred to as *nested loops*. Any of the loop patterns in Fig. 5-7 may be nested within any other. The effect is that an inner loop is completely executed each time an outer loop is performed.

For example, assume that we wish to determine the amount of time it will take for a bank deposit to double at interest rates varying from

```
      100 LET R=.03
  ┌── 110 IF R>.07 THEN 220
  │   120 LET B=1000
  │   130 LET Y=1
  │ ┌─ 140 IF B>=2000 THEN 200
  │ │ 150 LET I=R*B
  │ │ 160 LET B=B+I
  │ │ 170 PRINT Y,I,B
  │ │ 180 LET Y=Y+1
  │ └─ 190 GO TO 140
  │   200 LET R=R+.01
  └── 210 GO TO 110
      220 END
```

FIGURE 5-9.   The interest calculation program with
nested loops.

3% to 7% in 1% increments. One approach is to run the program in
Fig. 5-3 five times, each time using a different interest rate in the interest calculation. A better approach, however, is to put another loop in
the program that repeats the interest calculation five times, each with a
different rate. The resulting program is shown in Fig 5-9.

In this program statements 120 through 190 are the same as in the
previous program except for the line numbers and the use of the variable R for the interest rate in the interest calculation. The value of R is
controlled by a loop that surrounds this group of statements. Initially,
R is set equal to .03. Each succeeding time through the loop, R is
increased by .01. This loop is terminated when R becomes greater
than .07.

Notice in this program that the inner loop (statements 140 through
190) is completely contained within the outer loop (statements 110
through 210). (Brackets are used in the diagram to show the nested
loops.) Each time the outer loop is repeated, the inner loop is executed
completely. Since the outer loop is performed five times, the inner loop
is completely performed five times. Hence, the program produces five
tables, each similar to that shown in Fig. 5-3(b), but with a different
interest rate used in the calculation of each table.

*5-2.   WHILE LOOPS

A few versions of BASIC provide special statements for general loop
control. These are the DO WHILE and LOOP statements. Together
these statements form a loop that is called a *WHILE loop*. In this sec-

tion we describe these statements and demonstrate their use for loop control.†

The syntax of a WHILE loop is as follows:

ln DO WHILE *relational expression*

        .
        .
        .

    statements

        .
        .
        .

ln LOOP

The first statement, a DO WHILE statement, contains a relational expression. Following the DO WHILE statement is a sequence of statements that is to be repeatedly executed. At the end of the loop there must be a LOOP statement. For example, the following is a valid WHILE loop:

```
40 DO WHILE I<=10
50   PRINT I
60   LET I=I+1
70 LOOP
```

The effect of the WHILE loop is to execute repeatedly the statements in the loop as long as the relational expression in the DO WHILE loop is true. In the above example the PRINT and LET statements are repeatedly executed as long as I is less than or equal to 10. As soon as the relational expression becomes false, the computer branches out of the loop and continues with the next statement following the LOOP statement.

A WHILE loop is actually a pre-test loop. The pattern is shown graphically in Fig. 5–10. When a DO WHILE statement is encountered, the computer first evaluates the relational expression. If the expression is *false*, the computer branches to the next statement following the LOOP statement. If the expression is *true*, the computer executes the statements in the loop up to the LOOP statement. The relational expression is again evaluated and, if true, the loop is repeated. This continues until the relational expression becomes false. Control then transfers to the statement after the LOOP statement. Notice that because the expression is evaluated at the *beginning* of the loop, it is possible

---

†The statements described in this section are available in Dartmouth BASIC 7 and in related versions of BASIC.

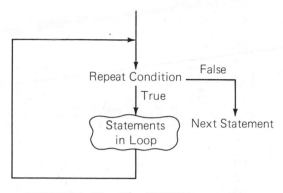

FIGURE 5-10.   The WHILE loop pattern.

that the loop will not be executed at all. If the relational expression is false when the DO WHILE statement is first encountered, the loop will be bypassed completely.

With a WHILE loop we do not need an IF statement or a GO TO statement for loop control. The testing and looping functions are built into the DO WHILE and LOOP statements. We can create the same effect, however, using an IF statement and GO TO statement in a pre-test pattern. To do this we must use the complement of the condition in the DO WHILE statement. Thus, the following sequence of statements is equivalent to the WHILE loop at the beginning of this section:

```
40 IF I>10 THEN 80
50    PRINT I
60    LET I=I+1
70 GO TO 40
80 (next statement)
```

In a WHILE loop there may be any number of statements between the DO WHILE and LOOP statements. The computer will repeatedly execute all statements while the logical expression is true. However, the LOOP statement is essential. If it is omitted, the computer will not know where the end of the loop is located.

Notice in our example that we have indented the statements in the loop. Although not required, this is a common programming style that makes it easier to see the loop structure in a program.

We can use a WHILE loop to control any of the types of loops discussed in the previous section. Sometimes, however, the structure of the program must be modified slightly. For example, to control an input loop with a trailer value, we must have *two* INPUT statements. One INPUT statement is outside the WHILE loop and accepts the first set of input data. The other INPUT statement is within the WHILE loop (usually the last statement) and accepts each successive set of

109

```
100 INPUT I,U
110 DO WHILE I<>9999
120    IF U<=12
130    THEN
140       LET T=350
150    ELSE
160       LET T=350+20*(U-12)
170    IFEND
180    PRINT I,T
190    INPUT I,U
200 LOOP
210 END
```

FIGURE 5-11.   The tuition calculation program with a
                WHILE loop.

```
10 LET B=1000
20 LET Y=1
30 DO WHILE B<2000
40    LET I=.05*B
50    LET B=B+I
60    PRINT Y,I,B
70    LET Y=Y+1
80 LOOP
90 END
```

FIGURE 5-12.   The interest calculation program with a
                WHILE loop.

input data. The relational expression in the DO WHILE statement checks for the absence of the trailer value. Figure 5-11 shows the pattern in the tuition-calculation program (Fig. 5-2). (Notice that we have used the structured decision statements in this program. Usually if a version of BASIC provides WHILE loops, it also allows structured decision statements.)

In this program, the first INPUT statement accepts the first set of input data. The DO WHILE statement tests the value of I to see whether it is *not* equal to 9999, the trailer value. When the loop is executed, the tuition is calculated and the output is printed. The INPUT statement at the end of the loop then accepts the next set of input data. The relational expression is checked again, and if true, the loop is repeated. Finally, after the last set of input data has been accepted and processed, the trailer value is entered with a value of 9999 for I. Since the relational expression is no longer true, execution continues with the next statement after the LOOP statement.

The interest-calculation program in Fig. 5-3 can easily be written with a WHILE loop. Since this program uses a pre-test loop, we can replace the IF statement with a DO WHILE statement using the complementary condition and replace the GO TO 30 statement with a LOOP statement. The modified program is shown in Fig. 5-12.

The program to total and average twenty test scores in Fig. 5-5 used a post-test counting loop. We can rewrite this program fairly easily with a WHILE loop. The result is shown in Fig. 5-13. The counter must be initialized outside the loop. Within the loop, the counter is incremented. The DO WHILE statement causes the loop to be repeated as long as the counter is less than or equal to 20.

WHILE loops may be nested. The only restriction is that each DO WHILE statement must have a corresponding LOOP statement. For example, the interest-calculation program in Fig. 5-9 uses nested loops. This program can be rewritten with WHILE loops as shown in Fig. 5-14. Notice that each DO WHILE statement has a matching LOOP statement. (Brackets are used in the diagram to show the nested loop

```
100 LET T=0
110 LET I=1
120 DO WHILE I<=20
130    INPUT S
140    LET T=T+S
150    LET I=I+1
160 LOOP
170 LET A=T/20
180 PRINT T,A
190 END
```

FIGURE 5-13.   A program to total and average twenty
test scores with a WHILE loop.

```
100 LET R=.03
110 DO WHILE R<=.07
120    LET B=1000
130    LET Y=1
140    DO WHILE B<2000
150       LET I=R*B
160       LET B=B+I
170       PRINT Y,I,B
180       LET Y=Y+1
190    LOOP
200    LET R=R+.01
210 LOOP
220 END
```

FIGURE 5-14.   A program with nested WHILE loops.

structure better.) The effect of execution is that the inner WHILE loop will be completely executed for each repetition of the outer WHILE loop.

One important thing to notice in all these examples of the use of WHILE loops is the lack of GO TO statements. If structured decision statements and WHILE loops are available in the version of BASIC being used, it is completely unnecessary to use GO TO statements. In general, this greatly reduces the complexity of programs. A program written with few or no GO TO statements is easier to understand, debug, and modify than an equivalent program written with many GO TO statements.

5-3. FOR LOOPS

Counting loops play an important role in programming. In Section 5-1 we saw several examples of the use of counting loops. Later chapters will show more examples. Because of the importance of this type of loop, BASIC provides two special statements, the FOR statement and the NEXT statement, for control of counting loops. A loop that is controlled by these statements is called a *FOR loop*. In this section we describe the FOR and NEXT statements and discuss programming with FOR loops.

The basic steps for controlling a counting loop involve initializing a counter, testing the counter to determine whether the loop should be terminated, and modifying the counter after the statements in the loop have been executed. The program to total and average fifty test scores in Fig. 5–5 illustrated these steps. The following is the main loop in this program:

```
110 LET I=1
120 IF I>20 THEN 170
130 INPUT S
140 LET T=T+S
150 LET I=I+1
160 GO TO 120
```

Using a FOR loop to control this loop, we can rewrite the sequence of statements as follows:

```
110 FOR I=1 TO 20 STEP 1
120    INPUT S
130    LET T=T+S
140 NEXT I
```

The first statement in this example is a FOR statement and the last is a NEXT statement. Whenever these statements are used, the statements that initialize, test, and modify the counter are not needed. Instead, the FOR and NEXT statements combine these functions. Here the effect is to cause the computer to execute repeatedly the statements following the FOR statement up to the NEXT statement (numbered 140). The first time that the loop is executed, I is assigned the value 1. On each succeeding pass through the loop, the value of I is increased by 1 until it exceeds 20. Then control transfers out of the loop to the statement following the NEXT statement.

The FOR and NEXT Statements

The syntax for a FOR loop is as follows:

ln FOR *control variable=initial value* TO *limit* STEP *increment*

.
.
.

statements

.
.
.

ln NEXT *control variable*

The FOR and NEXT statements always appear in pairs; there can never be a FOR statement without a corresponding NEXT statement and vice versa. A FOR loop begins with a FOR statement, contains any number of BASIC statements, and ends with a NEXT statement. In the FOR statement the *control variable* is a variable that serves as a counter. The NEXT statement must contain the same control variable as the FOR statement. The *initial value*, *limit*, and *increment* in the FOR statement are each a constant, variable, or complex numeric expression. They determine how many times the loop is executed.

As an example, consider the following FOR and NEXT statements:

```
10 FOR J=1 TO 50 STEP 1
                .
                .
                .
70 NEXT J
```

The control variable is J, which is the same in the FOR statement and the NEXT statement. The initial value is 1, the limit is 50, and the increment is 1.

The effect of a FOR loop is to execute repeatedly the statements between the FOR and NEXT statements. The first time that the statements are executed the control variable is assinged the initial value. Each succeeding time, when the NEXT statement is reached, the increment is added to the value of the control variable. When the value of the control variable becomes greater than the limit, the computer branches to the statement immediately following the NEXT statement.

In the previous example, the control variable, J, is assigned the initial value, 1, for the first execution of the loop. When the NEXT statement is executed, the increment, 1, is added to J making it equal to 2. Each succeeding time through the loop, J is increased by 1 until its value is greater than the limit, 50. Then the computer stops repeating the loop and goes on to the statement following statement 70 (the NEXT statement). Thus, this loop is executed exactly 50 times.

As another example, consider the following FOR loop:

```
15 FOR K=10 TO 20 STEP 3
          .
          .
          .
75 NEXT K
```

The control variable is K, the initial value is 10, the limit is 20, and the increment is 3. This loop is executed four times. The first time it is executed, K is 10. Then the control variable is incremented by 3 and assigned the value 13 for the second execution of the loop. Next K is incremented again by 3 to get 16 and the loop is executed a third time. Then 3 is added to K to obtain 19 for the fourth repetition of the loop. After this the increment is added to K to get 22. But since 22 is greater than the limit, 20, the loop is *not* repeated again. Instead, the computer branches to the statement following the NEXT statement.

With most FOR loops, the increment is 1. When this is the case, the word STEP and the increment can be omitted. For example, the following FOR statement is valid:

```
10 FOR J=1 TO 50
```

Since no increment is given, the computer assumes it is 1. However, if any increment other than 1 is needed, the STEP part must be included.

Besides constants, variables can be used for the initial value, limit, and increment. For example, the following FOR statement uses variables for the initial value and limit:

```
20 FOR L=I TO L STEP 5
```

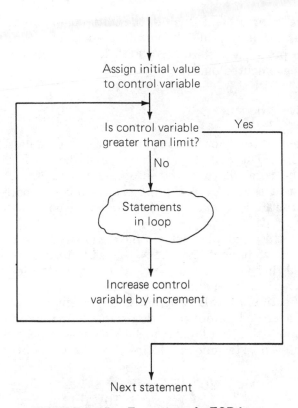

Assign initial value
to control variable

Is control variable
greater than limit?   Yes

No

Statements
in loop

Increase control
variable by increment

Next statement

FIGURE 5-15.   Execution of a FOR loop.

The values of the variables when the program is run determine the initial value and limit.

When a FOR loop is used, we do *not* have separate statements to initialize, test, and modify the counter. These operations are implied by the FOR and NEXT statements. However, the programmer must be aware of the order in which the computer performs these operations. Figure 5-15 shows the pattern that a FOR loop follows. First the control variable is initialized. Then the test is made to determine whether the control variable is greater than the limit. Next the statements in the loop are executed. Finally, the increment is added to the control variable and the loop is repeated.

Notice that this is a pre-test pattern, and it is therefore possible to code a FOR loop that is never executed. For example, consider the following loop:

```
25 FOR M=A TO B
          .
          .
          .
65 NEXT M
```

If A has a value of 50 and B is 40, the initial value is greater than the limit. Hence, the loop will not be executed at all. (Some versions of BASIC use a post-test pattern for a FOR loop, in which case the above loop would be executed once.)

Illustrative Programs

A program to total and average twenty test scores illustrates the use of a FOR loop. The complete program is shown in Fig. 5–16. After initializing the total, T, to zero, the program accumulates the total of the twenty test scores by accepting each score and adding it to the total. After the FOR loop is executed, the average is calculated and the results are printed.

Notice in this example that we have indented the statements between the FOR statement and the NEXT statement. This is a common program style that helps set off the statements in the loop so that the program is easier to understand.

A modification of this program is to accept the number of test scores to be averaged before the other data. This value determines the number of times that the loop is to be executed. The program in Fig. 5–17 illustrates this technique. Notice that the value of N is accepted

```
100 LET T=0
110 FOR I=1 TO 20
120    INPUT S
130    LET T=T+S
140 NEXT I
150 LET A=T/20
160 PRINT T,A
170 END
```

FIGURE 5-16.   A program to total and average twenty test scores using a FOR loop.

```
100 INPUT N
110 LET T=0
120 FOR I=1 TO N
130    INPUT S
140    LET T=T+S
150 NEXT I
160 LET A=T/N
170 PRINT T,A
180 END
```

FIGURE 5-17.   A program to total and average a given number of test scores using a FOR loop.

with the first INPUT statement. N is then used as the limit in the FOR statement.

In Fig. 5–4 we showed a program that prints a table giving the interest and balance on an original deposit of $1000 at 5% interest compounded annually. The program required a counting loop and thus can be written with a FOR loop. The equivalent program with a FOR loop is shown in Fig. 5–18. Notice that the value of Y is controlled with the FOR and NEXT statements. In addition, the value of this variable is printed each time through the loop.

This example illustrates the use of the control variable within the FOR loop. Any time the control variable is used in the loop, its value depends on the initial value, the increment, and the number of times the loop has been executed. Figure 5–19 shows another program that uses the control variable within the FOR loop. This program finds the sum of the even numbers from 2 to 20. In this example, the control variable is used in the LET statement that calculates the sum, S. Initially, zero is assigned to the variable S. With the first execution of the loop, the initial value of the control variable (2) is added to S and the result replaces the original value of S. Thus, after the first execution of the loop, S has a value of 0+2 or 2. With each succeeding execution of the loop, the current value of the control variable is added to S. After the second execution of the loop, S has a value of 0+2+4 or 6. After the third execution of the loop, S is 0+2+4+6 or 12. This continues until after ten executions of the loop the value of S is 0+2+4+6+8+10 +12+14+16+18+20, or 120. Then the control variable is incremented to a value greater than the limit and the loop is terminated.

```
10 LET B=1000
20 FOR Y=1 TO 10
30    LET I=.05*B
40    LET B=B+I
50    PRINT Y,I,B
60 NEXT Y
70 END
```

FIGURE 5-18.   The interest calculation program with a FOR loop.

```
10 LET S=0
20 FOR J=2 TO 20 STEP 2
30    LET S=S+J
40 NEXT J
50 PRINT S
60 END
```

FIGURE 5-19.   A program to find the sum of the even numbers from two to twenty.

```
100 LET T=0
110 LET P=0
120 FOR I=1 TO 20
130    INPUT S
140    IF S<60 THEN 170
150    LET T=T+S
160    LET P=P+1
170 NEXT I
180 LET A=T/P
190 PRINT T,A
200 END
```

FIGURE 5-20.   A program to total and average passing
test scores.

Occasionally within a FOR loop, it is necessary under certain conditions to bypass some of the statements in the loop and proceed directly to the modification and testing of the control variable. For example, assume as before that there are twenty test scores to be entered. This time, however, we wish to total and average only those scores that are 60 or greater (i.e., the passing scores). The program must accept a test score and determine whether it is greater than or equal to 60. If it is, the score must be added to the total; if not, the program must bypass the totalling step. In addition, a count of the number of scores greater than or equal to 60 must be kept for the averaging step.

Figure 5-20 shows a program that accomplishes this. Before entering the loop the program initializes T to zero. In addition, the variable P is initially set equal to zero. This variable is used to count the number of passing test scores (i.e., the number that are 60 or greater) and is used in the average calculation. In the FOR loop, the INPUT statement accepts a test score. The program must then check the score to determine whether it is greater than or equal to 60. If it is, the score must be added to T, and P must be increased by one. To do this the IF statement in the loop causes the computer to bypass the LET statements if S is less than 60. Notice that the IF statement branches to the *end* of the FOR loop (i.e., to the NEXT statement). A common mistake in this type of problem is to branch to the FOR statement. If this were done, the computer would reset the control variable to its initial value and restart the loop. Any time the computer branches to a FOR statement it initializes the control variable and starts processing the loop. If this were done in this example, the program would not process the loop in the required way.

Branching Into and Out of a FOR Loop

It is permissible to branch out of a FOR loop at any time. For example, assume that we wish to find the total and average of an unknown

```
100 LET T=0
110 FOR I=1 TO 100
120    INPUT S
130    IF S=0 THEN 160
140    LET T=T+S
150 NEXT I
160 LET N=I-1
170 LET A=T/N
180 PRINT T,A
190 END
```

FIGURE 5-21. A program to total and average an
unknown number of test scores.

number of test scores. Each score is to be entered through the terminal.
The last score is zero and serves as a trailer value. If we assume that
there are fewer than 100 test scores, a FOR loop that is executed 100
times may be used to accept the data and total the scores. However,
after each score is entered, a test for the trailer value must be made.
When the trailer value is detected, the program must branch out of the
FOR loop.

The program to accomplish this is shown in Fig. 5-21.[†] Notice that
after the program branches out of the loop, the number of test scores is
calculated by subtracting 1 from the control variable. The value of the
control variable is the last value assigned to it in the FOR loop. For
each score that is accepted, the variable is incremented by 1. Thus, the
control variable counts the number of input values. However, the trailer
value is not a test score and must not be included in the count. To
correct for this, the value of the control variable is reduced by 1 after
the program branches out of the loop. The number of test scores is then
used to calculate the average score.

Although it is permissible to branch out of a FOR loop at any time,
BASIC does not allow the program to branch into the middle of a FOR
loop. This does not mean, however, that branching to the FOR statement itself is restricted. The program can branch to a FOR statement
from outside the FOR loop at any time and thus begin the loop
processing.

Additional FOR Loop Features

In a FOR statement, the initial value, limit, and increment may be
any values within the limits of the computer. This means that any of
these may be positive, negative, or zero (although the increment should

---

[†]Although this program is valid in BASIC, we will see in Chapter 7 that it
violates certain principles of good program structure.

not be zero). For example, the following FOR statement is valid in BASIC:

$$30 \text{ FOR } I=-10 \text{ TO } 0 \text{ STEP } 1$$

The first time the FOR loop for this statement is executed, the value of I is -10. The 1 is added to I, making it -9 for the second execution of the loop. The value of I is incremented by 1 for each successive time through the loop. The last time the loop is executed, I is zero.

If the increment is negative, the FOR loop, in effect, counts backwards. For example, the following FOR statement causes the value of J to be decreased by 1 each time the loop is executed:

$$40 \text{ FOR } J=10 \text{ TO } 1 \text{ STEP } -1$$

When the increment is negative, the loop terminates when the value of the control variable is *less than* the test value. In this example, the value of J is 1 during the last execution of the loop. Then -1 is added to J, decreasing its value to zero. Since J is now less than 1, the limit, the loop is not repeated again.

The initial value, limit, and increment need not be whole numbers. For example, the following FOR statement is acceptable:

$$50 \text{ FOR } X=.05 \text{ TO } 1.00 \text{ STEP } .01$$

The initial value is .05, the limit is 1.00, and the increment is .01. Thus, the control variable, X, varies from .05 to 1.00 in increments of .01.

Besides constants and variables, complex numeric expressions can be used for the initial value, limit, and increment in a FOR loop. The value of any expression is evaluated at the time the FOR statement is encountered. The resulting value is then used for loop control. For example, consider the following FOR statement:

$$60 \text{ FOR } Y=A \text{ TO } A+B \text{ STEP } 2*C$$

If A is 5, B is 20, and C is 3 when this statement is executed, the initial value of Y is 5, the limit is 25, and the increment is 6.

Nested FOR Loops

Within a FOR loop may be another FOR loop. Such a combination is referred to as *nested FOR loops*. As an example of the use of nested

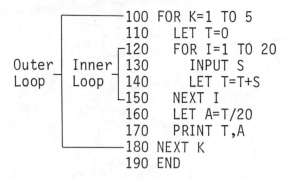

```
                   ┌─────100 FOR K=1 TO 5
                   │     110    LET T=0
                   │  ┌─120    FOR I=1 TO 20
  Outer │ Inner  │ 130      INPUT S
  Loop    Loop  │ 140      LET T=T+S
                   │  └─150    NEXT I
                   │     160    LET A=T/20
                   │     170    PRINT T,A
                   └─────180 NEXT K
                         190 END
```

FIGURE 5-22.   A program with nested FOR loops.

FOR loops, consider the problem of finding the total and average of five groups of twenty test scores each. One approach would be to execute the program in Fig. 5-16 five separate times. Each time, a different set of input data would be processed by the program. A better approach is to put another loop in the program to repeat the totalling and averaging statements five times. The resulting program is shown in Fig. 5-22. With this program all data can be processed at one time.

In this program, the first FOR statement initializes the control variable K to 1. The variable T is then assigned the value zero. The second FOR statement initializes the control variable I to 1. Next the inner FOR loop is executed. When the NEXT statement for the inner FOR loop is encountered, I is incremented. The inner loop is repeated until its control variable exceeds the limit. At that point the computer executes the statement following the NEXT statement of the inner FOR loop. In this case the average is computed and the output is printed. Then the NEXT statement for the outer loop is encountered, and the control variable K is incremented.

With the second execution of the outer FOR loop, the value of the variable T is reset to zero. The inner FOR statement is then encountered. This causes I to be set to 1 and the inner loop is executed twenty times. Next the average is calculated and the PRINT statement is executed. Then the outer loop's control variable is incremented. This continues for a total of five times. Each time the outer loop is executed, the statements in the inner loops are performed twenty times.

We can see from the example how nested FOR loops are executed. The basic rule is that each time an outer loop is performed, the inner loop is completely executed. In the previous example, the statements in the inner loop are executed a total of 100 times.

As another example, consider the following outline of nested FOR loops:

```
100 FOR L=11 TO 20
110   FOR M=1 TO 5
120     FOR N=2 TO 6 STEP 2
            .
            .
            .
200       NEXT N
210   NEXT M
220 NEXT L
```

In this example, the innermost loop is executed three times for each execution of the intermediate loop. The intermediate loop is executed five times for each execution of the outermost loop. Since the outermost loop is executed 10 times, the intermediate loop is executed a total of 50 times (10 × 5) and the innermost loop is performed 150 times (10 × 5 × 3).

Notice that the control variables of the loops in a nest are different. A unique variable must be used for the control variable of each loop in a nest of FOR loops.

When nested FOR loops are used, an inner loop must be completely contained within the next outer loop. Hence, the following pattern of FOR loops is invalid:

```
300 FOR I=1 to 20
310 FOR J=1 to 50
        .
        .
        .
400 NEXT I
410 NEXT J
```

This pattern is unacceptable because, if executed, the NEXT statement of the outer loop is encountered while performing the inner loop.

Nested FOR loops are extremely useful for manipulating certain types of data tables. We will see examples of this in Chapter 10.

REVIEW QUESTIONS

1. What is a trailer value?

2. Consider the following incomplete group of statements:

```
10 INPUT A,B,C
20
30 PRINT A,B,C
40 GO TO 10
```

These statements form a loop that is to be repeated until the input data contains a zero for the last value. What statement should appear at line 20?

3. Consider the program shown in Fig. 5-3. Assume that line 30 is changed to the following:

```
30 IF B>=1500 THEN 90
```

How many lines of output will be printed by the modified program?

4. How many times will statement 30 in the following group of statements be executed?

```
10 LET J=20
20 IF J<3 THEN 60
30 PRINT J
40 LET J=J-4
50 GO TO 20
```

5. Consider the program shown in Fig. 5-6 or 5-17. What output is printed if the following lines of input are entered?

```
? 3
? 70
? 83
? 75
```

6. The program structure in which one loop is contained within another loop is called _____.

7. Are WHILE loops available in the version of BASIC you are using?

8. Write a WHILE loop that prints the numbers 1 through 10 in a column.

9. Write a FOR loop that prints the numbers 20, 18, 16, . . . , 2 in a column.

10. How many lines will be printed by each of the following groups of statements?

(a)
```
10 FOR K=1 TO 10
20 PRINT K
30 NEXT K
```

(b)
```
10 FOR L=4 TO 15 STEP 2
20 PRINT L
30 NEXT L
```

(c) 10 FOR M=9 TO -9 STEP -3
    20 PRINT M
    30 NEXT M

(d) 10 FOR I=1 TO 9 STEP 3
    20 FOR J=8 TO 2 STEP -2
    30 PRINT I,J
    40 NEXT J
    50 NEXT I

11. During the execution of a FOR loop, when is the control variable modified and tested?

12. The following are the types of loops described in this chapter:

uncontrolled	counting	nested
input	pre-test	WHILE
processing	post-test	FOR

Indicate what type of loop is contained in each of the following sets of statements. All answers should come from the above list. However, some answers may require more than one word (e.g., a loop may be a pre-test processing loop or nested FOR loops).

(a) 10 INPUT X
    20 IF X=0 THEN 50
    30 PRINT X
    40 GO TO 10

(b) 10 LET A=-10
    20 PRINT A
    30 LET A=A+1
    40 IF A<0 THEN 10

(c) 10 LET Z=0
    20 PRINT Z
    30 GO TO 10

(d) 10 FOR I=1 TO 10
    20 LET J=1
    30 IF J>5 THEN 70
    40 PRINT I,J
    50 LET J=J+1
    60 GO TO 30
    70 NEXT I

(e)
```
10 INPUT X
20 DO WHILE X<>0
30 PRINT X
40 INPUT X
50 LOOP
```

(f)
```
10 LET P=1000
20 IF P<50 THEN 50
30 LET P=P-.1*P
40 GO TO 20
```

PROGRAMMING PROBLEMS

1. Complete the program for problem 2 or 5 in Chapter 4 with the modification that the program terminates when the customer number is 9999.

2. Complete the program for problem 4 in Chapter 4 with the modification that the total commission for all salespeople is accumulated and printed at the end of the regular output. Use a trailer value with zero for the salesperson number to control the input loop.

3. Write a BASIC program to print a table for converting Fahrenheit temperature to Celsius. (See problem 2 in Chapter 3 for the appropriate conversion formula.) The table should list the Fahrenheit temperatures from 32 to 212 degrees in two-degree increments and the equivalent of each temperature in Celsius.

4. A classic exercise in computer programming is sometimes called the "Manhattan Problem". It is based on the historical fact that in 1627 the Dutch purchased Manhattan Island from the Indians for the equivalent of $24. Currently the assessed value of Manhattan is over eight billion dollars. Did the Dutch make a good investment, or would it have been better to deposit the original $24 in a bank at a fixed interest rate and leave it for all these years?

Assume that the original $24 used to purchase Manhattan Island was deposited in a bank that paid 3% interest compounded annually. Write a BASIC program to determine the account total at the end of 1981 (355 years later). Do not use an interest formula to calculate the amount at the end of the time period; instead, accumulate the total one year at a time.

5. A company agrees to pay one of its employees in grains of rice instead of money. The employee receives one grain on the first day, two grains on the second day, four grains on the third day, eight grains

on the fourth day, and so forth. In other words, each succeeding day the employee receives twice as many grains as he or she did the day before. The employee works for the company for 15 days.

Write a BASIC program to determine the number of grains of rice that the employee receives on each day that he or she works. Also accumulate the total of the rice earnings. There is no input for this program. Output should consist of 15 lines each with the day number, the number of grains received on that day, and the accumulated number of grains received to date.

6. Assume that a pair of rabbits can produce a new pair in one month's time. Each new pair becomes fertile at one month of age and begins the cycle of reproducing a new pair every month. If rabbits never die, how many pairs of rabbits are produced from a single pair in N month's time?

If N ranges from 1 to some maximum value, the solution to this problem creates a sequence of numbers known as the Fibonacci sequence after the Italian mathematician who first posed the problem. For any N greater than 2, the value in the sequence is the sum of the two previous values. Thus, the sequence is as follows:

Number of Months	Number of Pairs of Rabbits
1	1
2	1
3	2
4	3
5	5
6	8
7	13
.	.
.	.
.	.

Let N range from 1 to 24. Write a BASIC program to compute and print a table of the number of rabbits produced from the original pair at the end of month N. There is no input for this program.

7. Complete the program for problem 12 in Chapter 4 with the modification that the total gross pay, withholding tax, social security tax, and net pay are accumulated and printed at the end of the regular output. Use a trailer value with 9999 for the employee number to control the input loop.

8. Write a BASIC program that produces a table of Fahrenheit and equivalent Celsius temperatures. The equation is given in problem 2 of

Chapter 3. The program should be designed to begin the table at any initial Fahrenheit temperature, end at any final temperature, and increment between the initial and final temperatures by any given value. Input for the program is the initial Fahrenheit temperature, the final temperature, and the increment. Use the following sets of input data to test the program:

Initial	Final	Increment
32	212	10
70	71	.1
40	30	-1
-10	0	2
0	0	0

The program should terminate if the increment is zero.

9. The value of e^x can be found from the following infinite series:

$$e^x = 1 + x + \frac{x^2}{2!} + \frac{x^3}{3!} + \frac{x^4}{4!} + \ldots = 1 + \sum_{i=1}^{\infty} \frac{x^i}{i!}$$

Notice that the nth term (where the first term is 1) is the previous term times $x/(n-1)$.

An approximation to the value of e^x can be computed by carrying out this summation to a finite number of terms. Write a BASIC program to approximate e^x using six terms in the summation. Print out the approximate value of e^x. Test the program with the following values of x:

$$1$$
$$0$$
$$-1$$
$$2.7183$$
$$5$$
$$-5$$

10. A tabulation of exam scores for students in a class is needed. The scores vary from 0 to 100. Write a BASIC program to determine the number of scores in the ranges 90 to 100, 80 to 89, 70 to 79, 60 to 69, and 0 to 59. Also determine the percentage of the total number of exam scores that fall in each range. Print all results.

Exam scores should be accepted one at a time until 999 is entered. Use the following exam scores to test the program:

85	100	80	76	42	65	89
91	90	37	72	83	88	69
94	85	48	66	92	45	100
73	87	70	60	80	72	59
61	78	61	91	75	78	74
82	76	75	85	91	79	75

11. A problem in timber management is to determine how much of an area to leave uncut so that the harvested area is reforested in a certain period of time. It is assumed that reforestation takes place at a known rate per year, depending on climate and soil conditions. The reforestation rate expresses this growth as a function of the amount of timber standing. For example, if 100 acres are left standing and the reforestation rate is .05, then at the end of the first year, there are 100 + .05 × 100 or 105 acres forested. At the end of the second year, the number of acres forested is 105 + .05 × 105 or 110.25 acres.

Assume that the total area to be forested, the uncut area, and the reforestation rate are known. Write a BASIC program to determine the percentage of the total area that is forested after 20 years. Output should give the input data plus the number of acres forested and the percentage of the total that this represents.

Use the following input data to test the program:

Area Number	Total Area	Uncut Area	Reforestation Rate
045	10,000	100	.05
083	1,000	50	.08
153	20,000	500	.10
192	14,000	3,000	.02
234	6,000	1,000	.01
416	18,000	1,500	.05
999 (trailer value)			

12. The rate of inflation is the annual percent increase in the cost of goods and services. For example, assume that an item costs $10.00 today and the rate of inflation is 10%. Then the cost of the item in one year is 10.00 + .10 × 10.00 or $11.00. In two years the item will cost 11.00 + .10 × 11.00 or $12.10.

Write a BASIC program to find the cost of a $12.00 item in fifteen years if the rate of inflation is 2%, 3%, 4%, and so forth up to 10%; that is, the program should give the cost after fifteen years at each inflation rate. Use nested loops. Do not use an interest formula.

Also determine the overall increase in the cost of the item. For example, if a $10.00 item costs $18.00 after fifteen years, the increase is 80%; if it costs $24.00, the increase is 140%. Compute the overall increase for the $12.00 item after fifteen years at each inflation rate.

There is no input for this program. Output should list the final results after fifteen years for each inflation rate.

6

INPUT AND OUTPUT PROGRAMMING

In Chapter 3 we introduced simple input and output programming. While this is sufficient for many programs, there are times when more complex I/O is required. In this chapter we describe additional input and output features of BASIC.

6-1. PRINTED OUTPUT

As we have seen, the PRINT statement causes the values of variables to be printed in fixed print zones. It is also possible to use the PRINT statement to print words or phrases to describe the output. In addition, the PRINT statement can print output anywhere on the print line, not just in the fixed zones. In this section we describe these and other features of the PRINT statement.

Character Output

Most programs print not only the results of processing but also words and phrases that describe the output. This is so that a person reading the output will know what the data represents. Sometimes a word or phrase is printed followed by the results of a computation. At other times, headings are printed above columns of output. Many variations are used to make the output more readable. We call this type of output *character output* since it consists of symbols (characters) other than just numbers.

To produce character output we put the words to be printed in quotation marks in the PRINT statement. For example, consider the following statement:

```
80 PRINT "THE ANSWER IS",X
```

Execution of this statement causes the computer to print the phrase THE ANSWER IS, followed by the value of the variable X. For example, if X is 125.25, the output appears as follows:

```
THE ANSWER IS 125.25
```

Notice that the quotation marks are *not* printed; only the characters between the quotation marks appear in the output.

There may be as many words or phrases in a PRINT statement as are needed. For example, the following statement prints two separate phrases and the values of two variables:

```
180 PRINT "AMOUNT=",A,"COUNT =",C
```

If A is 250 and C is 9, the output is as follows:

```
(Print Zone 1)(Print Zone 2)(Print Zone 3)(Print Zone 4)
AMOUNT =      250          COUNT =         9
```

Notice that the output in this example is spread out. This is because each value begins in the next print zone. The phrase AMOUNT = is printed in the first zone, the value of A is printed in the second zone, COUNT = is printed in the third zone, and the value of C is printed in the fourth zone.

If the word or phrase to be printed is longer than one print zone, it continues into the next zone. Anything else to be printed starts in the next zone. For example, consider the following statement:

```
280 PRINT X,"IS NOT GREATER THAN",Y
```

In this case the value of X is printed in the first print zone. Then the phrase IS NOT GREATER THAN is printed beginning in the second zone. But since this phrase requires nineteen print positions, printing continues into the third print zone. Finally, the value of Y is printed in the fourth zone. If X is 5 and Y is 6, the output appears as follows:

```
(Print Zone 1)(Print Zone 2)(Print Zone 3)(Print Zone 4)
  5           IS NOT GREATER THAN           6
```

We can use the PRINT statement to print just a word or a phrase without printing any other data. The following statement illustrates this:

```
380 PRINT "STATISTICAL DATA"
```

The effect of the execution of this statement is that the only output printed is the phrase STATISTICAL DATA. This approach is often used to print a *heading* to describe the output that follows.

Print zones can be used to arrange headings above columns of output. For example, if we wish to print two columns of data in the first two print zones with the titles AMOUNT and COUNT, the following statement can be used:

```
480 PRINT "AMOUNT","COUNT"
```

Since the words to be printed appear separately in the PRINT statement, they are printed in separate zones. AMOUNT is printed in the first print zone and COUNT is printed in the second zone.

Any printable characters except quotation marks can be printed with a PRINT statement. Letters, digits, and special characters including blanks are all permitted. Quotation marks are not allowed because they are used to set off the words to be printed. (Some versions of BASIC, however, have provisions for printing quotation marks.)

With the PRINT statement we can also print a line that contains nothing. This is accomplished by using a PRINT statement with nothing following the keyword PRINT, as in the following example:

```
580 PRINT
```

This tells the computer to print a line of blank spaces. It is often used to double-space printed output.

Figure 6-1(a) shows a program that produces character output. The output from running the program is shown in Fig. 6-1(b). This program lists the year, interest, and balance on a bank deposit of $1000 earning 5% interest compounded annually. The program stops when the balance is greater than or equal to $2000 (see Fig. 5-3). At the top of the output is printed a heading that describes the columns of data that are printed. Notice that the PRINT statement for the heading is outside the loop. If this statement were inside the loop, the heading would be printed each time the loop is repeated. There is also a final line printed after the loop terminates. Again, the PRINT statement for this line is outside the loop. Statements 110 and 210 print blank lines, so that extra space is included between the character output and the rest of the output.

```
100 PRINT "YEAR","INTEREST","BALANCE"
110 PRINT
120 LET B=1000
130 LET Y=1
140 IF B>=2000 THEN 200
150 LET I=.05*B
160 LET B=B+I
170 PRINT Y,I,B
180 LET Y=Y+1
190 GO TO 140
200 LET Y=Y-1
210 PRINT
220 PRINT "DOUBLING TIME",Y,"YEARS"
230 END
```

(a) The program

YEAR	INTEREST	BALANCE
1	50	1050
2	52.5	1102.5
3	55.125	1157.63
4	57.8813	1215.51
5	60.7753	1276.28
6	63.8141	1340.1
7	67.0048	1407.1
8	70.355	1477.46
9	73.8728	1551.33
10	77.5664	1628.89
11	81.4447	1710.34
12	85.517	1795.86
13	89.7928	1885.65
14	94.2825	1979.93
15	98.9966	2078.93

DOUBLING TIME	15	YEARS

(b) The output

FIGURE 6-1. The interest calculation program with character output.

Positioning Output

As we have seen, output is printed in fixed print zones spaced across the paper or CRT. This often leads to output that is difficult to read. However, it is possible to print the output closer together. This is done by using semicolons (;) instead of commas to separate the items in the PRINT statement. For example, consider the following statement:

70 PRINT X;Y;Z

Notice that semicolons separate the variables in the PRINT statement. This causes the values of X, Y, and Z to be printed close together, *not* in successive print zones. For example, if X is 35, Y is -27, and Z is 6.8, the output appears as follows:

35 -27 6.8

Each number is printed with a leading blank if it is positive or a minus sign if the number is negative. Following the value is a trailing blank.

If words or phrases are separated by semicolons in the PRINT statement, no spaces appear between the output. For example, the statement

170 PRINT "STATISTICAL";"DATA"

results in the output

STATISTICALDATA

Extra spaces can be provided in this output by including the spaces in the PRINT statement. Thus, if we wish to print the words STATISTICAL and DATA separated by two spaces, we can use the following statement:

170 PRINT "STATISTICAL ";" DATA"

Another approach in this case is to combine the two words in the PRINT statement as follows:

170 PRINT "STATISTICAL DATA"

The output will be the same in either case.

As another example of the use of semicolons, consider the following statement:

270 PRINT "AMOUNT =";A;"COUNT =";C

If A is 250 and C is 9, the output is as follows:

AMOUNT = 250 COUNT = 9

The extra spaces are provided in the output because numbers are always printed with a leading space (or a minus sign) and a trailing space.

Commas and semicolons can be combined in one statement. For example, consider the following statement:

```
370 PRINT X;Y,Z
```

In this case the values of X and Y are printed close together because a semicolon separates the variables, but Z is printed beginning in the next print zone. If X, Y, and Z are 35, -27, and 6.8, respectively, the output appears as follows:

```
|(Print Zone 1)|(Print Zone 2)|
| 35 -27       | 6.8          |
```

We can use commas and semicolons in other ways to position the output. Extra commas can be inserted in the PRINT statement to space over print zones. Each extra comma skips one zone. For example, the following statement prints the value of X in the second print zone and the value of Y in the fourth print zone:

```
370 PRINT ,X,,Y
```

The first comma causes the first print zone to be skipped. The extra comma between the variables causes the third print zone to be skipped.

If we put a comma or a semicolon at the *end* of a list of variables in a PRINT statement, a new line is *not* started when the next PRINT statement is executed. Instead, the output begins on the same line as the previous output. For example, consider the following statements:

```
470 PRINT X,Y,
475 PRINT Z
```

The comma at the end of line 470 means that the value of Z will be printed on the same line as the values of X and Y. Semicolons can be used for the same purpose, only the spacing of the output is different.

The TAB Function

Occasionally we want to print the output beginning in a specific print position. This can be done by using the TAB function in the PRINT statement. The TAB function consists of the word TAB followed by a constant, variable, or more complex numeric expression in parentheses. For example, the following statement uses the TAB function twice:

```
570 PRINT TAB(10);X;TAB(20);Y
```

The effect of the TAB function is to cause the printing mechanism to move or *tabulate* to the print position given in parentheses. Then printing begins at that position. In the above example the value of X is printed beginning in position 10 and Y is printed beginning in position 20.

Print positions are numbered beginning with 1 on the left. Thus, TAB(1) causes the output to begin as far to the left as possible. (In some versions of BASIC, the print positions are numbered beginning with 0. Then TAB(0) results in the leftmost output.)

As another example of the use of the TAB function, consider the following:

```
670 PRINT "A";TAB(6);"B";TAB(11);"C"
```

In this case the output will appear as follows:

```
A     B     C
```

The letter A is printed in the first print position, B is printed in the sixth print position, and C is printed in the eleventh print position.

Notice in these examples that a semicolon is used before and after the TAB function. If commas are used instead, the printing mechanism will move to the next print zone whenever a comma is encountered. This will usually result in output completely different from what the programmer wants.

It is not possible to move the printing mechanism backwards with the TAB function. For example, consider the following statement:

```
770 PRINT TAB(20);X;TAB(10);Y
```

After the value of X is printed beginning in the twentieth print position, TAB(10) is encountered. This does *not* move the printing mechanism back to print position 10 on the same line. Instead, a new line is started and the print mechanism is tabulated to print position 10. Then the value of Y is printed. Thus, the output appears on two separate lines. [With many versions of BASIC, the computer ignores the TAB(10) function and prints the value of Y on the same line in the next available space.]

If a variable or a more complex numeric expression is used in a TAB function, the value is rounded to determine the print position. For example, if X is 5.7, TAB(X) causes the output to be printed in the sixth print position and TAB(2*X) causes the output to begin in the eleventh print position. [With some versions of BASIC, the value of the expression is truncated rather than rounded; that is, the fractional part is dropped. Thus, if X is 5.7, TAB(X) tabulates to the fifth print position.]

Using a variable or numeric expression in a TAB function can produce interesting graphical output. For example, Fig. 6-2 shows a program that produces a graph of the equation $y = x^2$. The TAB function is used to move the printing mechanism so that the asterisk is printed at the value of x^2 for each value of x. (The +4 in the expression in the TAB function shifts the graph to the right.)

Input Prompts

In Chapter 3 we described how the INPUT statement prints or displays a question mark to prompt the terminal operator. Usually, however, we want to provide additional prompting in the form of a message that explains what input is required. For example, if the operator must enter a test score we may print the message ENTER TEST SCORE just

```
10 PRINT " X";TAB(13);"Y = X ^ 2"
20 PRINT TAB(4);"---------------------------"
30 FOR X=-5 TO 5 STEP 1
40    PRINT X;TAB(X^2+4);"*"
50 NEXT X
60 END
```

    (a) The program

```
 X              Y = X ^ 2
 ------------------------
-5                        *
-4                   *
-3              *
-2         *
-1    *
 0  *
 1  *
 2     *
 3        *
 4             *
 5                  *
```

    (b) The output

FIGURE 6-2.   A program that produces graphical output.

before the appropriate INPUT statement is executed. The following statements accomplish this:

```
70 PRINT "ENTER TEST SCORE"
80 INPUT S
```

On the terminal the sequence appears as follows:

```
ENTER TEST SCORE
? 85
```

The operator sees the message and the question mark and types the appropriate data (85 in this example).

Another approach is to use a semicolon at the end of the PRINT statement as follows:

```
70 PRINT "ENTER TEST SCORE";
80 INPUT S
```

The effect now is that the question mark appears on the same line as the message. The sequence appears as follows at the terminal:

```
ENTER TEST SCORE? 85
```

In some verions of BASIC, the message can be included in the INPUT statement. For example, the following statement may be used:

```
80 INPUT "ENTER TEST SCORE";S
```

The effect is the same as with the previous sequence. The message is printed followed by a question mark on the same line, after which the operator enters the data.

Printing Constants and Expressions

The PRINT statement may list variables and character output to be printed. In addition, constants and more complex numeric expressions can be used. For example, the following PRINT statement is valid:

```
60 PRINT X;1;X+1
```

This statement causes the computer to print the value of the variable X, the constant 1, and the value of the expression X+1. If X equals 5, the output appears as follows:

5   1   6

Any variable, constant, or numeric expression can appear in a PRINT statement. Thus, the following statements are valid:

```
160 PRINT A*B-C,.00057
260 PRINT 3.5847^3
360 PRINT 8.5E25,X/Y
460 PRINT B*(1+R)^N
```

The computer evaluates any expression using the current values of the variables and prints the result.

6-2. INTERACTIVE PROGRAM DESIGN

A program that involves interactive processing must be easy for the terminal operator to use. Basically this is accomplished by guiding the operator through the processing with messages and prompts. The operator should be told what to do at each step in the program. All input data should be requested with an appropriate prompt. All output

```
100 PRINT "TEST SCORE AVERAGING PROGRAM"
110 PRINT
120 PRINT "ENTER THE NUMBER OF SCORES TO BE AVERAGED";
130 INPUT N
140 PRINT
150 PRINT "ENTER";N;"TEST SCORES - ONE PER LINE"
160 LET T=0
170 FOR I=1 TO N
180    INPUT S
190    LET T=T+S
200 NEXT I
210 LET A=T/N
220 PRINT
230 PRINT "THE TOTAL IS";T
240 PRINT "THE AVERAGE IS";A
250 PRINT
260 PRINT "DO YOU WANT TO AVERAGE MORE SCORES"
270 PRINT "(TYPE 1 FOR YES, 0 FOR NO)";
280 INPUT R
290 IF R=1 THEN 110
300 END
```

FIGURE 6-3.   The interactive test score averaging program.

should be provided with an adequate description. It should be assumed that the terminal operator knows nothing about computers or programming and can only follow the printed or displayed instructions.

Figure 6–3 shows a test-score-averaging program that is designed for easy use. The terminal interaction that results from running the program is shown in Fig. 6–4.

This program first prints a title so that the operator knows which program is running. Then a prompt is printed requesting the number of test scores to be averaged. After the input is accepted, a message is printed stating how many test scores are to be entered. Notice that the input just entered (i.e., the value of N) is immediately printed out in this message. This is a common technique to remind the operator of what was entered. The program then accepts the required number of test scores, computing the total as the scores are entered. After the

```
TEST SCORE AVERAGING PROGRAM

ENTER THE NUMBER OF SCORES TO BE AVERAGED? 5

ENTER 5 TEST SCORES - ONE PER LINE
? 100
? 85
? 79
? 96
? 62

THE TOTAL IS 422
THE AVERAGE IS 84.4

DO YOU WANT TO AVERAGE MORE SCORES
(TYPE 1 FOR YES, 0 FOR NO)? 1

ENTER THE NUMBER OF SCORES TO BE AVERAGED? 3

ENTER 3 TEST SCORES - ONE PER LINE
? 57
? 89
? 72

THE TOTAL IS 218
THE AVERAGE IS 72.6667

DO YOU WANT TO AVERAGE MORE SCORES
(TYPE 1 FOR YES, 0 FOR NO)? 0
```

FIGURE 6-4.   Running the interactive test score averaging program.

average is computed, the total and average are printed with appropriate descriptions.

The program uses a common technique for determining whether to repeat the processing. This is shown in lines 260 through 290. The technique is to ask the operator whether he or she wishes to continue. The response, R, may be 1 or 0 in this example meaning yes or no, respectively. If R equals 1, the computer branches to the beginning of the program; otherwise the END statement is executed, stopping the program.

Notice that nothing is left for the operator to figure out during the processing. All input is requested with an appropriate message; all output is printed with the required description. In addition, blank lines are printed at appropriate places to make the output easier to read (see Fig. 6–4).

This program illustrates the basic principles of interactive program design. We will see other examples of interactive programs in later chapters.

6-3.   THE READ, DATA, AND RESTORE STATEMENTS

The INPUT statement is the main statement used for data input in BASIC. Its primary application is in interactive data processing. There are situations, however, where a batch of data needs to be processed. This can be done by using the INPUT statement to accept all of the data from the terminal. Another approach is to put the data in the program using a DATA statement and then to accept, or *read*, the data with a READ statement. In this section we describe these statements and their use in BASIC programs.

The READ and DATA statements are always used together in a program. The syntax of the READ statement is as follows:

ln READ *list of variables separated by commas*

For example, the following is a valid READ statement:

```
10 READ X,Y,Z
```

Notice that the syntax is the same as that of the INPUT statement with the exception of the keyword. The syntax of the DATA statement is as follows:

ln DATA *list of constants separated by commas*

For example, the following is a valid DATA statement:

```
15 DATA 78,95,82
```

Any acceptable constant can appear in a DATA statement, including constants in E-notation.

When a READ statement is executed, data is read from a DATA statement. Each variable in the READ statement is assigned a value from a DATA statement. The data is read in sequence, left-to-right. If the READ and DATA statements above appear in a program, then after execution of the READ statement, X is 78, Y is 95, and Z is 82.

There may be any number of DATA statements in a program and they may be placed anywhere before the END statement. When a DATA statement is encountered during the sequential execution of a program, it is ignored by the computer. A DATA statement is used only when a READ statement is executed.

When there is more than one DATA statement in a program, input begins with the data in the first statement and continues sequentially through the data in the other statements. For example, consider the following:

```
10 READ X
11 READ Y,Z
15 DATA 78,95
16 DATA 82
```

The first READ statement reads the first value in the first DATA statement. Thus, X is assigned the value 78. Then the second READ statement is executed. Input continues where the previous READ statement left off. Thus, 95 is read and assigned to Y. Now, since there are no more values in the first DATA statement, the computer automatically goes on to the second DATA statement. Hence, the value 82 is read for Z.

When a program is executed, the computer collects all of the data in sequence from the DATA statements to form a *data block*. For example, assume that a program contains the following DATA statements:

```
110 DATA 52, 85.3,-69
180 DATA 35.62
210 DATA 5.5E14,.0035,0,-2.69
```

Then the data block for this program is as follows:

```
52,85.3,-69,35.62,5.5E14,.0035,0,-2.69
```

The computer reads the data from the block in sequence. It keeps track of what data has been read by using what might be imagined as a *pointer* to point to the next available value in the data block. Initially the pointer points to the first value. Each time a value is read, the pointer automatically advances to the next value. In this way the computer always knows where to continue reading when a READ statement is executed.

As an example, assume that the following READ statements are executed in the program with the previous DATA statements:

```
120 READ A,B
130 READ C,D,E
```

After the first READ statement is executed, A is 52 and B is 85.3. Then the pointer points to the third value (−69) in the data block. After the second READ statement is executed, C is −69, D is 35.62, and E is 5.5×10^{14}. The pointer then points to the sixth value in the data block. The next READ statement begins at that point.

The pointer can be moved back to the beginning of the data block with the RESTORE statement. The syntax of this statement is as follows:

ln RESTORE

The effect of this statement is to restore the pointer to the first value in the data block. This is often done so that the same data can be assigned to different variables. For example, consider the following sequence of statements:

```
110 READ A,B
115 RESTORE
120 READ C,D,E
```

In this case, A and B are assigned the first two values in the data block. Then the RESTORE statement restores the pointer to the first value in the block. The second READ statement then reads the first two values of the data block again, assigning the values to C and D, and then reads the third value for E.

If a READ statement is executed and there is no more data in the data block, an execution error occurs and the program stops. This can cause a problem when reading sets of data from a DATA statement where the last set contains a trailer value. For example, assume that a program contains the following sequence:

```
10 READ X,Y,Z
20 IF X=999 THEN 200
```

```
10 READ I,U
20 IF I=9999 THEN 90
30 IF U>12 THEN 60
40 LET T=350
50 GO TO 70
60 LET T=350+20*(U-12)
70 PRINT I,T
80 GO TO 10
81 DATA 1001,15,1013,18,1026,8
82 DATA 1085,12,1117,20,1130,6
83 DATA 1147,3,1165,13.5,1207,11
84 DATA 1229,12.5,9999,0
90 END
```

FIGURE 6-5.   The tuition calculation program using
READ and DATA statements.

The trailer value is the value 999 for the variable X. Each time the READ statement is executed, three values are read from the data block. The last three values must be the trailer value for X and two arbitrary values such as zeros for Y and Z. If the last two values are not included, an execution error will occur even though the trailer value has been read.

Although DATA statements may be placed anywhere in a program, it is usually best to group all DATA statements together. This makes locating and changing the data easier. Most programmers put all DATA statements at the end of the program just before the END statement.

As an example of the use of READ and DATA statements in a program, consider the tuition-calculation program discussed in Chapter 5 (see Fig. 5-2). The same program using READ and DATA statements is shown in Fig. 6-5. Each time the READ statement is executed, the next two values are read from the data block. The first value read is a student's identification number and the second value is the number of units. Notice that the data appears in pairs in the DATA statement and that the last pair contains the trailer value (9999) for I and an arbitrary value (0) for U. In addition, all DATA statements are grouped together at the end of the program for easy reference.

*6-4. THE PRINT USING STATEMENT

With the PRINT statement, the value of a variable is printed in a standard format determined by the computer. The programmer does not have control over how the output appears, although the output would sometimes look better in a different format. For example, the output from the program in Fig. 6-1 would look better if the column of years were aligned on the right and two places were printed to the right of the decimal point for each interest and balance. These and other improvements can be made with the PRINT USING statement.

The PRINT USING statement is not available in all versions of BASIC, and its form and features vary considerably from one version of the language to another. In this section we introduce some of the features of one common form of the PRINT USING statement.[†] However, the programmer must refer to the appropriate reference manual for details of this statement in the version of BASIC being used.

The syntax of the PRINT USING statement is as follows:

ln PRINT USING *"format",list of variables*

The following is an example of a PRINT USING statement:

```
60 PRINT USING "####   ###.##",I,T
```

The statement consists of the keywords PRINT and USING, followed by the *format* (also called the *image*) which must be enclosed in quotation marks. In the format, special symbols are used to describe the arrangement of the output data. Following the format must be a comma and then a list of variables to be printed just as in a simple PRINT statement. When the PRINT USING statement is executed, the values of the variables are printed according to the specifications given in the format.

The special symbols used in the format determine how the output is printed. To print a number, the # symbol is used for each digit position in the number. For example, consider the following PRINT USING statement:

```
70 PRINT USING "###",X
```

This statement tells the computer to print the value of X using the format ###. This means that the value is to be printed in the first three print positions. If X is 128, this number is printed at the beginning of the output line. If the value of X requires fewer than three print positions, the number is printed so that it is aligned on the right; that is, the value is *right-justified.* For example, if X is 9, the output consists of two blank spaces and then the digit 9. If the value is negative, the minus sign is printed to the left of the first digit provided there are enough print positions. Thus, if X is -4, the output consists of a space, the minus sign, and the digit 4. When not enough print positions are pro-

---

[†]The features described are available in BASIC-PLUS on the DEC PDP 11 computer and in related versions of BASIC.

vided in the format, an error occurs. In this case the % symbol is printed followed by the value. For example, if X is 1024, the output appears as follows:

% 1024

To include a decimal point and a fractional part in the output, the decimal point is used in the format in the appropriate position. This is shown in the following example:

80 PRINT USING "###.##",Y

If Y is 486.37, the output consists of this number printed in the first six print positions with a decimal point in the fourth print position. (Notice that six print positions are needed because the decimal point requires one print position.) If the value has more places to the right of the decimal point than are indicated in the format, the output is rounded. Thus, if X is 486.376, the number printed is 486.38. When the value has fewer places to the right than indicated in the format, zeros are added to fill out the decimal positions. Thus, if X is 486.3, then 486.30 is printed.

If a comma is inserted anywhere to the left of the decimal point in the format, commas are printed every three digits in the output. For example, consider the following statement:

90 PRINT USING "#,#######.##",Z

If the value of Z is 5000000, the output appears as follows:

5,000,000.00

Notice that each comma requires a print position.

A dollar sign can be printed immediately preceding the first digit of a number by using two dollar signs at the beginning of the format. For example, consider the following statement:

100 PRINT USING "$$##.##",P

If the value of P is 500, the output printed is $500.00. However, if the value of P is 5, the output consists of two blank spaces and then $5.00. In effect, the double dollar sign causes one dollar sign to be printed just ahead of the first digit in the number.

If two asterisks are used at the beginning of a format, any print positions to the left of the number are filled with asterisks. The following statement illustrates this:

110 PRINT USING "**##.##",P

If P is 500, the output printed is *500.00. However, if P is 5, the output appears as ***5.00. Asterisks are often used in this way to protect dollar amounts on checks from alterations.

Figure 6-6 shows other examples of formats using the special symbols described here.

In all the examples given so far, the output begins in the first print position. To start in a different print position, blank spaces are used at the beginning of the format. For example, the following PRINT USING statement has four blanks at the beginning of the format:

120 PRINT USING "   ###",X

This causes the first four print positions to be skipped, and the output begins in the fifth print position.

When more than one number is to be printed on a line, the format contains the appropriate symbols to describe the arrangement of each number with the necessary blanks to spread out the values. For example, consider the following statement:

130 PRINT USING " ##   ##.##   #,###.##",A,B,C

This statement tells the computer to print the values of A, B, and C in the specified format. The output line contains two blanks, then the value of A in the format ##, then three spaces followed by the value of B in the format ##.##, then three more spaces and the value of C in the format #,###.##. If A is 20, B is 25.95, and C is 1482.38, the output appears as follows:

10   25.95   1,482.38

Format	Value	Output
"####"	1234	1234
"####"	56	56
"#,###"	1234	1,234
"#,###"	56	56
"##.###"	12.345	12.345
"##.###"	12.3456	12.346
"##.###"	56	56.000
"##.###"	123.456	% 123.456
"$$###"	1234	$1234
"$$###"	56	$56
"**#,###"	1234	**1,234
"**#,###"	56	*****56

FIGURE 6-6.   Examples of formats.

Notice that the horizontal positioning of the output is controlled by the format, not by the punctuation in the list of variables. Commas and seimcolons in the variable list have no effect on the placement of the output.

Words or phrases that are to be printed on the same line as the values of variables can be included in the format. Any characters that

```
100 PRINT "YEAR  INTEREST  BALANCE"
110 PRINT
120 LET B=1000
130 LET Y=1
140 IF B>=2000 THEN 200
150 LET I=.05*B
160 LET B=B+I
170 PRINT USING "  ##    $$##.##  $$,###.##",Y,I,B
180 LET Y=Y+1
190 GO TO 140
200 LET Y=Y-1
210 PRINT
220 PRINT USING "DOUBLING TIME ## YEARS",Y
230 END
```

(a) The program

```
YEAR  INTEREST  BALANCE

  1    $50.00  $1,050.00
  2    $52.50  $1,102.50
  3    $55.13  $1,157.63
  4    $57.88  $1,215.51
  5    $60.78  $1,276.28
  6    $63.81  $1,340.10
  7    $67.00  $1,407.10
  8    $70.36  $1,477.46
  9    $73.87  $1,551.33
 10    $77.57  $1,628.89
 11    $81.44  $1,710.34
 12    $85.52  $1,795.86
 13    $89.79  $1,885.65
 14    $94.28  $1,979.93
 15    $99.00  $2,078.93

DOUBLING TIME 15 YEARS
```

(b) The output

FIGURE 6-7. The interest calculation program with the PRINT USING statement.

are used in the format, except for characters with special meaning such as the # symbol, are printed exactly as they appear. For example, consider the following statement:

```
140 PRINT USING "TOTAL = ###, AVERAGE = ##.#",T,A
```

If T is 252 and A is 84, the output line appears as follows:

```
TOTAL = 252, AVERAGE = 84.0
```

Figure 6-7(a) shows a program that uses the PRINT USING statement. This is the interest-calculation program with headings and other descriptive output (see Fig. 6-1). In this program the values of Y, I, and B are printed in the format given in the PRINT USING statement at line 170. This format is designed to align the columns under the heading printed by the PRINT statement at line 100. A final output line with the doubling time is also printed with a PRINT USING statement (line 220). The output from running the program is shown in Fig. 6-7(b).

REVIEW QUESTIONS

1. Write a PRINT statement that prints the words OUTPUT DATA followed by the values of A and B.

2. Write a PRINT statement that prints a heading with the word NUMBER in the first print zone and the word TUITION in the second print zone.

3. Assume that the value of A is 2, B is 3, and C is 4. What is printed by each of the following statements? (Show the output in the exact print positions in which it will appear.)
   (a) 100 PRINT A,B;C
   (b) 200 PRINT "DATA";A;B;C
   (c) 300 PRINT A,,B;"DATA"
   (d) 400 PRINT TAB(5);A;B;TAB(15);C
   (e) 500 PRINT A;TAB(10);"DATA"
   (f) 600 PRINT 5;A*B;A-C

4. Assume that the value of A is 2, B is 3, and C is 4. What is printed by the following group of statements?

```
700 PRINT A;B,
710 PRINT C;
720 PRINT "DATA"
```

5. In the version of BASIC you are using, can an INPUT statement be used to print a message?

6. What are some ways in which an interactive program should be designed so that it is easy for the terminal operator?

7. Write a READ and DATA statement to read the values 2, 3, and 4 for the variables A, B, and C, respectively.

8. What are the values of the variables after the following group of statements is executed?

```
10 DATA 5,7,3
20 READ X,Y,Z,S
30 RESTORE
40 DATA 2,6,4
50 READ T,U
```

9. Consider the program shown in Fig. 6-5. What is printed on the first line of output?

10. Is the PRINT USING statement available in the version of BASIC you are using? If so, write a PRINT USING statement to print the values of A, B, and C. All values should be printed with three places to the left of the decimal point and one to the right. Two blank spaces should be provided between the output values.

PROGRAMMING PROBLEMS

Many of the problems given in previous chapters can be completed using the features described in this chapter. Some suggestions are made below, along with other exercises. Any of the problems in this or previous chapters can be completed using either the PRINT statement or the PRINT USING statement.

1. Complete the program for problem 2 or 5 in Chapter 4 with the modification that all output is printed with descriptive words or phrases.

2. Complete the program for problem 7 in Chapter 4 with the modification that the words FRESHMAN, SOPHOMORE, JUNIOR, or SENIOR are printed rather than the classification code.

3. Complete the program for problem 3, 5, or 6 in Chapter 5 with the modification that headings are printed for the columns of output.

4. Complete the program for problem 9, 10, or 12 in Chapter 4 with the modification that the program follows the approach to interactive design discussed in this chapter.

5. Complete the program for problem 10 or 11 in Chapter 5 with the modification that the READ and DATA statements are used for input.

6. The results of a questionnaire survey need to be printed in sentence form. The input consists of the sample identification number, the number of questionnaires processed, and the average age of the respondents. The output should appear as follows:

RESULTS FROM SAMPLE XXXXX
WITH XXX QUESTIONNAIRES PROCESSED,
THE AVERAGE AGE OF THE RESPONDENTS IS XX.X YEARS.

(Xs represent the locations of output values.)
Write a BASIC program to prepare the specified output from the input. Test the program using 10083 for the sample number, 253 for the number of questionnaires, and 37.3 for the average age.

7. Write a BASIC program to print your name in block letters. A sample of how the output might appear is as follows:

```
        X       XXX     X   X      X   X
        X      X   X    X   X      XX  X
        X      X   X    X   X      X   X
        X      X   X    XXXXX      X X X
        X      X   X    X   X      X   X
   X  X        X   X    X   X      X  XX
     XX         XXX     X   X      X   X
```

8. A graphical representation of a student's class schedule is as follows:

TIME	8-9	9-10	10-11	11-12	12-1	1-2	2-2	3-4
MONDAY	1	0	0	1	0	1	1	1
TUESDAY	0	1	1	1	0	0	0	0
WEDNESDAY	1	0	0	1	0	1	1	1
THURSDAY	0	1	1	1	0	0	0	0
FRIDAY	1	0	0	1	0	0	0	0

In this graph the digit 1 indicates hours when the student is in class; the digit 0 indicates hours when he or she is out of class.
Write a BASIC program that produces the graphical output for any student's class schedule. Input consists of one set of data for each day with the student's schedule for the day. The data is entered as a series

of ones and zeros. Use the data shown in the preceding graph to test the program.

9. Write a BASIC program to print a graph of the equation $y = 2x + 3$ between $x = 0$ and $x = 4$. Use increments of .5.

10. Write a BASIC program to print a graph of both the equations $y = 2x + 3$ and $y = -3x + 13$. Use different symbols for each line and a special symbol for the point of intersection.

11. In one business the commission paid to each salesperson is based on the product line sold and the total amount of sales. Assume that the product line is indicated by a code that can be either 5, 8, or 17. If the code is 5 or 8, the commission rate is 7½% for the first $5,000 of sales and 8½% for sales over $5,000. However, if the product-line code is 17, the commission rate is 9½% for the first $3,500 of sales and 12% for sales over $3,500.

Write a BASIC program to determine the commission for each salesperson. Input is the salesperson's number, product-line code, and total sales. Put all input data in DATA statements. Output should be the salesperson's number, total sales, and commission with appropriate headings.

Use the following data to test the program:

Salesperson's Number	Product-line Code	Total Sales
101	17	$2250
103	5	$4000
117	8	$7350
125	5	$6500
138	17	$6375
192	8	$8125
203	8	$3250
218	5	$5000
235	5	$5250
264	17	$4150
291	17	$ 750
999 (trailer value)		

12. Each student in a class of fifteen took two examinations. A program is needed to calculate the total and average test score for each student, the total and average for the entire class on each test, and the total and average of all thirty test scores. Input to the program is each student's identification number and score on each of the two tests. Output should list the input data and all required totals and averages. Supply headings and other descriptive information to identify the out-

put. Put the following data in DATA statements and use it to test the program:

Identification Number	Score on First Test	Score on Second Test
101	88	73
102	100	92
103	45	78
104	63	69
105	84	87
106	92	88
107	91	100
108	61	75
109	78	73
110	99	94
111	74	82
112	83	69
113	100	100
114	52	69
115	85	85

Notice that the data does not include a trailer value. The program should use a FOR loop to process exactly fifteen sets of input data.

7
PROGRAM DEVELOPMENT

In previous chapters we have discussed different aspects of the process of developing computer programs. Many of the ideas about program development were presented intuitively while illustrating some feature of BASIC. In this chapter we bring together these ideas and discuss program development in detail.

7-1. PROGRAM STRUCTURE

A central aspect of program development is the concept of program structure. The *structure* of a program is the way in which the instructions in the program are organized. When a programmer develops a BASIC program he or she builds a structure of BASIC statements. If the structure is well built, the program is correct, easy to understand, and easily modified. On the other hand, a poorly structured program may have errors that are difficult to detect, may be hard to read, and may be troublesome to change.

There are three basic structures of statements in a program: sequence structures, decision structures, and loop structures. They are illustrated in Fig. 7–1. In a *sequence structure*, the statements are executed in the order in which they are written, one after the other. For example, a series of LET statements that performs some calculation is a sequence structure. A *decision structure* (also called *selection* or *alternation*) is used to decide which of two other structures is to be executed next based on some condition. In BASIC the IF statement is used to create a decision structure. If the condition in the IF statement is true, one group of statements is executed; otherwise another set of

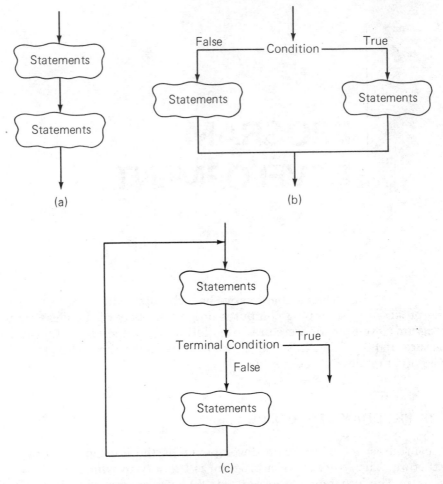

(a)

(b)

(c)

FIGURE 7-1. Basic program structures: (a) sequence
structure; (b) decision structure; (c) loop
structure.

statements is performed. (The structured decision statements discussed
in Section 4-4 also create a decision structure.) In a *loop structure*
(also called *repetition* or *iteration*), a group of statements is executed
repeatedly until some condition indicates that the loop should be
terminated. In BASIC we use a GO TO statement at the end of a set of
statements to branch to the beginning and thus create a loop. The loop
is controlled by checking a condition in an IF statement each time the
loop is executed. (Another loop structure is the WHILE loop discussed
in Section 5-2. In addition, the FOR and NEXT statements form a
special type of loop structure.)

Figure 7-1 summarizes the three basic structures. Figure 7-1(a)
shows a sequence structure in which one group of statements is performed after another. In Fig. 7-1(b) a decision structure is shown in

which one of two alternative groups of statements is executed based on some condition. We can also create a one-sided decision by not executing any statements when the condition is false (see Fig. 4-6). The loop structure in Fig. 7-1(c) is such that a group of statements is executed, a terminal condition is checked, and then another group of statements is executed before repeating the pattern. If no statements are performed in the loop before the terminal condition is checked, we have a pre-test pattern [see Fig. 5-7(b)]. Similarly, if the structure is such that no statements are executed after the condition is checked, the pattern is that of a post-test loop [see Fig. 5-7(c)].

One characteristic common to all these structures is that there is only one way of entering each structure and only one way of leaving; that is, it is not possible to branch into the middle of any of the structures or to branch out of any structure in more than one place. We say that each structure has one *entry point* and one *exit point*. We will see that this is an important characteristic of these structures.

Within a structure we can embed any other structure that we need. This is the idea of nesting discussed in relation to decisions and loops. In fact, we can nest any structure within any other. For example, within a loop we may have a sequence of statements, decision structures, and other loops. Within a decision structure we may have sequences, loops, and other decisions. In terms of the diagrams in Fig. 7-1, this means that we can substitute any structure for any block of statements within any structure.

We can use this idea of nesting to build a program as shown in Fig. 7-2. We might start with a single block and substitute a loop for it. Then we replace the statements at the beginning of the loop with a decision and the statements at the end with a sequence. Finally, we nest a loop in the decision. We can continue in this manner to build more complex programs. Notice, however, that because each structure has one entry point and one exit point, the final program has only one entry point (i.e., one point where execution of the program starts) and one exit point (i.e., one point where execution of the program stops).

There are other program structures that can appear in a program. For example, the ON-GO TO statement can be used to create a special type of selection known as a *case structure*. However, we can accomplish the same result using nested IF statements. In fact, *any* other structure can be created out of the three basic structures. This fact was proved by two computer scientists who showed that any program with a single entry point and a single exit point can be written using just the three basic structures.† Thus, if we know how to create these

---

†C. Böhm and G. Jacopini, "Flow Diagrams, Turing Machines and Languages with Only Two Formation Rules", *Communications of the ACM*, 9, 5(May 1966), 366-371. In proving their result, Böhm and Jacopini used a different loop structure from the one shown in Fig. 7-1(c). It can be shown, however, that the general loop structure in the text can be constructed from the Böhm and Jacopini structures.

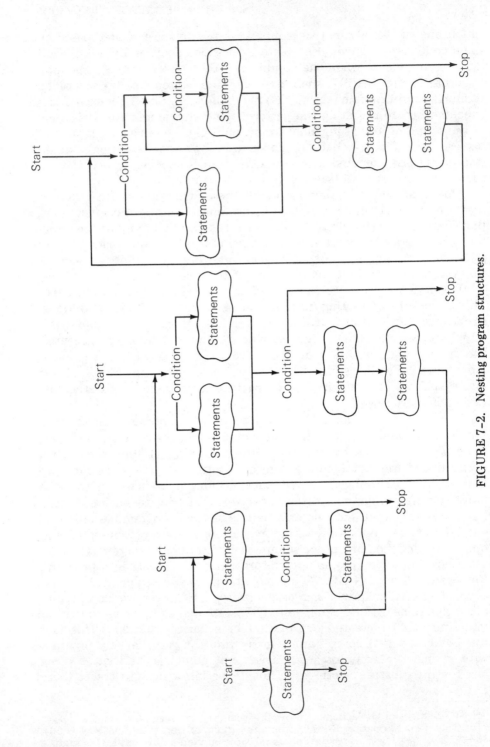

FIGURE 7-2. Nesting program structures.

structures in a programming language, we do not need any other structures.

7-2. PROGRAM UNDERSTANDABILITY

In Section 3-4 we discussed the importance of producing an understandable program. A program must be easily understood because people, including the original programmer, must understand the program in order to correct, modify, and enhance it.

Program structure can contribute greatly to program understandability. The problem with trying to understand the logic of a complex program is that there are really two versions of the program. One is the *static* version that is represented by the listing of the program on paper or the CRT. The other version is the *dynamic* form of the program that can be understood only by following the logic of the program as it is being executed. When a programmer reads a listing, he or she is reading the static form of the program. As with lines in a book, each statement is normally read in sequence from the top of the page down. The dynamic version may be different from the static version because the statements are not executed in the order in which they are written. For example, when a GO TO statement is encountered in a program, the next statement in the dynamic version of the program (i.e., the statement to which the program branches) is not the same as the next statement in the static version (which is the next statement in sequence). To understand the dynamic version, the programmer may have to skip all over the program listing instead of reading the program sequentially.

A basic principle of producing understandable programs is to make the dynamic version of the program resemble the static form as much as possible. Ideally, the program should execute from top to bottom just as it is read. However, if branching is required, this is not possible. The next best situation is to have the program execute from top to bottom through a sequence of basic program structures; that is, the program first executes the statements in one structure (e.g., a loop), then executes the statements in the next structure (such as a decision), and so on to the end of the program. Of course, other structures may be nested in these structures, as we saw in the last section. But this top-to-bottom execution using only the three basic program structures brings the dynamic version of the program as close as possible to the static form. In addition, we know that we can write any program using just these three structures.

The structure of a program can be greatly complicated by the uncontrolled use of GO TO statements. The problem with GO TO state-

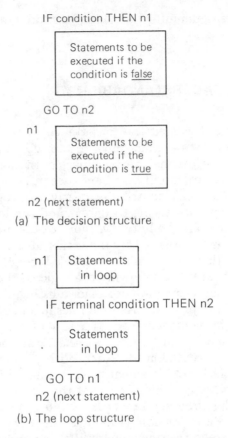

IF condition THEN n1

> Statements to be
> executed if the
> condition is <u>false</u>

GO TO n2

n1

> Statements to be
> executed if the
> condition is <u>true</u>

n2 (next statement)

(a) The decision structure

n1

> Statements
> in loop

IF terminal condition THEN n2

> Statements
> in loop

GO TO n1

n2 (next statement)

(b) The loop structure

FIGURE 7-3. Decision and loop structures in BASIC.

ments is that we do not always know where we came from. Although this may appear humorous, it makes a lot of sense. For example, assume that we are trying to understand the conditions under which a particular statement is executed. If it is possible to branch to that statement from a number of different points in the program, we will not know how we got to that statement without going back to all of the GO TO statements branching to it. The logic may become even more complex if there are multiple ways to get to each of these GO TO statements. (A famous letter entitled "GO TO Statement Considered Harmful" discusses this point of view.[†])

The ultimate situation would be to eliminate all GO TO statements from the program. In most versions of BASIC, this is not possible. GO

[†]Edsger W. Dijkstra, "GO TO Statement Considered Harmful", *Communications of the ACM*, 11 3(March 1968), 147–148. The letter begins with the statement, "For a number of years I have been familiar with the observation that the quality of programmers is a decreasing function of the density of *go to* statements in the programs they produce."

TO statements are needed to create decision and loop structures. The fundamental patterns are shown in Fig. 7-3 (see Figs. 4-8 and 5-8 for variations on the basic patterns). Although these structures require the use of the GO TO statement, the logic of the program is kept at the simplest level if we use the GO TO statement only in the particular ways shown.

In some versions of BASIC, structured decision statements and WHILE loops are available. Since the former is used for decision making and the latter for loop control, we can write any program we wish using these program structures. Such a program would not have any GO TO statements. For example, Fig. 5-11 showed a program using these structures. In general, structured decision statements and WHILE loops should be used if available instead of IF and GO TO statements. (Although it is not necessary, we may also want to use the FOR and NEXT statements for loop control.)

To summarize, the fundamental approach to producing understandable programs is to design the program so that it executes from top to bottom and uses only sequences, decisions, and loops.

7-3. PROGRAM STYLE

Program style refers to those characteristics of a program that make it easier to read and therefore easier to understand. In previous chapters we have mentioned a number of style rules. The following are some of the rules that have been discussed as well as a few that have not been mentioned:

1. Use meaningful variables. For example, use N for number, T for total, C for cost, and so forth. This helps the programmer remember what each name refers to.

2. Use line numbers of the same length. Usually this means using line numbers that are all three digits or all four digits. This helps to align the first part of each statement.

3. Assign line numbers in a logical pattern. For example, the statements in the first section of the program may be numbered between 1000 and 1990, the statements in the second section may be assigned numbers between 2000 and 2990, and so on for the other sections of the program. In addition, number the END statement with the largest line number of the length being used (e.g., 9999). This makes it easy to refer to the END statement.

4. Put all DATA statements at the end of the program and number them accordingly (e.g., with numbers between 9000 and 9990).

5. Use parentheses in expressions to show the order of evaluation even if they are not needed. This reduces confusion about how an expression is evaluated.

Program style can also help to display the structure of a program. If structured decision statements are used, the true and false parts should be indented. This enables the programmer to see the structure more quickly. Similarly, with WHILE loops the statements in the loop should be indented. Indentation should also be used with FOR loops.

When IF and GO TO statements must be used for decision and loop structures, indentation may help to show the structure or it may make the logic more confusing. We saw examples of this in Chapters 4 and 5. Some programmers advocate always branching to a REM statement. As we explained in Chapter 3, a REM statement is ignored when reached during the execution of the program. If we branch to a REM statement, the computer merely goes on to the next statement in sequence. Using this style and indentation, we could write the tuition-calculation program in Fig. 5–2 as shown in Fig. 7–4. Whether this style is used depends on the preference of the individual programmer.

Another way of improving the readability of a program is to use remarks to explain the function of different parts of the program. Remarks can be placed anywhere in the program by using the REM statement. We have purposefully avoided using remarks in our illustrative programs so as to concentrate on the logic of the program. However, as programs become more complex, remarks can help to explain them.

The basic function of a remark is to explain some characteristic of the program that is not immediately obvious. Usually there should be a remark at each important loop or decision in the program indicating the function of the code that follows. For example, in the program in

```
200 REM - BEGIN LOOP
210    INPUT I,U
220    IF I=9999 THEN 500
300    IF U>12 THEN 330
310       LET T=350
320       GO TO 350
330    REM
340       LET T=350+20*(U-12)
350    REM - END IF
400    PRINT I,T
410    GO TO 200
500 REM - END LOOP
999 END
```

FIGURE 7-4.   A program with branching to REM statements.

Fig. 7-4, we might insert the following remark at the beginning of the input loop:

```
205 REM - REPEAT INPUT LOOP UNTIL TRAILER VALUE IS ENTERED
```

While the information in this remark can be gleaned from the program, the remark makes the process of understanding the program easier. As another example, we may put the following remark before line 300 in the program in Fig. 7-4:

```
290    REM - CALCULATE TUITION
```

This remark describes the function of the decision structure that follows.

A common mistake in using remarks is simply to parrot the code that follows. For example, consider the following sequence that might be used in the program in Fig. 7-4:

```
309    REM - SET TUITION TO $350.00
310    LET T=350
```

The remark is unnecessary since it repeats the statement that follows. Another example of this unnecessary use of a remark is the following:

```
50 REM - INCREASE I BY 1
60 LET I=I+1
```

Again, the remark merely echoes the next statement.

A second common problem with the use of remarks is that a remark may state one thing while the program does something else. This may be because the programmer wrote the remark incorrectly or wrote a correct remark but incorrect code, or perhaps because the code was modified some time after the original program was written. When remarks are used, it is essential that they correctly describe the program. Otherwise the programmer may read the remark and think that the program does one thing while, in fact, it does something else. (Because of this, some programmers advocate deleting all remarks while debugging a program.)

One test that is sometimes applied to determine whether the remarks in a program are sufficient is to read just the remarks and not the code. If the basic logic of the program—but not the detail—can be understood from the remarks, they are sufficient. Unfortunately, this test may result in too many remarks or remarks containing too much detail. By remembering the objective that remarks should help to explain difficult parts of the program and not simply repeat the code, the best level of detail can be achieved.

Besides describing how a program works. remarks can be used to document important information about the program. This information includes such things as who wrote the program, when it was written, what the purpose of the program is, and what the variables in the program mean. Usually such information is put into a block of remarks at the beginning of the program. For example, the following remarks might be used at the beginning of the program in Fig. 7-4:

```
100 REM - TUITION CALCULATION PROGRAM
110 REM
120 REM - PROGRAMMER: ROBERT C. NICKERSON
130 REM - DATE: NOVEMBER 11, 1981
140 REM
150 REM - PURPOSE: THIS PROGRAM COMPUTES TUITION FOR A COLLEGE STUDENT
160 REM            BASED ON THE NUMBER OF UNITS THAT THE STUDENT IS TAKING.
170 REM
180 REM - VARIABLES:
182 REM      I = STUDENT IDENTIFICATION NUMBER (INPUT/OUTPUT)
184 REM      U = NUMBER OF UNITS (INPUT)
186 REM      T = TUITION (OUTPUT)
190 REM
```

Notice in this example that blank remark lines (i.e., lines with just the word REM) are used to separate groups of remarks. This helps make the remarks more readable. Blank lines may also be used to separate groups of statements in the program and thus improve the readability of the code.

In this section we have given a number of rules to improve the readability of a program, but many other rules of program style are advocated. As the programmer becomes more experienced, he or she should investigate alternative approaches to program style. The programmer should then select the style with which he or she is most comfortable and that at the same time makes the program readable and the logic understandable.[†]

7-4. PROGRAM REFINEMENT

Developing the logic of a complex program can be a difficult task. A technique that is often advocated is to develop the program through a sequence of refinement steps. The idea is to start with a general state-

---

[†]A good starting point is John M. Nevison's book, *The Little Book of BASIC Style*, published by Addison-Wesley. A more general and complete discussion of program style is found in the book by Brian W. Kernighan and P.J. Plauger entitled *The Elements of Program Style*, published by McGraw-Hill.

ment of the solution and to refine this statement gradually. Each refinement should bring the program closer to the final version. The last step in the process produces the coded program. This technique is often called *stepwise program refinement*.

To illustrate this technique, consider the problem of rearranging three numbers into ascending (or increasing) order. This process is called *sorting*. (In a later chapter we will see how to sort large amounts of data.) We assume that the three numbers to be sorted are input data. The numbers may be in any order initially. In the program we will refer to the numbers by the variables V1, V2, and V3. The program must accept values for V1, V2, and V3. Then it must rearrange the values so that V1 equals the smallest value, V2 is the middle value, and V3 equals the largest value. Finally, the sorted values must be printed.

As a first step in developing the program, we write the following:

```
100 INPUT V1,V2,V3
    Sort V1, V2, and V3 into ascending order.
400 PRINT V1,V2,V3
999 END
```

This program is complete except for the second line, which is written in English, not BASIC. If we can refine this line to a set of BASIC statements that accomplishes the sorting process, the program will be complete.

One way of sorting the three numbers is first to move the largest value to V3. The next largest value is then moved to V2. If this is done without destroying any of the values, V1 will be equal to the smallest value. Hence, the numbers will be sorted. For example, assume that initially the data is as follows:

$$V1 = 7$$
$$V2 = 9$$
$$V3 = 5$$

Moving the largest value, 9, to V3 results in the data being rearranged into the following order:

$$V1 = 7$$
$$V2 = 5$$
$$V3 = 9$$

Then moving the next largest value, 7, to V2 results in the following:

$$V1 = 5$$

```
            V2 = 7
            V3 = 9
```

Thus, the smallest value, 5, is automatically moved to V1. Incorporating this refinement into our program, we get the following:

```
100  INPUT V1,V2,V3
     Move largest value to V3.
     Move next largest value to V2.
400  PRINT V1,V2,V3
999  END
```

To move the largest value to V3, we first move the larger of V1 and V2 to V2, and then move the larger of V2 and V3 to V3. After doing this we move the next largest value to V2 by moving the larger of V1 and V2 to V2. Hence, the program can be refined again to the following:

```
100  INPUT V1,V2,V3
     Move larger of V1 and V2 to V2.
     Move larger of V2 and V3 to V3.
     Move larger of V1 and V2 to V2.
400  PRINT V1,V2,V3
999  END
```

To move the larger of V1 and V2 to V2, we compare V1 and V2. Then if V1 is larger than V2, we switch the values of V1 and V2. In effect, we are asking whether V1 and V2 are in proper sequence with respect to one another. If they are not, we switch their values. We do similar comparisons and switching for V2 and V3 and again for V1 and V2. Incorporating this refinement into the program we obtain the following:

```
100 INPUT V1,V2,V3
200 IF V1<=V2 THEN 250
        Switch V1 and V2.
250 IF V2<=V3 THEN 300
        Switch V2 and V3.
300 IF V1<=V2 THEN 400
        Switch V1 and V2.
400 PRINT V1,V2,V3
999 END
```

To complete the program, we need only to include the necessary satements to switch the values of the variables. Figure 7-5 shows how the switching is done for V1 and V2. First V1 is assigned to a temporary variable, T. Then V2 is assigned to V1. Finally, the value of T is assigned to V2. Thus, the following three statements are needed to switch the values of V1 and V2:

```
210 LET T=V1
220 LET V1=V2
230 LET V2=T
```

Writing similar sets of statements for the other switching steps and including these in the program, we get the final versions of the sorting program shown in Fig. 7-6.

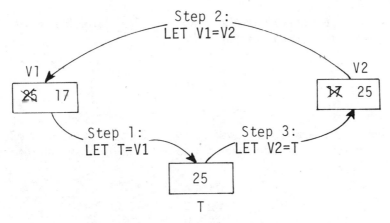

FIGURE 7-5.   Switching the values of two variables.

```
100 INPUT V1,V2,V3
200 IF V1<=V2 THEN 250
210 LET T=V1
220 LET V1=V2
230 LET V2=T
250 IF V2<=V3 THEN 300
260 LET T=V2
270 LET V2=V3
280 LET V3=T
300 IF V1<=V2 THEN 400
310 LET T=V1
320 LET V1=V2
330 LET V2=T
400 PRINT V1,V2,V3
999 END
```

FIGURE 7-6.   The sorting program.

To illustrate how the program works, consider the following worst possible case:

$$V1 = 9$$
$$V2 = 7$$
$$V3 = 5$$

The data is completely out of order. After the first switch the values will be as follows:

$$V1 = 7$$
$$V2 = 9$$
$$V3 = 5$$

That is, the larger of V1 and V2 is moved to V2. After the next switch the values will be in the following order:

$$V1 = 7$$
$$V2 = 5$$
$$V3 = 9$$

The larger of V2 and V3 is moved to V3. The effect of both switches is that the largest of all three is moved to V3. The final switch results in the following:

$$V1 = 5$$
$$V2 = 7$$
$$V3 = 9$$

The larger of V1 and V2 is moved to V2. In effect, the next largest of all three is moved to V2, and at the same time the smallest value ends up in V1. Hence, the data is sorted.

This example illustrates how the technique of stepwise refinement can be applied to a problem solution. The technique allows the programmer to concentrate on small parts of the program in successively more detail. The programmer does not try to find the entire solution at once, but rather thinks about the solution in pieces. This usually makes program development easier.

7-5. THE PROGRAMMING PROCESS

At the end of Chapter 2 we discussed briefly the process of preparing a computer program. We mentioned five activities that constitute the programming process. These activities are:

1. Understanding and defining the problem.
2. Designing the program.

3. Coding the program.
4. Showing that the program is correct.
5. Documenting the program.

In this section we discuss each of these activities in detail.

The five activities in the programming process are not necessarily performed in sequence. In fact, several activities usually take place at the same time. For example, later we will see that documenting begins while we are trying to understand and define the problem. Similarly, we can begin to show correctness of the program during the designing activity. The activities are listed not in the order in which they are *started* but rather in the order in which they are *finished*. For example, we cannot finish designing the program until we have finished understanding and defining the problem. However, we may have started the designing activity before the first activity is completed. Likewise, final coding cannot be completed until the program design is done; showing that the program is correct cannot be completed until the coding is done; and documentation cannot be finalized until all other activities have been completed.

Problem Definition

The first activity in the programming process is to understand and carefully define the problem to be solved. Frequently the most difficult step is recognizing that a problem exists for which a programmed solution is appropriate. However, it is usually not the programmer's responsibility to recognize the need for a program to solve a problem. Most often the programmer receives a general statement of the problem, either orally or in writing, and begins the programming process from that point.

At first the programmer should try to understand the problem as a whole. What does the problem require? Usually this involves determining what output is to be produced. What data is available? Answering this question often involves determining what input data is to be processed. The programmer tries to get a general understanding of the problem as a whole without going into details about the input, the output, and the calculations.

After the programmer has a general understanding of the problem, he or she should refine the problem definition to include specific information about input and output layouts, calculations, and logical operations. The refinement of the problem definition should continue until the programmer obtains sufficient detail to begin designing a solution. At a minimum the problem definition must give the following:

1. What output is to be produced and its layout.
2. What input data is available.

3. What computations are to be performed.

4. What logical conditions affect processing.

Sometimes the programmer may have difficulty understanding a problem. When this happens it often helps to isolate parts of the problem and work with each part separately. Another approach is to think of a simpler but similar problem and to understand it first. The programmer may get some insight from the simpler problem that helps explain the more complex problem.

Some problems cannot be solved with a computer. In mathematics there are a number of problems that do not have solutions. In addition, some problems may be too large for a computer or take too long to solve. Although problems that cannot be solved do not arise often, we must nevertheless be certain that it is reasonable to attempt a programmed solution.

As an example of the programming process, we will consider a variation of the test-score-averaging problem discussed in previous chapters. The problem is to calculate a weighted average of three test scores. We assume that the best test score counts 50%, the next best score is weighted 35%, and the worst test score counts only 15%. In addition to calculating the weighted average, the program must print the corresponding letter grade based on a straight percentage scale (i.e., 90% to 100% is an A; 80% to 89% is a B; 70 to 79% is a C; 60% to 69% is a D; and 59% or less is an F).

Already we begin to understand the problem. A program is needed that produces a report giving the weighted average and letter grade for each student in a class. The input to the program must be three test scores. In addition, there must be some way of identifying the student to whom the scores belong (such as a student identification number). The program must determine which test score is the best, which score is worst, and which score falls in between. Then the program must apply the appropriate percentages to arrive at the average. In addition, the program must determine which grade category the average falls into so that the appropriate letter grade can be printed.

We can refine the problem definition at this point to specify details about the input and output. We will assume that all input data is recorded in DATA statements. Output will be printed on paper. Variables can be assigned to the input and output data. For this program we will use the following variables:

Variable	Meaning
I	Student identification number
S1	Score on first test
S2	Score on second test
S3	Score on third test
A	Weighted average score

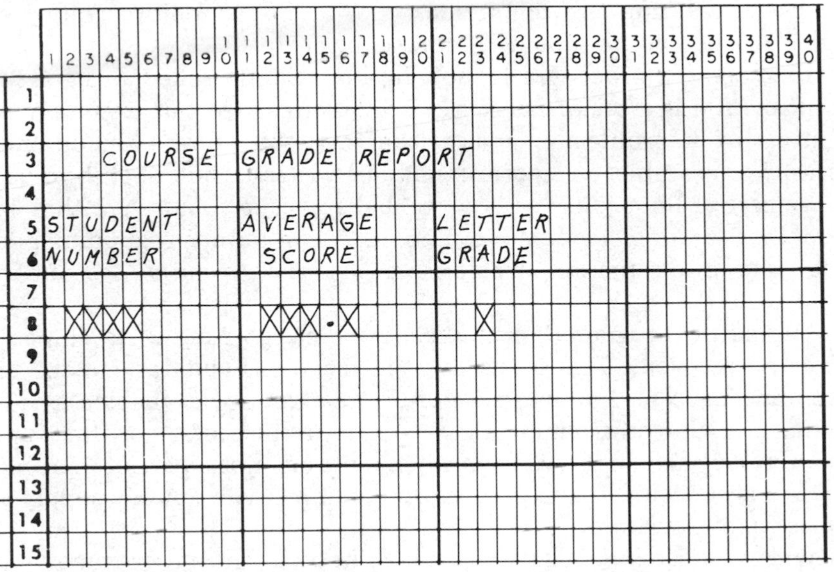

COURSE GRADE REPORT

STUDENT   AVERAGE   LETTER
NUMBER   SCORE   GRADE

XXXX   XXX.X   X

FIGURE 7-7. A print chart.

For the output we must consider the print positions in which the data is printed. A useful tool is to use a piece of graph paper or a special form called a *print chart* to sketch the output. Figure 7-7 shows the output format for this program on a print chart. The numbers across the top give the print positions. Headings are written on the chart exactly as they are to be printed. Variable information, such as the student's identification number, average score, and letter grade, is indicated by Xs in the print position in which it is to be printed.[†] By sketching the output format first on a chart such as this, it is much easier to code the necessary PRINT statements.

A question that has not been answered is how the input loop is to be controlled. As we have seen, there are a number of techniques for loop control. We will assume in this example that the last set of input data contains 9999 for the student number and use this to control the loop.

Program Design

After the problem has been carefully defined, we can begin to design an appropriate program. The objective during the program-designing activity is to devise a plan for a program that solves the problem. This does not mean that the program is coded at this stage,

---

[†]The variable output may not appear exactly in the format shown unless the PRINT USING statement is used.

because a solution procedure must be developed before coding can begin. The procedure should, of course, be correct.

In general, a procedure for solving a problem is called an algorithm. An *algorithm* is a set of instructions that, if carried out, results in the solution of a problem. An algorithm may be represented in many forms. For example, an algorithm may be written using English or using mathematical notation. A recipe to bake a cake is an algorithm in a form that is understandable to a cook. A computer programming language is used to represent an algorithm so that it can be carried out by a computer.

During the program-designing activity an algorithm is developed to solve the problem. This is usually the most difficult task in the programming process, but many helpful strategies are available. It is important for the programmer to have a repertoire of algorithms upon which he or she can draw. Then when a problem or a part of a problem requires a particular algorithm, the programmer can quickly supply the appropriate procedure.

When a necessary algorithm is not known, the programmer must devise one. The use of stepwise program refinement, discussed in the last section, can help to design an algorithm. In addition to producing the necessary algorithm, this procedure leads naturally to the use of the basic program structures in nested patterns as discussed in Section 7-1. If the programmer adheres to the basic structures during the refinement process, the final program will have a single entry point and a single exit point, and will flow from top to bottom through a sequence of loops and decisions. Thus, the program refinement strategy not only helps to devise an algorithm, but also leads to the most understandable program.

When developing an algorithm, the programmer should keep in mind the structure of the data. Although we have only worked with simple data structures so far, we can already see that an algorithm cannot be developed without knowing how the data is going to be organized. For example, the programmer must know the characteristics of the input and output data before developing an algorithm to do the necessary processing. In later chapters we will discuss more complex data structures and show that an algorithm depends on the structure of the data. Thus, the development of an algorithm is *not* independent of the development of the data structure.

Alternative algorithms are sometimes developed. Then the question of which algorithm to select becomes important. The objective is to select the best algorithm that will correctly solve the problem. However, which algorithm is "best" depends on trade-offs between such factors as speed of execution, storage utilization, and algorithm understandability.

Sometimes it is difficult to devise an algorithm for a problem. When this happens, it often helps to think of a related problem and develop an algorithm for it. Another approach is to simplify the problem by discarding some of the conditions and then to develop an algorithm for the simpler version. Sometimes it is necessary to return to the problem definition to determine whether anything has been omitted. Any of these approaches may help the programmer develop an algorithm for the problem.

Various tools are available to help in developing an algorithm. One such tool is the *flowchart* — a graphic representation of the logic in an algorithm. Many programmers find it helpful to draw a flowchart of the algorithm so that they can see the logic pictorially. The program can then be coded from the flowchart. In Appendix B we discuss program flowcharting in detail.

When a program is especially large, it often helps to divide the program into sections, or *modules.* Each module performs some function related to the overall processing of the program. The idea behind modular programming is that each module can be worked on separately. The programmer can develop an algorithm for each module without worrying about the logic of the other modules. In addition, each module can be individually coded and tested. This helps isolate errors.

With modular programming, each module can be regarded as a subalgorithm. The logic of a module can be developed through stepwise refinement. Using only the three basic program structures results in a module with only one entry point and one exit point. The exit point for one module then leads to the entry point of the next module. Thus, the complete program is a sequence of modules. (A related idea is the use of subroutines to modularize a program. BASIC subroutines are discussed in Chapter 12.)

To illustrate many of the ideas in this subsection, we continue with the development of the grade-report program. We might start by writing the overall algorithm as follows:

Print the headings.
Repeat the following until there is no more input data:
    Read a set of input data.
    Calculate the average score.
    Determine the grade category based on the average and print
        the output with the appropriate grade.

At this point we could begin to code some of the instructions in the program. However, before we do this and become entangled in details, we should continue to refine some of the steps that are not immediately obvious.

The step to calculate the average score needs further refinement. We recall that the average score is found by taking 50% of the best test score, 35% of the next best score, and 15% of the worst score. Hence, we must first determine the best score, the next best score, and the worst score. Thus, we could refine this step as follows:

> Find the best score.
> Find the next best score.
> Find the worst score.
> Compute the weighted average.

We can easily carry out the first three steps above by simply sorting the test scores into ascending order. Then the algorithm can be expressed as follows:

> Sort the test scores into ascending order.
> Compute the weighted average.

Since we already know a sorting algorithm for three numbers, we can use this algorithm in the first step. Thus, the refinement of the average calculation is complete (except for the final coding).

We should also refine the step that determines the grade category and writes the output. Since there are five grade categories, we can regard this as a selection process and refine it as follows:

> Select the appropriate grade category:
> > 90 - 100: Print output data with "A".
> > 80 - 89: Print output data with "B".
> > 70 - 79: Print output data with "C".
> > 60 - 69: Print output data with "D".
> > 0 - 59: Print output data with "F".

Although this does not resemble one of the three basic structures, we know that we can code it as nested decisions.

The only other step that needs some refinement is the input loop control. We wish to repeat the loop until there is no more input data. To refine this further, we need to know more about the structure of the input data. During the problem-definition stage, we decided that the last set of input data will contain 9999 for the student number. Hence, we can control the input by testing for this trailer value after each set of input is read.

Incorporating all of the refinements discussed here, we get the algorithm shown in Fig. 7-8. We can now begin the final program refinement, that of writing the code for the program.

Print the headings.
Repeat the following loop:
  Read a set of input data.
  If the trailer value is read, stop the program.
  Sort the test scores into ascending order.
  Compute the weighted average.
  Select the appropriate grade category:
    90–100: Print output data with "A".
    80– 89: Print output data with "B".
    70– 79: Print output data with "C".
    60– 69: Print output data with "D".
     0– 59: Print output data with "F".

FIGURE 7–8. Grade report algorithm.

Program Coding

The objective during the program-coding activity is to implement the algorithm in a specific programming language. In effect, this is the last step in program refinement. Each part of the algorithm must be translated into a group of statements. The final code will be correct if the algorithm is correct and the translation is done correctly.

Occasionally during the coding activity an error is discovered in the logic of the algorithm. When this happens, the programmer must redesign the program. It may even be necessary to return to the problem definition and work forward again if a serious error or misunderstanding is discovered.

During program coding, style rules, as discussed in Section 7-3, should be followed. This helps to make the program more readable and the structure more understandable. Remarks should be included as the program is coded. When the coding activity is complete, the program should be in its final form (except for the correction of possible errors).

The coding for the grade-report program is shown in Fig. 7–9. Each step in the algorithm is translated into one or more BASIC statements. For example, the sorting step results in twelve statements, while the average calculation requires only one statement. Notice that the remarks in the body of the program follow closely the algorithm given in Fig. 7–8. This is a common approach for organizing remarks in a program. Notice also the use of introductory remarks in the program.

The program is built from the basic program structures discussed in Section 7-1. The main logic is a sequence consisting of a step to print the heading and an input loop that is terminated when the trailer value is read. The loop contains a sequence of decisions for sorting, a calculation step for the average, and nested decisions for the output. Style rules have been followed to make the program more readable and understandable.

There are alternative ways of accomplishing different steps in this

```
1000 REM - GRADE REPORT PROGRAM
1010 REM
1020 REM - PROGRAMMER: ROBERT C. NICKERSON
1030 REM - DATE: NOVEMBER 18, 1981
1040 REM
1100 REM - PURPOSE: THIS PROGRAM COMPUTES A WEIGHTED AVERAGE OF THREE
1110 REM            TEST SCORES AND ASSIGNS APPROPRIATE LETTER GRADES
1120 REM
1200 REM - VARIABLES
1210 REM        I   = STUDENT IDENTIFICATION NUMBER (INPUT/OUTPUT)
1220 REM        S1  = SCORE ON FIRST TEST (INPUT)
1230 REM        S2  = SCORE ON SECOND TEST (INPUT)
1240 REM        S3  = SCORE ON THIRD TEST (INPUT)
1250 REM        A   = WEIGHTED AVERAGE SCORE (OUTPUT)
1260 REM        T   = TEMPORARY VARIABLE (INTERNAL)
2000 REM
2010 REM - PRINT HEADINGS
2020 REM
2100 PRINT "   COURSE GRADE REPORT"
2110 PRINT
2120 PRINT "STUDENT    AVERAGE    LETTER"
2130 PRINT "NUMBER      SCORE     GRADE"
2140 PRINT
3000 REM
3010 REM - BEGIN INPUT LOOP
3020 REM
3100 READ I,S1,S2,S3
3110 IF I=9999 THEN 9999
4000 REM
4010 REM - SORT TEST SCORES INTO ASCENDING ORDER
4020 REM
4100 IF S1<=S2 THEN 4200
4110 LET T=S1
4120 LET S1=S2
4130 LET S2=T
4200 IF S2<=S3 THEN 4300
4210 LET T=S2
4220 LET S2=S3
4230 LET S3=T
4300 IF S1<=S2 THEN 5000
4310 LET T=S1
4320 LET S1=S2
4330 LET S2=T
```

FIGURE 7-9. Grade report program (Part 1).

```
5000 REM
5010 REM - CALCULATE WEIGHTED AVERAGE
5020 REM
5100 LET A=.15*S1+.35*S2+.50*S3
6000 REM
6010 REM - SELECT GRADE CATEGORY AND WRITE OUTPUT
6020 REM
6100 IF A<90 THEN 6200
6110 REM - GRADE IS "A"
6120 PRINT I;TAB(12);A;TAB(23);"A"
6130 GO TO 7000
6200 IF A<80 THEN 6300
6210 REM - GRADE IS "B"
6220 PRINT I;TAB(12);A;TAB(23);"B"
6230 GO TO 7000
6300 IF A<70 THEN 6400
6310 REM - GRADE IS "C"
6320 PRINT I;TAB(12);A;TAB(23);"C"
6330 GO TO 7000
6400 IF A<60 THEN 6500
6410 REM - GRADE IS "D"
6420 PRINT I;TAB(12);A;TAB(23);"D"
6430 GO TO 7000
6500 REM - GRADE IS "F"
6510 PRINT I;TAB(12);A;TAB(23);"F"
7000 REM
7010 REM - REPEAT INPUT LOOP
7020 REM
7100 GO TO 3000
9000 REM - INPUT DATA
9010 DATA ...
  .
  .
  .
9999 END
```

FIGURE 7-9. Grade report program (Part 2).

program, depending on the language features that are available. For example, using some of the features discussed in Chapter 9, the printing of the letter grade can be simplified. The programmer should be familiar with as much of the programming language as possible and use those features that make the program easiest to code and as understandable as possible.

Program Correctness

In Chapter 2 we discussed the three types of errors that can occur in a program. These are syntax errors, execution errors, and logic errors. Syntax errors are detected by the computer while the program is being entered. An error message is printed for each syntax error. To correct such errors the programmer must interpret the error message and make appropriate changes in the program. Usually syntax errors result from the misuse of the programming language. Since these errors are detected by the computer, they are usually easy to correct.

Execution errors occur during the execution of the program. The program must not have any serious syntax errors in order to be executed. Thus, any execution error is the result of a condition that can be detected only during execution. Some examples of execution errors are dividing by zero, attempting to read when there is no more data in a DATA statement, and calculating a number that is too large for a variable. When such an error is detected, the computer normally stops execution of the program and prints an error message explaining the cause of the error. It is the programmer's responsibility to interpret the error message and to make the necessary correction.

If the program executes without errors, it may still not be correct. Errors may exist in the logic of the program, and these are the most difficult to detect. The usual approach is to make up test data and determine by hand what output is expected from the data. Then the program is run with the test data and the actual output is compared with the expected output. If the outputs do not agree, there is an error that must be located and corrected.

A program-testing procedure such as this shows only the *presence* of errors, not their *absence*. To show that a program is correct, we must demonstrate that under all circumstances the program produces the correct result. To do this by using test data would require running the program with all possible combinations of data and comparing the output with the expected output calculated by hand. In addition to being an enormous task, this would be senseless since then we would have all possible outputs calculated by hand and there would be no need for a program (except, perhaps, to check our hand calculations). We therefore need some other way of showing that the program is logically correct.

It is sometimes possible to prove that a program is correct in a mathematical sense, although this approach is usually too complex and tedious. We can, however, informally "prove" a program's correctness through the stepwise program-refinement process. Recall that in this approach we start with a general statement of the problem and then refine the statement by determining what must be done to accomplish it. At each step in the development, we refine the statements of the previous step until we reach the coded program. To show that a program is correct, we need to demonstrate that each refinement completes the task specified at the previous step.

As an example, consider the sorting program developed in Section 7-4. The problem is to sort three numbers into ascending sequence. The first step in the refinement includes the following statement:

Sort V1, V2, and V3 into ascending order.

We assume that this is a correct definition of the problem and begin to refine it. The first refinement results in the following:

Move largest value to V3.
Move next largest value to V2.

We can say that the program is correct at this point because we know that to sort the values we need only do the two steps listed above. We then refine each of these two steps separately and show that each refinement is a correct way of accomplishing the task that is being described. Thus, we can refine the first statement above to the following:

Move larger of V1 and V2 to V2.
Move larger of V2 and V3 to V3.

Then the program is correct at this level of refinement. We continue in this manner, showing that each successive step is a correct refinement of the previous step. Finally, we code the program and if there are no coding errors, the coded program is logically correct.

This method of showing program correctness through stepwise refinement is a very important part of programming. Most programmers do this even though they may not think they are "proving" that the program is correct. If it is done carefully and explicitly, the chance of serious logic errors in the program is greatly reduced. Thus, the development of the program is the most important step in the programming process.

Even if a program is developed in the manner described here, logic errors may occur. Details are often forgotten or a logical step in the development is passed over too quickly. A thorough testing of the program should therefore be performed to force out any hidden errors. The programmer should be merciless in testing the program. Some organizations have a different programmer do the testing so that the original programmer is not tempted to overlook possible weaknesses just to finish the job. The objective of program testing is to force errors to reveal themselves.

If the program is written in a modular fashion, each module can be tested separately. Sometimes testing can begin on an incomplete program by inserting "dummy" modules for incomplete parts of the program. After the modules are tested separately, the interaction among the modules can be tested. Pairs of modules can be tested, then three modules at a time, and so forth, until finally the entire program is tested as a whole.

The first tests of the program should be simple to insure that the program works in the simplest cases. Obvious errors such as misspelling of headings or nonalignment of columns can be corrected at this point. Then more complex tests can be performed.

At a minimum every statement in the program should be executed at least once using test data and the results compared with the expected output. This strategy, however, will not catch all obvious errors. For example, consider the following sequence of statements from the payroll program in Fig. 4-5:

```
110 IF H>40 THEN 150
120 LET G=4.50*H
130 LET W=.18*G
140 GO TO 170
150 LET G=180.00+6.75*(H-40)
160 LET W=.20*G
170 (next statement)
```

To test this section of code, we might supply two sets of test data, one with the hours equal to 35 and the other with the hours equal to 45. These data would cause every statement in this sequence to be executed at least once. Nevertheless, the sequence may still be in error. For example, assume that the IF statement has been incorrectly coded as follows:

```
110 IF H>=40 THEN 60
```

Then testing with only the two sets of inputs will not detect this error. We must also test the case where the hours are equal to 40.

We now have three sets of test data for this program. However, even with these data, errors may still be present. For example, the following erroneous IF statement would not be detected with these test data:

```
110 IF H>41 THEN 60
```

What we need is a test case that is just greater than 40, such as 40.1. Then this error would be detected.

We can see from this example the beginning of a general strategy for generating test data for this type of program. For this program the input value for the hours can range from zero to some practical limit such as eighty. We can divide this range into two subranges based on the calculations to be performed. If the hours are between zero and forty, one set of calculations should be performed. However, if the hours are greater than forty but less than or equal to the upper limit, another set of calculations should be carried out. Then the testing strategy is as follows: For each subrange, test the program with the maximum and minimum values in the subrange and with some representative value within the subrange. Applying this strategy to the payroll program, we would test the program with the hours equal to 0, 35, 40, 40.1, 45, and 80. If the program works for each of these cases, we are reasonably certain that it will work for others.

Generating test data for the grade-report program is much more complex. The best approach is to analyze the different parts of the program separately and to design appropriate test data for each part. We can apply the previous strategy to the grade-selection algorithm in the program. We note that the grade is based on the average test score. The actual grade depends on which of the following ranges the average falls into:[†]

$$90 - 100$$
$$80 - 89$$
$$70 - 79$$
$$60 - 69$$
$$0 - 59$$

We must select input data for the three test scores that will generate values for the average equal to the maximum and minimum value in each range and a value in between each set of limits. This results in fifteen test cases in all.

The sorting algorithm is more complex. We notice that the algorithm does not depend on whether any of the test scores are equal. Hence, for testing purposes we can assume that each score is different. Then there are six possible cases to test, based on the relative values of S1, S2, and S3. These cases are as follows:

Smallest		Largest
S1	S2	S3
S1	S3	S2
S2	S1	S3
S2	S3	S1
S3	S1	S2
S3	S2	S1

[†]Actually, the maximum value in each range should be as close to the minimum of the next range as possible (e.g., the second range should be 80–89.99). However, we will use the ranges given here to demonstrate the approach.

We must supply input test data for each of these cases. We can combine these six cases with the fifteen needed for the grade-selection algorithm. One additional case, with 9999 for the identification number, is needed to test the termination condition on the input loop.

A complete set of input data that satisfies these requirements is given in Fig. 7–10. Tests number 2, 3, 5, 6, 8, and 9 correspond to the six cases listed above for the sorting algorithm. For each set of data, the expected output is also shown. The test data should be shuffled so that the tests are not done in any particular order (except for the trailer value test). Then the program should be run with the data and the actual output compared with what is expected. Any discrepancy indicates an error. The output from running the program with this data is shown in Fig. 7–11.

The tests listed here will not detect all errors. For example, errors in input data, such as negative test scores or scores greater than 100, will not be detected by the program. In general, we should create special tests for the worst possible cases. Errors often occur at the beginning or end of processing. Hence, special tests should be made with the first and last set of input data. Tests should be made to see the results of too much or too little data. The program should also be run without any input data to see what happens.

When an error is detected, the programmer must locate the cause of the error in the program and correct it. Testing each module or section

Test Number	Input Test Data				Expected Output	
	I	S1	S2	S3	Average	Grade
1	1001	100	100	100	100	A
2	1002	83	93	100	95	A
3	1003	70	96	90	90	A
4	1004	90	88	88	89	B
5	1005	83	73	90	85	B
6	1006	86	60	80	80	B
7	1007	78	78	80	79	C
8	1008	73	80	63	75	C
9	1009	76	70	50	70	C
10	1010	68	70	68	69	D
11	1011	80	50	50	65	D
12	1012	45	75	45	60	D
13	1013	79	48	18	59	F
14	1014	40	40	70	55	F
15	1015	0	0	0	0	F
16	9999	0	0	0	—	—

FIGURE 7–10.   Test data and expected output for the grade report program.

COURSE GRADE REPORT

STUDENT NUMBER	AVERAGE SCORE	LETTER GRADE
1006	80	B
1011	65	D
1002	95	A
1009	70	C
1015	0	F
1004	89	B
1005	85	B
1013	59	F
1008	75	C
1001	100	A
1012	60	D
1010	69	D
1003	90	A
1007	79	C
1014	55	F

FIGURE 7-11.   Output from the grade report program.

separately helps to isolate errors. Since many errors are the result of incorrect input data, it is good practice during debugging to print all input data immediately after it is read. This is called *echo printing* and it allows the programmer to check that the desired input data has been read. Another technique is to print the values of variables that are not normally printed in the output. This allows the programmer to check the results of various intermediate calculations. A common technique is to *trace* the execution of the program; that is, to show the actual order of execution of various parts of the program. This can be done by inserting PRINT statements at different points in the program. The statements should print simple phrases that identify where in the program each statement is located, thereby allowing the programmer to compare the actual sequence of execution with what was expected.

The techniques discussed here can help to detect and locate errors in a program. However, if a program has been developed by following a logical, systematic approach, errors should be at a minimum. It is the programmer's responsibility to take whatever steps are necessary to guarantee that a program is correct. A program is correct when there are no logic errors as well as no syntax and execution errors.

Program Documentation

Documentation of a program provides information so that others can understand how to use the program and how the program works.

Documentation of how to use the program is provided mainly for people wishing to use the program to solve a particular problem. This is often called *user documentation*. It gives instructions for running the program on the computer, including what input to use and what to expect for output. (When this type of documentation is oriented toward computer operators, it is commonly called *operator documentation*.) Documentation on how the program works is provided for other programmers in the event that errors must be corrected or modifications in the program made. This is usually called *program documentation*. In this section we are concerned with this type of documentation.

Documenting the program begins during the problem-definition activity. Any written specifications of the program prepared at this stage are part of the documentation. For example, input and output data descriptions are part of the problem definition and should be included in the final program documentation. If, during program planning, flowcharts are prepared, they too should be included in the final documentation. Listings of the test data used and sample outputs should also be part of the program documentation.

This type of documentation is external to the program. However, much documentation can be included in the program itself. This is the primary purpose of remarks in the program. As we have seen, remarks can be used to describe the general features of the program and the detailed logic of the algorithm. A listing of the program with appropriate remarks is an important part of the documentation. The grade-report program in Fig. 7-9 illustrates such a program.

A complete documentation package for a program might contain the following:

1. A program summary or abstract that provides a brief statement of the overall function of the program.
2. A program narrative that describes the detailed logic of the program.
3. Program flowcharts, if prepared.
4. Input data descriptions.
5. Output data layouts.
6. A list of the test data used.
7. Sample output using the test data.
8. The program listing including all remarks.

The complete set of documents should be bound together with a title page and a table of contents. There should be one binder for each program, and the entire library of program documentation should be the responsibility of one or more documentation librarians. If a program is changed, it is important that the documentation be updated. No programmer should ever consider his or her job done until the final documentation is prepared or appropriately modified.

7-6. CONCLUSION

Computer programming is a process that includes several activities. One common misconception is that programming involves only the activity of writing the program. As we have seen, however, this activity, which is usually called coding, is just one part of the entire programming process. When we use the word "programming," we mean the whole set of activities associated with preparing a computer program. This includes the five activities discussed in the last section.

The approach to programming emphasized in this book is commonly called *structured programming*. There is considerable disagreement about what is meant by structured programming; a single definition does not exist. However, most people agree that structured programming involves a systematic process that results in programs that are well structured; that are easily understood, maintained, and modified; and that can be shown to be correct.

In this chapter we stressed developing programs through stepwise refinement. This approach helps us show the correctness of a program. Using the three basic program structures leads to programs that are well structured and easy to understand and change. The style rules discussed in this chapter also aid in producing readable programs.

Structured programming is really just good programming. By following the guidelines presented in this chapter, the programmer can produce good correct programs.

REVIEW QUESTIONS

1. What are the three basic structures of statements in a program?

2. What type of program structure is formed by each of the following groups of statements?

```
(a) 50 IF A>B THEN 80
    60 LET C=B
    70 GO TO 90
    80 LET C=A
(b) 50 FOR I=1 TO 10
    60 PRINT I
    70 NEXT I
(c) 50 LET A=5
    60 PRINT A
```

```
(d) 50 INPUT X
    60 IF X=0 THEN 80
    70 GO TO 50
```

3. Why is it important for each of the basic program structures to have a single entry point and a single exit point?

4. What principle of good program structure is violated by the program in Fig. 5–21?

5. The ON-GO TO statement can be used to form a _____ structure.

6. When we read the statements in a program in the order in which they are written on paper, we are reading the _____ version of the program. When we read the statements in a program in the order in which they are executed, we are reading the _____ version of the program.

7. Why can the uncontrolled use of GO TO statements make a program difficult to understand?

8. Give three rules of good program style.

9. What is wrong with the following group of statements?

```
50 REM - PRINT THE VALUES OF A, B, AND C
60 PRINT A,B,C
```

10. The process of developing a program by starting with a general statement of the problem and successively refining the statement until a program solution is obtained is called _____.

11. Consider the program shown in Fig. 7–6. Assume that the input is the numbers 8, 12, and 14. What is the value of all variables in the program *after* each statement in the program is executed?

12. Which activity in the programming process is begun during problem definition but finished after all other activities are completed?

13. A set of instructions that, if carried out, results in the solution of a problem is called a(n) _____.

14. Program testing can show that a program is correct. True or false?

15. Assume that the value of X can range from 100 to 200. Design test data following the strategy discussed in the chapter that tests the following program:

```
10 INPUT X
20 IF X<=125 THEN 50
30 LET Y=0
```

```
40 GO TO 60
50 LET Y=1
60 PRINT Y
70 GO TO 10
80 END
```

16. What is the purpose of program documentation?

17. What is the difference between coding and programming?

18. What is structured programming?

PROGRAMMING PROBLEMS

1. In the economic measurement of consumer behavior, the price elasticity of demand for a product is given by the following formula:

$$- \frac{(Q_2 - Q_1)/Q_1}{(P_2 - P_1)/P_1}$$

In this formula, Q stands for quantity sold and P for price.

If the elasticity is less than 1, the demand is said to be *inelastic*. If the elasticity equals 1, the demand is said to be *unit elastic*. If the elasticity is greater than 1, the demand is *elastic*.

Write a BASIC program to calculate the elasticity of demand for a particular product. Input is the product number and the relevant prices and quantities. Output from the program should be the product number, the elasticity of demand, and a statement of whether the demand is elastic, inelastic, or unit elastic.

Use the following data to test the program:

Product Number	P_1	Q_1	P_2	Q_2
103	25.00	100	17.50	135
108	20.00	200	10.00	300
112	125.00	35	95.00	37
115	32.50	512	27.00	713
128	44.00	80	33.00	100
132	15.75	72	10.25	63
999	(trailer value)			

2. A student is placed on the Dean's List of a college if his or her grade point average (GPA) is above a certain level. The minimum GPA necessary to make the Dean's List depends on the student's year in college. A freshman must have a GPA of 3.70 or greater to make the Dean's List. For a sophomore the minimum GPA is 3.50. Juniors and seniors must have a GPA of 3.30 or better to make the Dean's List.

Write a BASIC program to print data for all students who are on the Dean's List. There is one set of input for each student giving the student's identification number, year in school (1 = freshman, 2 = sophomore, 3 = junior, 4 = senior), and his or her GPA. Put all input data in DATA statements. Output should consist of the student's number and GPA for Dean's List students only. Supply appropriate headings for the output data.

Use the following data to test the program:

Student Number	Year	GPA
1012	2	3.61
1385	1	2.63
1472	3	3.95
1981	2	3.30
2061	4	2.91
2111	4	3.30
2385	1	3.85
2500	1	3.75
2911	2	3.50
3047	3	3.28
3568	3	3.00
3910	4	3.35
9999 (trailer value)		

3. The annual bonus paid to each employee of an organization is based on the number of years of service and the age of the employee. If the employee has 5 to 9 years of service and is between 25 and 34 years old, the annual bonus is $20. If he or she is 35 years or older, with 5 to 9 years of service, the bonus is $40. If the years of service are between 10 and 19, and the age is less than 40 years, the bonus is $50. If he or she has had 20 or more years of service, no matter what the age, the bonus is $60. For other employees, there is no bonus.

Write an interactive BASIC program to determine the annual bonus for any employee in the organization. Input for the program consists of the employee's identification number, age, and number of years of service. Output should include the employee's number and bonus for those employees who receive a bonus, or a phrase indicating no bonus if that is the case.

Use the following data to test the program:

Employee's Number	Age	Years of Service
1001	38	12
1121	52	28
1305	42	16
1457	29	8
1689	29	3
1810	37	9
1925	42	20
2008	33	10
2025	24	5
2133	54	23
2485	49	19
2561	24	6
2610	33	5

4. A theater sells tickets for $3.00 and averages 100 tickets sold for each performance. At this rate the theater's cost per patron is $1.20. The theater manager has estimated that for each 10¢ reduction in ticket price, the number of tickets sold will increase by 20 and the theater's cost per patron will increase by 4¢.

Write a BASIC program to calculate and print a table listing the ticket price, the number of tickets sold, the gross revenue (ticket price multiplied by the number of tickets sold), the theater's total cost (cost per patron times number of tickets sold), and the net profit (revenue minus theater's total cost) for each ticket price ranging from $3.00 to $2.00 in 10¢ increments.

As the ticket price decreases from $3.00 to $2.00, the profit will steadily increase to a maximum and then start to decrease. Use this fact to print the phrase MAXIMUM PROFIT on the line in the table that corresponds to the greatest profit.

5. Write a BASIC program to print student grade reports. Input to the program consists of a varying number of course grades for each student. Each set of input contains the student's identification number, course identification number, course units, and numeric course grade (equal to 4, 3, 2, 1, or 0). The input data is arranged in ascending numerical sequence by the students' identification numbers. All input data should be put in DATA statements.

The program must calculate the grade point average (GPA) for each student. This is done by multiplying the number of units for each course by the grade, totalling for all courses, and dividing by the total number of units taken.

The output from the program should list for each student the student's identification number, the number of units and grade for each course that the student took, and the student's GPA. In addition, if the GPA is 3.5 or greater, the message HONOR LIST should be printed. If the GPA is less than 1.5, the message PROBATION should be printed.

Design appropriate input data that thoroughly tests the program. Note that the number of courses taken by a student varies.

6. Given the slopes, s and t, and intercepts, a and b, of two lines — that is, the lines whose equations are

$$y = sx + a$$

$$y = tx + b$$

write a BASIC program to compute the coordinates of the point of intersection of the lines. Then print the name of the quadrant (FIRST, SECOND, THIRD, FOURTH) in which the point lies. If the point of intersection falls on an axis, print the name of the axis (X-AXIS or

Y-AXIS). If the point of intersection is the origin, print the word ORIGIN. Include a provision in the program to check whether the lines are parallel (i.e., s = t, a ≠ b) or whether the equations are for the same line (i.e., s = t, a = b), and print an appropriate phrase if either case holds.

Input to the program is the data identification number (ID) and the values of s, a, t, and b. Use the following data to test the program:

ID	s	a	t	b
101	2.00	8.00	−3.00	−2.00
102	4.38	4.25	−7.11	−18.92
103	.50	3.50	− .75	16.00
104	.50	0.00	− .50	0.00
105	.38	−15.79	.38	−28.35
106	.50	5.00	− .50	5.00
107	.50	5.00	− .50	−5.00
108	−5.63	28.91	6.21	14.35
109	4.87	.08	4.87	.08
110	−.50	−5.00	.50	−5.00
111	.50	−5.00	−.50	5.00
112	−.03	−16.92	1.72	24.38
113	−1.00	−4.00	−2.00	6.00

At the end of the input data, use a trailer value of 999 for the ID.

7. Write a program to calculate the accumulated amount of a bank deposit at any interest rate for any period of time. Input to the program is the depositor's number, the amount of his or her deposit, the interest rate that the deposit earns, and the number of years that the deposit is left. The basic problem assumes that interest is compounded annually. This means that the interest earned one year is added to the deposit and multiplied by the annual interest rate to get the next year's interest.

The following are the requirements for this program:

(a)   Read and print the input data. Output should include appropriate titles to identify each item. Execution should terminate when the depositor's number is zero.

(b)   For each set of input data, print, below appropriate headings, the year and the accumulated amount of the deposit at the end of the year. Assume that the deposit is made at the beginning of year 1. Then the accumulated amount of the deposit at the end of year 1 is the amount of the deposit plus the interest for that year. Continue the process for the other years, making certain that the interest is compounded annually.

(c)   In Part (b), we assumed that interest was compounded only once a year. It is possible to compound interest more frequently by incorporating a "compounding factor" into the program. This factor represents the number of times per year that interest is to be compounded. For example, a compounding factor of 4 means that interest is compounded four times per year (i.e., every three months). A compounding factor of 1 means that interest is pounded once per year (i.e., annually). When interest is compounded more than once a year, the interest rate used in the calculation is the annual interest rate divided by the compounding factor. For example, if the annual interest rate is 5% and the compounding factor is 4, the interest rate used to calculate interest every three months is 0.5/4 = .0125. Interest is calculated at this rate four times a year. Each time the interest is calculated, it is added to the deposit to obtain the new accumulated deposit that is used for the next interest calculation. Calculate the accumulated amount of the deposit at the end of each year for each set of input data, assuming compounding factors of 2, 4, 8, and 12. Note that these compounding factors are not input data but must be generated in the program. (Hint: It may be useful to use an ON-GO TO statement and a FOR loop.) For each compounding factor, print the factor and the *final* accumulated amount of the deposit with appropriate titles. Thus, in addition to the output already described, there will be four additional lines of output for each set of input data.

Use the following input data to test the program:

Depositor's Number	Amount of Deposit	Interest Rate	Time (Years)
10851	$1,000.00	5%	3
13721	1,000.00	4½%	3
18645	1,000.00	5¼%	3
19541	50.00	3¾%	25
24712	3,500.00	6¾%	10
24839	3,500.00	7%	10
26213	3,500.00	7¼%	10
28721	3,500.00	7%	5
00000 (trailer value)			

8. Develop an interactive program to help balance your checkbook each month.

9. Develop a program to compute a depreciation schedule for an asset based on the straight-line method, the declining balance method, and the sum of years' digits method.

10. Write a program to produce a home mortgage payment schedule. Input to the program should be the amount of the loan, the monthly payment, the annual interest rate, and the number of months that the loan runs. Output should be a table that gives for each month the amount of the payment applied to the principal, the amount applied to interest, and the balance due after payment. Yearly totals of interest paid should also be printed.

8
BASIC FUNCTIONS

A number of standard processing activities are commonly required in BASIC programs. For example, it is often necessary to find the square root of a number or to perform various trigonometric computations. In order to relieve the programmer of the responsibility of preparing the instructions necessary for such processing, BASIC supplies special built-in routines called *functions*. A function is a separate set of instructions that performs a specific task. Each function has a name that identifies it and is used in a numeric expression. In this chapter we describe the BASIC functions and show how they are used in programs.

The functions described here are built into the BASIC language. It is also possible for the programmer to prepare his or her own functions to do special tasks. This latter type of function is discussed in Chapter 12.

8-1. GENERAL CHARACTERISTICS

To illustrate the general characteristics of functions, we consider the square root function. The name of this function is SQR. The function is used by coding this name followed by a numeric expression enclosed in parentheses. The combination of function name and expression can then be used in certain statements in a program. For example, the following LET statement shows the use of the square root function:

```
20 LET C=SQR(A+B)
```

In evaluating the function the computer first determines the value of the numeric expression in parentheses. Then the SQR function finds the square root of the value. For example, if A is 9 and B is 7 in the previous statement, then A + B is 16 and SQR(A + B) is 4. This value is then assigned to C by the LET statement.

The expression in parentheses may be a constant, variable, or more complex numeric expression. Thus, any of the following statements is acceptable:

```
30 LET X=SQR(Y)
40 IF Z>SQR(100) THEN 200
50 LET R=(-B+SQR(B^2-4*A*C))/(2*A)
60 IF SQR(P)<=3*SQR(Q) THEN 300
```

Notice, however, that the function cannot be used by itself but only as part of another statement. In fact, the SQR function can be used only in place of a numeric expression in a statement or as part of a more complex numeric expression. The previous statements illustrate this.

The value of the expression in parentheses must not be negative since the computer cannot determine the square root of a negative number. In addition, only the non-negative square root is found [i.e., SQR(16) is 4 even though $\sqrt{16}$ is ± 4].

The program in Fig. 8-1 demonstrates the use of the square root function. The input to this program is the length (L) and width (W) of a piece of carpeting purchased to cover a floor. The problem is to compute the length of the side (S) of the largest square floor that can be covered by this amount of carpet. To do this, the program must first compute the area (A) of carpet purchased. This is done in statement 20. Then the square root of the area is computed in statement 30 to give the length of the side (S). Notice that if the value of A is not needed for output, statement 20 can be eliminated and statement 30 can be written as follows:

```
30 LET S=SQR(L*W)
```

In addition to the square root function, there are a number of other functions that are used in a similar fashion. These functions are listed

```
10 INPUT L,W
20 LET A=L*W
30 LET S=SQR(A)
40 PRINT L,W,A,S
99 END
```

FIGURE 8-1. A program to calculate floor dimensions.

Function	Meaning
ABS(X)	Absolute value of X
ATN(X)	Arctangent (in radians) of X
COS(X)	Cosine of X (X must be in radians)
EXP(X)	Exponential of X (that is, e^x)
INT(X)	Largest integer less than or equal to X
LOG(X)	Natural logarithm of X (that is, $\ln X$)
RND	Random number between 0 and 1
SGN(X)	Sign of X (that is, −1 if X < 0, 0 if X = 0, +1 if X > 0)
SIN(X)	Sine of X (X must be in radians)
SQR(X)	Square root of X
TAN(X)	Tangent of X (X must be in radians)

FIGURE 8-2. The BASIC functions.

in Fig. 8–2. Two of the functions in this list — the INT and RND functions — are discussed in more detail in the next two sections.

8-2. THE INTEGER FUNCTION

A very useful function is the INT, or integer, function. This function finds the largest *integer* (i.e., whole number) that is less than or equal to the value of the expression in parentheses. For example, consider the following statement:

$$110 \text{ LET } A=INT(B)$$

If B is 5.8, the INT function finds the largest integer that is less than or equal to 5.8. This integer is 5, which is assigned to A in the LET statement. Notice that the value is *not* rounded; the largest integer *less than or equal to* the value in parentheses is found. If the value is negative, the same rule applies. Thus, if B is –5.8 in the previous example, then INT(B) is –6, the largest integer less than or equal to –5.8. The following are additional examples of the result produced by the INT function:

B	INT(B)
3.1	3
7	7
−6.3	−7
−10	−10
0	0
.9999	0
−4.0001	−5

192

Notice that the INT function does not change the value of the variable in parentheses; it merely uses the value to find the appropriate integer. For example, assume that the following PRINT statement is executed after statement 110 above:

$$115 \ \text{PRINT} \ A,B$$

The value of A that is printed will be the largest integer that is less than or equal to B, but the value of B that is printed will be the original value of this variable. If B is 5.8, the numbers 5 and 5.8 are printed.

As with other functions, any numeric expression can be used with the INT function. For example, the following statements are valid:

```
120 LET X=INT(2.5*Y-7.3)
130 IF M>INT(N) THEN 300
140 LET C=3.5*INT(D/E)+8.4
150 IF INT(P)*INT(Q)<=R THEN 310
```

Any expression in parentheses is first evaluated before the INT function is used. Thus, if Y is 4 in statement 120 above, then 2.5*Y-7.3 is 2.7 and INT(2.5*Y-7.3) is 2, which is the value assigned to X. Notice also that the INT function can only be used in a statement in place of a numeric expression or as part of a more complex expression as shown in these examples.

As we have seen, the INT function does not round off the value in parentheses. However, a technique called *half-adjusting* can be used if rounding is necessary. With this technique, one-half (.5) is added to the value before the INT function is used. Thus, to half-adjust the value of B and assign the result to A, we can use the following:

$$160 \ \text{LET} \ A=\text{INT}(B+.5)$$

For example, if B is 5.8, then B+.5 is 6.3 and INT(B+.5) is 6. However, if B is 5.2, then B+.5 is 5.7 and INT(B+.5) is 5. Thus, the value of B is correctly rounded with this technique. Notice that the technique works even if B is negative.

There are many uses for the INT function. Figure 8–3 shows a modification of the program in Fig. 8-1. In this example we are again computing the length of a side of the largest square floor that can be covered by a certain amount of carpet. For this program, however, the length must be a whole number. Statement 40 in the program in Fig. 8-3 uses the INT function to produce the desired result. Notice that we could combine statements 30 and 40 and write one statement as follows:

$$40 \ \text{LET} \ S1=\text{INT}(\text{SQR}(A))$$

```
10 INPUT L,W
20 LET A=L*W
30 LET S=SQR(A)
40 LET S1=INT(S)
50 PRINT L,W,A,S1
99 END
```

FIGURE 8-3. A program to calculate floor dimensions.

```
10 INPUT E
20 LET D=INT(E/12)
30 LET R=E-D*12
40 PRINT E,D,R
99 END
```

FIGURE 8-4. The egg program.

As another example, the program in Fig. 8-4 calculates the number of dozen in a given number of eggs (E). After accepting the input, the program computes the number of dozen (D) by dividing E by 12. The INT function converts the result to a whole number. Then statement 30 finds the number remaining (R) after the number of dozen are removed. If the input value is 226 eggs, the output is 18 dozen with 10 remaining eggs.

There are many other uses of the INT function. In the next section we will see how it is used in conjunction with the RND function.

8-3. RANDOM NUMBERS

A number of computer applications require uncertainty or randomness in a program. For example, programs that play card or dice games need to produce random output such as would result from dealing cards or rolling dice. Programs that simulate real-world situations such as manufacturing processes or ecological systems also involve uncertainty. All of these programs require the computer to produce or *generate* numbers at random. In this section we see how this is done in BASIC.

A *random number* is a number that is as likely to be produced as any other number. For example, if we roll a die we get a random number (actually, a random integer) between 1 and 6 as indicated by the number of spots that are showing. If the die is fair, each integer between 1 and 6 is as likely to be produced as any other. If we want to write a program to play a dice game, we must be able to generate random intergers between 1 and 6. This is accomplished by using the RND function.

194

```
10 FOR I=1 TO 10
20    LET X=RND
30    PRINT X
40 NEXT I
99 END
```

(a) The program

```
.204935
.229581
.533074
.132211
.995602
.783713
.741854
.397713
.709588
.67811
```

(b) The output

FIGURE 8-5. A program to produce random numbers.

The RND function produces random numbers[†] between 0 and 1. Each time the function is used, a new random number that is greater than or equal to 0 but less than 1 is generated. Only the name of the function is required in a statement to generate a random number. (Some versions of BASIC require an expression in parentheses after the name.) For example, the following statement generates a random number and assigns it to the variable X:

```
210 LET X=RND
```

The number generated is between 0 and 1 including 0 but not including 1. Any number in this range is as likely to be generated as any other.

Figure 8-5(a) shows a program that produces a list of ten random numbers using the RND function. The actual output from the program is shown in Fig. 8-5(b). Notice that the numbers do not follow any pattern but appear to be entirely random.

Most often we are not interested in random numbers between 0 and 1 but rather numbers in some other range. The example of a dice-game program mentioned earlier illustrates this. In this case we need random

---

[†]Actually, these numbers are called *pseudorandom* numbers but the distinction is not important for this book.

integers between 1 and 6. To generate these we use a statement such as the following:

$$20 \text{ LET } D=INT(6*RND)+1$$

This statement works as follows:

1. First a random number between 0 and 1 is generated and multiplied by 6. This produces a random number between 0 and 6. Notice that since RND can generate 0, 6*RND can be 0. However, the largest value that RND can generate is just less than 1 (say .999999). Hence, 6*RND cannot be 6, but at most just less than 6 (i.e., 5.99999).
2. Next the integer part of 6*RND is found using the INT function. This gives a random integer between 0 and 5. Again, since 6 cannot be produced by 6*RND, INT(6*RND) cannot be 6.
3. Finally, 1 is added to get random integers between 1 and 6.

As an example, if RND produces .4, then 6*RND yields 2.4. INT(6*RND) is 2 and INT(6*RND)+1 is 3, which is the final result. Figure 8-6 shows a program that produces ten random integers between 1 and 6.

```
10 FOR I=1 TO 10
20    LET D=INT(6*RND)+1
30    PRINT D
40 NEXT I
99 END
```

(a) The program

```
2
2
4
1
6
5
5
3
5
5
```

(b) The output

FIGURE 8-6.   A program to produce random integers
between 1 and 6.

In general, to produce any random number (not just an integer) between A and B (including A but not including B) we use the following:

$$(B-A)*RND+A$$

For example, to produce random numbers between 5 and 15, we use:

$$10*RND+5$$

To generate random *integers* between A and B (including A *and* B) we use the following:

$$INT((B-A+1)*RND)+A$$

Thus, to produce random integers between 5 and 15 we use:

$$INT(11*RND)+5$$

There are other variations that can be used to produce numbers in different ranges.

One characteristic of the RND function is that each time a pro-

```
10 RANDOMIZE
20 FOR I=1 TO 10
30    LET D=INT(6*RND)+1
40    PRINT D
50 NEXT I
99 END
```

(a) The program

```
3
3
6
5
2
3
6
5
2
2
```

(b) The output

FIGURE 8-7. An example of the use of the RANDOMIZE statement.

gram is run using the function, the *same* sequence of random numbers is generated. For example, if we run the program in Fig. 8-6 again, the same output will be produced. This is done because it makes program testing and debugging easier. However, after the program is completed, it is usually desirable to produce a *different* sequence of random numbers. This is accomplished by using the RANDOMIZE statement. This statement is simply the keyword RANDOMIZE. (Some versions of BASIC use the word RANDOM instead.) The statement should appear at the beginning of the program. The effect of this statement is that each time the program is run, a *new sequence* of random numbers is generated. For example, the program in Fig. 8-7 is the same as the one in Fig. 8-6 but with the addition of the RANDOMIZE statement. Notice that the output shown is different from that of the previous program.

There are a number of uses of random numbers. In the next section we will see how random numbers are used in programs that play games. Then in Section 8-5 we will discuss simulation programs that require random numbers.

8-4. COMPUTER GAMES

One of the common uses of random numbers is in programs that play games. For example, programs that play card or dice games require the use of random numbers to "deal" cards or "roll" dice. In this section we introduce the basic ideas behind such game-playing programs.

In general, a game requires two or more "players". With a computer game, one of the players is a computer program and the other player (or players) is the person at the terminal. In some cases the computer's "play" is entirely determined by chance. This would be the situation with such games as "blackjack" or "craps". In other computer games, strategy is built into the program. For example, programs that play checkers or chess require complex strategy. Other computer games require a combination of chance and strategy. Many card-game programs (such as bridge) are of this nature.

In this section we discuss only programs that play games of chance. In such a program the computer must generate a chance event. For example, dice must be "rolled" or cards "dealt". Then the game is "played" with the result of the chance event. Eventually a "winner" is determined that may be the computer program or the person playing at the terminal.

To illustrate this idea, consider a simple dice game. The player must first guess what the next roll of a pair of dice will yield. If the player guesses correctly, he or she "wins"; otherwise the player "loses". The program in Fig. 8-8 shows how this is done. First, the player's guess, G, is accepted. Then the RND function is used twice to "roll" the dice. The total of the two rolls, T, is computed and compared with the guess. Finally, the program announces whether the player wins or loses. The actual results of playing the game several times are shown in Fig. 8-9.

While this program is relatively simple, the basic principle applies to other game-playing programs. For example, we could expand this program to include all of the rules of "craps". In addition, we could allow the player to bet different amounts and keep track of the total winnings over a period of time.

In a card game such as "blackjack", the computer must first "shuffle" a deck of cards and then "deal" the required hands. The terminal player plays one hand and the computer plays the other. The game proceeds according to the appropriate rules until a winner can be determined.

There are a number of games that can be programmed. In addition to card and dice games, we can program a computer to play other gambling games such as roulette and keno, sports games such as football

```
100 RANDOMIZE
110 PRINT "A SIMPLE DICE GAME"
120 PRINT
130 PRINT "GUESS THE TOTAL ON THE NEXT"
140 PRINT "ROLL OF A PAIR OF DICE."
150 PRINT
160 PRINT "WHAT IS YOUR GUESS";
170 INPUT G
180 LET D1=INT(6*RND)+1
190 LET D2=INT(6*RND)+1
200 LET T=D1+D2
210 PRINT
220 PRINT "FIRST DIE","SECOND DIE","TOTAL"
230 PRINT D1,D2,T
240 PRINT
250 IF G=T THEN 280
260 PRINT "YOU GUESSED WRONG. YOU LOSE."
270 GO TO 290
280 PRINT "YOU GUESSED RIGHT. YOU WIN."
290 PRINT
300 GO TO 130
999 END
```

FIGURE 8-8. A program to play a simple dice game.

```
A SIMPLE DICE GAME

GUESS THE TOTAL ON THE NEXT
ROLL OF A PAIR OF DICE.

WHAT IS YOUR GUESS? 7

FIRST DIE     SECOND DIE     TOTAL
  3               3             6

YOU GUESSED WRONG. YOU LOSE.

GUESS THE TOTAL ON THE NEXT
ROLL OF A PAIR OF DICE.

WHAT IS YOUR GUESS? 7

FIRST DIE     SECOND DIE     TOTAL
  5               2             7

YOU GUESSED RIGHT. YOU WIN.

GUESS THE TOTAL ON THE NEXT
ROLL OF A PAIR OF DICE.

WHAT IS YOUR GUESS? 10

FIRST DIE     SECOND DIE     TOTAL
  6               3             9

YOU GUESSED WRONG. YOU LOSE.
```

FIGURE 8-9. Playing the simple dice game.

and baseball, and various space games.[†] Some of these are described in the programming problems at the end of the chapter.

8-5. COMPUTER SIMULATION

Simulation is the technique of representing the functioning of one thing by using another. In the case of a computer simulation, we use a computer program to represent the operation of some process or sys-

---

[†]A very popular space game is based on the TV series "Star Trek".

tem. For example, we can write a program that simulates an oil-refining process. Other examples of computer simulations are programs that simulate the service of customers at a supermarket check-out stand or at a bank window. Computer programs that play games as described in the last section are also types of simulations. In fact, we can use a computer to simulate many things including manufacturing processes, business operations, ecological systems, games of chance, political situations, and economic systems.

There are several advantages to using computer simulations. For one, we can see how the system may behave without actually observing the real situation. Although the simulation cannot predict what will actually happen, it can give us some idea of the behavior of the system. We can also learn what may happen if we vary one or more of the factors that affect the system. For example, if we are simulating the customer check-out at a supermarket, we can see the effect of adding another check-out stand.

There are two basic types of simulation — *deterministic* simulation and *stochastic* (or *probabilistic*) simulation. The difference has to do with whether or not uncertainty or randomness is incorporated into the simulation. In the deterministic case, uncertainty is not included, while with stochastic simulation it is used. In this section we give an example of both types of simulation.

Deterministic Simulation

Assume that there are currently 5000 people living on an isolated island. If the birth rate is 7% per year and the death rate is 3% per year, what will the population of the island be after each of the next ten years? This problem involves simulating the population of the island. The birth and death rates are assumed to be fixed, and hence, there is no uncertainty about how many people will be born or will die each year. Thus, this is a deterministic simulation.

The program in Fig. 8–10(a) solves the problem. The variable P represents the population which is initially 5000. B is the number of births in a year (computed in statement 40) and D is the number of deaths (evaluated in statement 50). In statement 60 the number of births is added to the population and the number of deaths is subtracted to get the new population. The output from the program is shown in Fig. 8–10(b). The output shows the year and the population at the end of the year for each of the next ten years.

Besides using this program to answer the original question, we can use it to determine what would happen to the population if the birth or death rate were to change. For example, what would be the effect of a decreased birth rate (due, perhaps, to the introduction of family-planning techniques) or of an increased death rate (perhaps because of

```
10 LET P=5000
20 PRINT "YEAR","POPULATION"
30 FOR Y=1 TO 10
40    LET B=.07*P
50    LET D=.03*P
60    LET P=P+B-D
70    PRINT Y,P
80 NEXT Y
99 END
```

(a) The program

YEAR	POPULATION
1	5200
2	5408
3	5624.32
4	5849.29
5	6083.27
6	6326.6
7	6579.66
8	6842.85
9	7116.56
10	7401.22

(b) The output

FIGURE 8-10. A population simulation program.

a new disease)? Questions such as these can be answered by slight modifications in the program.

The problem that this program solves is relatively simple and can also be solved using a method other than simulation. Such methods are called *analytic solutions* and involve using mathematical formulas. However, as the problem becomes more complex, it is less likely that there will be an analytic solution and simulation must be used.[†]

This program demonstrates the basic idea of deterministic simulation. While most programs for such simulation are more complex, they all have the characteristic that uncertainty or randomness is not used in the program.

Stochastic Simulation

With stochastic simulation, random numbers are used to produce uncertainty in a program. As we have seen, the RND function generates

---

[†]An example of a complex deterministic simulation can be found in the book *Limits to Growth* by D. H. Meadows et al., published by Signet.

numbers at random. By using this function we can develop stochastic simulation programs.

Programs that play games of chance as discussed in the last section are examples of stochastic simulations. For example, we can think of a program that generates a random integer between 1 and 6 as simulating the roll of a die. Similar techniques are used to simulate the shuffling of a deck of cards, the spinning of a roulette wheel, and so forth.

Besides games we often use stochastic simulation to simulate the behavior of other types of systems. A common problem is to simulate a queuing system. A *queue* is a waiting line. For example, a queue is formed when customers wait to be checked out at a supermarket or for service by a bank teller. A *queuing system* consists of a queue plus the facility that serves the customers in the queue (for example, the supermarket checker or the bank teller). Figure 8-11 illustrates this idea. Customers arrive and go to the end of the queue. The service facility serves the first customer in the queue, who departs after being served. The queue increases in length when a customer arrives and decreases when a customer is served.

There are two main sources of uncertainty in a queuing system. One is the arrival of customers: we do not know for certain how often customers will arrive. The other source of uncertainty is the service facility: the amount of time that it takes to serve a customer may be unknown. Because of these uncertainties, any simulation of a queuing system requires the use of randomness in the program and hence is a stochastic simulation.

The objective in simulating a queuing system is to answer questions such as the following:

1. What is the average number of customers in the queue?
2. What is the average length of time that a customer must wait in the queue?
3. What percentage of the time will the service facility not be serving a customer (i.e., will the queue be empty)?

These questions can be answered by simulating the behavior of the queuing system.

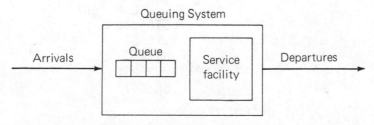

FIGURE 8-11. A queuing system.

To illustrate the technique, assume that in a five-minute period, it is equally likely that 1, 2, 3, or 4 customers arrive. In addition, assume that the service facility can serve 3 customers in a five-minute period. The service facility is open five hours per day. We need to write a stochastic simulation program that determines the average length of the queue on each day of a five-day week.

The program is shown in Fig. 8-12(a) and the output appears in Fig. 8-12(b). The program contains two FOR loops. The outer loop controls the value of D, which represents the day. The inner loop controls the value of C (for "clock"), which counts the number of five-minute periods in the day. (There are 60 five-minute periods in a five-hour day.) L represents the length of the queue and T stands for the total of all queue lengths. At the beginning of each day, the values of L and T are set to zero.

```
100 RANDOMIZE
110 PRINT "DAY","AVE QUEUE LENGTH"
120 FOR D=1 TO 5
130    LET L=0
140    LET T=0
150    FOR C=1 TO 60
160       LET N=INT(4*RND)+1
170       LET L=L+N
180       IF L>3 THEN 210
190       LET L=0
200       GO TO 220
210       LET L=L-3
220       LET T=T+L
230    NEXT C
240    LET A=T/60
250    PRINT D,A
260 NEXT D
999 END
```

(a) The program

DAY	AVE QUEUE LENGTH
1	.516667
2	1.56667
3	.816667
4	1.83333
5	.566667

(b) The output

FIGURE 8-12.   A queuing system simulation program.

During each five-minute period of the day, the number of arrivals (N) must be determined. Since it is equally likely that 1, 2, 3, or 4 customers arrive, we need to generate a random integer between 1 and 4 for the value of N. This is done in statement 160. Then, in statement 170, N is added to L to increase the queue length by the number of arrivals. Next we reduce the queue length by the number of customers served. If there are more than 3 customers in the queue, exactly 3 customers are served (statement 210). If there are 3 or fewer customers waiting, all are served, reducing the queue length to zero (statement 190). Finally, the total of all queue lengths (T) is increased by the value of L (statement 220).

After each day is completed, the value of T is divided by 60 (the number of five-minute periods in the day) to obtain the average queue length (A). This is printed along with the number of the day (D). Then the program repeats for the next day.

This program demonstrates the basic idea of stochastic simulation. The system simulated by this program is relatively simple, and in fact, there is an analytic solution to the problem of average queue length for this system; simulation is not really needed. For more complex systems, however, analytic solutions do not always exist and simulation must be used. The technique described in this section is the basis for more complex simulations.

REVIEW QUESTIONS

1. What built-in functions are available in the version of BASIC you are using?

2. Consider the program shown in Fig. 8-1. If the input is the numbers 18 and 8, what is the output?

3. Assume that the value of A is 3, B is 4, and C is 5. What is the result of each of the following functions?
   (a) SQR(B)
   (b) SQR(B*C+5)
   (c) SQR(A–B+1)
   (d) INT(C)
   (e) INT(B/A)
   (f) INT(A–C)
   (g) INT(C/A+.3333)
   (h) INT(–C/B)

4. Write a BASIC statement to half-adjust the value of X and assign the result to Y.

5. Consider the program shown in Fig. 8–3. If the input is the numbers 9 and 12, what is the output?

6. Consider the program shown in Fig. 8–4. If the input is the number 391, what is the output?

7. What is a random number?

8. Write a BASIC statement that generates a random number between 100 and 200.

9. Write a BASIC statement that generates a random integer between 1 and 52.

10. What does the RANDOMIZE statement do?

11. Think of a game not mentioned in the text. If a computer program were written to play the game, would the program determine the play by chance, by strategy, or by some combination of these?

12. What is the difference between deterministic simulation and stochastic simulation?

PROGRAMMING PROBLEMS

1. The economic order quantity represents the most economical quantity of inventory that should be ordered for each item in stock. The formula for calculating the economic order quantity is:

$$Q = \sqrt{\frac{2 \times R \times S}{H}}$$

In this formula Q is the quantity ordered, R is the demand rate, S is the set-up cost, and H is the inventory-holding cost. If C represents unit cost, the average cost per unit of inventory held is given by the following formula:

$$A = C + \frac{S}{Q} + \frac{H \times Q}{2 \times R}$$

Write a BASIC program to calculate the economic order quantity and the average cost per unit when this quantity is ordered. Input data is the inventory item number and the values of R, S, H, and C. Print the item number and the values of Q and A.

Use the following data to test the program:

Item Number	Demand Rate	Set-up Cost	Holding Cost	Unit Cost
12163	1025	$ 75	$ 60	$ 25
13841	500	$250	$150	$125
17213	2250	$120	$ 36	$ 10
19461	125	$450	$230	$195

2. If a projectile is fired with an initial velocity, v, and angle, θ, it reaches a maximum height, h, in time, t, given by the following equation:

$$h = \frac{1}{2} \frac{v^2 \sin^2 \theta}{32}$$

$$t = \frac{v \sin \theta}{32}$$

The sine of an angle is found using the function SIN; the angle must be in radians. (One radian equals 57.2958 degrees.)

Write a BASIC program that accepts the values of v and θ (in degrees), and computes h and t. Print the values of v, θ (in degrees), h, and t. Use the following input data to test the program:

Velocity	Angle
247.38	45
100.00	72.5
360.00	0
282.61	90
75.32	25.6

3. Using the equations in problem 2, write a BASIC program that prints a table listing the values of θ from 0 to 90 degrees in 5-degree increments along with the corresponding values of h and t. Use an initial velocity of 247.38 to test the program.

4. Write a BASIC program that converts seconds into hours, minutes, and seconds remaining. Input should be the amount of time in seconds. Output should be the number of seconds and its equivalent in hours, minutes, and seconds remaining. For example, 4,372 seconds is equivalent to one hour, twelve minutes, and fifty-two seconds. Test the program using 28,635 seconds.

5. There are 3.281 feet in a meter and 0.3937 inches in a centimeter. Write a program that accepts a distance in feet and inches, and com-

putes and prints the equivalent distance in meters and centimeters. Give the answer in whole meters and centimeters rounded to the nearest centimeter. Test the program with the distance 6 feet, 9 inches.

6. A classic problem in computer programming is the "automatic change-maker" problem. The problem involves determining the breakdown of a customer's change into various denominations.

Write an interactive BASIC program that solves the automatic change-maker problem. The program should accept the customer's number, the amount of a customer's bill, and the cash payment. Then the program should print the customer's number, the amount of the bill, the payment, and the change, if any. If there is no change, an appropriate message should be printed. Similarly, if the payment is less than the bill, a message should be printed.

For each transaction for which there is change, show the number and kind of each denomination in the change. The total number of bills and coins should be kept to a minimum. Assume that only pennies ($.01), nickels ($.05), dimes ($.10), quarters ($.25) and one-dollar bills are available for change.

Use the following data to test the program:

Customer's Number	Customer's Bill	Payment
11	$ 3.59	$ 5.00
22	8.00	8.00
33	14.95	14.00
44	21.03	25.00
55	9.95	50.00
66	.29	1.00

7. Write a BASIC program that finds the day of the week for any date in the twentieth century. Input to the program is the month, day, and year of any date between 1900 and 1999. The month should be numeric and the year should be two digits. For example, January 21, 1946, should be entered as 01 21 46. Output should give the day of the week for the given date (e.g., MONDAY).

The procedure to find the day of the week is as follows. Add the year, one-fourth of the year (truncated), and the day of the month, and the code for the month from the following table:

Month	Code
June	0
Sept., Dec.	1
April, July	2
Jan., Oct.	3
May	4
Aug.	5
Feb., March, Nov.	6

If the year is a leap year (i.e., if it is evenly divisible by four), the code is one less for January and February.

Subtract two from the sum and divide the result by seven. The remainder from the division is the day of the week with 0 denoting Saturday, 1 Sunday, 2 Monday, and so on.

For example, the day of the week for January 21, 1946, is found as follows:

Year		46
One-fourth of year		11
Day of month		21
Code		3
	Subtotal	81
Subtract		2
	Total	79

Dividing 79 by 7 gives 11 with a remainder of 2. Hence, January 21, 1946, was a Monday.

Test the program with the following dates:

October 25, 1978

March 7, 1944

December 6, 1973

April 18, 1906

January 1, 1984

February 29, 1952

Use a trailer value to terminate the program.

8. Write a program to generate 1,000 random numbers. In the program, count the number of random numbers that are between 0 and .1, between .1 and .2, between .2 and .3, and so forth. Print the counts.

9. Write a program to generate 10,000 tosses of a pair of dice. In the program, count the number of times that the dice show 2, 3, 4, . . . , 12. Divide each answer by 10,000 to get an estimate of the probability that the dice will show each total. Print the results.

10. This problem involves developing a program to assist a person in learning to add. The program should generate two random integers between 0 and 9. The integers should be printed in the form of an addition problem and the person at the terminal should be asked for the sum. The answer entered at the terminal should be compared with the correct answer computed by the program and a statement about the correctness of the answer should be printed. (You may wish to give

the person more than one try to get the right answer.) The program should repeat for a total of ten addition problems, keeping track of the number of correct and the number of incorrect answers.

11. Write a program to play a simple number guessing game. The program should generate a random integer between 1 and 100. The objective is for the player to guess what integer has been generated in as few guesses as possible. Each guess entered at the terminal should be compared to the random integer until the correct value is entered. Keep track of the number of guesses and print this amount once the random integer has been guessed.

12. Write a program to play roulette. Each spin of the wheel can be simulated by generating a random integer between –1 and 36 with –1 counting as 00. Assume that odd numbers are red and even numbers are black. The program should accept any bet and "pay off" according to the rules of the game.

13. Write a program to play the dice game "craps". The program should accept any bet and "pay off" according to the rules of the game.

14. This problem involves using arrays, which are discussed in Chapter 10. Set up a fifty-two element array to represent the fifty-two cards of a deck. Then "shuffle" the deck by generating random integers between 1 and 52 and assigning each integer to the next element of the array. You will have to use a second array to keep track of each integer that is generated so that the same number is not assigned to different elements of the array. Assume that the numbers 1 to 13 represent one suit, 14 to 26 represent another suit, and so forth. Then print out the shuffled deck with each card's value and suit.

15. Use the program logic developed in problem 14 to write a program to play "blackjack" (or "twenty-one"). The program should accept any bet and "pay off" according to the rules of the game.

16. Assume that rabbits reproduce at the rate of 20% per month until overpopulation occurs, at which time they begin dying at the rate of 15% per month. Rabbits continue to die at this rate until their population is reduced by one-third, at which time they begin reproducing again. Write a program to simulate the rabbit population for 48 months. Assume that there are initially 1,000 rabbits and overpopulation occurs when there are more than 3,000 rabbits.

17. Modify the simulation program in Fig. 8–12 to determine the percentage of time that the service facility is not serving a customer (i.e., that the queue is empty).

18. The simulation program in Fig. 8–12 assumes that the service facility can serve exactly 3 customers in a five-minute period. Modify the program to include the assumption that the number of customers served is 2, 3, or 4 with equal likelihood.

19. Develop a program to simulate a queuing system in which there are three service facilities and three queues. Design the program so that a customer goes to the end of the shortest queue. Determine the average length of time that the customer waits for service. Then modify the program so that there are three facilities but only one queue, with the customer at the front of the queue going to the next available facility. Again, determine the average amount of time that the customer waits for service.

20. Inventory is the stock of goods that a business has on hand. Assume that a business initially has 50 units in stock. Each day 1 to 5 units are sold with equal likelihood. When the stock falls below 10 units, another 50 are ordered. The order takes two, three, or four days to arrive with equal likelihood. Write a BASIC program to simulate the inventory over a period of 100 days. Print out the day number and the quantity on hand that day. Assume that if the inventory reaches zero for a day, no sales can be made on that day.

9 | STRINGS

In many programs it is necessary to process non-numeric data, that is, data that consists of letters and symbols other than numbers. For example, input and output of non-numeric data such as a person's name and address may be required in a program. As another example, a program may have to accept non-numeric data that is entered in response to an input prompt and then analyze the data to determine what is to be done next. In this chapter we describe the features of BASIC that are used for input, output, and processing of non-numeric data.

9-1. STRING CONSTANTS AND VARIABLES

A *character string*, or simply a *string*, is a group of characters. Any character that can be stored in the computer *except* a quotation mark can be in a string. For example, all of the following are strings:

```
ABC
X37Z$
JOHN'S
NEW YORK
1881
```

Notice that a blank space is a character and can be part of a string. In fact, one or more blanks without any other characters forms a string. It is also possible to have a string that does not have any characters in it.

This is called a *null string* or *empty string*. Finally, notice that a string can consist entirely of numbers as shown in the last example above.

A *string constant* is a string enclosed in quotation marks. For example, the following are valid string constants:

```
"ABC"
"X37Z$"
"JOHN'S"
"NEW YORK"
"1881"
" "
""
```

Notice that a number enclosed in quotation marks is a string constant and *not* a numeric constant. The next-to-last example above shows a string constant that consists of a single blank space. The last example has no characters between the quotation marks. This is a *null string constant* or *empty string constant*).

The length of the string in a string constant is usually limited by the length of the terminal's line. However, some versions of BASIC allow longer strings. In many cases there is a maximum string length (e.g., 255 characters is a common limit), while in other cases a string may be any length as long as there is space available in the computer's internal storage.

We have already seen one use of string constants in a program. In Section 6-1 we showed how character output can be produced by enclosing the words to be printed in quotation marks in a PRINT statement. In fact, we were using a string constant in the PRINT statement. For example, the following statement contains a string constant:

```
80 PRINT "THE ANSWER IS",X
```

Execution of this statement causes the string THE ANSWER IS to be printed followed by the value of X. Notice that the quotation marks are not part of the string and are not printed. We will see other uses of string constants in this chapter.

String Variables

A *string variable* is a variable that is used to refer to a string. A string variable consists of a single letter followed by a dollar sign. For example, A$, N$, and Z$ are string variables. Notice that because there are twenty-six letters of the alphabet, there are twenty-six valid string variables. (Some versions of BASIC allow string variables to be any variable followed by a dollar sign. For example, A1$ and X3$ are valid string variables in some versions of BASIC.)

We can assign a string to a string variable using a LET statement. For example, the following statement assigns the string THE ANSWER IS to the string variable A$:

70 LET A$="THE ANSWER IS"

Notice in the LET statement that a string variable appears on the left of the equal sign and a string constant is on the right. After execution of this statement, the value of the string variable A$ will be the string THE ANSWER IS. We can also assign the value of one string variable to another string variable. For example, the following statement assigns the value of A$ to B$:

75 LET B$=A$

The maximum length of a string that can be assigned to a string variable is 18 characters, not including the quotation marks. (Some versions of BASIC allow strings of any length to be assigned to a string variable.) We can also assign a null string (which has a length of zero) to a string variable as shown in the following example:

200 LET C$=""

It is important to distinguish between string variables and *numeric variables*, and between string constants and *numeric constants*. For example, consider the following statements:

210 LET X=15
210 LET X$="15"

The first statement assigns a numeric constant to a numeric variable, while the second statement assigns a string constant to a string variable. Even though the characters in the constants are the same (i.e., 15), they represent different types of data. The string constant ("15") can be assigned only to a string variable and the numeric constant (15) can be assigned only to a numeric variable. In addition, string constants and variables *cannot* be used in numeric calculations; only numeric constants and variables can be used for this purpose. Notice, however, that the same letter can be used for both a numeric variable and a string variable in a program without difficulty; the dollar sign is sufficient to distinguish between the two variables.

One use of a string variable is in the PRINT statement in place of a string constant. For example, consider the following statement:

80 PRINT A$,X

The effect of execution of this statement is that the value of the string variable A$ is printed followed by the value of the numeric variable X. If A$ is assigned the string THE ANSWER IS by statement 70 above, this string is printed when statement 80 is executed. As many string variables as are needed can be included in a PRINT statement. In addition, string and numeric variables can be intermixed without difficulty in one PRINT statement. Thus, a statement such as the following is valid:

```
90 PRINT S,T,B$,U,C$
```

We can accept a string as input data by using a string variable in an INPUT statement. For example, consider the following statement:

```
10 INPUT N$
```

When this statement is executed, a question mark prompt is printed on the terminal. Following the question mark the terminal operator must enter a string. In most cases, the string may be enclosed in quotation marks or the marks may be omitted. For example, the following input might be entered:

```
? JOHN
```

After the operator presses the RETURN key, the computer accepts the data and assigns it to the string variable N$.

Quotation marks are optional around the string input except when the data contains a comma or when spaces to the left or right are part of the string. For example, assume that the following statement is executed:

```
20 INPUT D$
```

The string input that is to be entered is a date containing a comma with two spaces to the left and three to the right. The data must then be enclosed in quotation marks as shown in the following example:

```
? "  SEPT. 1, 1980   "
```

Note that quotation marks can be used even when they are not required.

We can use string variables and numeric variables in the same INPUT statement. For example, the following statement is valid:

```
30 INPUT N,N$,D$,A
```

```
10 INPUT I,N$,H
20 LET G=6.50*H
30 LET W=.18*G
40 LET P=G-W
50 PRINT I,N$,G,W,P
60 GO TO 10
99 END
```

(a) The program

```
? 123,JOHNSON,40
 123          JOHNSON          260          46.8          213.2
? 456,SMITH,35
 456          SMITH            227.5        40.95         186.55
? 789,JONES,42.5
 789          JONES            276.25       49.725        226.525
```

(b) The input and output

FIGURE 9-1.   A payroll calculation program with string
input and output.

The important thing is for the data to be entered in the same order as the variables in the INPUT statement. Thus, in this example the first and last values entered must be numbers, while the second and third values must be strings.

Figure 9–1 shows an example of a program that uses string input and output. This is a simple payroll program that accepts and prints the employee's name along with other data. (This program is a variation of the one shown in Fig. 3–9.) Notice that the string variable N$ is used for the input and output of the name in statements 10 and 50.

The READ and DATA Statements with Strings

The READ and DATA statements, discussed in Section 6-3, can be used for string input. When this is done, a string variable is used in the READ statement and a string, either with or without quotation marks, appears in the DATA statement. For example, consider the following statements:

```
                    40 READ N$
                    45 DATA JOHN
```

When the READ statement is executed, the string JOHN is read from the DATA statement and assigned to N$.

216

Quotation marks around the string in the DATA statement are optional unless the string contains a comma, leading spaces, or trailer spaces. For example, consider the following statements:

```
50 READ D$
55 DATA " SEPT. 1, 1980    "
```

In this case, quotation marks must be used around the string input in the DATA statement.

Both string and numeric data can be read from a DATA statement. The only restriction is that the input data and the corresponding variables be of the same type. Thus, the following statements are valid:

```
60 READ N, N$,D$,A
65 DATA 123,JOHN,"  SEPT. 1, 1980    ",25
```

The first and last variables are numeric and the corresponding values in the DATA statement are numbers. The other variables are string variables and strings are used for their values in the DATA statement.

*The PRINT USING Statement with Strings

In Section 6-4 we discussed the PRINT USING statement. This statement is used to control the format of printed output. In the statement, special symbols describe the arrangement of the output data. In this subsection we show the symbols that are used in the PRINT USING statement for string output.[†]

If we wish to print a string, the backslash symbol (\) is used in the format in the PRINT USING statement to mark the beginning and end of the string output. For example, consider the following statement:

```
100 PRINT USING "\ \",N$
```

The format in this statement is \ \. This causes the value of N$ to be printed in the first four print positions. If the value of N$ is JOHN, this name is printed at the beginning of the output line.

Notice that the backslash marks the beginning and end of the output. The number of characters to be printed is determined by counting the number of spaces between the backslashes and adding two for the backslashes. Thus, in the previous example there are two spaces between the backslashes and hence four characters are printed.

[†]The features of the PRINT USING statement vary from one version of BASIC to another. The features described here are available in BASIC-PLUS on the DEC PDP 11 computer and in related versions of BASIC.

If the string to be printed is longer than the number specified in the format, only the left part of the string is printed. For example, if N$ is ROBERT when the previous statement is executed, only ROBE is printed. When the string is shorter than the number of characters in the format, extra spaces are added on the right. For example, if N$ is ED when statement 100 above is executed, the output printed is the string ED followed by two blank spaces.

The shortest string that can be printed using backslashes in the format is two characters. This is because backslashes must always appear in pairs. To print a one-character string, the exclamation point (!) is used. For example, consider the following statement:

```
110 PRINT USING "!",N$
```

In this case, the first character in the string assigned to N$ is printed. If N$ is JOHN, only the letter J is printed.

We can combine string output and numeric output in the same PRINT USING statement. For example, assume that F$, M$, and L$ are equal to an employee's first name, middle name, and last name, respectively, and that S is the employee's salary. Then the following statement prints the employee's first initial, middle initial, last name, and salary:

```
120 PRINT USING "! !\          \ $$#,###.##",F$,M$,L#,S
```

In this example we use exclamation points in the format for the initials, backslashes for the last name, and the # and other symbols for the salary.

9-2. COMPARING STRINGS

One of the common uses of string input is for a response to a prompt printed by the program. For example, a program is frequently designed so that the terminal operator is asked whether he or she wants the program to be repeated. The statements in the program to accomplish this might be something like the following:

```
250 PRINT "DO YOU WANT THE PROGRAM TO REPEAT";
260 INPUT R$
```

When the PRINT statement is executed, the prompt is printed followed by a question mark. The operator must then type a string such as YES or NO. For example, the sequence on the terminal might be as follows:

DO YOU WANT THE PROGRAM TO REPEAT? YES

Then the program accepts the string input and determines what to do next based on the response to the prompt.

To analyze string input as in this example, we need to compare the string variable with strings that could possibly be entered as input. This is accomplished with the IF statement. In general, we can use the IF statement to compare two string variables or a string variable and a string constant. The equal relational operator (=) can be used to determine whether two strings are identical, and the not equal relational operator (<>) can be used to determine whether the strings are not identical. For example, the following statement compares the values of the string variables A$ and B$ to determine whether they are the same:

```
100 IF A$=B$ THEN 150
```

The relational expression A$=B$ is true if the strings assigned to A$ and B$ are absolutely identical. If A$ and B$ differ at all, even if the difference is just extra blank spaces at the beginning or end, the expression is false. The following cases illustrate this:

A$	B$	A$=B$
"JEAN"	"JANE"	*false*
"JOHN"	"JOHN"	*true*
"JOHN"	"JOHN "	*false*

The following are other examples of the use of string comparison:

```
110 IF "JOHN"=B$ THEN 160
120 IF C$<>D$ THEN 170
130 IF E$<>"HELP ME" THEN 180
```

Notice that both the equal (=) and not equal (<>) operators can be used. Two strings are not equal if they are not absolutely identical. Notice also that both string variables and string constants can be used in the comparison.

In our example of a response to an input prompt given earlier, we must test the value of R$ to determine whether the response is YES. The complete sequence is as follows:

```
250 PRINT "DO YOU WANT THE PROGRAM TO REPEAT";
260 INPUT R$
270 IF R$="YES" THEN 100
999 END
```

If the response is YES, the program repeats. With any other input execution of the program is terminated. Besides testing for the YES response, we can also test for NO and print an error message when the input is neither YES nor NO. The following statements include this modification:

```
250 PRINT "DO YOU WANT THE PROGRAM TO REPEAT";
260 INPUT R$
270 IF R$="YES" THEN 100
280 IF R$="NO" THEN 999
290 PRINT "INVALID RESPONSE, TRY AGAIN"
300 GO TO 250
999 END
```

In this case the program will continue to repeat the question printed by statement 250 until a valid string is entered.

As we have stated, two strings are equal if they are absolutely identical, including any blank spaces. Some versions of BASIC make an exception for extra blanks that come at the end of a string. In these versions, such trailing blanks are ignored in the comparison. Thus, the strings JOHN and JOHN*b* (*b* = blank) are equal in some versions of BASIC.

The program in Fig. 9–2 shows another example of string comparison. This program is designed to analyze the results of a true-false questionnaire. There are ten questions and the terminal operator must answer T or F to each question. The program counts the number of answers that are true and prints the count in the final line.

*String Inequality

Many versions of BASIC allow the use of the less than ($<$), greater than ($>$), less than or equal to ($<=$), and greater than or equal to ($>=$) relational operators for string comparison. For example, the following statements are valid in many versions of BASIC:

```
20 IF A$<"JOHN" THEN 60
30 IF B$>C$ THEN 70
40 IF "B"<=D$ THEN 80
50 IF E$>=F$ THEN 90
```

In the relational expressions in these statements, the comparison is based on the ordering of the characters being compared. This ordering is called the *collating sequence*. If we just consider the letters of the alphabet, the collating sequence is the same as the alphabetical order; that is, one string is less than another if it appears before the other in an

```
100 PRINT "QUESTIONNAIRE ANALYSIS PROGRAM"
110 PRINT "ANSWER T OR F FOR EACH QUESTION"
120 LET N=0
130 FOR I=1 TO 10
140   PRINT "QUESTION";I;"ANSWER";
150   INPUT A$
160   IF A$="T" THEN 200
170   IF A$="F" THEN 210
180   PRINT "INVALID ANSWER, TYPE T OR F"
190   GO TO 140
200   LET N=N+1
210 NEXT I
220 PRINT
230 PRINT "TOTAL TRUE ANSWERS";N
999 END
```

(a) The program

```
QUESTIONNAIRE ANALYSIS PROGRAM
ANSWER T OR F FOR EACH QUESTION
QUESTION 1 ANSWER? T
QUESTION 2 ANSWER? F
QUESTION 3 ANSWER? T
QUESTION 4 ANSWER? T
QUESTION 5 ANSWER? R
INVALID ANSWER, TYPE T OR F
QUESTION 5 ANSWER? T
QUESTION 6 ANSWER? F
QUESTION 7 ANSWER? G
INVALID ANSWER, TYPE T OR F
QUESTION 7 ANSWER? F
QUESTION 8 ANSWER? T
QUESTION 9 ANSWER? T
QUESTION 10 ANSWER? F

TOTAL TRUE ANSWERS 6
```

(b) The input and output

FIGURE 9-2.   A program to analyze a true-false questionnaire.

alphabetical list. Thus, the string JEAN is less than JOHN, which is less than MARY. Hence, the expression A$<"JOHN" is true if A$ is JEAN, but false if it is JOHN or MARY.

The computer makes this evaluation by comparing the strings character-for-character, left-to-right. As soon as two corresponding characters are not equal to each other, the computer determines which string is the greater on the basis of which of the unequal characters is farther in the alphabet. Thus, in comparing JEAN and JOHN, the computer examines the first character of each and determines that they are equal. It then compares the second character of each and determines that they are not equal. Then, since the letter 0 is farther in the alphabet than E, the computer would indicate that JOHN is greater than JEAN.

If one string is shorter than the other and if all characters are the same up to the end of the shorter string, the shorter string is less than the longer one. Thus, JOHN is less than JOHNNY. If a string contains a blank, the blank is less than any other character. Hence, JOHN SMITH is less than JOHNNY JONES because the fifth character in the first string is a blank, which is less than the fifth character in the second string which is an N.

A string of digits is evaluated in the same way as a string of letters, with 0 less than 1, 1 less than 2, and so forth up to 9. Thus, 123 is less than 456, as we would expect. But because a blank is less than any other character, b9 is less than 8b (where b stands for a blank). Notice that comparing strings of digits can yield different results from comparing the corresponding numbers.

If we compare strings consisting of both letters and digits, the result depends on the computer being used. With many computers the collating sequence is such that all digits are less than all letters. Thus, the string X37Z is less than the string XM7Z since the digit 3 is less than the letter M. Figure 9-3 shows other examples of string comparison.

One common use of string comparison is to sort words or names into alphabetical order. In Section 7-4 we discussed a program that sorts the values of three numeric variables into ascending numerical order (see Fig. 7-6). By substituting string variables for the numeric variables, we have a program to sort strings into ascending alphabetical order. The program, shown in Fig. 9-4, accepts three strings as input.

Relational Expression	Truth Value
"ED JONES"<"ED SMITH"	true
"EDWARD JONES"<"ED SMITH"	false
"1234">"4567"	false
"1234">" 4567"	true
"LISA"=" LISA"	false
"X37Z"<>"2AY7"	true

FIGURE 9-3.   String comparison.

```
100  INPUT A$,B$,C$
200  IF A$<=B$ THEN 250
210  LET T$=A$
220  LET A$=B$
230  LET B$=T$
250  IF B$<=C$ THEN 300
260  LET T$=B$
270  LET B$=C$
280  LET C$=T$
300  IF A$<=B$ THEN 400
310  LET T$=A$
320  LET A$=B$
330  LET B$=T$
400  PRINT A$,B$,C$
999  END
```

(a) The program

```
? MARY,JOHN,JEAN
JEAN            JOHN            MARY
```

(b) The output

FIGURE 9-4.   A program to sort three strings.

The strings may be in any order initially. Through a series of comparisons, and switching of values, the strings are rearranged into the required sequence.

*9-3.   STRING FUNCTIONS

Most versions of BASIC provide special functions for strings. Among others there are usually functions to extract copies of a part of a string and to combine two strings to form a single string. The characteristics of the functions vary from one version of BASIC to another. In this section we describe the functions that are available in one common version of BASIC.† However, the programmer should refer to the appropriate reference manual for the details of the version of BASIC being used.

---

†The functions described in this section are available in BASIC-PLUS on the DEC PDP 11 computer and in related versions of BASIC.

*Substrings

A *substring* is a group of one or more adjacent characters in a string. For example, consider the string NEW YORK. The following are substrings of this string:

```
NEW
OR
YORK
EW YO
W
NEW YORK
```

Notice that any single character in a string is a substring, and that the entire string is a substring of itself. In addition, any group of characters that are adjacent to one another in a string form a substring. However, if a group of characters from the string are not adjacent to each other, they do not form a substring. Thus, NOR is *not* a substring of NEW YORK even though the characters come from the string.

In BASIC three functions may be used to extract a copy of a substring from a string. These are the LEFT, RIGHT, and MID functions.[†] The form of the LEFT function is LEFT(A$,N). This function produces the leftmost N characters of the string A$. For example, if A$ is the string ABCDEF, then LEFT(A$,3) is ABC. Notice that using this function (or any of the other functions) does *not* change the value of the original string; only a copy of the substring is extracted. Thus, after the function is used in this example, A$ is still the string ABCDEF. Notice also that this function (as well as others) is not a statement by itself but must be used in a statement. The function can be used anywhere that a string variable or string constant can be used. Thus the following statements are valid:

```
400 LET B$=LEFT(A$,3)
410 PRINT LEFT(A$,3)
420 IF C$=LEFT(A$,3) THEN 500
```

The form of the RIGHT function is RIGHT(A$,N). The function extracts the substring beginning with the Nth character in A$ through the end of A$. For example, if A$ is ABCDEF, then RIGHT(A$,3) is CDEF. Notice in this example that the function does *not* produce the rightmost three characters; rather, the third through last characters are extracted for a total of four characters. (In some versions of BASIC, this function would extract the rightmost three characters.)

[†]In some versions of BASIC, these functions are named LEFT$, RIGHT$, and MID$. In some cases the SEG$ function is used instead of the MID function.

224

The MID function yields a substring from the middle of a string. The form of the function is MID(A$,M,N). The function extracts the N characters from A$ beginning with the Mth character. For example, if A$ is ABCDEF, then MID(A$,2,3) is BCD, that is, the three characters beginning with the second character in the string.

Notice that we do not really need the LEFT and RIGHT functions although they are convenient. We can obtain the same results with just the MID function. For example, MID(A$,1,3) is the same as LEFT(A$,3) and MID(A$,3,4) is the same as RIGHT(A$,3).

Figure 9-5 shows other examples of substrings. Notice in the last example in this figure how a single character substring can be extracted.

In the examples cited so far, we have used numeric constants to indicate the position of the substring. We can also use variables and expressions. For example, MID(S$,I,J) is valid; the actual substring that is extracted depends on the values of I and J. Similarly, MID(S$,I+2,3*I-1) is acceptable. The expressions in this example are evaluated using the current value of I, and then the indicated substring is found.

One use of substrings is to locate the position of a particular character or group of characters in a string. For example, assume that we want to know the location of the first blank space in a string named N$. This can be accomplished with the following loop:

```
20 LET I=1
30 IF MID(N$,I,1)=" " THEN 60
40 LET I=I+1
50 GO TO 30
60 (next statement)
```

In this example the variable I is used to count through the characters in the string. I is initially set to 1 and incremented by 1 with each exe-

S$="WASHINGTON"

Function	Substring
MID(S$,3,5)	SHING
LEFT(S$,4)	WASH
MID(S$,1,4)	
RIGHT(S$,8)	TON
MID(S$,8,3)	
MID(S$,6,1)	N

FIGURE 9-5. Substrings.

```
10 INPUT N$
20 LET I=1
30 IF MID(N$,I,1)=" " THEN 60
40 LET I=I+1
50 GO TO 30
60 PRINT MID(N$,I+1,14-I);", ";MID(N$,1,I-1)
99 END
```

FIGURE 9-6.   A program to rearrange a name.

cution of the loop. In the loop, MID(N$,I,1) extracts the Ith character
in the string. When this character is a blank, the loop is terminated.
Then the value of I is the position of the blank character.

We can use this procedure to rearrange a person's name. Figure 9-6
shows a program to do this. The input to the program is a name consisting of 14 characters beginning with the first name, then a blank space,
and finally the last name. The program locates the position of the blank
space and then rearranges the name in the PRINT statement. The output
is printed with the last name first, a comma, and then the first name.
Thus, if the input name is ROBERT JOHNSON, the output that is
printed is JOHNSON, ROBERT.

*String Concatenation

Concatenation is the operation of combining two strings to form
one string. For example, concatenating the strings ABC and XYZ produces the string ABCXYZ. To concatenate two strings in BASIC, we
use the *concatenation operator.* This operator is a plus sign (+).[†] For
example, to concatenate ABC and XYZ, we can write the following:

```
"ABC"+"XYZ"
```

On each side of the operator may be a string constant, string variable,
or substring function. For example, each of the following are valid uses
of the concatenation operator:

```
S$+T$
U$+"1234"
"MY "+V$
MID(U$,4,4)+LEFT(S$,3)
RIGHT(V$,4)+T$
```

In each of these cases a new string is formed consisting of the string
identified by the constant, variable, or substring function on the left of

---

[†]Some versions of BASIC use an ampersand (&) as a concatenation operator.

226

the operator, followed by the string identified on the right. Thus, if S$ equals the string ABC and T$ equals the string XYZ, then S$+T$ is ABCXYZ and T$+S$ is XYZABC.

When we use a concatenation operator, we form a type of string expression. In general, a *string expression* is a string constant, string variable, substring function, or any of these in conjunction with the concatenation operator. In addition, we can have multiple concatenations in a string expression. For example, the following is a valid string expression:

$$U\$+"ABC"+MID(T\$,6,7)+S\$$$

The strings identified in the expression are concatenated left-to-right.

A string expression by itself is not a BASIC statement; rather it must be used as part of a statement. For example, we may assign the value of a string expression to a string variable with a LET statement. Thus, the following is a valid BASIC statement:

$$430 \ LET \ S\$=T\$+U\$+V\$$$

The strings identified in the string expression are concatenated and the resulting string is assigned to S$. We can also use a string expression in an IF statement and a PRINT statement.

As an example of the use of concatenation, consider the problem of rearranging the order of a person's name. Assume that L$, F$, and M$ are string variables that identify a person's last name, first name, and middle name, respectively. The problem is to create a string consisting of the person's first name followed by a space, then the person's middle initial followed by a period and a space, and finally the person's last name. The following statement accomplishes this:

$$440 \ LET \ N\$=F\$+" \ "+LEFT(M\$,1)+". \ "+L\$$$

Notice that we must put the period and spaces in the proper place in the expression so that the final result is the way we want it. Other examples of concatenation are shown in Fig. 9–7.

*String Length

Occasionally when we manipulate string data, we do not know the length of a string or substring. There are various ways to obtain this information in the program, but the easiest is to use the LEN function. The form of this function is LEN(A$). The function determines the number of characters in the string named in parentheses. For example,

Operation	Result
S$+" STATE"	WASHINGTON STATE
"GEORGE "+S$	GEORGE WASHINGTON
LEFT(S$,4)+MID(S$,5,3)+RIGHT(S$,8)	WASHINGTON
LEFT(S$,3)+" "+MID(S$,5,1)+MID(S$,8,1)+"?"	WAS IT?
MID(S$,10,1)+MID(S$,9,1)+MID(S$,8,1)	NOT

FIGURE 9-7. Concatenation.

the following statement assigns the length of the string S$ to the numeric variable L:

$$450 \text{ LET } L=LEN(S\$)$$

If S$ has eight characters in the string assigned to it, L will be equal to eight after execution of this statement. The entry in parentheses may be any string expression. For example, we can use LEN(RIGHT(S$,5)) to determine the length of the substring beginning with the fifth character through the end of the string S$.

*An Illustrative Program

To illustrate some of the string-manipulation features discussed in this chapter, we consider a text-analysis program. Input to the program is a line of text (i.e., a sentence). The program must count the number of blank spaces in the line and print this count.

Figure 9-8 shows a program that accomplishes this. The program first prints an input prompt and then accepts a line of text. The LEN function is used to determine the length of the line. Next a counter (C) is set equal to 0. The program then enters a loop that is repeated once for each character in the line. Each time through the loop, the next character in the line is examined to determine whether it is a blank. For each blank that is found, 1 is added to the counter (C). After branching out of the loop, the program prints the value of the counter. Then an input prompt is used to ask whether the program is to be repeated. If the response is YES, the computer branches to the beginning of the program; otherwise execution of the program is terminated.

This program illustrates one use of the string-manipulation features in BASIC. However, the program uses many features that are not standard in all versions of BASIC. The program may have to be modified to run on different computers.

There are numerous interesting and practical applications of strings

```
100 PRINT
110 PRINT "TYPE A LINE OF TEXT"
120 INPUT T$
130 LET L=LEN(T$)
140 LET C=0
150 LET I=1
160 IF I>=L THEN 210
170 IF MID(T$,I,1) <> " " THEN 190
180 LET C=C+1
190 LET I=I+1
200 GO TO 160
210 PRINT "THERE ARE";C;"BLANKS IN THIS LINE"
220 PRINT "DO YOU WANT TO TRY ANOTHER LINE";
230 INPUT R$
240 IF R$="YES" THEN 100
999 END
```

(a) The program

```
TYPE A LINE OF TEXT
? NOW IS THE TIME
THERE ARE 3 BLANKS IN THIS LINE
DO YOU WANT TO TRY ANOTHER LINE? YES

TYPE A LINE OF TEXT
? FOUR SCORE AND SEVEN YEARS AGO
THERE ARE 5 BLANKS IN THIS LINE
DO YOU WANT TO TRY ANOTHER LINE? YES

TYPE A LINE OF TEXT
? HELP
THERE ARE 0 BLANKS IN THIS LINE
DO YOU WANT TO TRY ANOTHER LINE? NO
```

(b) The input and output

FIGURE 9-8.   A text analysis program.

in computer programs. Some of these are discussed in the programming
problems at the end of the chapter.

REVIEW QUESTIONS

1. Which of the following are valid string constants?
   (a) "MY NAME IS"
   (b) "Z35X19$"

(c) 853.63

(d) JOHN

(e) " "

(f) "5,280"

2. Which of the following are valid string variables?

   (a) "A"

   (b) X3

   (c) M$

   (d) AMT$

3. What is a null string?

4. Write a statement that assigns the string 12345 to a variable.

5. Write an INPUT statement to accept three strings and a PRINT statement to print the strings in reverse order.

6. Write a READ statement and a DATA statement to assign your name and date of birth to string variables.

7. Assume that the value of A$ is AL, B$ is ALLAN, and C$ is ALFRED. What is the truth value of each of the following relational expressions?

   (a) A$=B$

   (b) B$<>C$

   (c) C$="ALFRED "

   (d) A$<B$

   (e) B$<=C$

   (f) A$>="AL"

8. What is the collating sequence for the version of BASIC you are using?

9. A group of one or more adjacent characters in a string is called a
_____ .

10. Assume that the value of X$ is XYZ123ABC. What is the value of each of the following functions?

   (a) LEFT(X$,6)

   (b) RIGHT(X$,6)

   (c) MID(X$,4,3)

   (d) MID(X$,1,4)

   (e) MID(X$,7,1)

   (f) LEN(X$)

11. The operation of joining together two strings to form one string is called _____ .

12. Assume that the value of X$ is XYZ, Y$ is 123, and Z$ is ABC. What is the result of each of the following operations?

(a) Z$+X$

(b) X$+" "+Y$+" "+Z$

(c) X$+"DEF"

(d) LEFT(X$,1)+MID(Y$,2,1)+RIGHT(Z$,3)

PROGRAMMING PROBLEMS

1. Rewrite the program for problem 2 or 5 in Chapter 4 with the modification that the customer's name is accepted and printed. Supply appropriate names with the test data.

2. Rewrite the program in Fig. 7–9 to use a string variable for the letter grade. Only one PRINT statement is needed for the final output.

3. In a political survey a number of people were given six statements about a political candidate's involvement in illicit campaign practices. Each person was asked to indicate whether he or she felt each statement was true or false by writing a T or F. A BASIC program is needed to analyze these data. The program should determine the answers to the following questions:

(a) What percentage of the people in the survey felt that the first two statements were true and the remainder false?

(b) What percent felt that all six statements were true?

(c) What percent felt that all six were false?

Output should give the answers to these questions with appropriate descriptive headings.

Input data consists of the six responses for each person. Use the following data to test the program:

Survey Responses	
TFTFFF	TTFTFF
TTFFFF	TTFFFF
TTTTT	TTFFFF
FFTTFF	FFFFFF
FFFFFF	TFFFFF
TTFTFT	TTTTT
FTFTFF	TTFFFF
FFFFFF	FTFFFF
TTFFFF	FFFFFF

4. A five-question true-false test needs to be graded. The correct answers are entered on the first line. On each succeeding line is entered a student's number and his or her answers to the five questions. Write a BASIC program to determine the number of correct answers for each student. The output for this program should give the correct answers followed by each student's number, his or her answers, and the number of correct answers.

Use the following data to test the program:

Correct answers: FTTFT

Student's Number	Student's Answers
101	FTFFT
102	TTTFF
103	TFFTF
104	FTTFT
105	TFTFT
106	FTTTT
107	FTFTF
108	TFFTF
109	FTTFT
999 (trailer value)	

5. Write a program that accepts a name from the terminal and prints the name on a diagonal. For example, the name ROBERT should print as follows:

```
R
 O
  B
   E
    R
     T
```

Supply several names to test the program.

6. Write a BASIC program that accepts a person's name with the last name first, followed by a space and then the first name. The length of the last name and the first name can vary. After accepting the data, the program should rearrange and print the name with the first name first, a space, and then the last name. Use the following input data to test the program:

WASHINGTON GEORGE
ADAMS JOHN
JEFFERSON THOMAS
MADISON JAMES
MONROE JAMES

7. Write a BASIC program to compute the average length of the words in a line of text. Assume that the line only contains alphabetic characters and blanks. Use the following lines to test the program:

NOW IS THE TIME FOR ALL GOOD MEN
THE QUICK BROWN FOX JUMPED OVER THE LAZY DOG
FOUR SCORE AND SEVEN YEARS AGO
PETER PIPER PICKED A PECK

8. Write a BASIC program to count the number of times that the word THE occurs in a line of text. Assume that the line contains only alphabetic characters and blanks. Use the following lines to test the program:

THE MAN WONDERED WHETHER THE THEATER WAS THERE
THEN THE MAN THOUGHT THAT IT WAS HERE
BUT IT WAS NOT THERE
THE THE THE TITHE THE THE THE

9. A palindrome is a word, phrase, or number that reads the same forward or backward. For example, RADAR is a palindrome. Write a BASIC program that accepts a character string and determines whether it is a palindrome. Print the string and a statement regarding whether it is a palindrome. Test the program with the following data:

RATS STAR
MOM
PALINDROME
A
11/5/11
ABLE WAS I ERE I SAW ELBA
ABABAB
1991

10. Write a program to compute final grades for a course. Input to the program is the student's identification number and five letter grades. In the program, convert each grade to its equivalent numerical grade according to the following table:

A+	4.3	C	2.0
A	4.0	C-	1.7
A-	3.7	D+	1.3
B+	3.3	D	1.0
B	3.0	D-	0.7
B-	2.7	F+	0.3
C+	2.3	F	0.0

The lowest of the five grades should be dropped and the remaining four should be averaged (weighted equally). Compute the numerical average and determine the final letter grade according to the following scale (where G is the numerical grade):

$G \geqslant 3.5$	A
$2.5 \leqslant G < 3.5$	B
$1.5 \leqslant G < 2.5$	C
$0.5 \leqslant G < 1.5$	D
$G < 0.5$	F

Output from the program should give the student's identification number, numerical grade, and letter grade with appropriate descriptive phrases. Use the following data to test the program:

Student Number	Grades
1015	B, C+, B+, A–, C–
1130	A, C–, C, D, D+
1426	B–, A–, B+, A+, A
1703	C, F+, D, F, D–
1827	D–, F, F, F+, D–
1933	A+, A+, A, A, A+

11. Write a BASIC program that right-justifies a line of text (i.e., aligns the right margin). Input to the program should be a line of no more than forty characters including blanks. Assume that the line contains only alphabetic characters and blanks. Output from the program should be the same line with the first word beginning in position one and the last word ending in position 40 (i.e., left- and right-justified). This may involve inserting extra blanks between words so that the line is properly aligned.

Make up several lines of input to test the program. There should be one test line that is exactly 40 characters long. All other test lines should be less than 40 characters long. There should be at least one line that is less than 30 characters long.

12. The Roman numeral system uses the following seven symbols: M (value 1,000), D (value 500), C (value 100), L (value 50), X (value 10), V (value 5), and I (value 1). The Arabic value of each symbol is shown in parentheses. The value of a Roman numeral expressed as an Arabic numeral is found by adding the Arabic value of each Roman symbol. However, if a C, X, or I is to the left of a symbol with a greater value, the Arabic value of C, X, or I is subtracted, not added. For example, the Roman numeral MCDLXXVI is 1476 in the Arabic system.

Write a BASIC program to convert Roman numerals to Arabic numerals. The program should accept a string of Roman numerals, determine the equivalent in the Arabic system, and print the Roman numeral and its Arabic equivalent.

Use the following data to test the program:

> CMXCIX
> MDCCLXVI
> DCCCXXXIV
> MMDCCCLXXXVIII
> MCMLXXIV
> MCDXLII
> CCIII
> MMDXXII
> (trailer value − all blank)

10

ARRAYS

Frequently it is necessary to store and process a large amount of data in a program. For example, we may need to process a list of fifty numbers, all of which must be available in the program at the same time. With the techniques discussed so far, it is necessary to use a separate variable for each number in the list. Hence, fifty variables are needed for the data.

Another approach to this type of problem is to identify the entire list of data by a single variable. Then each list value is referred to by indicating its position in the list. In this chapter we examine this approach and its use in BASIC.

10-1. ARRAYS AND ARRAY ELEMENTS

A list of data that is identified by a single variable in a program is called an *array*. A variable that refers to an array is called an *array variable*. For example, Fig. 10–1(a) shows an array of ten numbers that is identified by the variable A. Each value in an array is called an *array element*. In Fig. 10–1(a) the number 23.2 is an array element. Similarly, 17.5, –10.8, and so forth are each elements of the array A. There are ten elements in this array.

An array is identified by a variable that consists of a single letter. Thus, A, M, and X are array variables. Since there are twenty-six letters of the alphabet, there can be twenty-six array variables in a program. (Some versions of BASIC allow any variable to be used for an array. For example, A5, M9, and X1 can be used as array variables in some

236

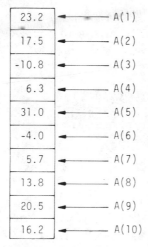

(a) The Array A   (b) Subscripted Variables

FIGURE 10-1.   An array.

versions of BASIC.) The same variable cannot be used both as an array variable and as a simple numeric variable. Thus, we cannot use A to identify an array and to refer to a single number in the same program. (Some versions of BASIC do not make this restriction.)

An array variable refers to the entire array, not to the individual values in the array. However, usually we are interested in processing the elements of an array separately. In a program we think of the array elements as being numbered. The first element is numbered 1, the second is numbered 2, and so on throughout the array. The array in Fig. 10-1(a) has ten elements; thus, the last element is numbered 10. In a program an array element is identified by coding the array variable, followed immediately by the number of the element in parentheses. For example, the first array element shown in Fig. 10-1(a) is identified by A(1); the fifth element is A(5); the last is A(10). A variable of this sort is called a *subscripted variable*. The number in parentheses following the array variable is called a *subscript*. A subscripted variable such as A(5) is read "A sub five". The complete list of subscripted variables for the array in Fig. 10-1(a) is shown in Fig. 10-1(b).

It is important not to confuse an array element with its subscript. A subscript specifies which value in an array is being identified. The actual value is the array element. Thus, A(5) identifies the fifth value in the array A. The corresponding array element from Fig. 10-1(a) is 31.0.

The data in an array is referred to collectively by the array variable. However, an array variable cannot be used by itself in a BASIC program. An array variable must always be followed by a subscript to identify an element of the array. A subscripted variable may be used like any other variable. Thus, subscripted variables may be used in

INPUT and PRINT statements and in numeric expressions. For example, assume that X and Y identify arrays of ten elements each. Then the following statements are valid examples of the use of subscripted variables:

```
10 INPUT X(1),Y(1)
40 IF Y(5)>X(10) THEN 200
80 LET W=X(3)+X(5)+X(7)
90 PRINT W,X(7),X(5),X(3)
```

Array Bounds

Although not shown in Fig. 10-1, each array used in a program has an element numbered 0; that is, A(0), X(0), and Y(0) are all valid subscripted variable names. Thus, the array in Fig. 10-1 has eleven elements, not ten. (Some versions of BASIC do not provide for an element numbered 0.)

Unless the programmer specifies otherwise in a program, each array has a maximum of eleven elements. The elements are numbered 0, 1, 2, and so forth up to 10. If we do not need all eleven elements, then we do not have to use them. For example if all we need is a five-element array, we can use A(1), A(2), A(3), A(4), and A(5). The other elements in the array A are available but they do not have to be used.

If we need more than eleven elements in an array or if we need to use subscripts greater than 10, we must specify the array in a DIM or dimension statement. The syntax of the DIM statement is as follows:

ln DIM *list of array declarations separated by commas*

In the DIM statement, each array declaration consists of an array variable followed by a whole number enclosed in parentheses. For example, the following statement contains two array declarations:

```
10 DIM B(50),C(25)
```

The number in parenthesis is *not* a subscript, but rather specifies the maximum subscript that is acceptable for the array. In this example, the subscript for array B may be between 0 and 50, while the subscript for array C may be between 0 and 25.

Notice that the number of elements in an array is always one more than the number given in the array declaration. This is because of the element numbered 0. Thus, in the example above B contains fifty-one elements and C has twenty-six elements. Even though this is the case, we commonly ignore the element numbered 0. Thus, we would regard

B and C as being fifty- and twenty-five-element arrays, respectively. We will follow this practice in this chapter.[†]

As many arrays as are needed can be declared in a DIM statement (up to the limit of the number of array variables). All arrays can be declared in one DIM statement or several statements can be used. For example, the following statements could be used in a program:

```
10 DIM Z(100)
20 DIM S(50),T(200),U(84)
30 DIM W(320),D(39)
```

Note, however, that we cannot declare the same array in more than one DIM statement.

DIM statements may appear anywhere in a program as long as each array is declared before it is used in the program. Most programmers group all DIM statements together at the beginning of the program. This makes it easier to refer to the statements and to check whether an array has been declared.

A DIM statement is not required for an array if the subscript does not exceed 10. However, the DIM statement can be used even when it is not needed. Thus, if A is an array with a maximum subscript of 5 and X has a maximum subscript of 10, these arrays can be declared as follows:

```
10 DIM A(5),X(10)
```

Although these array declarations are not needed, they can be used. In fact, many programmers declare all arrays whether or not it is needed.

Subscripts

A subscript indicates which element of an array is being identified. As we have seen, a subscript may be a numeric constant. A subscript may also be a numeric variable. For example, A(I) is a valid subscripted variable. This is read "A sub I". The element of the array A identified by this variable depends on the value of I. For example, if the value of I is 3, the third element of the array A is identified by A(I).

The use of a variable as a subscript is a powerful technique in BASIC programming. As an example, assume that the input to a program consists of twenty numbers. The program must store the numbers

---

[†]In some versions of BASIC, the element numbered 0 can be eliminated from all arrays by including the following statement at the beginning of the program:

```
10 OPTION BASE 1
```

```
100 DIM B(20)
    (Read data for array)
150 LET T=0
160 FOR I=1 TO 20
170   LET T=T+B(I)
180 NEXT I
    (Print array data)
230 PRINT T
999 END
```

FIGURE 10-2.   An array processing program.

in an array, accumulate the total of the numbers, print the array data, and then print the total. The program in Fig. 10–2 shows how this can be done. The program is complete except for the input and output of the array data. (Array input and output are discussed in the next section.)

The first line in this program is a DIM statement for the array B. The array contains twenty elements (plus the element numbered 0 which is not used in the program). Processing in the program begins with the input of the array data. The total of the array elements is then accumulated by successively adding each element to the variable T. This is accomplished in a FOR loop by using the control variable as the subscript to identify an array element. Initially the value of T is set to zero. With the first execution of the loop, the control variable I is one and hence the value of $B(1)$ is added to T. The second execution of the loop causes the value of $B(2)$ to be added to T. This continues for the remaining executions of the loop. Upon completion of the FOR loop, the value of T is $0+A(1)+A(2)+...+A(20)$. The program terminates after printing the array data and the total.

In addition to constants and variables, numeric expressions can be used as subscripts. For example, $A(2*I-1)$ is a valid subscripted variable. If I is 5, this variable refers to the ninth element of A. Any valid numeric expression can be used as a subscript.

The value of a subscript, whether a constant, variable, or more complex expression, must be between 0 and the maximum subscript value declared in the DIM statement (or 10 if a DIM statement is not used). Thus, a subscript cannot be negative. Similarly, if A has a maximum subscript of 10, $A(15)$ is invalid.

The value of a subscript need not be a whole number. For example, $A(X)$ where the value of X is 3.25 is acceptable. When the subscript is not a whole number, its value is rounded. Thus, if X is 3.25, $A(X)$ is interpreted as $A(3)$ while if X is 3.75, $A(X)$ is $A(4)$. [Some versions of BASIC do not round the subscript but rather chop off or *truncate* any fraction. In such a case, $A(X)$ where X is 3.75 is interpreted as $A(3)$.]

Arrays are very powerful ways of organizing and processing data in a program. We will see a number of examples of array processing in this chapter.

10-2. INPUT AND OUTPUT OF ARRAY DATA

The most straightforward technique for input and output of array data is to list each subscripted variable in an INPUT, READ, or PRINT statement. For example, assume that C is an array with five elements. We can use the following statement to accept five input values and assign them to the elements of C:

```
10 INPUT C(1),C(2),C(3),C(4),C(5)
```

When this statement is executed, the terminal operator must enter five values after the queston mark prompt. We can use the same technique with the READ statement. For example, the following READ statement reads the five values for the array C from the accompanying DATA statement:

```
10 READ C(1),C(2),C(3),C(4),C(5)
20 DATA 78,95,84,36,67
```

To print the values of C, we can use this approach in a PRINT statement as in the following example:

```
30 PRINT C(1),C(2),C(3),C(4),C(5)
```

The problem with this technique is that if the array is very large, the list of subscripted variables in the INPUT, READ, or PRINT statement is quite long and tiresome to code. A better approach is to use a loop to control the input or output operation. For example, the following sequence of statements uses a FOR loop to control the input process:

```
10 FOR I= 1 TO 5
20   INPUT C(I)
30 NEXT I
```

The control variable in this loop is used as a subscript for the array. With each execution of the loop, the INPUT statement is executed and a new value is accepted from the terminal. Thus, with the first execution of the loop, the value of C(1) is accepted. Then the control variable is incremented and the value of C(2) is accepted during the second execution of the loop. This continues until the loop is terminated. Notice that because the INPUT statement is executed five times, five question mark prompts are displayed. Thus, each value is entered on a separate line.

We can use this technique with a READ statement or a PRINT statement. For example, the following program segment reads the five values for C from a DATA statement and then prints the values on five lines:

```
10 FOR I=1 TO 5
20    READ C(I)
30 NEXT I
40 FOR I=1 TO 5
50    PRINT C(I)
60 NEXT I
90 DATA 78,95,84,36,67
```

Using a loop to control the input and output of array data is most useful for large arrays or when there is an unusual arrangement of the data. For example, assume that the 100 elements of an array named M are to be entered two at a time. The data can be accepted using a FOR loop that is executed 50 times as shown in the following statements:

```
10 FOR I=1 TO 99 STEP 2
20    INPUT M(I),M(I+1)
30 NEXT I
```

The control variable I in the FOR loop ranges from 1 to 99 in steps of two. With each execution of the FOR loop, two elements of the array are accepted. The use of the control variable in the subscripts I and I+1 causes the data to be assigned to the proper subscripted variables.

As another example, consider the problem of printing two arrays in adjacent columns. Assume that X and Y are two twenty-element arrays. The following statements cause the data in the arrays to be printed in columns along with another column for the value of the FOR loop control variable:

```
70 FOR J=1 TO 20
80    PRINT J,X(J),Y(J)
90 NEXT J
```

If array data is to be accepted until a trailer value is entered, a looping technique must be used. For example, assume that the array named N has at most 150 elements. Each element is to be entered on a separate line. The last value entered is a trailer value equal to zero. To accept the data, a loop must be used with a test for the trailer value included in the loop. The following statements accomplish this:

```
10 DIM N(151)
20 LET J=1
30 INPUT N(J)
40 IF N(J)=0 THEN 80
50 LET J=J+1
70 GO TO 30
80 (next statement)
```

Notice in this example that N has a maximum subscript of 151. This is because there can be at most 150 elements entered for N plus the trailer value. When the loop is terminated, J is equal to the number of elements entered plus one for the trailer value. Hence, to find the actual number of data values in the array, J must be decreased by one.

10-3. ARRAY-PROCESSING TECHNIQUES

The use of arrays is one of the most powerful features of the BASIC programming language. With the proper use of loops and subscripts, extensive processing can be accomplished with just a few statements. This section illustrates a number of array-processing techniques. While many of the examples may seem simple, the techniques appear often in complex array-processing programs. For the examples we assume that the arrays X, Y, and Z have twenty elements each.

Often it is necessary to set each element of an array to an initial value. For example, assume that the elements of the array X must be initialized to zero, and the elements of Y and Z are each to be given an initial value of one. Then the three arrays may be initialized in one loop as follows:

```
110 FOR I=1 TO 20
120    LET X(I)=0
130    LET Y(I)=1
140    LET Z(I)=1
150 NEXT I
```

Sometimes it is necessary to copy the data from one array into another. As a result, the original data can be saved in one array while it is manipulated or modified in the other. For example, assume that data has been entered for array X. The data is then copied into array Y by the following statements:

```
210 FOR J=1 TO 20
220   LET Y(J)=X(J)
230 NEXT J
```

Occasionally a copy of the array data is necessary with the elements in reverse order. In other words, the first element of one array is assigned to the last element of another array, the second element of the first array is assigned to the next-to-last element of the other array, and so forth until the last element of the first array is assigned to the first element of the other array. To accomplish this, the subscript of the first array must be incremented from 1 to the maximum, while the subscript of the second array is decremented from the maximum to 1. The following statements accomplish this for arrays X and Y:

```
310 LET J=20
320 FOR I=1 TO 20
330   LET Y(J)=X(I)
340   LET J=J-1
350 NEXT I
```

Notice that the variable J is initialized to 20 and then decreased by 1 with each execution of the FOR loop. Thus, with the first execution of the loop, X(1) is assigned to Y(20). The value of the control variable is then incremented to 2, while the value of J is decremented to 19. The second execution of the loop causes the value of X(2) to be assigned to Y(19). This continues until the last execution of the loop when the value of X(20) is assigned to Y(1).

Array elements are often processed arithmetically. For example, the following statements add the corresponding elements of the arrays X and Y and assign the results to the array Z:

```
410 FOR K=1 TO 20
420   LET Z(K)=X(K)+Y(K)
430 NEXT K
```

On occasion it is necessary to determine how many times a particular value occurs in an array. For example, we may wish to know the number of elements of Y that are zero. The following statements accomplish this:

```
510 LET N=0
520 FOR I=1 TO 20
530   IF Y(I)<>0 THEN 550
540   LET N=N+1
550 NEXT I
```

At the end of execution of this sequence, the variable N will be equal to the number of elements of Y that are equal to zero. A similar situation occurs when we want to know the number of elements in one array that are equal to corresponding elements in a second array. For example, we may want to know how many elements of X and Z are the same. The following statements accomplish this:

```
560 LET N=0
570 FOR J=1 TO 20
580   IF X(J)<>Z(J) THEN 600
590   LET N=N+1
600 NEXT J
```

Often it is necessary to locate the largest or smallest element in an array. For example, assume that it is necessary to find the smallest element in the array X. The following statements accomplish this:

```
610 LET S=X(1)
620 FOR L=2 TO 20
630   IF X(L)>=S THEN 650
640   LET S=X(L)
650 NEXT L
```

Initially we assume that the first element of the array is the smallest, and its value is assigned to the variable S. This value is then compared with each succeeding element to determine whether there is one smaller. If an element is smaller, its value is assigned to S, replacing the previous value. If an element is not smaller than the current value of S, this assignment is bypassed. At the end of the execution of the loop, the value of the variable S is the smallest element of the array.

10-4. SEARCHING AND SORTING

Two common problems in array processing are searching and sorting. Searching involves locating a specific value in an array. Sorting is the process of rearranging the data in an array into a specific order. In this section we give algorithms[†] for searching and sorting arrays.

Searching

There are many situations that involve searching. In the simplest case a value is given and the first occurrence of an equivalent value is to

---

[†]Recall from Section 7-5 that an algorithm is a set of instructions that solves a problem.

be located in an array. For example, the following statements search the array X (which we assume has twenty elements) for the first element whose value is equal to that of V:

```
110 LET I=1
120 IF X(I)=V THEN 150
130 LET I=I+1
140 GO TO 120
150 PRINT "VALUE FOUND AT ELEMENT";I
```

In this sequence, I is used as a subscript. Initially the value of I is 1. Each time through the loop, I is increased by 1. The loop is terminated when X(I) is equal to V. The value of I at this time is the number of the first element in X that has a value equal to V. This value of I is printed along with an appropriate message when the loop is terminated.

The problem with this sequence of statements is that it does not take into account the case where the value of V is not in the array. However, we can modify the statements to print an error message if the value is not found. The following sequence of statements accomplishes this:

```
210 LET I=1
220 IF X(I)=V THEN 280
230 IF I=20 THEN 260
240 LET I=I+1
250 GO TO 220
260 WRITE "VALUE NOT FOUND"
270 GO TO 290
280 WRITE "VALUE FOUND AT ELEMENT";I
290 (next statement)
```

In this sequence the loop is terminated when X(I) equals V *or* when X(I) does not equal V but I equals 20. The latter case occurs when we reach the end of the array without finding the value. After branching out of the loop, an error message is printed. Notice that if V is found, statement 280 prints the corresponding value of I.

Frequently we need to search one array and retrieve the corresponding element of another array. For example, we may wish to search array X for value V and print the corresponding value of array Y when V is found. The only modification in the previous sequence of statements that is necessary is that Y(I) is printed instead of I in statement 280.

To illustrate the use of searching in an actual program, consider the problem of locating the price of an item in a table. For example, Fig. 10–3 shows a table of item numbers and prices. The problem is to store the pricing table in two arrays, one for the item numbers and one for

Item Number	Unit Price
1001	$2.95
1023	$3.64
1045	$2.25
1172	$0.75
1185	$1.50
1201	$1.95
1235	$4.85
1278	$9.95
1384	$6.28
1400	$4.75

FIGURE 10-3. A pricing table.

the prices. Then the program must accept an item number and a value that represents the quantity of the item purchased from the terminal, locate the item's price in the table, and compute the cost by multiplying the price by the quantity. Fig. 10-4 shows a program that accomplishes this.

In this program, N is the item number array and P is the array of corresponding prices. The program begins by reading the data for these

```
100 DIM N(10),P(10)
110 FOR I=1 TO 10
120    READ N(I),P(I)
130 NEXT I
140 INPUT N1,Q
150 IF N1=9999 THEN 999
160 LET I=1
170 IF N(I)=N1 THEN 240
180 IF N(I)>N1 THEN 220
190 IF I=10 THEN 220
200 LET I=I+1
210 GO TO 170
220 PRINT "ITEM";N1;"NOT FOUND"
230 GO TO 140
240 LET C=P(I)*Q
250 PRINT "ITEM";N1;"COST";C
260 GO TO 140
900 DATA 1001,2.95,1023,3.64,1045,2.25,1172,0.75,1185,1.50
910 DATA 1201,1.95,1235,4.85,1278,9.95,1384,6.28,1400,4.75
999 END
```

FIGURE 10-4. A pricing program with a sequential search.

arrays from DATA statements. A FOR loop with a READ statement accomplishes this. Each execution of the READ statement in the loop reads the next two values from a DATA statement and assigns the values to the next two elements of N and P. Notice that the data appears in pairs in the DATA statements. The first pair is the first item number and price, then comes the second item number and price, and so on.

After the data is read into the pricing table arrays, the program accepts an item number, N1, and quantity, Q, from the terminal. It then searches the item number array for an element that is equal to N1. The program assumes that the item numbers are in increasing order in the array and branches out of the searching loop when N(I) is either equal to N1 or greater than N1. This latter case occurs when the search has gone beyond the value of N1 in the array. (If the item numbers are not in increasing order, statement 180 would be omitted from the program.) The loop is also terminated if we reach the end of the array without finding N1 (i.e., when I is equal to 10). If the program branches out of the loop because N1 is found in the array, the quantity, Q, is multiplied by the item's price, P(I), to get the cost, and the result is printed. If the loop is terminated because the item number is not found in the array, an error message is printed.

This example illustrates a common algorithm for "table look-up", the process of looking something up in a table. In this algorithm we search through the array elements in sequence. This approach is called a *sequential search*. In a sequential search we begin by examining the first element of the array, then the second, then the third, and so on until the desired element is found or until we can determine that the item is not in the array.

Binary Search

Another algorithm for searching for an element in an array is called a *binary search*. In a binary search the array elements *must* be in ascending or descending order. We will assume that the elements of the array to be searched are in ascending order. Then with a binary search we first look at the *middle* element of the array and determine whether this is the desired element. If we have *not* found the element that we want, we determine whether it is located before or after the middle one. We then search the appropriate half of the array by examining the middle element of that half. Again we determine whether the element is the one we want or whether we should search above or below the middle element. We continue to search by examining the middle of smaller and smaller sections of the array until the desired element is found or until we can determine that the element is not in the array.

To illustrate this algorithm, assume that the twenty elements of array X are in ascending order. We wish to use a binary search to locate

the element with a value equal to V. The following sequence of statements accomplishes this:

```
310 LET B=1
320 LET T=20
330 LET M=INT((B+T)/2)
340 IF X(M)=V THEN 430
350 IF B=T THEN 410
360 IF V<X(M) THEN 390
370 LET B=M+1
380 GO TO 330
390 LET T=M-1
400 GO TO 330
410 PRINT "VALUE NOT FOUND"
420 GO TO 440
430 PRINT "VALUE FOUND AT ELEMENT";M
440 (next statement)
```

In this sequence, B equals the number of the bottom element of the
part of the array being searched and T equals the number of the top
element. Initially these are 1 and 20, respectively. The number of the
middle element of the part of the array being searched is computed and
assigned to M in statement 330. Each time through the loop, we check
whether X(M) equals V and branch out of the loop if this is the case.
If V is not found, we check whether V is less than X(M). If this is the
case, we let T be one less than M. If V is greater than X(M), then B is
M plus 1. Then we compute a new M and repeat the process. The loop
terminates either when we find the desired element or when B equals T,
in which case the element is not in the array. Figure 10-5 shows how a
binary search compares with a sequential search.

We can use a binary search algorithm in the pricing table program.
Figure 10-6 shows the complete program. Notice that after the appropriate item is found, the cost is determined by multiplying Q by P(M).

For large arrays, a binary search is much faster than a sequential
search. For example, if an array contains 1,000 elements, then on the
average a sequential search will require about 1000/2 or 500 repetitions
of the loop. For a binary search, however, the loop will be repeated no
more than $\log_2$ 1000 or about ten times. Clearly for large arrays, the
extra complexity required to program a binary search results in considerable savings in execution time of the program.

Sorting

Sorting is the process of rearranging a set of data into a particular
order. For example, given a list of numbers, we may wish to sort the
numbers into ascending or descending order. There are many times

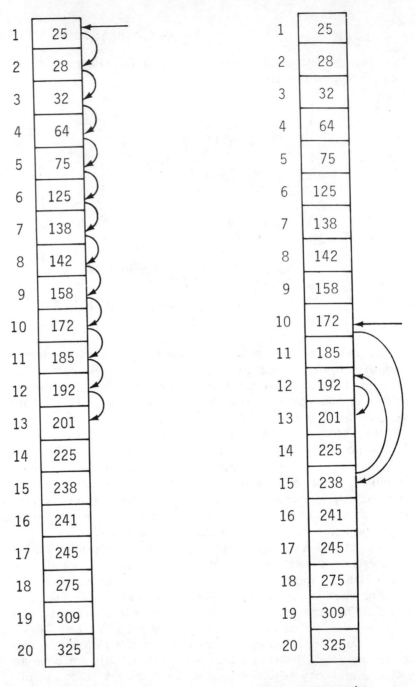

Sequential Search
for V = 201

Binary Search
for V = 201

FIGURE 10-5. Sequential vs. binary search.

```
100 DIM N(10),P(10)
110 FOR I=1 TO 10
120   READ N(I),P(I)
130 NEXT I
140 INPUT N1,Q
150 IF N1=9999 THEN 999
160 LET B=1
170 LET T=10
180 LET M=INT((B+T)/2)
190 IF N(M)=N1 THEN 280
200 IF B=T THEN 260
210 IF N1<N(M) THEN 240
220 LET B=M+1
230 GO TO 180
240 LET T=M-1
250 GO TO 180
260 PRINT "ITEM";N1;"NOT FOUND"
270 GO TO 140
280 LET C=P(M)*Q
290 PRINT "ITEM";N1;"COST";C
300 GO TO 140
900 DATA 1001,2.95,1023,3.64,1045,2.25,1172,0.75,1185,1.50
910 DATA 1201,1.95,1235,4.85,1278,9.95,1384,6.28,1400,4.75
999 END
```

FIGURE 10-6. A pricing program with a binary search.

when sorted data is needed. For example, we may want to produce a list of students in a class in order by student identification number. This requires sorting if the data is not already in order. In the last subsection we saw that an array must be in ascending or descending order if the binary search algorithm is to be used. If the array is not in the appropriate order, it must be sorted before it can be searched.

There are many algorithms for sorting. In this subsection we discuss *bubble* sorting. (This type of sorting is also called *pushdown* sorting, *interchange* sorting, and *exchange* sorting.) As we will see, bubble sorting gets its name from the fact that data "bubbles" to the top of the array.

The basic principle of bubble sorting is to compare adjacent elements of the array to be sorted. If any two adjacent elements are found to be out of order with respect to each other, they are interchanged (i.e., their values are switched). For example, assume that the array C has five elements that are to be sorted into ascending order. The following loop will pass through the array once, exchanging elements that are not in the proper order:

```
110 FOR I=1 TO 4
120    IF C(I)<=C(I+1) THEN 160
130    LET T=C(I)
140    LET C(I)=C(I+1)
150    LET C(I+1)=T
160 NEXT I
```

Notice that the loop is repeated *four* times. Each time through the loop, C(I) is compared with C(I+1). Thus, the first time through the loop, C(1) is compared with C(2). Then C(2) is compared with C(3). Next C(3) and C(4) are compared. Finally, C(4) and C(5) are compared. If any two adjacent elements are not in ascending order, they are switched. (See Section 7-4 for a discussion of switching the values of two variables.) Figure 10–7 shows what takes place for a particular set of data.

This loop will cause the largest element of the array to be "pushed down" to the last position in the array. At the same time, smaller elements start to "bubble up" to the top of the array. We must now repeat the loop to cause the next largest element to be pushed to the next-to-last position in the array. The loop must then be repeated for the next-to-next largest element, and so forth. In all, this loop must be repeated four times. The last time, the smallest element will automatically appear in the first position of the array. This repeated execution of the loop can be accomplished by nested FOR loops as follows:

```
100 FOR J=1 TO 4
110    FOR I=1 TO 4
120       IF C(I)<=C(I+1) THEN 160
130       LET T=C(I)
140       LET C(I)=C(I+1)
150       LET C(I+1)=T
160    NEXT I
170 NEXT J
```

Figure 10–8 shows how the array appears after each execution of the outer loop. Notice that large values in the array are "pushed down" and small values "bubble up".

We can make the algorithm more efficient by recognizing that with each successive "pass" through the inner loop one less comparison is required. This is because once the largest element has been pushed to the end of the array, we do not need to include it in any subsequent comparisons. The same holds true for the next largest element and so forth. The following sequence of statements includes this modification:

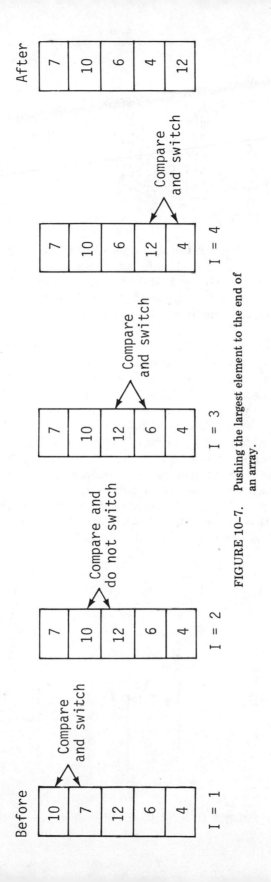

FIGURE 10-7. Pushing the largest element to the end of an array.

```
100 FOR K=4 TO 1 STEP -1
110   FOR I=1 TO K
120     IF C(I)<=C(I+1) THEN 160
130     LET T=C(I)
140     LET C(I)=C(I+1)
150     LET C(I+1)=T
160   NEXT I
170 NEXT K
```

Notice that the test value for the inner loop is the value of the variable named K. Initially K is 4 and the inner loop is executed four times. Then K is decremented by 1 and the inner loop is done only three times. We can see that K is one less for each successive time through the inner loop. Hence, one fewer comparison is carried out with each repetition of the loop.

We can use bubble sorting to sort the pricing table used in the examples in the previous subsection. This is required if a binary search is to be done and the table is not read in ascending order by item number. The only necessary modification is that each time two item numbers are found out of sequence and are switched, the corresponding prices must be switched. This is done to maintain the relationship between the item numbers and prices. The sequence of statements to accomplish this is shown in Fig. 10–9.

The examples so far demonstrate *ascending* order sorts. To sort an array into descending order, the less-than or equal-to condition in the IF statement must be changed to a greater-than or equal-to condition. The effect is that the smaller elements are pushed to the end of the array and the larger elements "bubble up" to the beginning of the array.

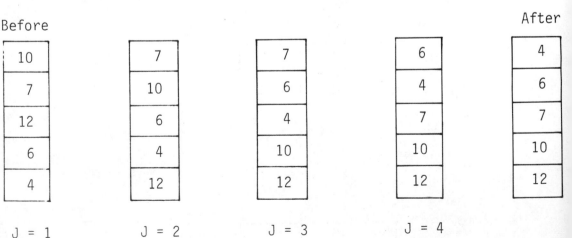

FIGURE 10–8. Sorting a five-element array.

```
110 FOR K=9 TO 1 STEP -1
120    FOR I=1 TO K
130       IF N(I)<=N(I+1) THEN 200
140       LET T=N(I)
150       LET N(I)=N(I+1)
160       LET N(I+1)=T
170       LET T=P(I)
180       LET P(I)=P(I+1)
190       LET P(I+1)=T
200    NEXT I
210 NEXT K
```

FIGURE 10-9.   Sorting a pricing table.

Bubble sorting is just one of many ways to sort an array. A number of algorithms are considerably faster than bubble sorting for large arrays. However, these algorithms are also more difficult to program. As the programmer finds more situations where sorting is required, other techniques should be explored.[†]

*10-5. STRING ARRAYS

In most versions of BASIC, an array may contain string data. When this is the case, the array variable must be followed by a dollar sign. Then each element in the array is a string. For example, A$ can be used as a variable for an array of string data. Then A$(1) is the first element in the array, A$(2) is the second element, and so forth. If the maximum subscript for the array is greater than ten, the array must be declared in a DIM statement. Thus, if the array A$ is to contain twenty elements, the following DIM statement would have to be used in the program:

```
10 DIM A$(20)
```

A subscripted string variable can be used in a string expression just like a simple string variable. For example, the following statements use subscripted string variables:

```
20 LET A$(5)=A$(4)
40 IF A$(I)="END" THEN 90
50 PRINT A$(18),A$(19),A$(20)
60 LET A$(I+2)=A$(I+1)+A$(I)
80 LET B$=MID(A$(10),3,5)
```

[†]Most textbooks on data structures include sections on sorting. A very complete reference is by Donald Knuth, entitled *The Art of Computer Programming: Vol. 3, Sorting and Searching*, published by Addison-Wesley.

```
100 DIM S$(50),P(50)
110 FOR I=1 TO 50
120   READ S$(I),P(I)
130 NEXT I
140 INPUT N$
150 IF N$=" " THEN 999
160 LET I=1
170 IF S$(I)=N$ THEN 230
180 IF I=50 THEN 210
190 LET I=I+1
200 GO TO 170
210 PRINT "INVALID STATE NAME"
220 GO TO 140
230 PRINT N$;" HAS A POPULATION OF";P(I)
240 GO TO 140
900 DATA ALABAMA,3444000,ALASKA,302000,...
      :
      :
999 END
```

FIGURE 10-10. A string array program.

To illustrate the use of string arrays in a program, assume that the data in a group of DATA statements consists of the names of the fifty states and their corresponding populations. A program must read the data into two arrays, one for the state names and one for the populations, to create a population table. Next, the program must accept a state's name as input from the terminal. Then the population table must be searched for the corresponding state name, and the state's population must be printed. Figure 10-10 shows a program to accomplish this. The program is complete except for the data in the DATA statements.

REVIEW QUESTIONS

1. Define each of the following terms:
   (a) array
   (b) array variable
   (c) array element
   (d) subscripted variable

2. Write one DIM statement to declare a hundred-element array named X and a fifty-element array named Y.

3. Consider the array, A, shown in Fig. 10-1. Assume that the value of J is 4 and K is 3. What is the value of each of the following subscripted variables?
   (a) A(9)

(b) A(J)

(c) A(J+K)

(d) A(J/K)

4. Write a sequence of statements to read the data for the twenty-element array A from a group of DATA statements.

5. Write a sequence of statements to print the twenty elements of the array A in a column in reverse order.

6. Write a sequence of statements to assign the numbers 1, 2, 3, . . . , 20 to the corresponding twenty elements of the array A.

7. Write a sequence of statements to accumulate the total of the odd-numbered elements of the twenty-element array A.

8. What is the difference between a sequential search and a binary search?

9. Consider the program shown in Fig. 10-4. What is the output from this program for each of the following sets of input?
   (a) 1172, 5
   (b) 1270, 10

10. Consider the program shown in Fig. 10-6. What is the output from this program for each of the following sets of input?
   (a) 1025, 10
   (b) 1384, 7

11. Consider the sorting algorithm discussed in Section 10-4 and the five-element array, C, shown in Fig. 10-7. This figure shows the order of the data in C for each value of I during the *first* execution of the sorting loop. Draw the equivalent figure for the *second* repetition of the sorting loop.

12. Consider the program segment shown in Fig. 10-9. What modifications would have to be made in the program for a descending order sort?

PROGRAMMING PROBLEMS

1. Write a BASIC program that reads hourly temperatures for a day into a twenty-four-element array. The first element of the array gives the temperature at 1:00 a.m., the second element is the temperature at 2:00 a.m., and so forth. Note that the thirteenth element is the temperature at 1:00 p.m. Then search the array for the maximum and minimum temperatures. Print these temperatures along with the times at which they occur. Supply appropriate input data to test the program.

2. An inventory table contains information about the quantity of inventory on hand for each item stocked. Assume that there are fifteen

items in the inventory. Then the inventory table contains fifteen entries, each consisting of an item number and the quantity of the item that is in stock. The data is in increasing order by item number.

Write a BASIC program to do the following:

(a) Read the inventory table into two arrays, one for the item numbers and one for the quantities. Then print the inventory data in columns below appropriate headings.

(b) Accept an item number, an amount received, and an amount sold from the terminal. Search the inventory table for the corresponding item using either a sequential search or a binary search. Then update the quantity on hand by adding the amount received to the amount from the table and subtracting the amount sold. Repeat this step until 9999 is entered for an item number. Be sure to account for the case where the item is not in the table.

(c) After all items have been updated, print the inventory data in columns below appropriate headings.

Use the following data for the inventory table:

Item Number	Quantity On Hand
1102	100
1113	25
1147	37
1158	95
1196	225
1230	150
1237	15
1239	105
1245	84
1275	97
1276	350
1284	82
1289	125
1351	138
1362	64

Use the following data to update the inventory table:

Item Number	Quantity Received	Quantity Sold
1230	25	100
1113	0	15
1255	16	42
1289	50	0
1405	26	5
1102	100	75
1239	25	25

3. The following tax rate schedule is used to compute income tax for a single taxpayer:

SCHEDULE X—Single Taxpayers Not Qualifying for Rates in Schedule Y or Z

Use this schedule if you checked **Box 1** on Form 1040—

If the amount on Schedule TC, Part I, line 3, is:		Enter on Schedule TC, Part I, line 4:
Not over $2,200............		—0—

Over—	But not over—		of the amount over—
$2,200	$2,700	14%	$2,200
$2,700	$3,200	$70+15%	$2,700
$3,200	$3,700	$145+16%	$3,200
$3,700	$4,200	$225+17%	$3,700
$4,200	$6,200	$310+19%	$4,200
$6,200	$8,200	$690+21%	$6,200
$8,200	$10,200	$1,110+24%	$8,200
$10,200	$12,200	$1,590+25%	$10,200
$12,200	$14,200	$2,090+27%	$12,200
$14,200	$16,200	$2,630+29%	$14,200
$16,200	$18,200	$3,210+31%	$16,200
$18,200	$20,200	$3,830+34%	$18,200
$20,200	$22,200	$4,510+36%	$20,200
$22,200	$24,200	$5,230+38%	$22,200
$24,200	$28,200	$5,990+40%	$24,200
$28,200	$34,200	$7,590+45%	$28,200
$34,200	$40,200	$10,290+50%	$34,200
$40,200	$46,200	$13,290+55%	$40,200
$46,200	$52,200	$16,590+60%	$46,200
$52,200	$62,200	$20,190+62%	$52,200
$62,200	$72,200	$26,390+64%	$62,200
$72,200	$82,200	$32,790+66%	$72,200
$82,200	$92,200	$39,390+68%	$82,200
$92,200	$102,200	$46,190+69%	$92,200
$102,200	....	$53,090+70%	$102,200

The tax is based on the individual's taxable income. For example, if the taxable income is $17,500, the income tax is $2,605 plus 30% of the difference between $17,500 and $15,000, or $3,355.

Write a BASIC program that reads the tax rate schedule into several arrays. One approach is to use three arrays, one for the first column and two for the third column. Then the program should accept a taxpayer's identification number and taxable income, compute the income tax, and print the results.

Use the following data to test the program:

Taxpayer Number	Taxable Income
1234	$ 17,500
1332	6,200
1424	10,201
2134	1,500
2432	47,300
3144	154,000
3223	23,350

4. The results of a random survey of households in an area of a city need to be analyzed. The data consists of the following information for each household: an identification number, the annual income of the head of the household, and the number of people living in the household. The last set of data contains 9999 for the identification number. Write a BASIC program to analyze this data according to the following specifications:

(a) Read the survey results into three arrays, one for the identification numbers, one for the annual incomes, and one for the number of people living in the households. Assume that there are no more than fifty households in the survey and dimension all arrays accordingly. However, there may be fewer than fifty households, so a count of the number of households must be kept as the data is read. Finally, print the array data in columns below appropriate headings.

(b) Calculate the average income and average number of people for all households. Print the results with appropriate headings.

(c) Print the identification numbers and annual incomes of all households where the income is below the average.

(d) Determine the percentage of the households in the area that have incomes below the poverty level. The poverty level depends on the number of people living in the household. If there is one person, the poverty level income is $3,500. If there are two people, the poverty level is $4,500. For a household with more than two people, the poverty level is $4,500 plus $750 for each additional person.

Use the following data to test the program:

Identification Number	Annual Income	Number of People
1011	$ 8,750	3
1020	3,250	2
1083	6,000	5
1141	6,500	1
1157	12,300	4
1235	7,000	6
1347	8,350	7
1508	2,350	1
1512	4,900	3
1513	5,600	4
1584	6,385	2
1631	4,300	2
1690	15,200	4
1742	13,350	5
1755	3,700	1
1759	6,300	3
1763	5,250	8
1809	8,250	1
1853	10,500	2
1899	12,000	6
1903	1,500	1
1952	3,250	3
9999 (trailer value)		

5. This problem involves analyzing product sales information. Input consists of the identification number and quantity sold for each of twenty-five products. Write a BASIC program to do the following:

(a) Read the identification numbers and quantities into two arrays. After all data has been read, print the arrays in columns below appropriate headings.

(b) Calculate and print the average of the quantities sold.

(c) Determine the number of products whose sales fall into each of the following categories:

500 or more
250 to 499
100 to 249
0 to 99

Print the results with appropriate headings.

(d) Sort the quantity array into descending order (largest to smallest) using the bubble-sort algorithm. Note that there are two arrays, although only the quantity array is to be sorted. However, whenever two elements of the quantity array are out of order and need to be switched, the corresponding identification numbers must be switched. After the array is sorted, print the two arrays in columns with appropriate headings.

(e) Sort the identification number array into ascending order (smallest to largest). Again note that any exchange of elements in one array must be accompanied by an exchange of corresponding elements in the other array. After the array is sorted, print the two arrays in columns below appropriate headings.

Use the following data to test the program:

Identification Number	Quantity Sold
208	295
137	152
485	825
217	100
945	250
607	435
642	500
735	36
300	163
299	255
435	501
116	75
189	0
218	63
830	617
695	825
708	416
325	99
339	249
418	237
225	712
180	328
925	499
455	240
347	378

6. Two important applications of computers in statistics are tabulation of data and calculation of the mean. Tabulation involves counting the number of items in a set of data that falls into various categories. For example, given a set of test scores, we may wish to count the number of scores that fall between 90 and 100, between 80 and 89, between 70 and 79, and so forth.

The mean is merely the average of the data. For example, given a set of test scores, the mean is calculated by adding the scores and dividing by the number of tests.

Write a BASIC program to read student test-score data into an array, calculate the mean of the test scores, tabulate the test scores, and sort the test scores into descending order.

Input data consists of a student's identification number and a test score for an unknown number of students. Put all input data in DATA statements. The last set of input data consists of 999 for the student's number and zero for the test score. Use this fact to control the input process. Assume that there are no more than 99 sets of input (not counting the final set) and dimension any arrays accordingly.

Prepare the program according to the following specifications:

(a) Read the identification numbers and the test scores into two separate arrays. It is necessary to count the data as it is read to obtain a count of the number of test scores to be processed. Finally, list below appropriate headings the data in the identification number and test-score arrays. At the end, print a statement of the number of test scores in the data.

(b) Accumulate and print the total of the test scores. Calculate and print the mean of the test scores.

(c) Determine the number of scores that fall into each of the following categories:

$$90\text{--}100$$
$$80\text{--}89$$
$$70\text{--}79$$
$$60\text{--}69$$
$$0\text{--}59$$

Print the results with appropriate titles.

(d) Sort the test scores into descending order (largest to smallest). Print a list of the identification numbers and test scores in descending order. Use the bubble-sort algorithm to sort the test-score data. Note that there are two arrays, although only the test-score array is to be sorted. However, when two elements of the test-score array are out of order and need to be switched, the corresponding identification numbers must be switched.

(e) Determine and print the median of the test scores. The median is the middle value of a set of data. Fifty percent of the data values are greater than or equal to the median, and fifty percent are less than or equal to the median. In order to determine the median, the data must first be sorted into ascending or descending order. Then the median is the middle value of the sorted data when there is an odd number of items or the average of two middle values when there is an even number of items. Be sure to make the program sufficiently general to handle both cases.

Use the following input data to test the program:

Identification Number	Test Score	Identification Number	Test Score	Identification Number	Test Score
282	99	283	83	240	73
115	75	116	72	145	74
124	76	123	71	267	74
215	77	114	74	294	91
275	69	287	96	232	75
208	78	201	79	206	75
225	85	242	71	150	76
113	77	119	63	133	83
205	76	142	78	255	70
122	89	219	84	250	77
137	78	248	72	210	70
185	75	173	79	233	80
235	100	261	85	166	71
138	74	265	71	202	61
298	74	281	72	176	81
217	62	139	55	257	72
104	82	141	73	256	14
108	73	266	65	230	73
191	79	110	81	129	89

7. Write a BASIC program to score a twenty-five question true-false test. Input to the program is the correct answers, followed by one set of data for each student giving the student's identification number and his or her answers. The program should print for each student the student's identification number, followed by a listing in adjacent columns of the correct answers, the student's answers, and an X opposite any incorrect answer. At the end of this output, print the percentage of the answers that are correct.

Use the following data to test the program:

Correct answers: FTTTFFTFTTTFTFFFTFTTFFTFFT

Student's Number	Student's Answers
11301	FTTFTFTFTTTFTFFTFTTFFFTFT
11302	FFTTTTFFTTFTTFFTTFTFFTFFF
11303	FTTTFFTFTTTFTFFFTFTTFFTFFT
11304	TFTTFFTFTTTFFFFFFFTTFTTFTT
11305	TTTTFFFFTTFTFFFTFTFFFTFFT
11306	FFFFFFTFTTTTTFFFTFFTFTFFF
11307	TTTFFFFTTTFTFFFTTFTFTTFFT
11308	FTFTFTFTFTFTFTFTFTFTFTFTF
11309	TFTFTFTFTFTFTFTFTFTFTFTFT
11310	TTTTTTTTTTTTTTTTTTTTTTTTT
11311	FFFFFFFFFFFFFFFFFFFFFFFFF
11399 (trailer value)	

8. Using the data in problem 7, write a program that determines the percentage of the students in the class that answered each question cor-

rectly; that is, determine and print the percentage of the students that answered the first question correctly, the percentage that answered the second question correctly, and so forth.

9. Each state has a two-letter abbreviation authorized by the Postal Service. For example, the abbreviation for California is CA and the abbreviation for New York is NY. (See a Zip Code directory for a complete list.)

Write a BASIC program that reads a complete table of state abbreviations and corresponding state names. Use one array for the abbreviations and another array for the names. Then print the arrays below appropriate headings. Next, accept a state abbreviation from the terminal and search the table for the corresponding state's name. Print the abbreviation and the name. Repeat this part of the program until an abbreviation of XX is entered. Supply appropriate input data to test the program.

10. Write a BASIC program that reads an array of twenty names and sorts them into alphabetical order. Each name consists of the last name followed by a comma and then the first name. It will be necessary to separate the names into two arrays before doing the sorting and then to reconstruct the names in the appropriate format after the sorting is completed. Print the sorted array of names. Supply an appropriate list of twenty names to test the program.

11

TWO-DIMENSIONAL ARRAYS AND MATRIX OPERATIONS

The type of array described in Chapter 10 is called a *one-dimensional array.* This is because we think of the data in the array as being organized in one direction, like a column (for example, see Fig. 10–1). BASIC also allows two-dimensional arrays. (Some versions of BASIC permit even higher dimensional arrays.) In this chapter we examine two-dimensional arrays and their use in BASIC. We also discuss special operations for processing array data.

11-1. TWO-DIMENSIONAL ARRAYS

A *two-dimensional array* is often regarded as a table of data organized into rows and columns. Figure 11–1 shows a two-dimensional array of four rows and three columns. In an actual case this data may represent the test scores of four students on three different exams. For example, the data in row one represents the three test scores of student number 1. The score on the first test for this student is 91; this score is found in column 1 or row 1. In row 1, column 2 is the score of this student on the second test (78). The third test score for this student is found in row 1, column 3. Similarly, test scores for the other students are found in the other rows.

Like a one-dimensional array, a two-dimensional array is identified by an array variable. The array variable may be any single letter such as A, S, or Z. (Some versions of BASIC allow any variable to be used as a two-dimensional array variable.) The same array variable cannot be used in a program to identify both a one-dimensional array and a two-

	1	2	3
1	91	78	85
2	95	90	96
3	85	100	89
4	69	75	68

Row Numbers

FIGURE 11-1. A two-dimensional array.

dimensional array. Thus, we cannot use A as an array variable for both types of arrays.

To identify an element of a two-dimensional array, both the row number and the column number of the element must be given; that is, a subscripted variable is formed from the array variable and *two* subscripts. The subscripts are separated by commas and enclosed in parentheses. The first subscript is the row number and the second subscript is the column number. For example, assume that the array in Fig. 11-1 is identified by the variable S. Then the element in row 1, column 2 is referred to by the subscripted variable S(1,2). The element in row 3, column 1 is S(3,1). Figure 11-2 shows the subscripted variables for all elements in this two-dimensional array.

The subscripts for a two-dimensional array may be constants, variables, or more complex numeric expressions. For example, S(I,J) refers to the element in the "Ith row" and "Jth" column. Similarly, S(3,K+2) refers to the element in the third row and column K+2. As with one-dimensional arrays, if the subscript is not a whole number, its value is rounded to locate the array element. (Some versions of BASIC truncate rather than round the subscript.)

We can use a two-dimensional subscripted variable like any other

Column Numbers

	1	2	3
1	(1, 1)	(1, 2)	(1, 3)
2	(2, 1)	(2, 2)	(2, 3)
3	(3, 1)	(3, 2)	(3, 3)
4	(4, 1)	(4, 2)	(4, 3)

Row Numbers

FIGURE 11-2. Subscripted variables for a two-dimensional array.

variable. For example, all of the following statements are acceptable in BASIC:

```
100 INPUT S(1,1),S(1,2),S(1,3)
130 LET A=S(I,J)+S(I,K)
160 PRINT S(X+3,2*Y-1)
190 IF S(I,3)>90 THEN 300
```

Two-dimensional Array Bounds

In the last chapter we saw that a one-dimensional array has an element numbered 0. Similarly, a two-dimensional array has a "0 row" and a "0 column". For example, in the array shown in Fig. 11-2, the "0 row" contains the elements $S(0,0)$, $S(0,1)$, $S(0,2)$ and $S(0,3)$. The "0 column" has the elements $S(0,0)$, $S(1,0)$, $S(2,0)$, $S(3,0)$ and $S(4,0)$. Although these elements exist, they are not used in programming except in certain special situations. (Some versions of BASIC do not provide for a "0 row" and a "0 column".)

Unless we specify otherwise in a program, the maximum row subscript of a two-dimensional array is 10 and the maximum column subscript is also 10. If we need to use subscripts greater than 10, the array must be specified in a DIM statement. For example, assume that the array T is to have 25 rows and 8 columns. The following DIM statement can be used to declare the array:

```
10 DIM T(25,8)
```

The numbers in parentheses are the maximum values of each subscript. The first number gives the maximum row subscript and the second number is the maximum column subscript. The array T in this example is said to be a "25-by-8" array.

Notice that we can always use a DIM statement even if it is not needed. Thus the following statement is valid:

```
20 DIM A(10,10)
```

In fact, most programmers declare all arrays in DIM statements.

We can use one- and two-dimensional arrays in the same program as long as each array is identified by a different array variable. In addition, the same DIM statement can be used for both one- and two-dimensional arrays. For example, the following statement declares three arrays:

```
30 DIM X(20,30),Y(50),Z(5,100)
```

The first array is a 20-by-20 two-dimensional array, the second array is a fifty-element one-dimensional array, and the third array is a 5-by-100 two-dimensional array.

Processing Two-dimensional Arrays

A two-dimensional array is often processed by using a nest of two FOR loops. The control variable of the outer loop is used as one subscript for the array and the control variable of the inner loop is used for the other subscript. With an appropriate initial value, limit, and increment for each loop, part or all of the array can be processed. For example, assume that it is necessary to initialize all of the elements of the 4-by-3 test-score array, S, to zero. The following statements accomplish this:

```
110 FOR I=1 TO 4
120   FOR J=1 TO 3
130     LET S(I,J)=0
140   NEXT J
150 NEXT I
```

In this example the control variable of the outer loop is used in the subscripted variable in the LET statement to indicate the row number. The outer loop is executed with the control variable incremented from one to the maximum number of rows in the array. The control variable of the inner loop indicates the column number. It is incremented from one to the maximum number of columns. Thus, for each execution of the outer loop, the inner loop causes the elements in one row to be set to zero. Since the outer loop is executed four times, once for each row, all elements of the array are set to zero by these statements.

Occasionally it is necessary to find the total of the elements in each row of the array. This can be accomplished most easily by using a one-dimensional array of four elements where each element is used to accumulate the total of a row. Assume that this one-dimensional array is called R. Since this array is used to accumulate totals, it must first be initialized to zero. Then the elements in each row of the test-score array are successively added to the appropriate element of the row-total array. The following statements show how this is done:

```
210 FOR I=1 TO 4
220   LET R(I)=0
230 NEXT I
240 FOR I=1 TO 4
250   FOR J=1 TO 3
260     LET R(I)=R(I)+S(I,J)
270   NEXT J
280 NEXT I
```

When execution of this sequence of statements is completed, the elements of the array R will contain the totals of the elements in each row of the test-score array.

A similar approach can be used to calculate the total of the elements of each column of the test-score array. Assume that C identifies a one-dimensional, three-element array. After setting the elements of C to zero, the following sequence of statements accumulates the total of each column of the test-score array and assigns the results to elements of the array named C:

```
310 FOR J=1 TO 3
320   LET C(J)=0
330 NEXT J
340 FOR J=1 TO 3
350   FOR I=1 TO 4
360     LET C(J)=C(J)+S(I,J)
370   NEXT I
380 NEXT J
```

Notice in this example that the outer loop of the nested FOR loops controls the column number. The inner loop controls the row number and is executed four times for each execution of the outer loop. At the end of the execution of this sequence of statements, the elements of the C array will contain the correct column totals.

In searching a two-dimensional array for a specific value, we include a test for the value in the nested FOR loops. For example, assume that it is necessary to print the student number and test number for any student who scored 90 or more on any test. The following statements accomplish this:

```
410 FOR I=1 TO 4
420   FOR J=1,3
430     IF S(I,J)<90 THEN 450
440     PRINT I,J
450   NEXT J
460 NEXT I
```

In this example, the PRINT statement is executed only if the student's test score is 90 or above. The current values of the control variables for each FOR loop are printed and indicate the student number and test number.

Frequently when we search a two-dimensional array, we search one column (or row) for a specific value and use the information from the other columns (or rows). For example, assume that we wish to calculate and print the average of the second and third test scores for each student who scored 90 or above on the first test. The following statements accomplish this:

```
510 FOR I=1 TO 4
```

```
520   IF S(I,1)<90 THEN 550
530   LET A=(S(I,2)+S(I,3))/2
540   PRINT I,A
550 NEXT I
```

In the IF statement, S(I,1) refers to the first column of the Ith row of the array. Hence, each time through the loop, we check the first score to see whether it is less than 90. If this is not the case, we compute the average of the other two scores for that student and print the student's number and average.

We can sort the elements in one row or column of a two-dimensional array. If it is necessary to maintain the correspondence between elements in a row or column during the sorting process, then any time two elements in one column (or row) are switched, the corresponding elements in the other columns (or rows) must be switched. For example, the following sequence of statements sorts the first column of the test-score array into descending order:

```
610 FOR K=3 TO 1 STEP -1
620   FOR I=1 TO K
630     IF S(I,1)>=S(I+1,1) THEN 690
640     FOR J=1 TO 3
650       LET T=S(I,J)
660       LET S(I,J)=S(I+1,J)
670       LET S(I+1,J)=T
680     NEXT J
690   NEXT I
700 NEXT K
```

The sorting is done on the first column since the second subscript in each subscripted variable used in the IF statement is one. The innermost loop switches all the elements of two rows if the elements in the first column are out of order with respect to each other.

Input and Output of Two-dimensional Array Data

Input and output of a two-dimensional array can be accomplished by listing the subscripted variables for the array in an INPUT, READ, or PRINT statement. For example, assume X is a 2-by-3 array. The following statements can be used to accept input data for X and then to print the array:

```
10 INPUT X(1,1),X(1,2),X(1,3),X(2,1),X(2,2),X(2,3)
20 PRINT X(1,1);X(1,2);X(1,3);X(2,1);X(2,2);X(2,3)
```

The problem with this technique is that if the array is large, the list of subscripted variables will be long. Because of this the usual approach is to use some sort of looping technique. For example, assume that the data for the 4-by-3 test-score array, S, is to be entered at the terminal one row at a time. The following loop can be used to accept the data:

```
100 FOR I=1 TO 4
110   INPUT S(I,1),S(I,2),S(I,3)
120 NEXT I
```

Execution of this loop causes the INPUT statement to be executed four separate times. Each time the statement is executed, a question mark prompt is displayed on the terminal. The terminal operator must then enter three test scores after each prompt. Each set of input data is stored in one row of the array.

We can use nested FOR loops for the input operation. The following statements show how this is done for the test-score array:

```
200 FOR I=1 TO 4
210   FOR J=1 TO 3
220     INPUT S(I,J)
230   NEXT J
240 NEXT I
```

In this case the INPUT statement is executed twelve times. Hence, twelve prompts will be displayed on the terminal. Following each prompt, the terminal operator must enter one test score. The first three scores entered must be the data for the first row, then the data for the second row must be entered, and so forth.

Nested FOR loops are often used to read data for a two-dimensional array using a READ statement and DATA statements. For example, the following statements can be used to read the test-score data:

```
110 FOR I=1 TO 4
120   FOR J=1 TO 3
130     READ S(I,J)
140   NEXT J
150 NEXT I
      .
      .
      .
900 DATA 91,78,85,95,90,96
910 DATA 85,100,89,69,75,68
```

Notice that the data is recorded in the DATA statements in order by rows since this is the order in which the data is read in the nested FOR loops.

To print a two-dimensional array we can use a FOR loop. For example, the following statements print the test-score array with each row on a separate line:

```
200 FOR I=1 TO 4
210    PRINT S(I,1),S(I,2),S(I,3)
220 NEXT I
```

We can also use nested FOR loops as in the following example:

```
300 FOR I=1 TO 4
310    FOR J=1 TO 3
320       PRINT S(I,J)
330    NEXT J
340 NEXT I
```

In this case, however, the elements of the array are printed one per line on twelve lines.

To print a two-dimensional array with one row per line using nested FOR loops requires a special technique. Recall from Chapter 6 that a comma or a semicolon at the end of a PRINT statement causes the next value printed to appear on the same line as the previous value. We can use this fact in the last example above to print the data in rows. We start by modifying statement 320 as follows:

```
320 PRINT S(I,J),
```

Notice that a comma has been added to the PRINT statement after the subscripted variable. Then each time the PRINT statement is executed, the array element is printed on the same line as the previous element provided there is room on the line. Once a line is full, the next value is automatically printed at the beginning of the next line. In this case, five values are printed on each line because there are five print zones. (If a semicolon is used instead of a comma, the values are printed closer together and more data is printed on a line.)

This approach still does not print one row per line unless there are five elements in each row. However, by including a PRINT statement that prints nothing between the two NEXT statements, we obtain the desired result. This is shown in the program in Fig. 11–3. In this program, the comma in the PRINT statement causes each value in a row to be printed on the same line as the previous value. But after a complete row is printed, the PRINT statement at line 240 causes the printer to advance to the next line. Thus, each row is printed on a separate line.

```
100 DIM S(4,3)
110 FOR I=1 TO 4
120    FOR J=1 TO 3
130       READ S(I,J)
140    NEXT J
150 NEXT I
200 FOR I=1 TO 4
210    FOR J=1 TO 3
220       PRINT S(I,J),
230    NEXT J
240    PRINT
250 NEXT I
900 DATA 91,78,85,95,90,96
910 DATA 85,100,89,69,75,68
999 END
```

(a) The program

91	78	85
95	90	96
85	100	89
69	75	68

(b) The output

FIGURE 11-3.   A program with two-dimensional array
input and output.

There are other approaches to the input and output of array data, but the techniques can be quite complex. In general, it is best to use the simplest approach that works so that the data is processed in the desired order.

An Illustrative Program

To illustrate the use of two-dimensional arrays in a program, consider the problem of tabulating test scores. Assume that there are twelve students in a class and each student took four tests. The problem is to count for each test the number of students who scored between 90 and 100, between 80 and 89, between 70 and 79, and less than 70. Figure 11-4 shows a program that accomplishes this.

In this program, S is a 12-by-4 array of test scores. Statements 200 through 240 read the data for S from the DATA statements. The 4-by-4 array T is used to keep count of the number of test scores in each category. The first row of this array is used for the number of scores between 90 and 100 on each of the four tests, the second row is used for the scores between 80 and 89, and so on.

```
100 DIM S(12,4),T(4,4)
200 FOR I=1 TO 12
210    FOR J=1 TO 4
220      READ S(I,J)
230    NEXT J
240 NEXT I
250 FOR I=1 TO 4
260    FOR J=1 TO 4
270      LET T(I,J)=0
280    NEXT J
290 NEXT I
300 FOR I=1 TO 12
310    FOR J=1 TO 4
320      IF S(I,J)<90 THEN 350
330      LET T(1,J)=T(1,J)+1
340      GO TO 420
350      IF S(I,J)<80 THEN 380
360      LET T(2,J)=T(2,J)+1
370      GO TO 420
380      IF S(I,J)<70 THEN 410
390      LET T(3,J)=T(3,J)+1
400      GO TO 420
410      LET T(4,J)=T(4,J)+1
420    NEXT J
430 NEXT I
500 FOR I=1 TO 4
510    FOR J=1 TO 4
520      PRINT T(I,J);
530    NEXT J
540    PRINT
550 NEXT I
901 DATA 74,84,86,67,100,94,95,89
902 DATA 82,87,67,91,35,48,52,63
903 DATA 65,84,75,72,91,84,72,95
904 DATA 72,78,81,69,84,75,80,79
905 DATA 70,69,72,73,55,62,70,38
906 DATA 90,85,91,82,75,81,78,72
999 END
```

(a) The program

```
3  1  2  2
2  6  3  2
4  2  5  4
3  3  2  4
```

(b) The output

FIGURE 11-4.   A test-score tabulation program.

Initially, the elements of T must be set to zero. This is accomplished in statements 250 through 290. Then the nested FOR loops in statements 300 through 430 cause the elements of S to be examined one at a time. When it is determined that the score for a student on a test falls in a particular range, one is added to the appropriate element of T. After all of the counts are accumulated, statements 500 through 550 cause the elements of T to be printed.

*Two-dimensional String Arrays

Most versions of BASIC allow two-dimensional arrays of string data. In this case the array name must be followed by a dollar sign. For example, the following DIM statement declares a 3-by-5 string array:

```
10 DIM T$(3,5)
```

We can use a two-dimensional subscripted string variable in a string expression. For example, the following statements are valid:

```
30 LET T$(2,4)="HELP"
60 INPUT T$(I,J)
90 IF T$(K+1,3)=T$(K-1,3) THEN 200
```

In general, all of the techniques for processing two-dimensional numeric arrays can be adapted to two-dimensional string arrays.

*11-2. MATRIX OPERATIONS

An array is sometimes called a *matrix*. In general, a matrix is a group of data that is organized into rows and columns. The two-dimensional test-score array in Fig. 11–1 is organized this way and can be regarded as a matrix. A one-dimensional array is also a matrix because it can be regarded as composed of a number of rows and *one* column.

Many versions of BASIC provide special statements that perform various operations on an entire matrix. These are called the MAT or matrix operations. The characteristics of these operations vary from one version of BASIC to another. In this section we describe the matrix operations for one common version of BASIC.[†]

[†]The operations described in this section are available in BASIC-PLUS on the DEC PDP 11 computer and in related versions of BASIC.

*Elementary Matrix Operations

To illustrate the characteristics of the matrix operations, assume that S is a 4-by-3 matrix (i.e., array). If we wish to initialize all of the elements of S to 0, we can write the following nested FOR loops:

```
110 FOR I=1 TO 4
120   FOR J=1 TO 3
130     LET S(I,J)=0
140   NEXT J
150 NEXT I
```

However, with a matrix operation we can achieve the same result with one statement as follows:

```
110 MAT S=ZER
```

The effect of this statement is to set all elements of the matrix S (except the elements in the 0-row and 0-column) to zero.

The syntax of the matrix zeroing statement is as follows:

ln MAT *array variable* = ZER

The statement must begin with the keyword MAT. An array variable without a subscript must appear to the left of the equal sign. For example, the following statement sets all of the elements of the matrix T to zero:

```
250 MAT T=ZER
```

The matrix zeroing statement illustrates the general characteristics of the matrix operations. All matrix operations accomplish in one statement what normally requires several statements. Each matrix operation statement begins with the keyword MAT. The matrix operation affects all elements in the matrix *except* the elements in the 0-row and 0-column. These elements are not changed by any of the matrix operations.

A matrix operation can be used with a one-dimensional or a two-dimensional array. For example, assume that X is a one-dimensional array with twenty elements. The following matrix operation statement sets each element of X to zero:

```
210 MAT X=ZER
```

In general, any array that is processed by a matrix operation should be declared in a DIM statement. This is done so that the number of elements affected by the operation is explicitly stated in the program. It is possible to leave out the DIM statement for some arrays when using the matrix operations. However, the rules for determining the size of the array that is used in the matrix operation are complex, and this situation should be avoided.

The matrix zeroing statement sets all elements of a matrix to zero. We can also set all elements to one with a matrix operation. The syntax of the statement that does this is as follows:

ln MAT *array variable* = CON

For example, the following statement initializes all elements of S to one:

120 MAT S=CON

If we wish to copy one matrix into another, we can use a matrix assignment statement. The syntax of this statement is as follows:

ln MAT *array variable* = *array variable*

For example, the following statement copies the elements of X into Y:

220 MAT Y=X

Whenever a matrix assignment statement is used, the two arrays must be the same size.

*Matrix Input

Input of matrix data can be accomplished with the MAT INPUT or MAT READ statements. The MAT INPUT statement accepts input data for a matrix from the terminal. The syntax of this statement is as follows:

ln MAT INPUT *list of array variables separated by commas*

For example, the following statement can be used to accept the data for the 4-by-3 test-score matrix S:

110 MAT INPUT S

When the MAT INPUT statement is executed, a question mark prompt is displayed on the terminal. Following the prompt, the terminal operator must enter all the data for the matrix. The data must be entered in order by rows with the elements separated by commas. For example, the data for S would be entered as follows:

? 91,78,95,95,90,96,85,100,89,69,75,68

Notice that the first three values are the elements for the first row; then comes the data for the second row, and so forth. If the end of the terminal line is reached before all data has been entered, the LINE FEED key (*not* the RETURN key) should be pressed. The data entry is then continued on the next line. Notice that data is not entered for the 0-row and 0-column since the elements in this row and column are not affected by any of the matrix operations.

We can use the MAT INPUT statement for one-dimensional array input. For example, the following statement accepts input data for the five-element array Z:

210 MAT INPUT Z

After the question mark prompt is displayed, all five elements of Z must be entered separated by commas.

We can list more than one array variable in a MAT INPUT statement. For example, the following statement can be used to accept input for both S and Z:

220 MAT INPUT S,Z

All data for S must be entered followed by the data for Z. We can also use the MAT INPUT statement for one- and two-dimensional string arrays. For example, assume that T$ is a 3-by-5 string array. The following statement can be used to accept input data for the array:

230 MAT INPUT T$

Each input element entered must be a string and the data must be entered in order by rows.

Matrix data can be read from DATA statements using the MAT READ statement. The syntax of the MAT READ statement is as follows:

ln MAT READ *list of array variables separated by commas*

For example, the following statements can be used to read the data for the test-score matrix:

```
110 MAT READ S
900 DATA 91,78,95,95,90,96
910 DATA 85,100,89,69,75,68
```

The data in the DATA statements is in order by rows. This is required with the MAT READ statement. Notice also that data is not provided for the 0-row and 0-column.

As with the MAT INPUT statement, the MAT READ statement can be used to read one-dimensional array data, multiple arrays, and string arrays. Thus, if Z and S are one- and two-dimensional arrays, respectively, and T$ is a string array, the following statement is valid:

```
240 MAT READ Z,S,T$
```

The corresponding DATA statements must contain all of the data for Z, followed by all of the data for S, and then the string data for T$.

*Matrix Output

Matrix output can be printed with the MAT PRINT statement.[†] The syntax of this statement is as follows:

ln MAT PRINT *array variable*

For example, to print the test score matrix, we can use the following statement:

```
120 MAT PRINT S
```

When this statement is executed, all of the data in the matrix S (except the data in the 0-row and 0-column) is printed. Notice that there can be only one array variable in the MAT PRINT statement.

When there is no punctuation in the MAT PRINT statement, each element is printed on a separate line. Thus, if S is a 4-by-3 matrix, twelve lines are printed by the previous statement. The first three lines contain the data from the first row, then comes the data from the second row, and so forth.

To print the data in tabular form with one row per line, the array variable in the MAT PRINT statement should be followed by a comma or a semicolon. For example, either of the following statements could be used:

```
120 MAT PRINT S,
120 MAT PRINT S;
```

A comma causes the data to be printed with one element in each print

---

[†]Some versions of BASIC also have a MAT PRINT USING statement.

```
100 DIM S(4,3)
110 MAT READ S
120 MAT PRINT S,
900 DATA 91,78,95,95,90,96
910 DATA 85,100,89,69,75,68
999 END
```

(a) The program

91	78	95
95	90	96
85	100	89
69	75	68

(b) The output

FIGURE 11-5. A matrix input and output program.

zone (i.e., five elements per line). A semicolon causes the data to be printed as close together as possible.

Figure 11-5 shows a program that contains matrix imput and output. The input data is read from DATA statements using a MAT READ statement. The output is printed using a MAT PRINT statement. Notice that a comma is used to print the data with one row per line. If a semicolon were used instead of a comma, the data would be printed closer together.

The MAT PRINT statement can also be used to print one-dimensional arrays and string arrays. For example, to print the five elements of the one-dimensional array Z in a column, we can use the following statement:

```
130 MAT PRINT Z
```

Matrix input and output statements can be used in programs that do not involve other matrix operations. This can often simplify the input and output steps in a program that requires one- and two-dimensional arrays.

*An Illustrative Program

Figure 11-4 showed a program that tabulated test scores. Several of the steps in this program can be simplified by using matrix operations. Statements 200 through 240 can be replaced by a MAT READ

281

statement. A matrix zeroing statement can be used in place of statements 250 through 290. The output steps in statements 500 through 550 can be accomplished with a MAT PRINT statement. These modifications are shown in the program in Fig. 11–6. Notice that the output is the same as for the previous version of the program.

```
100 DIM S(12,4),T(4,4)
200 MAT READ S
250 MAT T=ZER
300 FOR I=1 TO 12
310    FOR J=1 TO 4
320       IF S(I,J)<90 THEN 350
330       LET T(1,J)=T(1,J)+1
340       GO TO 420
350       IF S(I,J)<80 THEN 380
360       LET T(2,J)=T(2,J)+1
370       GO TO 420
380       IF S(I,J)<70 THEN 410
390       LET T(3,J)=T(3,J)+1
400       GO TO 420
410       LET T(4,J)=T(4,J)+1
420    NEXT J
430 NEXT I
500 MAT PRINT T;
901 DATA 74,84,86,67,100,94,95,89
902 DATA 82,87,67,91,35,48,52,63
903 DATA 65,84,75,72,91,84,72,95
904 DATA 72,78,81,69,84,75,80,79
905 DATA 70,69,72,73,55,62,70,38
906 DATA 90,85,91,82,75,81,78,72
999 END

(a) The program

3  1  2  2

2  6  3  2

4  2  5  4

3  3  2  4

(b) The output
```

FIGURE 11–6.   The test-score tabulation program using matrix operations.

*Other Matrix Operations

A number of matrix operations are used for various mathematical computations. To understand these operations fully, the programmer should be familiar with elementary matrix algebra. In this subsection we explain and illustrate these operations.

Besides setting the elements of a matrix to zero or one, we can also initialize a matrix to the identity matrix. An identity matrix has ones along the main diagonal and zeros elsewhere. The syntax of the statement that accomplishes this is as follows:

$$ln \text{ MAT } array\ variable = \text{IDN}$$

For example, to initialize the matrix X to the identity matrix, we use the following statement:

```
110 MAT X=IDN
```

Only a square matrix (i.e., a matrix with the same number of rows and columns) can be initialized to the identity matrix. Figure 11-7 shows a sample program that initializes and prints an identity matrix.

The corresponding elements of two matrices can be added or subtracted and the result assigned to a third matrix using special matrix statements. The syntax of these statements is as follows:

$$ln \text{ MAT } array\ variable = array\ variable + array\ variable$$

$$ln \text{ MAT } array\ variable = array\ variable - array\ variable$$

```
100 DIM X(4,4)
110 MAT X=IDN
120 PRINT "IDENTITY MATRIX"
130 MAT PRINT X;
999 END

(a) The program

IDENTITY MATRIX
 1  0  0  0

 0  1  0  0

 0  0  1  0

 0  0  0  1

(b) The output
```

FIGURE 11-7.   A program to print an identity matrix.

For example, to add the elements of the matrices A and B and assign the results to the matrix C, we use the following statement:

130 MAT C=A+B

Similarly, if the difference between the elements of A and B must be computed and assigned to D, we use the statement:

140 MAT D=A-B

Figure 11-8 shows a sample program that includes these operations. Note that whenever matrix addition or subtraction is used, the sizes of all matrices must be the same; that is, the matrices that are added or subtracted and the matrix to which the result of the operation is assigned must all have the same number of rows and columns.

All elements of a matrix can be multiplied by the same value by using a scalar multiplication statement. The syntax of this statement is as follows:

ln MAT *array variable* = (*numeric expression*) * *array variable*

The numeric expression in parentheses can be a constant, a variable, or a more complex numeric expression. For example, to double the elements of the matrix A and assign the result to the matrix B, we can use the following statement:

120 MAT B=(2)*A

Figure 11-9 shows the effect of this statement in a program. Notice that A and B must be the same size (i.e., they must have the same number of rows and columns). The following are other examples of scalar multiplication:

210 MAT C=(K)*B
220 MAT C=(K+5)*C

Two matrices can be multiplied using a special matrix operation. Matrix multiplication does *not* involve multiplication of the corresponding elements of two matrices; rather, it involves a special form of multiplication.[†] Figure 11-10 shows an example of matrix multiplication. Notice that in matrix multiplication the number of columns in the

---

[†]Most college algebra texts explain matrix multiplication in detail.

```
100 DIM A(2,3),B(2,3),C(2,3),D(2,3)
110 MAT READ A
120 MAT READ B
130 MAT C=A+B
140 MAT D=A-B
150 PRINT "MATRIX A"
160 MAT PRINT A,
170 PRINT "MATRIX B"
180 MAT PRINT B,
190 PRINT "MATRIX C=A+B"
200 MAT PRINT C,
210 PRINT "MATRIX D=A-B"
220 MAT PRINT D,
900 DATA 5,7,9,2,4,6
901 DATA 3,5,7,6,4,2
999 END
```

(a) The program

```
MATRIX A
 5              7              9

 2              4              6


MATRIX B
 3              5              7

 6              4              2


MATRIX C=A+B
 8             12             16

 8              8              8


MATRIX D=A-B
 2              2              2

-4              0              4
```

(b) The output

FIGURE 11-8.   A program with matrix addition and sub-
              traction.

```
100 DIM A(2,3),B(2,3)
110 MAT READ A
120 MAT B=(2)*A
130 PRINT "MATRIX A"
140 MAT PRINT A,
150 PRINT "MATRIX B=(2)*A"
160 MAT PRINT B,
900 DATA 5,7,9,2,4,6
999 END
```

(a) The program

```
MATRIX A
  5              7              9

  2              4              6


MATRIX B=(2)*A
  10            14            18

  4              8             12
```

(b) The output

FIGURE 11-9.   A program with scalar multiplication.

$$\begin{pmatrix} 2 & 4 & 6 \\ 1 & 3 & 5 \end{pmatrix} \times \begin{pmatrix} 1 & 5 \\ 4 & 2 \\ 3 & 6 \end{pmatrix}$$

$$= \begin{pmatrix} 2 \times 1 + 4 \times 4 + 6 \times 3 & 2 \times 5 + 4 \times 2 + 6 \times 6 \\ 1 \times 1 + 3 \times 4 + 5 \times 3 & 1 \times 5 + 3 \times 2 + 5 \times 6 \end{pmatrix}$$

$$= \begin{pmatrix} 2 + 16 + 18 & 10 + 8 + 36 \\ 1 + 12 + 15 & 5 + 6 + 30 \end{pmatrix}$$

$$= \begin{pmatrix} 36 & 54 \\ 28 & 41 \end{pmatrix}$$

FIGURE 11-10.   Matrix multiplication.

first matrix must be the same as the number of rows in the second matrix (i.e., the matrices must be *conformable*). The product contains the same number of rows as the first matrix and the same number of columns as the second matrix.

The syntax of the matrix multiplication statement in BASIC is as follows:

In MAT *array variable = array variable * array variable*

For example, to multiply matrices A and B and assign the result to C, we use the following statement:

130 MAT C=A*B

Figure 11-11 shows a sample program that includes this statement.

```
100 DIM A(2,3),B(3,2),C(2,2)
110 MAT READ A
120 MAT READ B
130 MAT C=A*B
140 PRINT "MATRIX A"
150 MAT PRINT A,
160 PRINT "MATRIX B"
170 MAT PRINT B,
180 PRINT "MATRIX C=A*B"
190 MAT PRINT C,
900 DATA 2,4,6,1,3,5
901 DATA 1,5,4,2,3,6
999 END
```

(a) The program

```
MATRIX A
  2           4           6

  1           3           5


MATRIX B
  1           5

  4           2

  3           6


MATRIX C=A*B
 36          54

 28          41
```

(b) The output

FIGURE 11-11. A program with matrix multiplication.

Notice that A is a 2-by-3 matrix, B is a 3-by-2 matrix, and C is a 2-by-2 matrix.

The *transpose* of a matrix is the matrix whose columns are the same as the rows of the original matrix. For example, consider the following matrix:

$$\begin{pmatrix} 2 & 4 & 6 \\ 1 & 3 & 5 \end{pmatrix}$$

The transpose of this matrix is as follows:

$$\begin{pmatrix} 2 & 1 \\ 4 & 3 \\ 6 & 5 \end{pmatrix}$$

To form the transpose of a matrix in BASIC, we use the TRN function. For example, the following statement assigns the transpose of matrix A to the matrix B:

```
120 MAT B=TRN(A)
```

This statement is used in the sample program in Fig. 11–12.

The *inverse* of a matrix is the matrix that, when multiplied by the original matrix, yields the identity matrix. Only a square matrix (i.e., a matrix with the same number of rows and columns) can have an inverse and then only if certain other conditions hold. In BASIC the INV function is used to form the inverse of a matrix. For example, the following statement finds the inverse of the matrix A and assigns it to the matrix B:

```
120 MAT B=INV(A)
```

Figure 11–13 shows a program that uses this statement to find the inverse of a matrix and then multiplies the result by the original matrix to obtain the identity matrix.

Matrix inversion can be used to solve systems of simultaneous linear equations. For example, consider the following equations:

$$2x_1 + 1x_2 = 5$$
$$3x_2 - 2x_2 = 4$$

These equations can be written in the following form:

```
100 DIM A(2,3),B(3,2)
110 MAT READ A
120 MAT B=TRN(A)
130 PRINT "MATRIX A"
140 MAT PRINT A;
150 PRINT "MATRIX B=TRN(A)"
160 MAT PRINT B;
900 DATA 2,4,6,1,3,5
999 END
```

(a) The program

```
MATRIX A
 2  4  6

 1  3  5


MATRIX B=TRN(A)
 2  1

 4  3

 6  5
```

(b) The output

FIGURE 11-12.   A program to find the transpose of a
matrix.

$$\begin{pmatrix} 2 & 1 \\ 3 & -2 \end{pmatrix} \begin{pmatrix} x_1 \\ x_2 \end{pmatrix} = \begin{pmatrix} 5 \\ 4 \end{pmatrix}$$

Alternatively, if A is the 2-by-2 matrix of coefficients, X is the 2-by-1 matrix of unknowns, and B is the 2-by-1 matrix of right-hand side values, the equations can be written as follows:

$$A*X = B$$

If we multiply both sides of this equation by the inverse of A, we obtain the following:

$$INV(A)*A*X = INV(A)*B$$

```
100 DIM A(2,2),B(2,2),C(2,2)
110 MAT READ A
120 MAT B=INV(A)
130 MAT C=A*B
140 PRINT "MATRIX A"
150 MAT PRINT A,
160 PRINT "MATRIX B=INV(A)"
170 MAT PRINT B,
180 PRINT "MATRIX C=A*B"
190 MAT PRINT C,
900 DATA 2,1,3,2
999 END
```

(a) The program

```
MATRIX A
  2              1

  3              2


MATRIX B=INV(A)
  2             -1

 -3              2


MATRIX C=A*B
  1              0

  0              1
```

(b) The output

FIGURE 11–13.   A program to find the inverse of a
matrix.

However, the inverse of A times A is the identity matrix and the identity matrix times X is X. Hence, we have the following:

$$X = INV(A)*B$$

We can use this final equation to find the solution to a system of simultaneous linear equations. Figure 11–14 shows a program that does this. Notice in this program that it is first necessary to assign the inverse of A to another matrix, C, and then to multiply C by B. This is because

```
100 DIM A(2,2),X(2),B(2),C(2,2)
110 MAT READ A
120 MAT READ B
130 MAT C=INV(A)
140 MAT X=C*B
150 PRINT "MATRIX A"
160 MAT PRINT A,
170 PRINT "MATRIX B"
180 MAT PRINT B
190 PRINT "MATRIX X=INV(B)*A"
200 MAT PRINT X
900 DATA 2,1,3,-2
901 DATA 5,4
999 END
```

(a) The program

```
MATRIX A
 2             1

 3            -2



MATRIX B
 5
 4

MATRIX X=INV(B)*A
 2
 1
```

(b) The output

FIGURE 11-14.   A program to solve a system of simultaneous linear equations.

most versions of BASIC do not allow more than one matrix operation in a single statement.

The matrix operations discussed in this subsection can be used in a wide variety of problems. Their use can often greatly simplify complex processing steps.

REVIEW QUESTIONS

1. What are the differences between one-dimensional arrays and two-dimensional arrays?

2. Consider the two-dimensional array, S, shown in Fig. 11–1. Assume that the value of I is 2, J is 3, and K is 4. What is the value of each of the following subscripted variables?

    (a) S(3,2)

    (b) S(K,1)

    (c) S(I,J)

    (d) S(I*J–4,K/2)

3. Write one DIM statement to declare a 5-by-15 array and a 100-by-2 array.

4. Write a sequence of statements to set each of the elements of the third row of the 10-by-5 array W to one.

5. Write a sequence of statements to find the total of all of the elements of the 4-by-12 array X.

6. Consider the 100-by-2 array Y. Write a sequence of statements that counts the number of corresponding elements in the two columns of the array that are equal.

7. Write a sequence of statements to print the elements of the 10-by-4 array Z with the last row on the first line, the next-to-last row on the second line, and so forth.

8. Consider the program shown in Fig. 11–3. Assume that the statements at lines 110 and 120 were switched and the statements at lines 140 and 150 were switched. What output would be printed by the resulting program?

9. Assume that A and B are each 10-by-4 arrays. Write a matrix operation statement to do each of the following:

    (a) Initialize the elements of A to one.

    (b) Assign the elements of A to B.

    (c) Print the elements of B in a column.

    (d) Read the elements of A from DATA statements.

    (e) Initialize the elements of B to zero.

    (f) Print the elements of A in rows.

10. Assume that the following DIM statement appears in a program:

```
100 DIM C(10,10),D(10,5),E(10,5),F(10,5),G(5,10),H(10,10)
```

Write a matrix operation statement to do each of the following:

    (a) Add the elements of D and E and assign the result to F.

    (b) Multiply each of the elements of F by 5 and assign the result to E.

    (c) Set C to the identity matrix.

(d) Form the transpose of D, assigning the result to G.

(e) Multiply E by G and assign the result to C.

(f) Form the inverse of C, assigning the result to H.

PROGRAMMING PROBLEMS

1. A company sells five products with four models for each product. The following table gives the unit price of each model of each product:

Model Number

		1	2	3	4
	1	10.50	16.25	21.00	23.75
	2	4.95	5.95	6.50	6.95
Product number	3	.38	.47	.59	.62
	4	8.75	8.95	9.10	9.22
	5	1.52	1.75	1.95	2.25

Write a BASIC program to read the pricing table from DATA statements and store the data in a two-dimensional array. Then print the pricing table with appropriate headings. Next, accept from the terminal a customer number, product number, model number, and quantity ordered. From this information, compute the sales amount by multiplying the unit price for the product from the table by the quantity ordered. Print the customer number, product number, model number, quantity ordered, unit price, and sales amount.

To test the program, use the data in the pricing table above and the following sales data:

Customer Number	Product Number	Model Number	Quantity Ordered
10113	2	1	10
11305	5	4	35
11412	1	1	100
11516	2	3	125
11603	4	2	75
11625	4	1	65
11735	3	3	50
11895	1	3	130
11899	2	4	20
11907	5	2	82
00000 (trailer value)			

2. The data for problem 6 in Chapter 10 consists of student's identification numbers and test scores. The first digit of a student's identification number indicates his or her year in school (1 = freshman, 2 = sophomore). A tabulation of test scores by score category and school year is needed. The score categories are 90 to 100, 80 to 89, 70 to 79, 60 to 69, and 0 to 59.

Write a BASIC program to create a two-dimensional array of five rows and two columns where the rows represent the score categories and the columns indicate the year in school; that is, the array should appear as follows:

	Freshman	*Sophomore*
90–100		
80–89		
70–79		
60–69		
0–59		

Tabulate the number of scores that fall into each classification. Print the results of the tabulation with appropriate headings. After the data has been tabulated, determine the total number of freshmen and the total number of sophomores who took the test. Print the results.

Use the data for problem 6 of Chapter 10 to test the program. (Hint: To obtain the year in school, divide the student's identification number by 100 and use the INT function.)

3. The data gathered from scouting a football team can be analyzed by a computer. In a simple system, assume that four characteristics of each offensive play are recorded by the scout. The characteristics are the down, the yards to go for a first down, the type of play (where 0 identifies a pass and 1 indicates a run), and the number of yards gained or lost (where a negative value indicates lost yardage). The information for each play can be recorded in one row of a two-dimensional array. The first element in the row is the down, the second element is the yards to go, the third is the play, and the final element is the yards gained or lost. In all, twenty-five plays are to be analyzed.

Write a BASIC program to read the scouting data from DATA statements and to store it in a two-dimensional array. Print the scouting data in columns with appropriate headings. Then find and print the answers to the following questions:

(a) What was the average yards gained per play?

(b) What was the average yards gained per running play?

(c) Of all running plays, what percent gained yardage, what percent lost yardage, and what percent gained zero yardage?

(d) What was the average yards gained per passing play?

(e) What percent of the plays were passes?

(f) What percent of first-down plays were passes?

(g) What percent of second-down plays were passes?

(h) What percent of third-down plays were passes?

(i) Of third-down plays with less than five yards to go, what percent were passes?

Use the following data to test the program:

Down	Yards to Go	Play	Gain (+) or Loss (−)
1	10	Run	+4
2	6	Pass	0
3	6	Pass	+8
1	10	Run	−3
2	13	Run	+8
1	10	Run	0
2	10	Pass	+8
3	2	Pass	+15
1	10	Pass	+12
1	10	Run	−15
2	25	Pass	+5
3	20	Pass	0
1	10	Run	+2
2	8	Run	+4
3	4	Run	+1
1	10	Pass	0
2	10	Run	+6
3	4	Pass	+12
1	10	Pass	0
2	10	Run	+6
3	4	Run	+2
1	10	Pass	−3
2	13	Run	−5
1	10	Run	+2
2	10	Run	−16

4. An airline flies between six cities. Whether or not there is a direct flight from one city to another is indicated in the following table:

		To:					
		1	2	3	4	5	6
	1	0	1	1	0	0	1
	2	1	0	1	0	0	1
From:	3	0	0	0	1	0	0
	4	0	1	0	0	1	0
	5	0	1	0	1	0	0
	6	0	1	0	0	1	0

On the left and across the top are the numbers of the cities. If there is a 1 at the intersection of a row and a column, there is a direct flight from the city marked on the left to the city indicated at the top. A 0 indicates that there is no direct flight between the two cities.

This table can be used to determine whether a flight pattern is possible. A flight pattern consists of five digits indicating the cities between which the customer wishes to fly. For example, the pattern 1, 3, 4, 2, 6 indicates that the customer wishes to fly from city 1 to city 3, then from city 3 to city 4, then to city 2, and finally to city 6. If the customer has fewer than five cities in his or her flight pattern, the remaining digits are zeros. Thus, a pattern of 6, 2, 0, 0, 0 indicates that the customer wishes to fly from city 6 to city 2 and does not wish to continue beyond that.

Write a BASIC program to read the data for the flight table from DATA statements. Then print the table with appropriate headings. Next, accept from the terminal a customer number and a requested flight pattern. Determine whether the flight pattern is possible. Print the customer's number, his or her requested flight pattern, and a statement as to whether a ticket may be issued for the desired pattern.

Use the following input data to test the program:

Customer Number	Flight Pattern
10123	1,3,4,2,6
11305	6,2,0,0,0
13427	4,2,3,2,0
18211	5,2,5,0,0
19006	3,4,2,1,2
20831	6,5,4,2,6
21475	3,2,0,0,0
22138	4,3,6,2,1
24105	1,3,4,2,4
24216	6,5,2,3,1
25009	3,4,2,5,0
00000 (trailer value)	

5. A telephone company charges varying rates for a long-distance call between two cities. The rate charged depends on the time of day the call is made and how the call is placed. There is a fixed charge for the first three minutes and a charge for each additional minute or fraction thereof. The following table outlines the rate structure:

How Placed	Time of Day			
	Day	Evening	Night	Weekend
Direct-dialed	.79	.58	.52	.49
	.26	.23	.21	.15
Station-to-station — operator assisted	.95	.73	.64	.57
	.30	.25	.24	.21
Person-to-person	1.55	1.55	1.55	1.55
	.52	.52	.52	.52

For any given time of day and method of placing the call, two figures are shown. The top figure represents the charge for the first three minutes or fraction thereof; the bottom figure represents the charge for each additional minute or fraction thereof. For example, a night call that is station-to-station, operator-assisted is charged $.64 for the first three minutes, and $.24 for each additional minute.

Write a BASIC program to read and print the rate table using two two-dimensional arrays. One array should be used for the charges for the first three minutes and the other array for the charges for each additional minute. Then accept from the terminal a customer's number, a "how placed" code (1 for direct-dialed, 2 for station-to-station, 3 for person-to-person), a "time of call" code (1 for day, 2 for evening, 3 for night, and 4 for weekend), and the length of the call. From this information determine the charge for the customer. Print the customer's number, the length of the call, and the charge.

To test the program, use the data in the preceding rate table and the following customer data:

Customer Number	"How Placed"	"Time of Call"	Length
9606	1	1	3.84
2160	3	4	2.50
6100	2	2	3.00
1820	3	3	4.00
9215	2	1	8.50
2111	1	3	6.32
1452	2	3	2.15
6658	1	2	1.05
1138	3	2	9.72
6886	2	4	6.35
3552	3	1	3.51
7111	1	4	5.75
9999 (trailer value)			

6. Write a BASIC program that does the following *without* using the special matrix operations discussed in Section 11-2.

(a) Read two matrices from DATA statements. Assume that both matrices are the same size but that the size is not known when the program is written. The first data read should be the number of rows and the number of columns. Assume that the matrices have no more than ten rows and eight columns, and dimension all arrays accordingly.

(b) Compare the two matrices to determine whether they are equal; that is, determine whether the corresponding elements in the two matrices are the same.

(c) If the matrices are equal, print an appropriate message, multiply one of the matrices by two, and print the result.

(d) If the matrices are not equal, print an appropriate message, add the matrices, and print the result.

Use the following pairs of matrices to test the program:

$$
\text{I.} \quad \begin{bmatrix} 8.35 & 6.25 \\ 7.91 & -5.32 \end{bmatrix} \quad \begin{bmatrix} 8.35 & 6.24 \\ 7.91 & -5.32 \end{bmatrix}
$$

$$
\text{II.} \quad \begin{bmatrix} 1.62 & 4.35 & -2.13 & 7.62 \\ -8.35 & -12.72 & 6.51 & 8.39 \\ -1.82 & 4.21 & 7.83 & -0.71 \end{bmatrix} \quad \begin{bmatrix} -4.71 & 5.63 & 7.81 & -1.22 \\ 17.39 & 8.42 & 5.61 & -2.22 \\ -5.81 & 3.92 & 8.35 & 1.11 \end{bmatrix}
$$

7. Write a BASIC program to multiply two matrices *without* using the special matrix operations. Print the result. Test the program with the following matrices:

$$
\begin{bmatrix} 2 & -3 & 1 \\ -5 & 6 & 4 \\ -1 & 0 & 5 \\ 3 & -2 & -4 \end{bmatrix} \quad \begin{bmatrix} 7 & 0 & 3 & -4 & -2 \\ 4 & 6 & -6 & -1 & 5 \\ -5 & -3 & 1 & 2 & -7 \end{bmatrix}
$$

8. Do problem 7 using the matrix operations discussed in Section 11-2.

9. Consider the following matrices:

$$
X = \begin{bmatrix} 1 & 6 & 3 \\ 5 & 2 & 8 \\ 4 & 7 & 9 \end{bmatrix} \quad Y = \begin{bmatrix} 8 & 5 & 4 \\ 7 & 9 & 1 \\ 3 & 2 & 6 \end{bmatrix}
$$

Write a program to compute and print the following:
(a) $3X^2 - 4XY - 2Y^2$
(b) $(X-2Y)(3X+Y)$
(c) XY
(d) YX

10. Consider the following matrix:

$$
P = \begin{bmatrix} .5 & .25 & .25 \\ .5 & 0 & .5 \\ .25 & .25 & .5 \end{bmatrix}
$$

Write a BASIC program to read and print this matrix. Then compute and print P^2, P^3, P^4, and P^5.

11. A method of solving simultaneous linear equations is called the Gauss elimination method. It is described in many algebra textbooks. Write a BASIC program that uses this method to solve the following system of four equations in four unknowns:

$$1.0x_1 + 7.3x_2 + 12.6x_3 + 11.2x_4 = 31.3$$

$$0.2x_1 - 4.74x_2 - 6.78x_3 - 36.82x_4 = -76.82$$

$$-0.2x_1 - 1.46x_2 + 0.88x_3 - 15.84x_4 = -38.90$$

$$0.3x_1 + 2.29x_2 + 4.03x_3 + 1.79x_4 = 6.17$$

12. Write a BASIC program that uses the techniques discussed at the end of Section 11-2 to solve the system of simultaneous linear equations given in problem 11.

12

USER-DEFINED FUNCTIONS AND SUBROUTINES

When we write a program it is sometimes necessary to repeat a statement or a group of statements at several points in the program. For example, it may be necessary to perform the same computation several times. As another example, a set of input or output statements may have to be used at a number of points in a program. Repeating a group of statements each time they are needed can make the program tiresome to code. It would simplify the process if the necessary statements could be coded once and then referred to each time they are needed. The effect of referring to the statements would be the same as if the statements were placed in the program at the point where they are referenced.

This is the purpose of *functions* and *subroutines*. Functions and subroutines consist of one or more BASIC statements that can be referred to at different points in a program. Each time that a function or a subroutine is referenced we say that it is *called*. We can call a function or a subroutine from the main part of a program or from another function or subroutine. The effect of calling a function or subroutine is the same as if the statements in the function or subroutine were coded in the program at the calling point.

In this chapter we describe the programming and use of functions and subroutines. We also discuss the development of large programs and the design of complex interactive programs.

12-1. USER-DEFINED FUNCTIONS

In Chapter 8 we discussed functions that are built into the BASIC language. The SQR, INT, and RND functions are examples of these. To call such a function, we use the name of the function followed by a numeric expression enclosed in parentheses. For example, the SQR function is called in the following statement:

$$30 \ \text{LET} \ X=SQR(Y)$$

A function computes a value (in this case, the square root of Y) and returns the value to the statement in which the function is called.

Besides the built-in functions, a programmer can code his or her own functions and call them when needed in the program. Such a *user-defined function* is specified with a function-defining or DEF statement in the program. The syntax of the DEF statement is as follows:

ln DEF FN*letter*(*variable*) = *numeric expression*

For example, the following is a DEF statement that specifies a user-defined function:

$$100 \ \text{DEF} \ FNY(X)=3*X^2-2*X+4$$

The DEF statement begins with the keyword DEF. Following this comes the name of the function. The name of a user-defined function always begins with the letters FN and contains one other letter. Thus, in the example above, FNY is the function's name. Similarly, FNA, FNM, and FNZ are valid function names. Notice that because there are only twenty-six letters of the alphabet there can be only twenty-six functions. (Some versions of BASIC allow function names that contain a letter or a letter followed by a digit, that is, a variable. Thus FNA1 and FNX3 are valid function names in some versions of BASIC.)

Following the function name is a single variable enclosed in parentheses. This variable is called the *parameter* (or *dummy argument*) of the function. We can also define a function without a parameter. Some versions of BASIC allow more than one parameter. We will see examples of these cases and how parameters are used below.

Following the parameter is an equal sign and then a numeric expression. The expression indicates what computation the function is to perform. The parameter is usually used in the expression. The expression can be any valid numeric expression in BASIC.

The DEF statement defines a function but does *not* cause it to be executed. Usually all of the DEF statements are placed at the beginning of the program. When the computer reaches a DEF statement during the normal sequential execution of the program, it goes on to the next statement in sequence without doing anything. The function defined in a DEF statement is executed only when it is called.

A user-defined function is called in the same way that a built-in

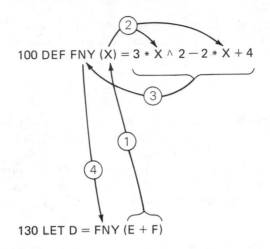

Steps:
1 Value of argument is computed and assigned to parameter.
2 Parameter value is used in expression.
3 Value of expression is computed and assigned to function name.
4 Result is returned to calling statement.

FIGURE 12-1. Calling a function.

function is called; we use the name of the function followed by a numeric expression enclosed in parentheses. For example, consider the FNY function defined previously:

```
100 DEF FNY(X)=3*X^2-2*X+4
```

The following LET statement calls this function:

```
130 LET D=FNY(E+F)
```

The effect of calling a function is that first the value of the expression in parentheses is computed. Then this value is assigned to the parameter in the function. Next the expression in the function is computed using the parameter's value. Finally, the result is assigned to the function's name and returned to the statement in which the function is called. This sequence is shown in Fig. 12-1 for the FNY function. In this example, if E is 3 and F is 2, the value of the function is 69. This value is assigned to the variable D in the LET statement.

The expression in parentheses following the function name when the function is called is the *argument* (or *actual argument*). The argument can be a constant, variable, or more complex numeric expression. For example, the following are valid calls of the FNY function:

302

```
160 LET S=FNY(3)
170 LET T=FNY(Z)
180 LET U=FNY(3*Z+5)
```

In each case the value of the argument is assigned to the parameter of the function when the function is called.

We can call a function as many times as needed in a program. We can even call a function more than once in a single statement. In fact, we can use a function call in a program wherever a variable or a constant can be used. For example, all of the following are valid uses of the FNY function:

```
190 IF FNY(G)>10 THEN 400
200 LET H=7.5*FNY(I+2)-FNY(J)
210 PRINT FNY(1),FNY(2),FNY(3)
```

The only restriction is that any function must be defined before it is called. This means that it is usually best to define all functions at the beginning of the program. Figure 12-2 shows a complete program that calls the FNY function several times.

The variable that is used as a parameter in a DEF statement can also be used in the rest of the program. When this is done, there is no relationship between the parameter and the same variable elsewhere in the program. We say that the parameter is a *local variable* in the function. For example, consider the following statements:

```
100 DEF FNY(X)=3*X^2-2*X+4
      .
      .
      .
220 LET X=5
230 LET Y=FNY(6)
```

In this case we set the value of X in the program to 5 and then call the FNY function with an argument of 6. This causes the value of X *in the function* to be assigned the value 6 for the purpose of evaluating the function. However, it does *not* change the value of X in the rest of the program. If we were to print the value of X after statement 230 is executed, the number 5 would be printed.

Besides using a local variable in a function definition, we can also use other variables. These other variables are not local to the function but are used throughout the program. They are called *global variables*. For example, consider the following DEF statement:

```
110 DEF FNZ(X)=A*X^2+B*X+C
```

```
100 DEF FNY(X)=3*X^2-2*X+4
110 LET E=3
120 LET F=2
130 LET D=FNY(E+F)
140 LET D1=FNY(4)
150 LET D2=FNY(E)
160 PRINT D,D1,D2
999 END
```

(a) The program

69   44   25

(b) The output

FIGURE 12-2.   A program that calls a function.

In this function, X is a *local* variable, but A, B, and C are *global* variables. When the function is called, the value of the argument is assigned to X. The values of A, B, and C that are used in the function evaluation are the values of these variables at the time the function is called. For example, assume that A is 3, B is 2, and C is 1, and that the following statement is executed:

```
150 PRINT FNZ(4)
```

Then the value printed will be $3 \times 4^2 + 2 \times 4 + 1$ or 57.

A function can be defined without a parameter. Then all of the variables in the function definition are global. For example, consider the FNA function defined by the following DEF statement:

```
120 DEF FNA=(X+Y+Z)/3
```

This function computes the average of three values identified by the global variables X, Y, and Z. Whenever this function is called, no argument is used. For example, the following statement computes the average of X, Y, and Z, and assigns the result to A:

```
130 LET A=FNA
```

Many versions of BASIC allow more than one parameter. Sometimes a maximum number of parameters (such as five) is allowed. When more than one parameter is used, the parameters are separated by commas and enclosed in parentheses following the function name. For example, the FNA function described above can be defined with three parameters as follows:

```
120 DEF FNA(X,Y,Z)=(X+Y+Z)/3
```

In this case, X, Y, and Z are local variables. When the function is called, three arguments must be given. For example, to find the average of S, T, and 25, we can write the following:

$$130 \text{ LET } A=FNA(S,T,25)$$

In this case, the value of S is assigned to X, the value of T is assigned to Y, and 25 is assigned to Z. These values are then used to compute the average which is returned to the statement where the function is called.

We can define as many functions as are needed in a program (up to the limit of the number of valid function names). We can even define one function in terms of another. For example, the following DEF statements could be included in a program:

```
100 DEF FNS(A)=A+2
110 DEF FND(A)=A-2
120 DEF FNC(A)=2*FNS(A)+3*FND(A)
```

Then if we write the statement

$$200 \text{ PRINT } FNS(5),FND(4),FNC(3)$$

the output printed will be the numbers 7, 2, and 13.

Functions can be useful when a complex computation needs to be carried out several times with different parameter values. However, their use is limited to computations that require only a single line. In Section 12-2 we will describe multiple-line functions that are available in some versions of BASIC.

*User-defined String Functions

Most versions of BASIC that provide sophisticated string processing also allow user-defined string functions. The name of such a function must end with a dollar sign; that is, the name must consist of FN followed by a string variable. The result produced by a string function is a string and not a numeric value. However, the parameters may be string variables or numeric variables.

As an example of a user-defined string function, consider the following DEF statement:

```
200 DEF FNC$(F$,M$,L$)=F$+" "+LEFT(M$,1)+". "+L$
```

This function creates a string consisting of a person's first name (F$), followed by the person's middle initial (the first letter of M$), and then the person's last name (L$). To call this function, arguments that are string constants or string variables must be supplied for the three parameters. For example, the following statement could be used to call the function:

$$150 \text{ LET N\$=FNC\$(A\$,B\$,"SMITH")}$$

Notice that when the function is called, the result is a string and the value must therefore be assigned to a string variable.

User-defined string functions can be extremely useful in simplifying complex string operations. The example above demonstrates just one case in which an appropriate string function can simplify a program.

*12-2. MULTIPLE-LINE FUNCTIONS

One of the restrictions on user-defined functions is that they can only be a single line, which greatly limits the type of processing that can be performed by such a function. To overcome this limitation some versions of BASIC allow multiple-line functions. In this section we describe the characteristics of such functions for one common version of BASIC.†

The syntax of a multiple-line function definition is as follows:

ln DEF FN*variable(parameters)*

.

.

.

(BASIC statements)

.

.

.

ln FNEND

For example, Fig. 12–3 shows the definition of a function that finds the maximum of three numbers.

The function definition begins with a DEF statement that gives the name of the function. The function name consists of the characters FN, followed by a single letter or a letter and a digit (i.e., a variable). If the function is a string function, a dollar sign must come at the end of the name. In the example in Fig. 12–3, the function name is FNM. Following the function name is the list of parameters. There can be between zero and five parameters separated by commas and enclosed in paren-

---

†The features described in this section are available in BASIC-PLUS on the DEC PDP 11 computer and in related versions of BASIC.

```
100 DEF FNM(A,B,C)
110 LET L=A
120 IF B<=L THEN 140
130 LET L=B
140 IF C<=L THEN 160
150 LET L=C
160 LET FNM=L
170 FNEND
```

FIGURE 12-3.   A multiple line function.

theses. In the example in Fig. 12-3, there are three parameters A, B, and C. Notice that the DEF statement does *not* contain an equal sign or a numeric expression; the computation to be performed by the function is given by the statements following the DEF statement.

The function definition ends with the FNEND statement. When this statement is executed, the computer returns to the point where the function is called.

Between the DEF statement and the FNEND statement can be any number of BASIC statements that perform the processing required of the function. However, one statement is required in the function. This is a LET statement that assigns a value to the *name* of the function. This statement is required because the name of the function is used to return a value to the point where the function is called. The value to be returned must be assigned to the function name at some time in the function. In the example function in Fig. 12-3, statement 160 assigns a value to the function name, FNM.

We can now understand how the function in Fig. 12-3 works. The purpose of this function is to find the largest of the three variables A, B, and C. The technique used is to assume that A is the largest. The value of this variable is assigned to L. Then L is compared with B and C. If either is larger than the current value of L, the larger value is assigned to L. Finally, the value of L is assigned to the name of the function, FNM. The FNEND statement then causes the computer to return to the point in the program where the function is called.

A multiple-line function is called in the same way that a single-line function is called. For example, if we wish to find the maximum of S, T, and 25, we can use the following statement:

```
200 LET M=FNM(S,T,25)
```

The function is executed with the values of the arguments assigned to the parameters, and the result is returned to the calling statement.

A multiple-line function, like a single-line function, must appear before any statement that calls the function. Usually it is best to put all functions at the beginning of the program. When the program is executed, the computer passes over all functions to reach the first executable statement in the program. A function is executed only when it is called.

All of the rules about local and global variables for single-line functions apply to multiple-line functions. The parameters are local variables in the function. Any other variable is global. In the function in Fig. 12-3, A, B, and C are local variables, but L is a global variable. This means that the value of L will be modified when the function is executed, which could cause problems in the program if L is used for another purpose.

There can be as many multiple-line functions in a program as needed. One function can be called from another function. However, the program should never branch out of a function with a GO TO or IF statement. The only way that the execution of a function should be terminated is with the FNEND statement.

Multiple-line functions can be very useful in a complex program. They can simplify programming by allowing a set of computations to be coded once and then called whenever needed.

12-3. SUBROUTINES

A function computes a single value and returns that value to the statement in which the function is called. While this can be useful, there are situations where we wish to compute several values and make the results available in another part of the program. Although several functions could be utilized for this, we will find it convenient to use another approach. This other approach involves using subroutines.

A *subroutine* is a group of statements that can be executed from different points in a program. The form of a subroutine is as follows:

ln (first statement in subroutine)

.

.

.

(statements in subroutine)

.

.

.

ln RETURN

For example, the following is a simple subroutine that finds the total and average of three numbers:

```
200 LET T=X+Y+Z
```

```
210 LET A=T/3
299 RETURN
```

A subroutine can begin at any statement in the program. The subroutine is identified by the *number* of the first statement in the subroutine. In the example above, the subroutine begins at statement 200. There can be any number of statements in a subroutine. The last statement executed in a subroutine must be a RETURN statement. It consists merely of the keyword RETURN. When executed, the RETURN statement causes the computer to return to the point where the subroutine is called.

As a matter of style, it is usually best to begin a subroutine with a REM statement. This sets off the subroutines more clearly from the rest of the program. For example, we could code the previous subroutine as follows:

```
200 REM - SUBROUTINE TO TOTAL AND AVERAGE 3 NUMBERS
210 LET T=X+Y+Z
220 LET A=T/3
299 RETURN
```

To call a subroutine, we use a GOSUB statement. The syntax of the GOSUB statement is as follows:

ln GOSUB *ln*

The effect of this statement is to execute the subroutine that begins at the line number given after the keyword GOSUB. For example, to call the subroutine defined above, we can use the following GOSUB statement:

```
140 GOSUB 200
```

The GOSUB statement causes the computer to branch to the subroutine whose number is given in the statement. Then the statements in the subroutine are executed. When the RETURN statement is reached, the computer branches back to the *next statement following* the GOSUB statement. This is illustrated in Fig. 12–4. Notice that when the computer branches to a REM statement at the beginning of the subroutine, it merely continues with the next statement in sequence.

The advantage of using a subroutine is that it can be called from several points in the program; that is, we can have more than one GOSUB statement that calls the same subroutine. When a RETURN statement in a subroutine is executed, the computer branches back to the next statement following the GOSUB statement that called the sub-

```
 ┌─140 GOSUB 200
 │►150 (next statement)
 │
 │
 │
 └►200 REM - SUBROUTINE TO TOTAL AND AVERAGE 3 NUMBERS
   210 LET T=X+Y+Z
   220 LET A=T/3
  ─299 RETURN
```

FIGURE 12-4.   Calling a subroutine.

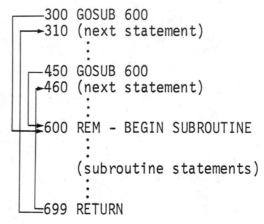

FIGURE 12-5.   Calling a subroutine more than once.

routine. This is illustrated in Fig. 12-5, in which a subroutine is called twice in a program.

A subroutine is normally placed at the end of a program just before the END statement. So that the subroutine is not executed in the normal sequential processing of the program, there must be a GO TO statement just ahead of the subroutine that branches to the END statement. Figure 12-6 shows a complete program that includes a subroutine. The subroutine is called twice in this program. Notice that the GO TO statement at line 160 causes the computer to branch around the subroutine to the END statement. (In place of this GO TO statement, a STOP statement can be used in some versions of BASIC. This statement is merely the keyword STOP. It causes the computer to stop execution of the program.)

Notice that all variables in a subroutine are global. There is no use of parameters that are local variables, as is the case with functions. Because of this, any variable used in the subroutine must be assigned a value before the subroutine is called. In the example in Fig. 12-6, the subroutine uses the variables X, Y, and Z. The values for these variables are supplied through an INPUT statement just before the subroutine is called.

310

```
100 INPUT X,Y,Z
110 GOSUB 200
120 PRINT X,Y,Z,T,A
130 INPUT X,Y,Z
140 GOSUB 200
150 PRINT X,Y,Z,T,A
160 GO TO 999
200 REM - SUBROUTINE TO TOTAL AND AVERAGE 3 NUMBERS
210 LET T=X+Y+Z
220 LET A=T/3
299 RETURN
999 END
```

FIGURE 12-6.   A program that uses a subroutine.

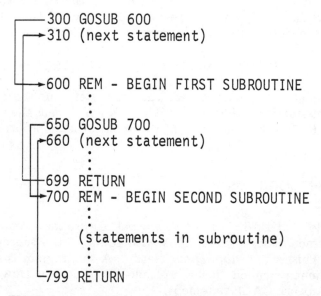

```
 300 GOSUB 600
 310 (next statement)


 600 REM - BEGIN FIRST SUBROUTINE
       .
       .
       .
 650 GOSUB 700
 660 (next statement)
       .
       .
       .
 699 RETURN
 700 REM - BEGIN SECOND SUBROUTINE
       .
       .
       .
     (statements in subroutine)
       .
       .
       .
 799 RETURN
```

FIGURE 12-7.   Calling a subroutine from a subroutine.

We can have as many subroutines as we need in a program. Each subroutine begins at a unique statement number and ends with a RE-TURN statement. All subroutines should be placed at the end of the program. A subroutine can do any type of processing required in a program. Often subroutines contain sets of input or output statements or statements for complex computations.

We can call a subroutine from any point in a program. We can even call one subroutine from another. This is illustrated in Fig. 12-7. All that is needed to call a subroutine is a GOSUB statement with the number of the first statement of the subroutine. When the RETURN statement of the called subroutine is reached, the computer branches back to the point where the subroutine was called.

There are many uses of subroutines. In Section 12-5 we will see how subroutines can be used in the development of large programs, and in Section 12-6 we will discuss the design of complex interactive programs using subroutines.

*The ON-GOSUB Statement

Some versions of BASIC provide the ON-GOSUB statement, which functions much like the ON-GO TO statement. The syntax of the ON-GOSUB statement is as follows:

In ON *numeric expression* GOSUB *ln,ln*, . . .

The effect of this statement is to call one of the subroutines whose numbers are listed after the word GOSUB based on the value of the numeric expression. For example, consider the following statement:

```
250 ON K GOSUB 400,500,600,700
```

When this statement is executed, the computer calls the subroutine beginning at statement 400 if the value of K is 1; it calls the subroutine at statement 500 is K is 2, and so forth for the other subroutines.

*12-4. SUBPROGRAMS

A few versions of BASIC provide a special feature that combines some of the characteristics of functions with some of the aspects of subroutines.[†] This is the *subprogram* feature. A subprogram is a separate set of statements much like a multiple-line function. However, it is called by a special CALL statement.

The syntax of a subprogram is as follows:

In SUB *name(parameters)*

.

.

(statements in subprogram)

.

.

In SUBEND

[†]The features described in this section are available in BASIC-PLUS-2 on the DEC PDP 11 computer, in Dartmouth BASIC 7, and in related versions of BASIC.

For example, Fig. 12–8 shows a subprogram that finds the total and average of three numbers.

A subprogram begins with a SUB statement that contains the name of the subprogram. The name is usually limited in length to six characters. Following the name is a list of parameters separated by commas and enclosed in parentheses. As we will see, the parameters are used both to send data to the subprogram and to return data to the point where the subprogram is called. The subprogram contains any BASIC statements necessary to perform the processing required of the subprogram. The last statement of the subprogram must be a SUBEND statement. When this statement is executed, the computer returns to the point where the subprogram is called.

To call a subprogram, the CALL statement is used. The syntax of the CALL statement is as follows:

ln CALL *name(arguments)*

The statement gives the name of the subprogram and the arguments to be assigned to the parameters of the subprogram. For example, to call the subprogram TOTAVE in Fig. 12–8, we could use the following statement:

```
150 CALL TOTAVE(A,B,C,S,M)
```

When a CALL statement is executed, the values of the arguments are assigned to the parameters in the subprogram. In this example, the value of A is assigned to X, the value of B is assigned to Y, and so on. Notice that there must be the same number of arguments as there are parameters and that the arguments must be in the same order as the parameters. After the argument values are assigned to the parameters, the computer branches to the first statement in the subprogram.

The subprogram is executed until the SUBEND statement is reached. Then the values of the parameters are assigned to the arguments. In the example, the value of X in the subprogram is assigned to A, the value of Y is assigned to B, and so forth. In this case, the values of A, B, and C are unchanged by the process, but the arguments S and M are assigned the new values of T and A computed by the subprogram. This is how the results are returned to the point where the subprogram is called. After the parameter values are assigned to the arguments, the

```
1000 SUB TOTAVE(X,Y,Z,T,A)
1010 LET T=X+Y+Z
1020 LET A=T/3
1099 SUBEND
```

FIGURE 12-8.   A subprogram.

computer branches back to the next statement following the CALL statement. This process is summarized in Fig. 12–9.

The arguments used in a CALL statement can be constants, variables, or more complex expressions. For example, the following statement could be used to call the TOTAVE subprogram:

$$250 \ \text{CALL TOTAVE(A+B,35,X,T,A)}$$

When an argument is not a variable, the value of the parameter is *not* returned to the program that called the subprogram. This is because a value cannot be assigned to a constant or an expression, only to a variable.

Arrays can also be used as parameters and arguments. To indicate an array parameter, parentheses are used after the array variable. For example, consider the subprogram shown in Fig. 12–10. This subprogram finds the average, A, of an N-element array, X. X is an array variable because of the parentheses following the variable in the list of parameters. To call this function, we must use an array variable fol-

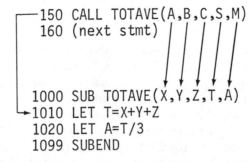

(a) Calling a subprogram

(b) Returning from a subprogram

FIGURE 12-9.   Calling a subprogram.

```
2000 SUB AVE(A,X(),N)
2010 LET T=0
2020 FOR I=1 TO N
2030   LET T=T+X(I)
2040 NEXT I
2050 LET A=T/N
2099 SUBEND
```

FIGURE 12-10.   A subprogram with an array parameter.

lowed by parentheses in the CALL statement. The following statement shows how this can be done:

```
350 CALL AVE(M,D(),L)
```

When a subprogram is used, the subprogram is placed *after* the END statement of the program. This is because the subprogram is a separate, distinct program. As a result, all of the variables used in a subprogram are *local;* that is, any variable that is not a parameter can be used without affecting the same variable outside the subprogram. For example, the variable T in the subprogram in Fig. 12-10 is distinct from the same variable in the main program. Changing the value of T in the subprogram does not change the value of T elsewhere.

We can use as many subprograms as needed by a program. All subprograms come after the END statement. A subprogram can be called as often as required with different arguments. We can even call one subprogram from another.

Subprograms are very useful for developing a large program. While they are currently available only in a few versions of BASIC, we can expect their availability to increase in the future.

12-5. DEVELOPING LARGE PROGRAMS

In Chapter 7 we discussed a number of aspects of program development, including program structure, style, and understandability, and the activities in the programming process. We saw that following the guidelines in Chapter 7 resulted in programs that were well structured, easily understood, and correct.

As programs become larger, their development becomes more complex. In Chapter 7 we introduced the idea of modular programming in which a large program is divided into sections or modules. Each module performs some function related to the overall processing of the program. The modules for a program can be developed separately and then combined to form a complete program after all modules are finished.

With functions and subroutines we have a convenient mechanism for modularizing a program. The approach is to code each module as a separate function or subroutine. Then the main program is composed of a series of calls to the functions and subroutines.

To illustrate this approach, consider the problem of updating a pricing table. In an example in Section 10-4, we showed a table that consisted of two ten-element arrays, one for item numbers and one for the corresponding unit prices (see Fig. 10–3). Assume now that some of the prices in the table have changed. We need a program to make the appropriate modifications in the table (i.e., to *update* the table). In addition, we want a printed copy of the table before and after the changes are made.

We can see that the program must basically do the following:

1. Read the pricing table.
2. Print the pricing table.
3. Update the pricing table.
4. Print the updated table.

Following our approach of using functions and subroutines to modularize the program, we can code each of these steps as a separate subroutine. However, since the second and fourth steps merely involve printing the pricing table, we only need three subroutines — one to read the pricing table, one to print the table, and one to update the table. The main part of the program calls these three subroutines in order and then calls the printing subroutine again to print the updated table.

Assume that we have coded the three subroutines and that they begin at lines 400, 500, and 600, respectively. The main part of the program to call the subroutines in the proper sequence is shown in Fig. 12-11. Notice the simplicity of this part of the program; it is just a sequence of four GOSUB statements. REM statements are included to document further which subroutine is called at each point.

The input and output subroutines can be coded fairly easily. Each involves a loop to read or print the elements of two arrays — one for the item numbers and one for the prices. The subroutines are shown in Fig. 12-12. Notice that the DATA statements containing the pricing data are in the input subroutine. Although this is not required, it simplifies the process of locating these statements.

The updating process has not been fully defined. Assume that new prices along with corresponding item numbers are to be entered at the terminal. There are any number of changes that need to be made, and the input data is not entered in any particular order. The updating process is to repeat until the terminal operator indicates that no more prices are to be changed.

```
100 REM - THIS PROGRAM UPDATES THE UNIT PRICING TABLE
110 REM
120 REM - THIS IS THE MAIN PART OF THE PROGRAM
130 REM
200 DIM N(10),P(10)
210 REM - CALL READ TABLE SUBROUTINE
220 GOSUB 400
230 REM - CALL PRINT TABLE SUBROUTINE
240 GOSUB 500
250 REM - CALL UPDATE TABLE SUBROUTINE
260 GOSUB 600
270 REM - CALL PRINT TABLE SUBROUTINE
280 GOSUB 500
399 GO TO 999
      .
      .
      .
    (subroutines go here)
      .
      .
      .
999 END
```

FIGURE 12-11.   The main part of the program for the
table updating problem.

```
400 REM - READ TABLE SUBROUTINE
410 FOR I=1 TO 10
420    READ N(I),P(I)
430 NEXT I
490 DATA 1001,2.95,1023,3.64,1045,2.25,1172,0.75,1185,1.50
491 DATA 1201,1.95,1235,4.85,1278,9.95,1384,6.28,1400,4.75
499 RETURN


500 REM - PRINT TABLE SUBROUTINE
510 PRINT "ITEM NUMBER","UNIT PRICE"
520 PRINT
530 FOR I=1 TO 10
540    PRINT N(I),P(I)
550 NEXT I
560 PRINT
599 RETURN
```

FIGURE 12-12.   The table input and output subroutines.

The updating subroutine must do the following:

1. Accept an item number and new price.
2. Find the corresponding item in the pricing table.
3. Make the necessary change in the pricing table.

Assume that we have a subroutine beginning at line 800 that finds the location (i.e., the element number) of a given item in the item-number array. If the item number is found, the subroutine sets the variable L to its location; otherwise the value of L is set to zero.

We can use this item-locating subroutine in the table-updating subroutine shown in Fig. 12–13. First, an item number and new price are accepted from the terminal. Then the item-locating subroutine is called. Next the value of L is tested to determine whether it is zero. If it is, an error message is printed; otherwise the new price is assigned to P(L) thereby modifying the pricing table.

The only step that remains in completing the program is to develop the item-locating subroutine. This subroutine searches the item-number array for a given value. We could use a sequential search, or a binary search if the array is in ascending order. We will assume that this is not necessarily the case and search sequentially. The complete subroutine is shown in Fig. 12–14. Notice that the variable L in the subroutine is

```
600 REM - UPDATE TABLE SUBROUTINE
610 PRINT "ENTER ITEM NUMBER";
620 INPUT N1
630 PRINT "ENTER NEW PRICE";
640 INPUT P1
650 PRINT
660 REM - CALL LOCATE ITEM SUBROUTINE
670 GOSUB 800
680 IF L=0 THEN 730
690 LET P(L)=P1
700 PRINT "ITEM";N1;"UPDATED"
710 PRINT
720 GO TO 750
730 PRINT "ITEM";N1;"NOT FOUND IN TABLE"
740 PRINT
750 PRINT "DO YOU WANT TO UPDATE MORE PRICES";
760 INPUT R$
770 PRINT
780 IF R$="YES" THEN 610
799 RETURN
```

FIGURE 12–13.   The table updating subroutine.

assigned the subscript of the matching element if the item is found in the table; otherwise it is assigned a value of zero.

The subroutines in Figs. 12-12, 12-13, and 12-14 can now be included in the program in Fig. 12-11. The result is a complete program to update the pricing table.

We can see from this example several advantages of using subroutines to modularize a program. For one, this approach allows us to develop the program in a *top-down* fashion. This is similar to the idea of stepwise program refinement discussed in Section 7-4. We start by designing the overall logic of the program. Each basic operation that the program is to perform becomes a subroutine (or possibly a function). The main part of the program contains a series of calls to the subroutines. (There may be other statements in the main part of the program besides those that call subroutines. For example, loop control or decision-making statements may be needed to control the order of execution of the subroutines.) We then design each subroutine in a similar top-down fashion. Eventually we reach the point where the basic operations of the program can be coded.

One way of displaying the top-down design of a program is to draw a diagram showing the relationship between the main part of the program and the subroutines. Figure 12-15 shows such a diagram for the table-updating program. The box at the top represents the main part of the program. Each box below signifies a subroutine. A line connects two boxes if one part of the program calls the other. Thus, Fig. 12-15 shows that the main part of the program calls the read-table, print-table, and update-table subroutines, and that the update-table subroutine calls the item-locating subroutine.

This diagram also shows how we can regard the program in terms of *levels*. At the highest level, we can think of the program as the sequence of activities that takes place in the main part of the program. If we wish, we can understand the program just at this level and not examine any of the subroutines. However, if we wish to understand the program at a deeper level, we can look at the subroutines that are called by the main part of the program. Even further, we can examine the next level of subroutines and so forth until we reach the bottom of the diagram.

```
800 REM - LOCATE ITEM SUBROUTINE
810 LET L=1
820 IF N(L)=N1 THEN 899
830 IF L=10 THEN 860
840 LET L=L+1
850 GO TO 820
860 LET L=0
899 RETURN
```

FIGURE 12-14.   The item-locating subroutine.

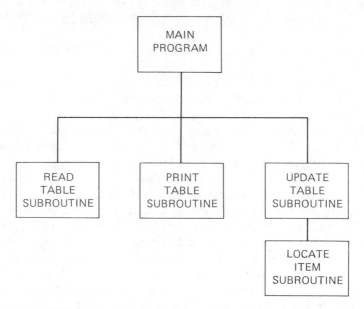

FIGURE 12-15. The calling hierarchy for the table-
updating program.

Besides designing the program in a top-down fashion, we can also follow a *top-down coding and testing* pattern. In this approach, we code the main part of the program first. Then for each subroutine called by the main part of the program we code a "dummy" subroutine (sometimes referred to as a *stub*) that simulates, but does not actually perform the function of the subroutine. Usually each stub just prints a line stating that the subroutine was executed. We can then run the program with the nonfunctioning subroutines to make certain that the logic of the main part of the program is correct. Next we follow the same procedure for the first subroutine, coding stubs for any subroutines that it calls. We then test the program with the completed first subroutine. This process is repeated for all subroutines until the complete program is coded and tested.

An alternative strategy is called *bottom-up coding and testing*. In this approach we design the program in a top-down fashion, but then start coding and testing with the lowest level subroutine. This requires writing programs (sometimes called *exercisers*) to call and test the subroutines. We build the program from the bottom up until we finally reach the top level, which is the main part of the program.

A final advantage of using subroutines to modularize a program is that the subroutines can often be used in other programs. For example, assume that we need a program that computes the cost of an order by multiplying the quantity purchased times the price. Since we already have a subroutine to read the pricing table and one to locate an item in the table, we can use these in a pricing program. The main part of the program to do this is shown in Fig. 12-16. The program first reads the pricing table using the read-table subroutine. It then accepts an item number and quantity from the terminal. Next the program uses the item-locating subroutine to find the location of the desired item in the table. The value of L is then checked to determine whether the item was found. If it was, the price for the item is multiplied by the quantity to obtain the cost, and the output is printed. If the item was not found, an error message is printed. This main part of the program, together with the read-table and item-locating subroutines, forms a complete pricing program.

We can see from these examples a number of advantages to using subroutines. In fact, most large programs are developed in the manner described here. For any complex program, the programmer should consider using the techniques in this section.

```
100 REM - THIS PROGRAM COMPUTES TOTAL COST GIVEN THE QUANTITY PURCHASED
110 REM
120 REM - THIS IS THE MAIN PART OF THE PROGRAM
130 REM
200 DIM N(10),P(10)
210 REM - CALL READ TABLE SUBROUTINE
220 GOSUB 400
230 PRINT "ENTER ITEM NUMBER";
240 INPUT N1
250 PRINT "ENTER QUANTITY";
260 INPUT Q
270 PRINT
280 REM - CALL LOCATE ITEM SUBROUTINE
290 GOSUB 800
300 IF L=0 THEN 340
310 LET C=P(L)*Q
320 PRINT "ITEM";N1;"UNIT PRICE";P(L);"QUANTITY";Q;"COST";C
330 GO TO 350
340 PRINT "ITEM";N1;"NOT FOUND IN TABLE"
350 PRINT
360 PRINT "DO YOU WANT TO COMPUTE MORE ORDER COSTS";
370 INPUT R$
380 PRINT
390 IF R$="YES" THEN 230
399 GO TO 999
        .
        .
        .
    (subroutines go here)
        .
        .
        .
999 END
```

FIGURE 12-16.   The main part of the pricing program.

12-6. INTERACTIVE PROGRAM DESIGN REVISITED

In Section 6-2 we introduced basic principles for the design of interactive programs. Such devices as input prompts and descriptive output make a program easier for the terminal operator to use. However, as programs become more complex, new techniques are needed. In this section we describe a common approach to the design of sophisticated interactive programs.

Many programs allow the terminal operator to select which of several tasks he or she wants the program to perform. For example, a pricing program, similar to the one discussed in the last section, may require the operator to indicate whether the pricing table is to be printed, whether prices are to be updated, or whether the cost of an order is to be computed. The program must be designed so that the terminal operator has complete control over which task is selected and the order in which a group of tasks is performed.

This type of program usually operates in the following way. First a list of the tasks that the program can perform is printed. This list is called a *menu*. For example, Fig. 12-17 shows a menu for a pricing program. Each task in the list has a code associated with it. In the example in Fig. 12-17, the codes are numbers (1, 2, 3, and 9) but letters can also be used. Notice that one of the codes (9 in this example) is used to indicate that the program should stop.

Following the menu, the program prints an input prompt which requests the code for the desired task. The terminal operator must enter one of the codes from the menu. Then the program analyzes the code to determine what is required. Usually each task is performed by a subroutine in the program. The input code is analyzed and the program calls the appropriate subroutine. If the code indicates that execution should stop, the program branches to the END statement. If an invalid code is entered, an error message is printed and the menu is displayed again. After a task is performed by a subroutine, the program displays the menu once again and asks for the next task. This way the computer operator has complete control over the computer's activities.

Figure 12-18 shows a complete pricing program that incorporates

```
SELECT ONE TASK:
 1 PRINT PRICING TABLE
 2 UPDATE PRICES
 3 COMPUTE ORDER COST
 9 STOP

WHICH TASK?
```

FIGURE 12-17. The menu for a pricing program.

```
1000 REM - ITEM PRICING PROGRAM
1010 REM
1100 REM - THIS IS THE MAIN PART OF THE PROGRAM
1110 REM
1200 DIM N(10),P(10)
1210 PRINT "ITEM PRICING PROGRAM"
1220 PRINT
1230 REM - CALL READ TABLE SUBROUTINE
1240 GOSUB 2400
1250 REM - CALL DISPLAY MENU SUBROUTINE
1260 GOSUB 2100
1270 IF T=9 THEN 9999
1280 IF T=1 THEN 1400
1290 IF T=2 THEN 1370
1300 IF T=3 THEN 1340
1310 PRINT "INVALID TASK"
1320 PRINT
1330 GO TO 1250
1340 REM - CALL COMPUTE ORDER COST SUBROUTINE
1350 GOSUB 2200
1360 GO TO 1250
1370 REM - CALL UPDATE TABLE SUBROUTINE
1380 GOSUB 2600
1390 GO TO 1250
1400 REM - CALL PRINT TABLE SUBROUTINE
1410 GOSUB 2500
1420 GO TO 1250
2000 REM
2010 REM - SUBROUTINES
2020 REM
2100 REM - DISPLAY MENU SUBROUTINE
2110 PRINT "SELECT ONE TASK:"
2120 PRINT " 1 PRINT PRICING TABLE"
2130 PRINT " 2 UPDATE PRICES"
2140 PRINT " 3 COMPUTE ORDER COST"
2150 PRINT " 9 STOP"
2160 PRINT
2170 PRINT "WHICH TASK";
2180 INPUT T
2190 PRINT
2199 RETURN
```

FIGURE 12-18.   The pricing program (Part 1 of 3).

```
2200 REM - COMPUTE ORDER COST SUBROUTINE
2210 PRINT "ENTER ITEM NUMBER";
2220 INPUT N1
2230 PRINT "ENTER QUANTITY";
2240 INPUT Q
2250 PRINT
2260 REM - CALL LOCATE ITEM SUBROUTINE
2280 GOSUB 2800
2290 IF L=0 THEN 2330
2300 LET C=P(L)*Q
2310 PRINT "ITEM";N1;"UNIT PRICE";P(L);"QUANTITY";Q;"COST";C
2320 GO TO 2340
2330 PRINT "ITEM";N1;"NOT FOUND IN TABLE"
2340 PRINT
2350 PRINT "DO YOU WANT TO COMPUTE MORE ORDER COSTS";
2360 INPUT R$
2370 PRINT
2380 IF R$="YES" THEN 2210
2399 RETURN
2400 REM - READ TABLE SUBROUTINE
2410 FOR I=1 TO 10
2420   READ N(I),P(I)
2430 NEXT I
2490 DATA 1001,2.95,1023,3.64,1045,2.25,1172,0.75,1185,1.50
2491 DATA 1201,1.95,1235,4.85,1278,9.95,1384,6.28,1400,4.75
2499 RETURN
2500 REM - PRINT TABLE SUBROUTINE
2510 PRINT "ITEM NUMBER","UNIT PRICE"
2520 PRINT
2530 FOR I=1 TO 10
2540   PRINT N(I),P(I)
2550 NEXT I
2560 PRINT
2599 RETURN
```

FIGURE 12-18.   The pricing program (Part 2 of 3).

this approach. The main part of the program calls subroutines to read the pricing table, display the menu, and perform the appropriate task based on the code that is entered. The process of displaying the menu and analyzing the code is repeated until a code of 9 is entered, indicating that the program should stop.

The rest of the program consists of six subroutines to perform the various processing required of the program. The subroutines are as follows:

324

```
2600 REM - UPDATE TABLE SUBROUTINE
2610 PRINT "ENTER ITEM NUMBER";
2620 INPUT N1
2630 PRINT "ENTER NEW PRICE";
2640 INPUT P1
2650 PRINT
2660 REM - CALL LOCATE ITEM SUBROUTINE
2670 GOSUB 2800
2680 IF L=0 THEN 2730
2690 LET P(L)=P1
2700 PRINT "ITEM";N1"UPDATED"
2710 PRINT
2720 GO TO 2750
2730 PRINT "ITEM";N1;"NOT FOUND IN TABLE"
2740 PRINT
2750 PRINT "DO YOU WANT TO UPDATE MORE PRICES";
2760 INPUT R$
2770 PRINT
2780 IF R$="YES" THEN 2610
2799 RETURN
2800 REM - LOCATE ITEM SUBROUTINE
2810 LET L=1
2820 IF N(L)=N1 THEN 2899
2830 IF L=10 THEN 2860
2840 LET L=L+1
2850 GO TO 2820
2860 LET L=0
2899 RETURN
9999 END
```

FIGURE 12-18.   The pricing program (Part 3 of 3).

Line	Subroutine
2100	Display Menu
2200	Compute Order Cost
2400	Read Pricing Table
2500	Print Pricing Table
2600	Update Pricing Table
2800	Locate Item in Table

The last four subroutines are the same as the subroutines used in the last section but with new line numbers. The order-cost-computation subroutine is derived from the main part of the program shown in Fig. 12-16. The menu-displaying subroutine is new to this program. The calling hierarchy for the program is shown in Fig. 12-19.

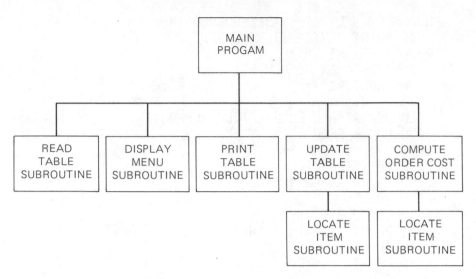

FIGURE 12-19. The calling hierarchy for the pricing
program.

A sample run of the pricing program is shown in Fig. 12-20. Notice that after each task is performed, the menu is displayed again so that a new task code can be entered. The program terminates when 9 is entered for the task code.

The program-design approach described in this section is commonly used for complex interactive programs. If a program can perform many tasks, the selection of which is under the control of the terminal operator, this approach should be considered.

```
SELECT ONE TASK:
 1 PRINT PRICING TABLE
 2 UPDATE PRICES
 3 COMPUTE ORDER COST
 9 STOP

WHICH TASK? 1

ITEM NUMBER    UNIT PRICE

 1001          2.95
 1023          3.64
 1045          2.25
 1172          .75
 1185          1.5
 1201          1.95
 1235          4.85
 1278          9.95
 1384          6.28
 1400          4.75

SELECT ONE TASK:
 1 PRINT PRICING TABLE
 2 UPDATE PRICES
 3 COMPUTE ORDER COST
 9 STOP

WHICH TASK? 2

ENTER ITEM NUMBER? 1172
ENTER NEW PRICE? .85

ITEM 1172 UPDATED

DO YOU WANT TO UPDATE MORE PRICES? YES

ENTER ITEM NUMBER? 1234
ENTER NEW PRICE? 5.25

ITEM 1234 NOT FOUND IN TABLE

DO YOU WANT TO UPDATE MORE PRICES? YES

ENTER ITEM NUMBER? 1235
ENTER NEW PRICE? 5.25

ITEM 1235 UPDATED

DO YOU WANT TO UPDATE MORE PRICES? NO
```

FIGURE 12-20.   Running the pricing program (Part 1 of 3).

```
SELECT ONE TASK:
  1 PRINT PRICING TABLE
  2 UPDATE PRICES
  3 COMPUTE ORDER COST
  9 STOP

WHICH TASK? 4

INVALID TASK

SELECT ONE TASK:
  1 PRINT PRICING TABLE
  2 UPDATE PRICES
  3 COMPUTE ORDER COST
  9 STOP

WHICH TASK? 1

ITEM NUMBER      UNIT PRICE

  1001             2.95
  1023             3.64
  1045             2.25
  1172              .85
  1185             1.5
  1201             1.95
  1235             5.25
  1278             9.95
  1384             6.28
  1400             4.75
```

FIGURE 12–20.   Running the pricing program (Part 2 of 3).

```
SELECT ONE TASK:
 1 PRINT PRICING TABLE
 2 UPDATE PRICES
 3 COMPUTE ORDER COST
 9 STOP

WHICH TASK? 3

ENTER ITEM NUMBER? 1023
ENTER QUANTITY? 12

ITEM 1023 UNIT PRICE 3.64 QUANTITY 12 COST 43.68

DO YOU WANT TO COMPUTE MORE ORDER COSTS? YES

ENTER ITEM NUMBER? 1279
ENTER QUANTITY? 20

ITEM 1279 NOT FOUND IN TABLE

DO YOU WANT TO COMPUTE MORE ORDER COSTS? YES

ENTER ITEM NUMBER? 1278
ENTER QUANTITY? 20

ITEM 1278 UNIT PRICE 9.95 QUANTITY 20 COST 199

DO YOU WANT TO COMPUTE MORE ORDER COSTS? NO

SELECT ONE TASK:
 1 PRINT PRICING TABLE
 2 UPDATE PRICES
 3 COMPUTE ORDER COST
 9 STOP

WHICH TASK? 9
```

FIGURE 12-20.   Running the pricing program (Part
3 of 3).

REVIEW QUESTIONS

1. What are the differences between functions and subroutines?

2. When a function or subroutine is referenced in a program it is said to be _____.

3. Write a DEF statement to define a function that computes

$$A = B(1+R)^Y$$

The parameter of the function is B.

4. Write a statement to call the function defined in question 3 with 1000 as the argument. The statement should assign the result to X.

5. The parameter of a function is a (global/local) _____ variable. All other variables used in a function are (global/local) _____ variables.

6. What is printed by the following sequence of statements?

```
10 DEF FNA(B)=A+B
20 LET A=5
30 LET B=10
40 LET A=FNA(A)
50 LET B=FNB(B)
60 PRINT A,B
```

7. Are multiple-line functions available in the version of BASIC you are using? If they are, write a multiple-line function that computes Z as follows:

if $X < Y$, then $Z = Y - X + 10$

if $X > Y$, then $Z = X - Y + 20$

if $X = Y$, then $Z = 30$

8. The last statement executed in a subroutine must be a _____ statement.

9. Write a statement to call a subroutine that begins at line 500.

10. What is the next statement to be executed after a RETURN statement is executed?

11. Consider the program shown in Fig. 12-6. What output is printed if the first set of input is 70, 90, 80, and the second set of input is 85, 60, 75?

12. All variables in a subroutine are (global/local) ——————.

13. Are subprograms available in the version of BASIC you are using? If they are, write a subprogram to compute the sum and the difference of the values of two variables. Write a statement to call the subprogram.

14. Consider the program shown in Fig. 12-11 including the sub-routines in Figs. 12-12, 12-13, and 12-14. Assume that we wish to use the program to update the price of item 1172 to $1.25 and the price of item 1245 to $5.50. What output would be printed by the program for each of these cases? What changes would be made in the pricing table?

15. What is meant by top-down coding and testing?

16. Draw a hierarchy diagram (similar to the one in Fig. 12-15) for the program in Fig. 12-16.

17. A list of tasks that a program can perform is called a ——————.

18. Consider the program shown in Fig. 12-18 and the run shown in Fig. 12-20. How many times is the LOCATE ITEM subroutine called in this run?

PROGRAMMING PROBLEMS

1. Write a function to convert Fahrenheit temperature to Celsius temperature. The formula is given in problem 2 of Chapter 3. Write a program that accepts a temperature in Fahrenheit, calls the function, and prints the result. Use the data in problem 2 of Chapter 3 to test the program.

2. The present value of an amount, A, received Y years in the future is given by the following formula:

$$\text{Present value} = \frac{A}{(1+R)^Y}$$

In this formula, R is called the discount rate. Write a function to compute the present value given any amount. The discount rate and the number of years are not parameters of the function. Write a program to accept an amount, discount rate, and number of years; call the function; and print the present value. Test the program with an amount of $1,000, a discount rate of 6%, and ten for the number of years.

3. Write a program for problem 7 in Chapter 3 using two functions, one to find the interest and the other to compute the maturity value.

4. Write a multiple-line function that uses a loop to accumulate the balance in a bank account for a given initial balance, interest rate, and

number of years. Assume that interest is compounded annually. Write a program that accepts the initial balance, interest rate, and number of years; calls the function; and prints the balance computed by the function. Test the program with several sets of input data.

5. Write a multiple-line function to find the Nth Fibonacci number (see problem 6 in Chapter 5 for a description of Fibonacci numbers). Write a program that accepts a value of N, calls the function, and prints the result. Test the program with N equal to 5, 12, 1, 25, 2, 8, and 3.

6. Write a multiple-line function to find e^x using the series given in problem 9 of Chapter 5. Write a program that accepts a value of x, computes e^x using the function, and prints the result. Test the program with several values of x.

7. The tuition charged a student at a small private college is based on the number of units that the student is enrolled for during a quarter. The tuition is $200 plus $25 per unit for each of the first eight units and $32.50 per unit for all units over eight. Write a subroutine to determine the tuition given the number of units.

Prepare a program that reads a student's number and the number of units taken for each of three quarters. Then, using the subroutine described in the previous paragraph, calculate the tuition for each quarter. Print these results along with the student's number.

Use the following input data to test the program:

Student Number	Units Taken		
	Fall Quarter	Winter Quarter	Spring Quarter
1018	7.0	18.0	15.0
1205	15.0	12.5	6.0
1214	15.5	15.5	15.5
1218	8.0	7.0	5.0
1293	8.5	7.5	4.0
1304	6.0	6.0	6.0
1351	10.5	18.5	0.0
1354	0.0	15.0	6.0
9999 (trailer value)			

8. Prepare a subroutine to determine the expected population of a group in ten years given the current population and the annual growth rate. Prepare a program that reads population data for two socio-economic groups in each area of a city; uses the subroutine to calculate the expected population of each group in ten years; and prints the area number, the expected population of each group, and the total expected population for the area.

Use the following data to test the program:

| Area Number | Group A | | Group B | |
	Current Pop.	Growth Rate	Current Pop.	Growth Rate
001	14,500	3.5%	6,300	4.1%
002	18,251	2.3%	2,215	2.9%
003	6,205	4.0%	8,132	3.9%
004	3,738	5.4%	12,730	2.7%
005	12,100	3.0%	10,150	3.0%
000 (trailer value)				

9. Prepare a program for problem 10 in Chapter 4 using subroutines. There should be four subroutines that accept one, two, three, or four test scores, respectively; calculate the average of the number of scores accepted; and print the results. Use the data in problem 10 of Chapter 4 to test the program.

10. Adding amounts of time expressed in hours and minutes requires special manipulation because there are sixty minutes in an hour. Write a subroutine that finds the sum of two amounts of time. For each time to be added and for the sum, two variables are needed — one for the hours and the other for the minutes.

Prepare a program that reads the time that an employee worked on each day of the week. Then use the subroutine described in the previous paragraph to calculate the total time worked by the employee for the week. This requires four calls of the subroutine. Print all input data and the total of the times.

Use the following data to test the program:

| Employee Number | Time Worked | | | | | | | | | |
| | Monday | | Tuesday | | Wednesday | | Thursday | | Friday | |
	Hr	Min	Hr	Min	Hr	Min	Hr	Min	Hr	Min
10011	8	0	7	30	8	0	7	30	7	30
10105	7	45	7	55	6	30	5	0	8	45
10287	10	0	8	5	6	25	8	0	7	15
10289	9	45	8	0	6	10	8	30	0	0
10304	0	0	0	0	8	0	8	25	7	45
10455	6	35	8	40	0	0	0	0	11	55
00000 (trailer value)										

11. Do problem 10 using a subprogram rather than a subroutine. There are six parameters for the subprogram, two for each amount of time to be added and two for the sum.

12. Prepare the following subroutines:

(a) *Calculate charge.* This subroutine determines the total gas utility charge based on the number of gas therms used (gas consumption is measured in therms). The charge is $0.09 per therm for the first 200 therms, $0.08 per therm for the next 300 therms, $0.07 per therm for the next 500 therms, and $0.065 per therm for all gas used over 1,000 therms.

(b) *Print output.* This subroutine prints with appropriate headings the customer number, the gas used in therms, and the charge for one month.

Prepare a program that reads the customer number and the gas consumed for three separate months. Then, through three separate calls of the first subroutine, calculate the charge for each of the three months. Print the results for each month using three calls of the second subroutine.

Use the following data to test the program:

Customer Number	Therms Used		
	1st Month	2nd Month	3rd Month
1182	425	172	253
1397	665	892	1283
1482	45	572	313
1921	1562	973	865
2841	200	500	1000
3108	0	300	600
9999 (trailer value)			

13. Assume that F, G, and H are polynomials defined as follows:

$$F(X)=A(1)+A(2)*X+A(3)*X \wedge 2+ \ldots +A(N+1)*X \wedge N$$

$$G(X)=B(1)+B(2)*X+B(3)*X \wedge 2+ \ldots +B(M+1)*X \wedge M$$

$$H(X)=C(1)+C(2)*X+C(3)*X \wedge 2+ \ldots +C(L+1)*X \wedge L$$

Note that the degrees of these polynomials are N, M, and L, respectively. Assume a maximum of twenty for each of these and dimension any arrays accordingly. Note also that the coefficient of $X \wedge I$ has subscript I+1.

Prepare the following subroutines:

(a) *Read polynomial.* This subroutine reads an array A of the coefficients of a polynomial of degree N from a DATA statement. Input data should include the degree of the polynomial followed by the coefficients. Note that a polynomial of degree N has N+1 coefficients.

(b) *Print polynomial.* This subroutine prints the array A of the coefficients of a polynomial of degree N. The coefficients should be neatly arranged and labeled.

(c) *Scalar multiply.* This subroutine multiplies a polynomial of degree N with array A of coefficients by the constant D producing a polynomial of degree N with array C of coefficients.

(d) *Add polynomials.* This subroutine adds a polynomial of degree N with coefficient array A and a polynomial of degree M with coefficient array B producing a polynomial with coefficient array C and degree L.

Prepare a main program that uses these subroutines to do the following:

> Read F(X)
> Print F(X)
> Read G(X)
> Print G(X)
> Compute H(X)=F(X)+2*G(X)
> Print H(X)
> Compute a new F(X)=3*H(X)
> Print the new F(X)

Use the following data to test your program:

Polynomial F(X) N=5	Polynomial G(X) M=2
A(1)=1.0	B(1)=7.0
A(2)=17.6	B(2)=3.1
A(3)=0.0	B(3)=-1.0
A(4)=2.0	
A(5)=-3.6	
A(6)=1.0	

14. Problem 6 in Chapter 10 involves writing a program to process student test-score data. Rewrite this program as the following series of subroutines:

(a) *Read array.* This subroutine reads identification numbers and test scores into two arrays. The subroutine must count the data as it is read to obtain a count of the number of test scores to be processed. Note that the value of the count should not include the trailer value.

(b) *Print arrays.* This subroutine prints in columns below appropriate headings the array of identification numbers and the array of test scores.

(c) *Calculate mean.* This subroutine calculates the mean of the test scores. The mean is simply the average.

(d) *Tabulate scores.* This subroutine tabulates (i.e., counts) the number of test scores in various categories. The subroutine should determine the number of scores in each of the following categories:

> 90–100
> 80–89
> 70–79
> 60–69
> 0–59

The subroutine also prints the results with appropriate titles.

(e) *Sort test scores.* This subroutine sorts the *test-score array* into descending order (largest to smallest). Be certain that the correspondence between the identification-number array and the test-score array is maintained during the sorting.

(f) *Find median.* This subroutine determines the median of the test scores. The subroutine should handle both the case where the number of test scores is even and the case where the number of scores is odd.

Prepare a program that uses these subroutines to process the test-score data. The main program should call the subroutines to do the following:

> Read the arrays
> Print the arrays
> Calculate the mean
> Tabulate the test scores
> Sort the test scores
> Print the arrays
> Find the median

Notice that after sorting, the arrays are printed using the output subroutine. The program also requires other output operations. The mean must be printed by the main program after it is calculated. The median must be printed after it is found. All output should be printed with appropriate headings or descriptive comments. Use the data in problem 6 of Chapter 10 to test the program.

15. Develop an interactive program to compute a depreciation schedule for an asset based on the straight-line method, the declining balance method, and the sum-of-years' digits method. The program should be designed so that the terminal operator can select the desired method from a menu. Test the program with a number of sets of input data.

16. Modify the program described in problem 14 so that the terminal operator can select the desired task from a menu. Include the following tasks:

> Accept student identification number and test score
> Print arrays
> Update test score
> Calculate mean
> Tabulate scores
> Sort scores
> Find median

Notice that one of the tasks is to accept a student's identification number and test score. This allows the data to be entered at the terminal instead of being read from DATA statements. The data that is entered should be added to the end of the array and the count of the number of students should be increased by one. There is also a task that allows the terminal operator to update (i.e., change) a test score for any student after the score has been entered.

Test all of the tasks in the program using appropriate test data.

13

FILES

In Chapter 1 we described the auxiliary storage component of a computer (see Fig. 1-1). A common type of auxiliary storage is magnetic disk (see Figs. 1-5 and 1-6). Information is stored on the surface of the disk by using patterns of magnetic spots. Another type of auxiliary storage is magnetic tape (see Fig. 1-7). Magnetic spot patterns are also used for data storage on tape. Although both tape and disk serve as auxiliary storage, disk is the more common and we will be concerned only with its use in this chapter.

One of the purposes of auxiliary storage is to store *programs* that are not currently being executed by the computer. When a program is saved (i.e., when the SAVE command is typed), the program that is currently in internal storage is stored in auxiliary storage. A program that is saved will remain in auxiliary storage until it is erased. A saved program can be retrieved as many times as necessary.

Another purpose of auxiliary storage is to store *data* that is not currently being processed by the computer. This could be data not needed immediately by the program that is executing or it could be data used by another program. Such data can be stored in auxiliary storage as long as necessary and retrieved whenever it is needed.

A collection of data that is stored in auxiliary storage is called a *data file* or simply a *file*. Data files are used for several reasons. Sometimes a large amount of data needs to be processed by a program. There may be so much data that not all of it can be stored in the computer's internal storage at one time. For example, a statistical program may have to analyze a large amount of experimental data. In such a case, the data can be stored in a file and then processed by the program piecemeal.

338

Another reason for utilizing files is that data may have to be saved for use by a program more than once. For example, personnel data for a business has to be processed by a payroll program every time the payroll is prepared. By storing the personnel data in a file, the data does not have to be reentered at the terminal each time it is needed.

Finally, data files can be used when several programs process the same data. For example, if student test scores are kept in a file, one program can be used to compute totals and averages for each student, another program can tabulate data for all students, and a third program can print grade reports. These programs can be run without reentering the data for each program.

In this chapter we discuss the programming necessary for the use of data files in BASIC. We describe how data files are created and how information is retrieved from a file. While the general concepts apply to all versions of BASIC, the characteristics of the statements vary from one version of BASIC to another. The programmer must refer to the appropriate reference manual for the details of the version of BASIC being used.

13-1. FILE CONCEPTS

A file is a collection of data stored in auxiliary storage. Each individual data value in a file is called a *field*. For example, a file of personnel data will contain fields for each employee's name, social security number, and pay rate. Related fields are grouped together to form a *record*. For example, a personnel record would contain the fields for one employee (i.e., one employee's name, number, and rate). A *file* is a group of related records. Thus, all of the personnel records, one for each employee, form the personnel file.

Figure 13-1 shows a listing of the data in an inventory file. Inventory is the stock of goods that a business has on hand. Each line in Fig. 13-1 is a separate record in the inventory file. Each record contains information about one item that the business stocks. The information is contained in the fields in the records. Notice that the fields are separated by commas just as the data values entered at a terminal are separated by commas.

The first field in each inventory record in Fig. 13-1 is the item's identifying number. The second field is the item's description. The next field is the unit price. The last field is the stock on hand. Notice that the fields in each record are in the same order. In fact, as we will see, we must know the order of the fields in the records when we write a program to process the data in the file.

Usually in a file each record has one field that identifies the record. This is called the *key field*. For example, in a personnel file the key

```
1001 ,SCREWS, 2.95 , 15
1023 ,NAILS, 3.64 , 7
1045 ,BOLTS, 2.25 , 0
1172 ,WASHERS, .75 , 32
1185 ,NUTS, 1.5 , 4
1201 ,HOOKS, 1.95 , 11
1235 ,GLUE, 4.85 , 3
1278 ,CLAMP, 9.95 , 0
1384 ,HANGER, 6.28 , 12
1400 ,TAPE, 4.75 , 0
9999 ,X, 0 , 0
```

FIGURE 13-1. An inventory file.

field might be the employee's social security number. In the inventory file in Fig. 13-1, the key field is the item number. Usually each record has a unique key field; that is, the key field in each record is different. As we will see, this helps us to retrieve specific records in the file.

The last record in the file in Fig. 13-1 has 9999 in the key field. This is a trailer value used to signal the end of the file. Sometimes this last record is called a *trailer record*. Notice that the other fields in the trailer record must contain some data. In this case, the item description is merely the letter X, and the price and quantity are both zero.

Physically the data in a file is stored as patterns of magnetic spots on an auxiliary storage device such as magnetic disk. The surface of a disk is organized into concentric circles called *tracks*. Each track can store a certain amount of data. The records in a file are recorded one after another along a track, as shown in Fig. 13-2. Once one track is full, the file is continued onto the next track. More than one file can be stored on a disk if there is room. In fact, it is not uncommon to have many files on one disk.

A magnetic disk is mounted in a disk drive (see Figs. 1-5 and 1-6), where it is attached to a spindle that rotates the disk at a high speed. As the disk rotates, a mechanism called a *read/write head* moves over the surface of the disk. The read/write head can be positioned over any track. Then, as the disk rotates, the head can retrieve data from the track or record data on the track.

One of the advantages of storing data on magnetic disk is that the data can be changed if necessary; that is, we can erase the data in a file and replace it with new data. This is possible because the data is stored in magnetic form. The magnetic patterns that represent the data can be easily changed by the disk drive.

File Processing

There are several things that we need to be able to do when we use data files. One is to *create* a file; that is, we need to be able to put data

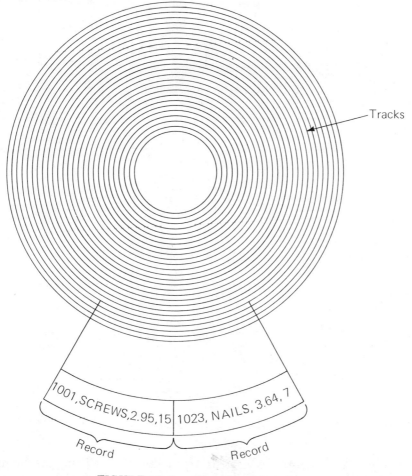

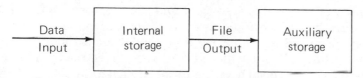

FIGURE 13-2. Magnetic disk storage.

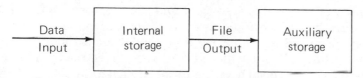

| Data Input | Internal storage | File Output | Auxiliary storage |

FIGURE 13-3. Creating a file.

into a file. The data that goes into a file must come from some other source. This data could be accepted from the terminal or be read from a DATA statement. It is even possible to obtain the data from another file. In any case, the data must first be brought into the computer's internal storage and then sent to the file. This is shown in Fig. 13-3. Notice that *input* data must be obtained from another source and that *output* data is sent to the file. Usually this is done one record at a time.

After a file is created, we can *access* the data in the file. By this we

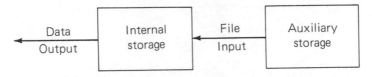

FIGURE 13-4.   Accessing a file.

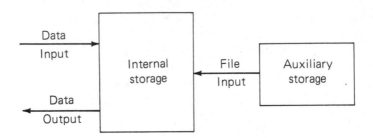

FIGURE 13-5.   Searching a file.

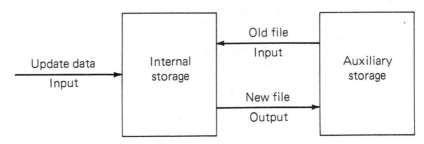

FIGURE 13-6.   Updating a file.

mean that we can retrieve records from the file and process them in internal storage. Usually this is done one record at a time and some sort of printed output is produced for each record in the file. This is shown in Fig. 13-4. In this case the *input* data is from the file and the *output* goes to the CRT, printer, or some other device.

We may also need to *search* for a particular record in a file. In this case the information about which record is to be retrieved must come from some other source such as the terminal. Then the required record must be located in the file and processed, and the appropriate output produced. Figure 13-5 shows this concept. *Input* data comes from the terminal and is used to locate the desired record in the file. The record that is retrieved is *input* data to the internal storage. The *output* then goes to the CRT or printer.

Finally, we may need to *update* the data in a file — to change the data in one or more records in a file in order to bring the information up to date. Figure 13-6 shows this process. The update information is *input* data that comes from the terminal, a DATA statement, or another file. The file to be updated contains old data that needs to be changed. This is also *input* data, since each record to be updated must be brought into internal storage for the necessary changes to be made. After the record is updated, the *output* data for the new file is sent to auxiliary storage.

In all of the situations described here, data must be transferred between the internal storage and the file in auxiliary storage. Data can be processed only if it is in the computer's internal storage. When data is brought into internal storage from a file, the process is viewed as an *input* operation. When data is sent from the internal storage to a file, the process involves an *output* operation. Usually input and output of file data is done one record at a time.

Notice also that a program can use more than one file. In fact, we could have several input files and several output files processed by the same program. This provides a great deal of versatility in what can be accomplished using files.

File Organization

There are two basic ways of organizing the records in a file — sequential file organization and random access file organization. In a *sequential file* the records are stored in the file in the order in which they are put into the file; that is, the first record that is created becomes the first physical record in the file. The second record created is put immediately after the first record. Then comes the third record, the fourth record, and so on for the other records in the file. For example, the file in Fig. 13-1 is a sequential file.

The records in a sequential file can be accessed only in the order in which they were created. This is called *sequential access*. Thus, we can access all of the records in a sequential file in order beginning with the first record in the file. However, if we only want to locate a particular record, such as the fifth record, we must access all of the preceding records in order until we find the one we need.

In a *random access file* records are not necessarily stored in sequence, but are put in particular record locations in the file. The location of a record is determined when the record is created, usually by using the key field of the record; that is, the key field indicates whether the record is the first record in the file, or the fifth record, or the tenth record or whatever record. Then to locate a particular record, we need only know the key field; the desired record can be retrieved without going through the other records in the file. This is called *random access* or *direct access*.

There are advantages and disadvantages to both types of file organization. In general, programs that process sequential files are easier to write. Sequential files, however, can only be accessed sequentially. On the other hand, the records in a random access file can be processed in any order, although random access programming can be quite complex.

In the next section we discuss sequential file processing and sequential access. Then in Section 13-3 we introduce some of the concepts associated with random access files.

*13-2. SEQUENTIAL FILES

In this section we describe the BASIC statements that are used to create and access sequential files.[†] We also explain the program logic for searching and updating a sequential file.

*Accessing a Sequential File

File processing is easiest to understand if we begin with file access. We will assume that a sequential file has already been created on disk and we need a program to retrieve the records in the file. For example, assume that the inventory file shown in Fig. 13-1 is stored on disk. We need to write a program to list the data in this file.

When a file is created, it is given a *name*. A file name must be one to six characters in length. For example, the name of the inventory file is INVEN. A name is required because it is possible to store more than one file on a disk. The computer must be given the name of the file so that it knows which file to access.

Before a file can be accessed, it must be "opened". Opening a file involves, among other things, telling the computer the name of the file. The computer checks whether a file with the given name exists. If an attempt is made to open a file that is not on the disk, an execution error occurs. The records in a file cannot be retrieved until the file is opened.

To open a file, we use an OPEN statement. The syntax of this statement is as follows:

ln OPEN *"file name"* FOR INPUT AS FILE *number*

For example, to open the inventory file, we could use the following statement:

```
100 OPEN "INVEN" FOR INPUT AS FILE 1
```

The OPEN statement begins with the keyword OPEN, followed by

[†]The statements described in this section are available in BASIC-PLUS on the DEC PDP 11 computer and in related versions of BASIC.

the name of the file enclosed in quotation marks. Then the words FOR INPUT indicate that the data in the file will be brought into the computer's internal storage. In other words, the file is an *input* file. (We will see that different words are used when we create a file.) Finally, the words AS FILE followed by a number indicate the "channel" that is to be used for the file. A channel can be regarded as a connection between the internal storage and the auxiliary storage. There are twelve channels numbered 1, 2, . . . , 12. One of these numbers must be used in the OPEN statement. In our example we use channel number 1, but any number between one and twelve is acceptable.

The reason for twelve channels is that there are times when we need to open more than one file in a program. We will see an example of this when we discuss file updating. Each file must be opened with a separate OPEN statement and must use a different channel number. Thus, we can have at most twelve open files at one time in a program.

After a file is opened, we can access records from the file one at a time. To retrieve a record, we use a special form of the INPUT statement. The syntax of this statement is as follows:

ln INPUT #*number,list of variables separated by commas*

For example, to retrieve one record from the inventory file, we could use the following statement:

```
130 INPUT #1,N,D$,P,S
```

In this form of the INPUT statement, the number following the # sign is the channel number for the file. This must be the same number that is given in the OPEN statement for the file. In this example, the file is opened as file 1. Thus, we must "input" from file #1. Notice that only the channel number makes this form of the INPUT statement different from the terminal INPUT statement.

The list of variables used in the INPUT statement must correspond to the fields in the records in the file. When we access a file, we must know how many fields there are in each record and the order of the fields. In the inventory file we know that the first field is the item number. The first variable (N) in the INPUT statement identifies this field. The second field is the item description, and the variable D$ is used for this field. The third and fourth fields are the unit price and the stock on hand; the variables P and S are used for these fields. Notice that the type of the variable must correspond to the type of data in the fields; that is, a numeric variable must be used for numeric data and a string variable must be used for string data.

Each time an INPUT statement for a file is executed, the next record in the file is retrieved. Input begins with the first record in the file and proceeds sequentially through the records in the file. We cannot access records out of sequence or in reverse order.

After we finish processing a file, we must "close" the file. This renders the file no longer available for processing. The statement that accomplishes this is the CLOSE statement. Its syntax is as follows:

ln CLOSE *number*

The number following the word CLOSE must be the channel number for the file. For example, to close the inventory file (channel number 1), we could use the following statement:

170 CLOSE 1

We can close more than one file at a time by listing several channel numbers in a single CLOSE statement. For example, the following statement closes three files:

800 CLOSE 3,8,11

Figure 13-7 shows a complete program that uses the file-processing statements described here to list the data in the inventory file. The first statement opens the file so that it can be accessed. Then headings for the output are printed. Next comes a loop consisting of statements 130 through 160. The first statement in the loop is an INPUT statement that retrieves one record from the file. Then statement 140 tests for a trailer value. Recall from Fig. 13-1 that the last record in the inventory file contains 9999 in the item number field. The IF statement tests for this value and branches out of the loop when this is the case. If the trailer value is not detected, the data in the inventory record is printed and the loop is repeated. When the loop is terminated, the CLOSE statement at line 170 is executed and the program ends. Notice that the OPEN statement and CLOSE statement are outside the loop. The file must be *opened once before* the first record in the file is accessed and *closed once after* processing is finished.

In the example in Fig. 13-7, one line is printed for each record in the file (except the trailer record). This is not always the case. For example, Fig. 13-8 shows a program that prints a line only if the amount of stock on hand is zero. In this case, only three lines are printed, each with the item number and description. Notice that a variable for the price (P) must appear in the proper place in the INPUT statement even though the price is not needed in the program. This is because each execution of the INPUT statement causes a complete record to be retrieved and a variable must be provided for each field in the record.

```
100 OPEN "INVEN" FOR INPUT AS FILE 1
110 PRINT "ITEM NUMBER","DESCRIPTION","PRICE","STOCK"
120 PRINT
130 INPUT #1,N,D$,P,S
140 IF N=9999 THEN 170
150 PRINT N,D$,P,S
160 GO TO 130
170 CLOSE 1
999 END
```

(a) The program

ITEM NUMBER	DESCRIPTION	PRICE	STOCK
1001	SCREWS	2.95	15
1023	NAILS	3.64	7
1045	BOLTS	2.25	0
1172	WASHERS	.75	32
1185	NUTS	1.5	4
1201	HOOKS	1.95	11
1235	GLUE	4.85	3
1278	CLAMP	9.95	0
1384	HANGER	6.28	12
1400	TAPE	4.75	0

(b) The output

FIGURE 13-7. A program to list a sequential file.

```
100 OPEN "INVEN" FOR INPUT AS FILE 1
110 PRINT "THE FOLLOWING ITEMS ARE OUT OF STOCK"
120 INPUT #1,N,D$,P,S
130 IF N=9999 THEN 170
140 IF S>0 THEN 120
150 PRINT N,D$
160 GO TO 120
170 CLOSE 1
999 END
```

(a) The program

```
THE FOLLOWING ITEMS ARE OUT OF STOCK
  1045          BOLTS
  1278          CLAMP
  1400          TAPE
```

(b) The output

FIGURE 13-8. A program to process a sequential file.

*Creating a Sequential File

Before the programs in Figs. 13-7 and 13-8 can be run, a file must exist on disk. There are several ways of creating a file. Some versions of BASIC have special system commands that can be used to help create a file. These commands vary considerably from one computer to another.

One approach to creating a sequential file is to write a program that stores the records in the file one at a time. Such a program would obtain the data for one record from some other source, such as the terminal or a DATA statement. It would then store the data record in the file in auxiliary storage. This sequence would be repeated until all of the records, including the trailer record, are stored in the file.

To create a file, the file must first be opened. The syntax of the OPEN statement used is as follows:

ln OPEN *"file name"* FOR OUTPUT AS FILE *number*

For example, the following OPEN statement could be used in a program that creates the inventory file:

100 OPEN "INVEN" FOR OUTPUT AS FILE 1

The OPEN statement gives a name to the file. The name must be one to six characters long and is made up by the programmer. Whenever the file is accessed, the same name must be used. The OPEN statement also indicates that records will be stored in the file; that is, that the file is an *output file*. This is the meaning of the words FOR OUTPUT in the OPEN statement. Finally, the OPEN statement specifies the channel number that is used for the file. This must be a number between 1 and 12. The same number does *not* have to be used when the file is accessed.

After a file is opened, we can store records in the file one at a time. The statement used for this is a special form of the PRINT statement. The syntax is as follows:

ln PRINT #*number,output list*

For example, to store one record in the inventory file, we could use the following statement:

120 PRINT #1,N;",";D$;",";P;",";S

The number following the # sign in this form of the PRINT statement is the channel number for the file. This must be the same number that is given in the OPEN statement for the file. Notice that it is basi-

348

```
100 OPEN "INVEN" FOR OUTPUT AS FILE 1
110 READ N,D$,P,S
120 PRINT #1,N;",";D$;",";P;",";S
130 IF N<>9999 THEN 110
140 CLOSE 1
901 DATA 1001,SCREWS,2.95,15
902 DATA 1023,NAILS,3.64,7
903 DATA 1045,BOLTS,2.25,0
904 DATA 1172,WASHERS,0.75,32
905 DATA 1185,NUTS,1.50,4
906 DATA 1201,HOOKS,1.95,11
907 DATA 1235,GLUE,4.85,3
908 DATA 1278,CLAMP,9.95,0
909 DATA 1384,HANGER,6.28,12
910 DATA 1400,TAPE,4.75,0
911 DATA 9999,X,0,0
999 END
```

FIGURE 13-9.   A program to create a sequential file.

cally the channel number that differentiates this form of the PRINT statement from the PRINT statement for CRT or printer output.

Following the channel number is a list of the data that is to appear in one record in the file. There is one variable in this list for each field. Semicolons are used so that the fields are as close together as possible. (Commas can also be used, but then the fields are spread out in the record and the file requires more space on disk.) Notice that between each variable in the PRINT statement the string "," appears. This causes a comma to be placed in the record between each field. These commas appear in the file (see Fig. 13-1) and are necessary because the input operation that accesses a record requires commas between the data. If the commas are omitted, the computer cannot know where each field ends and thus cannot assign the data to the proper variables.[†]

Figure 13-9 shows a program that creates the sequential inventory file. The first statement in the program opens the file. Then the READ statement reads the data for one record from a DATA statement. Notice that four values are read for the four fields in a record. (This input data could also be accepted from a terminal or retrieved from another file.) Next, the special form of the PRINT statement is used to store one record in the file. The READ and PRINT statements are repeated in a loop until the trailer record is stored in the file. Notice that the last DATA statement contains the data that is to go into the trailer

---

[†]Some versions of BASIC automatically insert commas between the fields when the file is created. In this case, commas are not used in the PRINT statement.

record. This record must be stored in the file by the program that creates the file. The IF statement at line 130 repeats the READ/PRINT loop until *after* the trailer record is read and stored. Finally, the CLOSE statement closes the file. This is required after all file processing is completed.

*Searching a Sequential File

Occasionally it is necessary to retrieve a specific record from a file. For example, we may wish to locate the record for a particular item in the inventory file. Usually the record to be retrieved is specified by giving the key field for the record. Recall that the key field is the field that identifies the record. In the inventory file this is the item number. Thus, to retrieve a particular inventory record, we would give the number for the item whose record is to be located.

Locating a record in a file involves searching the file until the record with the desired key field is found. The search is done by retrieving one record at a time beginning with the first record in the file. Each time a record is retrieved, we compare its key field with the desired key. If they are the same, the search stops; otherwise we continue to the next record. The processing stops either when the desired record is found or when the end of the file is reached without finding the record.

Figure 13-10 shows a sample program that involves file searching. The purpose of this program is to compute the cost of an order by multiplying the quantity purchased by the unit price for an item. The terminal input and output for this program are shown in Fig. 13-11. The item number and quantity are entered from the terminal; statements 100 through 130 are used to accept this input data. Then the file is searched for a matching item number. First, the file is opened (statement 150). Then statement 160 retrieves one record from the file. In statement 180 the item number entered at the terminal is compared with the item number from the file. If these are the same, the quantity ordered is compared to the stock on hand (statement 200). If insufficient stock is available, a message is printed; otherwise the cost is computed and the output is printed (statements 230 through 250).

Searching continues until either the desired item is found in the file or the trailer record is reached. In the latter case we know that the item is not in the file and a message indicating this is printed (statement 270).

After the search is completed, the file is closed by statement 280. The terminal operator is then asked whether he or she wishes to repeat the processing. If more costs are to be computed, the computer branches to statement 100 and the program is repeated.

Notice that the program is designed so that the file is closed and then reopened when more than one item is to be located in the file. This must be done so that the computer begins accessing the file with

```
100 PRINT "ENTER ITEM NUMBER";
110 INPUT N1
120 PRINT "ENTER QUANTITY";
130 INPUT Q
140 PRINT
150 OPEN "INVEN" FOR INPUT AS FILE 1
160 INPUT #1,N,D$,P,S
170 IF N=9999 THEN 270
180 IF N1=N THEN 200
190 GO TO 160
200 IF Q<=S THEN 230
210 PRINT "INSUFFICIENT STOCK ON HAND FOR ITEM";N1
220 GO TO 280
230 LET C=P*Q
240 PRINT "ITEM";N1;D$
250 PRINT "UNIT PRICE";P;"QUANTITY";Q;"COST";C
260 GO TO 280
270 PRINT "ITEM";N1;"NOT FOUND IN FILE"
280 CLOSE 1
290 PRINT
300 PRINT "DO YOU WANT TO COMPUTE MORE ORDER COSTS";
310 INPUT R$
320 PRINT
330 IF R$="YES" THEN 100
999 END
```

FIGURE 13-10. A program to search a sequential file.

the first record each time the file is to be searched. If we do not close and reopen the file, processing will continue with the next record following the last record retrieved.[†]

In this program the records in the file are searched in order beginning with the first record in the file. This is called a *sequential search*. The search stops either when the desired record is located or when the trailer record is retrieved indicating an unsuccessful search. If the records are sorted in increasing order by key field, an unsuccessful search can be detected before reaching the trailer record. This can be done in the program in Fig. 13-10 by changing statement 170 to the following:

```
170 IF NI<N THEN 270
```

In this case the search stops if the desired item number is less than the

---

[†]Some versions of BASIC have a statement such as RESET #1 or RESTORE #1 that can be used to restart file access with the first record in the file.

```
ENTER ITEM NUMBER? 1201
ENTER QUANTITY? 5

ITEM 1201 HOOKS
UNIT PRICE 1.95 QUANTITY 5 COST 9.75

DO YOU WANT TO COMPUTE MORE ORDER COSTS? YES

ENTER ITEM NUMBER? 1045
ENTER QUANTITY? 10

INSUFFICIENT STOCK ON HAND FOR ITEM 1045

DO YOU WANT TO COMPUTE MORE ORDER COSTS? YES

ENTER ITEM NUMBER? 1225
ENTER QUANTITY? 8

ITEM 1225 NOT FOUND IN FILE

DO YOU WANT TO COMPUTE MORE ORDER COSTS? YES

ENTER ITEM NUMBER? 1023
ENTER QUANTITY? 1

ITEM 1023 NAILS
UNIT PRICE 3.64 QUANTITY 1 COST 3.64

DO YOU WANT TO COMPUTE MORE ORDER COSTS? NO
```

FIGURE 13–11.   The input and output for the file searching program.

item number from the input file. This indicates that we have gone beyond the required item in the file and that the item is not in the file.
Again, this approach assumes that the records are organized in increasing order by key fields.

While a sequential search is useful, it can be very slow. This is because each time that a file INPUT statement is executed, the computer
must retrieve a record from the disk. Such disk access is time-consuming
in comparison to other types of processing that the computer can do.

An alternative approach to file searching is to retrieve all of the
records in the file at one time and to store the data in internal storage.
This can be done only if the file is small enough to fit in internal storage, which in many realistic situations is not possible. When this is
possible, however, the file is brought into internal storage and stored in

several arrays, one for each field. For example, to retrieve the ten records from the inventory file and to store the data in four arrays, we could use the following statements:

```
100 DIM N(10),D$(10),P(10),S(10)
110 OPEN "INVEN" FOR INPUT AS FILE 1
120 FOR I=1 TO 10
130   INPUT #1,N(I),D$(I),P(I),S(I)
140 NEXT I
150 CLOSE 1
```

Once the file of data is in internal storage, it can be searched very quickly. We can use a sequential search or, if the data is in increasing order by key field, a binary search. (These approaches to array searching were discussed in Section 10-4.) It is important to remember, however, that this approach works only if the file is sufficiently small to fit in internal storage.

*Updating a Sequential File

File updating involves changing the data in one or more records in a file. For example, it may be necessary to update the stock on hand for several times in an inventory file to reflect withdrawals from and additions to inventory. To update a file, we must locate the records that are to be changed. Essentially this involves searching the file for the desired records. After finding a record that is to be updated, individual fields in the record can be modified.

One problem with updating a sequential file is that we cannot change a record in the file itself; that is, once a sequential file is created, we cannot change the data in the file without erasing the entire file and recreating it. This is because we cannot open the file as an input file *and* an output file at the same time. Thus, to update a sequential file, we must create a *new* file which contains all of the records from the *old* (nonupdated) file with any changes made in the data.

We call the file that is to be updated the *old master file*. The updated file is called the *new master file*. We assume that the records in the old master file are in increasing order by key field. The data that indicates what changes are to be made in the master file is called the *transaction data* because it represents "transactions" that have taken place and that need to be reflected in the records of the master file. The transaction data may be entered at the terminal, may be read from DATA statements, or may be retrieved from another file. In the last situation the file is called the *transaction file*. In any case, the transaction data must contain the key fields of the records to be updated and the data must be in increasing order by key field.

As an example, assume that we wish to update the inventory stock on hand by subtracting the amount withdrawn from stock and adding the amount added to stock. The old master file is the inventory file shown in Fig. 13-1. The transaction data consists of three values for each item to be updated. These are the item number, the amount withdrawn, and the amount added. For example, if, for item 1172, the amount withdrawn is 4 and the amount added is 15, the new stock on hand is the old stock (which is 7 in Fig. 13-1) minus 4 plus 15 or 18. This is the amount that would go into the new master file for this item.

Usually the transaction data does not contain transactions for each record in the old master file. In the inventory example there would be no transaction data for an item if stock was not withdrawn or added. In such a case, however, the record from the old master file must still be put on the new master file; otherwise the record would be lost from the file.

There can also be transaction data for records that do not exist in the master file. This would be the case if an error were made in the transaction data or if a record had not yet been added to the master file for an item. If such a situation occurs, a message should be printed indicating the condition so that corrective action can be taken.

Figure 13-12 shows a program that incorporates the concepts discussed here to update the inventory file. The old master file is the file named INVEN with the data shown in Fig. 13-1. This is an input file and is opened as such in statement 110. The new master file is named NEWINV and is opened as an output file in statement 120. Notice that different channel numbers are used for the files; when more than one file is opened at a time in a program, each file must use a different channel.

The transaction data is contained in the DATA statements. Each set of transaction data consists of an item number (which is the key field), the amount withdrawn from inventory, and the amount added to inventory. Notice that the data is in increasing sequence by key field and that there is a set of trailer data with 9999 for the key field. Recall also that the old master file is in increasing order by key field and has a trailer record. In order for the program to work correctly, both the master data and the transaction data *must* be in increasing sequence by key field.

The program in Fig. 13-12 consists of a main loop (statements 200 through 380) that is repeated until either the end of the master file or the end of the transaction data is reached. Essentially this loop reads a set of transaction data and then searches the master file for a record with the same key field. If one is found, the stock on hand is updated and the record is stored in the new master file (statements 270 and 280). Any master record with a key field less than the key in the transaction data is stored in the new master file without modification (state-

```
100 REM - SEQUENTIAL FILE UPDATE PROGRAM
110 OPEN "INVEN" FOR INPUT AS FILE 1
120 OPEN "NEWINV" FOR OUTPUT AS FILE 2
200 REM - MAIN UPDATE LOOP
210 INPUT #1,N,D$,P,S
220 READ N1,W,A
230 IF N=9999 THEN 450
240 IF N1=9999 THEN 400
250 IF N<>N1 THEN 300
260 REM - KEYS MATCH; UPDATE RECORD
270 LET S=S-W+A
280 PRINT #2,N;",";D$;",";P;",";S
290 GO TO 200
300 IF N>N1 THEN 350
310 REM - MASTER KEY LESS THAN TRANSACTION KEY
320 PRINT #2,N;",";D$;",";P;",";S
330 INPUT #1,N,D$,P,S
340 GO TO 230
350 REM - MASTER KEY GREATER THAN TRANSACTION KEY
360 PRINT "ITEM";N1;"NOT IN FILE"
370 READ N1,W,A
380 GO TO 240
400 REM - FINISH MASTER FILE
410 IF N=9999 THEN 500
420 PRINT #2,N;",";D$;",";P;",";S
430 INPUT #1,N,D$,P,S
440 GO TO 400
450 REM - FINISH TRANSACTION FILE
460 IF N1=9999 THEN 500
470 PRINT "ITEM";N1;"NOT IN FILE"
480 READ N1,W,A
490 GO TO 450
500 PRINT #2,9999;",";"X";",";0;",";0
510 CLOSE 1,2
900 REM - TRANSACTION DATA
901 DATA 1023,4,15
902 DATA 1172,30,0
903 DATA 1193,12,20
904 DATA 1201,0,15
905 DATA 1225,0,30
906 DATA 1235,0,0
907 DATA 9999,0,0
999 END
```

FIGURE 13–12. A program to update a sequential file.

ment 320). If the key field in the master record is greater than that in
the transaction data, an error message is printed indicating that the item
is not in the file (statement 360).

To see how the updating proceeds, assume that the master file and
transaction data contain records with the following key fields:

Master Key	Transaction Key
1001	1023
1023	1172
1045	1193
1172	1201
1185	
1201	

The processing sequence for this data is as follows:

1. $1001 < 1023$; store old master record without updating in new
    master file
2. $1023 = 1023$; update old master record and store in new master
    file
3. $1145 < 1172$; store old master record without updating in new
    master file
4. $1172 = 1172$; update old master record and store in new master
    file
5. $1185 < 1193$; store old master record without updating in new
    master file
6. $1201 > 1193$; print error message
7. $1201 = 1201$; update old master record and store in new master
    file

When the end of either the old master file or the transaction data is
reached, the update loop is terminated. However, if the end of the
transaction data is reached before the end of the old master file, there
will still be master records that must be stored in the new master file.
This is accomplished in statements 400 through 440. Similarly, if the
end of the old master file is reached before the end of the transaction
data, there will still be transaction data that requires an error message
to be printed. Statements 450 through 490 accomplish this.

Finally, after all data is processed, a trailer record must be stored in
the new master file. This is done in statement 500. Then both files are
closed (statement 510) and the program is terminated.

The actual processing of the program in Fig. 13-12 results in the
printed output shown in Fig. 13-13(a). This is a list of the item numbers from the transaction data for items that were not found in the old

```
ITEM 1193 NOT IN FILE
ITEM 1225 NOT IN FILE
```

(a) The printed output

```
1001 ,SCREWS, 2.95 , 15
1023 ,NAILS, 3.64 , 18
1045 ,BOLTS, 2.25 , 0
1172 ,WASHERS, .75 , 2
1185 ,NUTS, 1.5 , 4
1201 ,HOOKS, 1.95 , 26
1235 ,GLUE, 4.85 , 3
1278 ,CLAMP, 9.95 , 0
1384 ,HANGER, 6.28 , 12
1400 ,TAPE, 4.75 , 0
9999 ,X, 0 , 0
```

(b) The new master file

FIGURE 13-13.   The output from the file updating
program.

master file. Figure 13-13(b) shows the contents of the new master file. Notice that the stock on hand for several items has been updated.

A file-updating program such as this is used whenever the data in a sequential file changes. Additional statements can be included in the program to add new records to the file and to delete out-of-date records. These would be required in a complete file maintenance program.

*13-3. RANDOM ACCESS FILES

In a random access file the records are not necessarily stored physically one after the other as in a sequential file. Instead, the records are stored at various locations in the file depending on the key field. In this section we discuss the concepts necessary to understand random access files. However, since the details vary considerably from one version of BASIC to another, we do not describe the statements that are used for random access files. The programmer will have to refer to the appropriate reference manual for the specifics of the version of BASIC being used.

The basic idea of a random access file is that a certain number of record locations are set aside for the file on disk. Each record location can store one record in the file. The record locations are numbered in sequence from 1 up to the total number of locations. For example, Fig. 13-14 shows the space for a random access file that contains 100 record locations. The locations are numbered 1, 2, 3, . . . , 100.

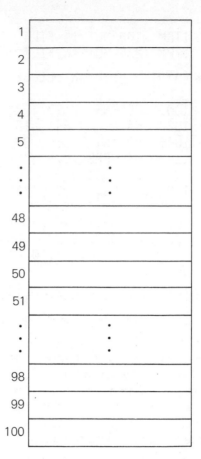

FIGURE 13-14.   The file space for a random access file
with 100 record locations.

To create a random access file, each record is stored in the file at a specific record location that is determined from the key field. (We will discuss how this is done below.) When we store a record in the file, we specify the *number of the location* where the record is to go. Thus, if we want to store a record at the fifth location, we would write a statement that essentially says "store the record at location number 5". This can be done without having previously stored records at locations one through four. We can then store the next record at another location which is not necessarily the next location in sequence. In other words, with a random access file records can be stored anywhere in the file, not just in sequential order.

Figure 13-15 shows several inventory records stored in a random access file. Notice in this figure that some record locations do not contain data. In a random access file, sufficient record locations must be set aside for the maximum number of records that the file can contain, although not all record locations have to be used.

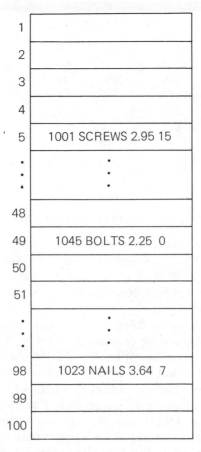

1	
2	
3	
4	
5	1001 SCREWS 2.95 15
⋮	⋮
48	
49	1045 BOLTS 2.25 0
50	
51	
⋮	⋮
98	1023 NAILS 3.64 7
99	
100	

FIGURE 13-15.   Inventory records stored in a random
access file.

Records are accessed in a random access file by specifying the location of the desired record. For example, to retrieve the fifth record in the file, we would write a statement such as "retrieve the record at location number 5". We can retrieve a record at any location in the file, not just the next location in sequence, and we do not have to start with the first record in the file. This is what is meant by *random access*. We can access the records in random order, not only in sequential order.

To understand how random access files are used, we need to know how a key field can determine the record location. One approach is to let the value of the key field be the record location. For example, in the inventory file shown in Fig. 13-1, the key field is the item number. The first record in the file has a key field of 1001. This record could be stored in a random access file at record location 1001. Similarly, the second record, with a key field of 1023, could be stored at record location 1023.

Key Field	Record Location
1001	5
1023	98
1045	49
1172	28
1185	20
1201	82
1235	79
1278	46
1384	51
1400	24

FIGURE 13-16.   An index for the inventory file.

The problem with this approach is that a very large space for the file may be required. For the inventory file, if we assume that each item number has four digits, 9999 record locations would be required. Most of these locations would not contain a data record since only a few item numbers are used.

Another approach is to keep a table containing key fields and locations of the corresponding records in the file. This type of table is often called an *index*. For example, Fig. 13-16 shows an index for the inventory data. Notice that the record locations in the index do not have to be in sequence. Such an index is set up when the file is created and can be stored in a sequential file on disk. The index can be retrieved whenever it is needed. In internal storage the index can be stored in two arrays and searched very rapidly (perhaps with a binary search). To retrieve a specific record in the file, the index is searched for the key field of the record. The record is then retrieved from the location specified in the index.

A third approach to using the key field to indicate a record location in a random access file is called *hashing* or *randomizing*. Basically this involves using the value of the key field in a mathematical computation that yields the record location. The technique is complex because of special cases that can occur. We will not cover this approach in the present book.†

With a random access file, not all of the record locations will necessarily contain data records. Records can be scattered throughout the file with empty locations in between. Because of this, the idea of sequential access does not apply to a random access file. In addition, there is no trailer record since the end of the file is determined by the last record location.

---

†See the article by W. D. Mauer and T. G. Lewis, "Hash Table Methods", in the March, 1975 issue of *Computing Surveys* for a complete discussion of this approach.

Records in a random access file are created and accessed randomly. Searching for a specific record is no more complex than accessing any record. We merely use the key field of the desired record to indicate the record's location. Updating a random access file is also done randomly. In contrast to sequential files, with random access files a new file does not need to be created when old data is updated. We simply retrieve the record to be updated, make the necessary changes, and store the record in its record location, thereby erasing the old record.

We can see that some aspects of random access file processing are simpler than sequential file processing. The main difficulty comes in using the key field to indicate the record's location. However, once this part of the problem is solved, random access files can be very useful.

*13-4. CHAINING

Sometimes a program is too large to fit into the computer's internal storage. When this is the case, it is necessary to break the program into sections and save each section on disk. Essentially each section becomes a separate program and is given a name when it is saved. Then execution is begun by bringing the first section of the program into internal storage and running it. At the end of this section, a special statement is executed that brings the second section into internal storage, erasing the first section and continuing with execution. This can be repeated for as many program sections as required. The process is called *chaining*.

The statement that is used to bring in the next section of a program is the CHAIN statement.[†] The syntax of this statement is as follows:

ln CHAIN *"program name"*

For example, to bring in a program section named SEC2, we could use the following statement:

```
830 CHAIN "SEC2"
```

Execution of this statement causes the computer to replace the program currently in internal storage with the one named SEC2. Processing then continues with the first statement in SEC2.

We can use the CHAIN statement to execute any program section that is saved. We can even return to the first section of the program and repeat it. Each program section that is brought in by the CHAIN state-

---

[†]This statement is available in BASIC-PLUS on the DEC PDP 11 computer and in related versions of BASIC.

ment replaces the current program section in internal storage. Hence, we can use the same statement numbers and variables in different program sections; the computer will treat each program section as if it were a new program.

One problem with chaining is that any *data* stored in a program section is lost when the next section is brought in. To solve this problem, we can create a file containing all of the data that needs to be used by the next section just before the CHAIN statement is executed. Then the file can be accessed at the beginning of the next program section and processing can continue without loss of data.

For example, assume that the values of the variables A, B, C, and D are determined in the first section of a program and are needed in the next section (SEC2). The following statements can then be executed at the end of the first section:

```
800 OPEN "FILE1" FOR OUTPUT AS FILE 1
810 PRINT #1,A;",";B;",";C;",";D
820 CLOSE 1
830 CHAIN "SEC2"
```

At the beginning of the second section, we would have statements such as the following:

```
100 OPEN "FILE1" FOR INPUT AS FILE 1
110 INPUT #1,A,B,C,D
120 CLOSE 1
```

Thus, the values of A, B, C, and D would be transferred from one program section to the other by use of a file.

Chaining can be very useful in large programs, especially interactive programs involving many tasks. Each task can be stored as a separate program section and brought in as needed. This not only makes it possible to write large programs, but also simplifies the development of programs that perform many different operations.

REVIEW QUESTIONS

1. Auxiliary storage is used to store _____ and _____.

2. Give three reasons for storing data in files in auxiliary storage.

3. An individual data value in a file is called a _____.

4. A group of related fields is called a _____.

5. What is a key field?

6. Data is stored on the surface of a disk in concentric circles called
_____.

7. When a file is created, it is an (input/output) _____ file.

8. When a file is accessed, it is an (input/output) _____ file.

9. When data in a file is to be updated, the old file is an (input/output) _____ file, and the new, updated file is an (input/output) _____ file.

10. What is the difference between sequential access and random access?

11. Assume that a sequential file named FILEX exists on disk. Each record in the file has five fields. Write statements to do the following:
  (a) Open the file.
  (b) Retrieve one record from the file.
  (c) Close the file.

12. Assume that it is necessary to create a new sequential file on disk to be named FILEY. Each record in the file has three fields. Write statements to do the following:
  (a) Open the file.
  (b) Store one record in the file.
  (c) Close the file.

13. What is the purpose of a trailer record in a sequential file?

14. Consider the program shown in Fig. 13-10. What would happen if the OPEN statement were moved to line 90 and the CLOSE statement were moved to line 340?

15. When a file is searched beginning with the first record in the file and continuing one record at a time, the process is called a _____ search.

16. The data that indicates what changes are to be made in a master file is called the _____.

17. Consider the program shown in Fig. 13-12. How many times will each of the following statements be executed when this program is run?
  (a) The statement at line 280.
  (b) The statement at line 320.
  (c) The statement at line 420.

18. How are records stored in a random access file?

19. Describe two techniques that can be used to relate key fields and record locations in a random access file.

20. Write a statement to appear in a program named PROGX that causes a program named PROGY to be retrieved from auxiliary storage and executed.

PROGRAMMING PROBLEMS

1. Write a BASIC program to create a sequential file of payroll data. Each record in the file contains a field for the employee's number, employee's name, hourly pay rate, number of exemptions, and year-to-date gross pay. The records are in ascending order by employee number. Store the following data in the file:

Employee Number	Employee Name	Hourly Pay Rate	Number of Exemptions	Year-to-date Gross Pay
1234	SMITH	5.25	2	13,528.32
1345	JONES	6.10	2	18,452.00
1456	BROWN	5.75	0	17,152.25
1567	JOHNSON	4.75	3	10,295.30
1678	ANDREWS	5.20	5	14,252.85
1789	MCDONALD	6.10	0	17,025.00
2123	WHITE	4.90	1	15,302.00
2234	KNIGHT	7.25	1	17,305.41
2345	DAVIS	8.15	6	24,505.25
2456	EMERY	4.00	3	17,225.36
2567	HOLT	5.50	0	12,250.00
2678	COLE	6.00	3	9,845.00

2. Write a BASIC program to list the payroll file created in problem 1. Supply appropriate headings and print one line for each record in the file.

3. Write a BASIC program to print the employee number and name for each employee in the payroll file created in problem 1 who has zero exemptions.

4. Write a BASIC program to print any employee's record from the payroll file created in problem 1 given the employee's number. Test the program for several employees. Be sure to test the case where there is no matching employee number in the file.

5. Write a BASIC program to process payroll transaction data against the payroll file created in problem 1. Transaction data consists of the employee's number and hours worked for a number of employees. The data is in increasing order by employee number. The program should produce a payroll summary report. The report should list the following fields for each employee for which there is transaction data: employee number, employee name, gross pay, withholding tax, social security tax, net pay, and new year-to-date gross pay. Supply appropriate headings for the columns of output. If there is transaction data for an employee for whom there is no record in the payroll file, print the employee's number and an appropriate message. The gross pay, withholding tax, social security tax, net pay, and new year-to-date gross pay are computed as follows:

(a) Gross pay is hours times rate with "time and one-half" for all hours over forty worked in a week.

(b) Withholding tax = 22.5% of [gross pay - (exemptions $\times$ 13.5)].

(c) Social security tax is 6.05% of gross pay. Employees are exempt from social security tax once their year-to-date gross exceeds $17,300.

(d) Net pay is gross pay less withholding tax and social security tax.

(e) New year-to-date gross pay is the year-to-date gross pay from the payroll file plus the current gross pay.

Use the following transaction data to test the program:

Employee Number	Hours Worked
1345	35
1678	40
1789	50
1890	37
2234	42
2235	40
2456	45
2460	48
2567	20

6. Modify the program in problem 5 to create a new payroll file in addition to printing the payroll summary report. The new payroll file should be the same as the old payroll file with the exception that the year-to-date gross pay is updated to the new year-to-date gross pay where appropriate. Modify the program in problem 2 to list the new payroll file after it is created.

7. Write a BASIC program to create a file of test-score data. Each record in the file has two fields — an identification-number field and a test-score field. The records in the file are not in any particular order. Store the data in problem 6 of Chapter 10 in the file.

8. Write a BASIC program to print the data in the test-score file created in problem 7.

9. Write a BASIC program to process the data in the test-score file created in problem 7 as follows:

(a) Accumulate and print the total of the test scores.

(b) Calculate and print the mean of the scores.

(c) Determine and print the number of scores that fall into each of the following categories:

90–100
80–89
70–79
60–69
0–59

10. Write a BASIC program to create a sorted test-score file from the file created in problem 7. The data in the sorted file should be in ascending order by identification number. (Hint: Retrieve all of the records in the file, storing the data in two arrays in the program. Then sort the identification-number array and store the sorted data in a new file.) Modify the program in problem 8 to print the sorted test-score file.

11. Write a BASIC program to create a sequential name-and-address file. Each record in the file has six fields: identification number, name, street address, city, state, and zip code. The records are in increasing order by identification number. Supply a list of ten to twenty names and addresses to store in the file.

12. Write a BASIC program to print "mailing labels" from the records in the name-and-address file created in problem 11. Each mailing label consists of three lines with the name on the first line, the street address on the second line, and the city, state, and zip code on the third line.

13. Write a BASIC program to print any name and address from the file created in problem 11 given the identification number. Test the program with several identification numbers. Be certain to test the case where there is no matching record in the file.

14. Write a BASIC program to create a random access name-and-address file. Each record in the file contains an identification number, name, street address, city, state, and zip code.

15. Write a BASIC program to retrieve randomly and print any name and address from the random access file created in problem 14 given the identification number. Test the program with several identification numbers. Be certain to test the case where there is no matching record in the file.

16. Write a BASIC program to update the random access file created in problem 14. Update data is entered at the terminal and begins with an update code. The update codes and their meanings are as follows:

Code	Meaning
1	Add a record to the file
2	Delete a record from the file
3	Change a record in the file

4.   Create a file

If a code of 1 is entered, the program should accept the name-and-address data from the terminal and add a record with this data to the file. If a code of 2 is entered, the program should accept an identification number and delete the corresponding record from the file. If a code of 3 is entered, the program should accept new name-and-address data from the terminal and replace the corresponding record in the file with the new data. Test the program by making several additions, deletions, and changes. Then use the program in problem 15 to check that all updating has been done correctly.

SUMMARY
OF BASIC

This appendix summarizes the BASIC language. The characteristics of both ANS minimal BASIC and the common extensions discussed in the text are presented. Any item that is marked with an asterisk (*) is not available in ANS minimal BASIC. The actual syntax of a nonstandard item may vary from one version of BASIC to another. The programmer must consult the appropriate reference manual for the characteristics of the version of BASIC being used.

The information in this appendix is presented in three tables as follows:

TABLE 1: Fundamental Elements of BASIC
TABLE 2: BASIC Statements
TABLE 3: Built-in Functions

Each entry in the tables describes the syntax of an item, shows an example, and gives the number of the section in the text in which the item is discussed. Occasionally an item is listed more than once in a table. Each listing describes a different form of the item.

TABLE 1
FUNDAMENTAL ELEMENTS OF BASIC

Element	Syntax	Examples	Section Reference
array variable	a letter	A	10-1
*array variable**	any numeric variable	A5	10-1
*concatenation operator**	+	+	9-3
line number	a number between 1 and 9999	100	2-1
numeric constant	one or more digits possibly with a decimal point and possibly preceded by a sign	25 -48.56	3-1
numeric constant (E-notation)	a simple numeric constant followed by the letter E and an exponent (one or two digits possibly preceded by a sign)	-3.58E15 856E-8	3-1
numeric expression	a numeric constant, variable, or function, or any group of these combined with numeric operators and possibly containing parentheses	5 X3 A+(B-2.5)*C	3-2, 8-1
numeric operator	+,-,*,/,∧	+	3-2
numeric variable	a letter or a letter followed by a single digit	A B5	3-1
relational expression	a numeric expression followed by a relational operator followed by a numeric expression	A+B>=3.5	4-1
relational expression	a string constant or variable followed by = or <> followed by a string constant or variable	R$="YES"	9-2
*relational expression**	a string expression followed by a relational operator followed by a string expression	N$>="JOHN"	9-2, 9-3
relational operator	<,<=,>,>=,=,<>	<	4-1
*string array variable**	array variable followed by a dollar sign	S$	10-5
string constant	a group of characters enclosed in quotation marks	"THE END"	9-1
*string expression**	a string constant, variable, or function, or any group of these combined with the concatenation operator	"ABC" S$ "ABC"+S$	9-3
string variable	a letter followed by a dollar sign	A$	9-1
*string variable**	any numeric variable followed by a dollar sign	X5$	9-1
*subscripted string variable**	string array variable followed by a numeric expression enclosed in parentheses	S$(5) S$(K) S$(X+3)	10-5

(continued)

369

TABLE 1—*Cont.*

Element	Syntax	Examples	Section Reference
subscripted variable	array variable followed by a numeric expression enclosed in parentheses	A(5) A(K) A(X+3)	10–1
subscripted variable	array variable followed by two numeric expressions separated by commas and enclosed in parentheses	A(5,6) A(K,X+3)	11–1

TABLE 2
BASIC STATEMENTS

Statement	Syntax	Example	Section Reference
CALL*	ln CALL name (arguments)	300 CALL TOT(1,2,X)	12–4
CHAIN*	ln CHAIN "program name"	480 CHAIN "PROG2"	13–4
CLOSE*	ln CLOSE number,number, . . .	250 CLOSE 1,2	13–2
DATA	ln DATA list of constants	800 DATA 1,2,3	6–3
DEF	ln DEF FNletter(variable)=numeric expression	100 DEF FNT(A)=A+B	12–1
DEF*	ln DEF FNvariable(list of variables)=numeric expression	110 DEF FNT(A,B)=A+B	12–1
DEF*	ln DEF FNstring variable(list of variables)=string expression	120 DEF FNS$(A$,B$)=A$+B$	12–1
DEF/FNEND*	ln DEF FNvariable(parameters) statements ln FNEND	130 DEF FNT(A,B) 140 LET FNT=A+B 150 FNEND	12–2
DIM	ln DIM list of array declarations	100 DIM A(20),B(15,5)	10–1, 11–1
DO WHILE/ LOOP*	ln DO WHILE relational expression statements ln LOOP	270 DO WHILE A>B 280 LET A=A–1 290 LOOP	5–2
END	ln END	999 END	3–3
FOR/NEXT	ln FOR control variable=initial value TO limit STEP increment statements ln NEXT control variable	300 FOR I=1 TO 20 STEP 2 310 PRINT I 320 NEXT I	5–3
GO TO	ln GO TO ln	140 GO TO 110	3–3
GOSUB	ln GOSUB ln	350 GOSUB 400	12–3
IF	ln IF relational expression THEN ln	160 IF A>B THEN 200	4–1
IF*	ln IF relational expression GO TO ln	160 IF A>B GO TO 200	4–3
IF*	ln IF relational expression THEN statement	160 IF A>B THEN LET C=A–B	4–3
IF-THEN-ELSE*	ln IF relational expression THEN $\begin{Bmatrix} statement \\ ln \end{Bmatrix}$ ELSE $\begin{Bmatrix} statement \\ ln \end{Bmatrix}$	160 IF A>B THEN 200 ELSE LET C=B–A	4–3

IF/THEN/
ELSE/IFEND*
	ln IF relational expression
	ln THEN
	   statements
	ln ELSE
	   statements
	ln IFEND
		160 IF A>B
		170 THEN
		180 LET C=A–B
		190 ELSE
		200 LET C=B–A
		210 IFEND
			4–4

(continued)

371

TABLE 2 — Cont.

Statement	Syntax	Example	Section Reference
IF/THEN/ IFEND*	ln IF relational expression ln THEN 　　statements ln IFEND	220 IF A>B 230 THEN 240　　LET C=A–B 250 IFEND	4-4
INPUT	ln INPUT list of variables	110 INPUT B,C	3-3
INPUT #*	ln INPUT #number, list of variables	150 INPUT #1,A,B,C	13-2
LET	ln LET numeric variable=numeric expression	120 LET A=B+C	3-2
LET	ln LET string variable=string constant or string variable	220 LET S$="ABC"	9-1
LET*	ln LET string variable=string expression	230 LET S$="ABC"+T$	9-3
MAT addition*	ln MAT array variable=array variable+array variable	410 MAT C=A+B	11-2
MAT assignment*	ln MAT array variable=array variable	420 MAT A=B	11-2
MAT constant*	ln MAT array variable=CON	430 MAT A=CON	11-2
MAT identity*	ln MAT array variable=IDN	440 MAT A=IDN	11-2
MAT multipli- cation*	ln MAT array variable=array variable*array variable	450 MAT C=A*B	11-2
MAT scalar multiplication*	ln MAT array variable=(numeric expression)*array variable	460 MAT B=(2)*A	11-2
MAT subtraction*	ln MAT array variable=array variable–array variable	470 MAT C=A–B	11-2
MAT zero*	ln MAT array variable=ZER	480 MAT A=ZER	11-2
MAT INPUT*	ln MAT INPUT list of array variables	490 MAT INPUT A,B	11-2
MAT PRINT*	ln MAT PRINT array variable	500 MAT PRINT A	11-2
MAT READ*	ln MAT READ list of array variables	510 MAT READ A,B	11-2
ON-GO TO	ln ON numeric expression GO TO ln,ln, . . .	170 ON K GO TO 100,250,200,250	4-5

372

Statement	Syntax	Example	Reference
ON-GOSUB*	ln ON numeric expression GOSUB ln,ln,...	260 ON K GOSUB 400,500,600	12-3
OPEN*	ln OPEN "file name" FOR {INPUT / OUTPUT} AS FILE number	100 OPEN "ABFILE" FOR INPUT AS FILE 1	13-2
OPTION BASE	ln OPTION BASE {0 / 1}	100 OPTION BASE 1	10-1
PRINT	ln PRINT output list	130 PRINT A,B,C	3-3, 6-1
PRINT #	ln PRINT #number,output list	160 PRINT #2,X;"";Y	13-2
PRINT USING*	ln PRINT USING "format",list of variables	360 PRINT USING "### ###",A,B	6-4
RANDOMIZE	ln RANDOMIZE	100 RANDOMIZE	8-3
READ	ln READ list of variables	130 READ A,B,C	6-3
REM	ln REM remark	100 REM - ADD TWO NUMBERS	3-3
RESTORE	ln RESTORE	150 RESTORE	6-3
RETURN	ln RETURN	799 RETURN	12-3
STOP	ln STOP	500 STOP	12-3
SUB/SUBEND*	ln SUB name(parameters) statements ln SUBEND	800 SUB TOT(A,B,C) 810 LET C=A+B 820 SUBEND	12-4

TABLE 3

BUILT-IN FUNCTIONS

Function	Meaning	Section Reference
TAB(X)	Tabulate to print position X	6-1
SQR(X)	Square root of X	8-1
ABS(X)	Absolute value of X	8-1
ATN(X)	Arctangent (in radians) of X	8-1
COS(X)	Cosine of X (X must be in radians)	8-1
EXP(X)	Exponential of X (that is, e^X)	8-1
LOG(X)	Natural logarithm of X (that is, lnX)	8-1
SGN(X)	Sign of X (that is, -1 if $X<0$, 0 if $X=0$, $+1$ if $X>0$)	8-1
SIN(X)	Sine of X (X must be in radians)	8-1
TAN(X)	Tangent of X (X must be in radians)	8-1
INT(X)	Largest integer less than or equal to X	8-2
RND	Random number between 0 and 1	8-3
LEFT(A$,N)*	Left N characters of A$	9-3
RIGHT(A$,N)*	Right part of A$ beginning with the Nth character	9-3
MID(A$,M,N)*	Middle N characters of A$ beginning with the Mth character	9-3
LEN(A$)*	Number of characters in A$	9-3
TRN(A)*	Transpose of matrix A	11-2
INV(A)*	Inverse of matrix A	11-2

B

FLOWCHARTING

A tool often used to help design a computer program and to document a program is a *program flowchart*. A flowchart is a diagram of the logic in a computer program. As an example, Fig. B–1 shows a flowchart of the interest-calculation program discussed in Chapter 3 (see Fig. 3–5). This program accepts a bank balance and interest rate, calculates the interest and end-of-year balance, and prints the results. Notice that the flowchart depicts this sequence of steps. The flowchart is drawn by using special symbols connected by lines. Within each symbol is written a phrase that describes the activity at that step. The lines connecting the symbols show the sequence in which the steps take place.

During the program-designing activity the programmer may prepare rough flowcharts of how he or she thinks the program should work. Sometimes several flowcharts are drawn so that different designs can be compared. After the program logic is worked out with the rough diagrams, a final flowchart is drawn. The programmer can then code the program directly from the flowchart.

When the program is being tested, errors may be detected in the logic. If this happens, changes need to be made not only in the program but also in the flowchart. The final flowchart should depict precisely the logic in the completed program and serve as documentation to enable other programmers to understand this logic more easily.

Flowchart Symbols

In a flowchart the shape of the symbol indicates the type of activity that is to take place. Figure B–2 shows the standard program flowchart

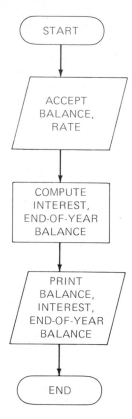

FIGURE B-1.   Flowchart of the interest calculation
program.

symbols adopted by the American National Standards Institute (ANSI).
The *process symbol* is used to represent any general processing activity
such as an arithmetic calculation or a manipulation of data. The *input/
output symbol* is used for any step that involves input or output of
data. The *decision symbol* is used whenever a decision is made in the
program. The *terminal point symbol* appears at the beginning and at the
end of the flowchart. The *connector symbol* is used to connect parts of
a flowchart. *Flowlines* show the direction of the flow of logic in the
flowchart. The normal direction is from top to bottom and left to
right. Arrowheads on the lines are optional (but generally used) if the
normal flow is followed and required if the direction of flow is other
than normal. Finally, the *annotation symbol* is used for additional
comments or notes. This symbol may be open on either the right or the
left, with the dashed line extending to the symbol that requires comment. All of these symbols are illustrated in flowcharts in this appendix.

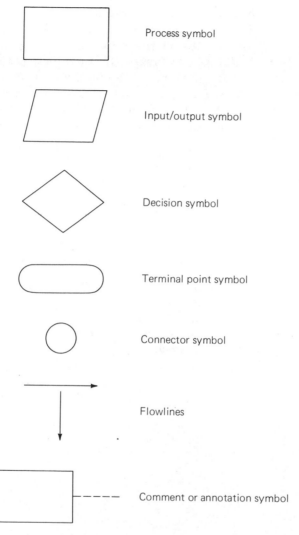

Process symbol

Input/output symbol

Decision symbol

Terminal point symbol

Connector symbol

Flowlines

Comment or annotation symbol

FIGURE B-2. ANSI flowchart symbols.

Simple Flowcharts

Figure B-1 illustrates a simple flowchart using some of these symbols. The terminal point symbol is used to mark the point where the flowchart logic starts and where it ends. The input/output symbol shows where the input data is accepted and the output is printed. The process symbol is used for the calculation step. Notice that the flowchart symbols do not necessarily correspond directly to individual instructions in the program. For example, the process symbol in the flowchart in Fig. B-1 corresponds to two arithmetic calculations in the program. However, the *sequence* of symbols does follow exactly the *sequence* of instructions in the program. By beginning with the symbol marked START and following the flowlines through the flowchart to the END symbol, the logic of the program can be understood.

Another example of a simple flowchart is shown in Fig. B-3. This is the flowchart of the payroll-calculation program discussed in Chapter 3 (see Fig. 3-9). In this flowchart, each calculation is shown as a sepa-

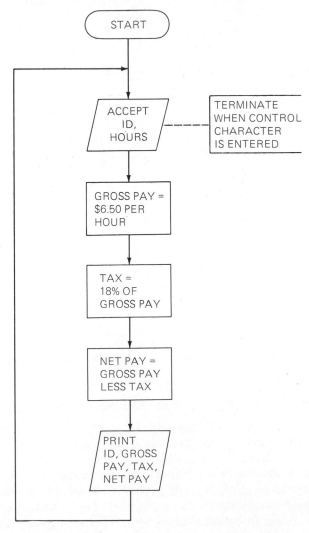

FIGURE B-3.   Flowchart of the payroll calculation
program.

rate step. Notice that the order of these steps corresponds to the order of the LET statements in the program.

This figure also demonstrates how a loop is represented in a flowchart. A loop is shown by a flowline extending from the end of the loop to its beginning. Notice that there is no separate symbol for a GO TO statement; branching from one point to another is simply indicated by a flowline. There is also no symbol in this flowchart to show where the flowchart logic ends. The loop in this flowchart does not contain any step that automatically stops the repetition. Instead, the loop is terminated when a special control character is entered. This fact is clarified in the flowchart by the use of an annotation symbol.

Flowcharting Decisions

The flowchart in Fig. B-4 depicts the logic in the tuition-calculation program discussed in Chapter 4 (see Fig. 4-1). This flowchart uses the decision symbol to show the test of whether the number of units is greater than twelve. Whenever a decision symbol is used, two or more flowlines *must* leave the symbol. These lines represent possible answers to the question asked in the symbol. The flowlines leaving a decision symbol *must* be labeled with the possible answers. The decision symbol in Fig. B-4 asks whether the number of units is greater than twelve and the possible answers — yes and no — are written above the flowlines leaving the symbol.

This flowchart depicts the basic decision logic discussed in Chapter 4. If a condition is true, one thing is done; otherwise something else is done. After the necessary processing, the logical flow comes together to continue with the next step.

A nested decision can be depicted in a flowchart. Figure B-5 shows a flowchart for the tuition-calculation program with a nested decision (see Fig. 4-9). Notice that after the first decision is made, a second decision is required. The nesting of the decisions shows up very clearly in the flowchart.

This flowchart also shows the use of the connector symbol. This symbol is used when it is necessary but inconvenient to connect distant parts of a flowchart with a flowline or when it is necessary to continue a flowchart onto another page. When the connector symbol is used, it appears once where the flow logic leaves one part of the chart and again where the logic enters the other part. An identifying letter or number is placed within each set of connectors. In Fig. B-5, the letter A identifies the pair of connectors. If another set of connector symbols is needed for another part of the flowchart, a different letter or symbol such as B is used.

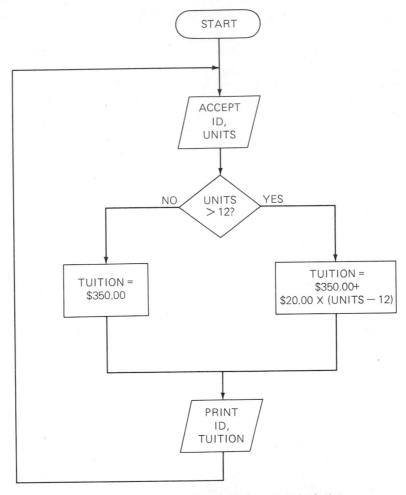

FIGURE B-4.   Flowchart of the tuition calculation
program.

Flowcharting Loop Control

When a loop is controlled by any of the techniques discussed in
Section 5-1, the condition that determines when the loop is to be
terminated is indicated by a decision within the loop. For example,
Fig. B-6 shows the flowchart for the tuition-calculation program with
the input loop controlled by a trailer value (see Fig. 5-2). The first
step after the input operation is to check for the trailer value. If the
value of ID is 9999, the processing stops. This step is shown in the
flowchart by a decision symbol.

Figure B-7 shows the flowchart for the interest-calculation program

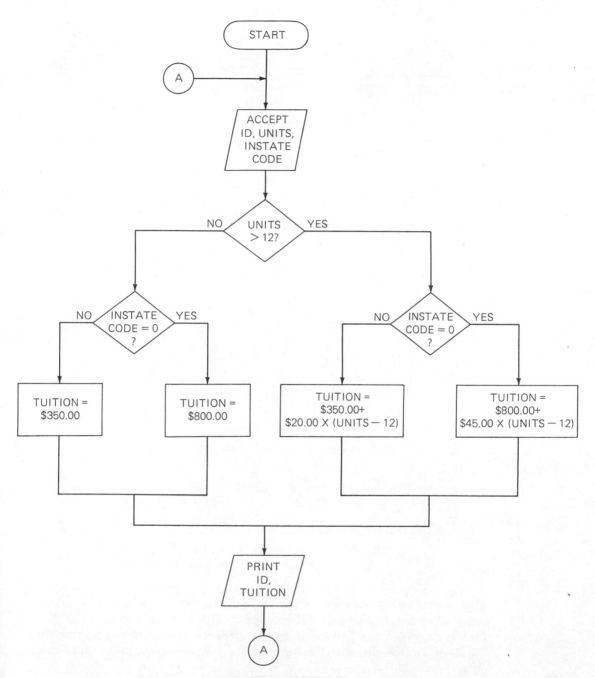

FIGURE B-5. Flowchart of the tuition calculation
program with nested decisions.

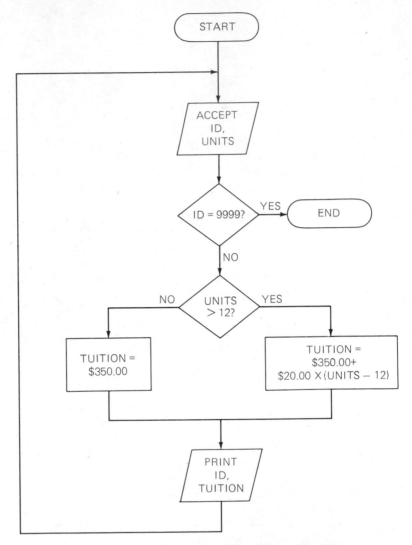

FIGURE B-6. Flowchart of the tuition calculation
program with input loop control.

with a processing loop (see Fig. 5-3). In this program the loop terminates when the bank balance becomes greater than or equal to $2000.
This is shown in the flowchart by the decision step at the beginning of
the loop. Notice also that the balance and year are initialized before the
loop is entered.

When a program includes a counting loop, the corresponding flowchart must show the steps that initialize the counter, modify the
counter, and test the counter. Figure B-8 is a flowchart of the program
that finds the total and average of twenty test scores (see Fig. 5-5).

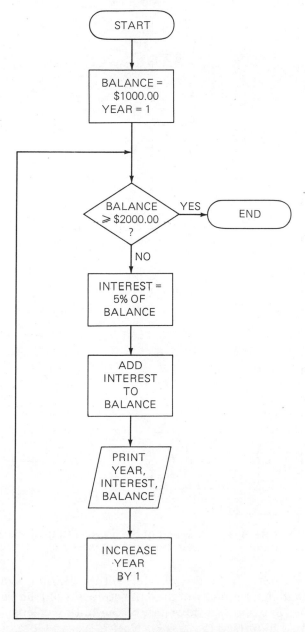

FIGURE B-7.   Flowchart of the interest calculation
              program with a processing loop.

The loop is executed exactly twenty times. The counter is initialized
to one before the loop is entered. Each time through the loop, the
counter is increased by one and tested to determine whether it is
greater than twenty.

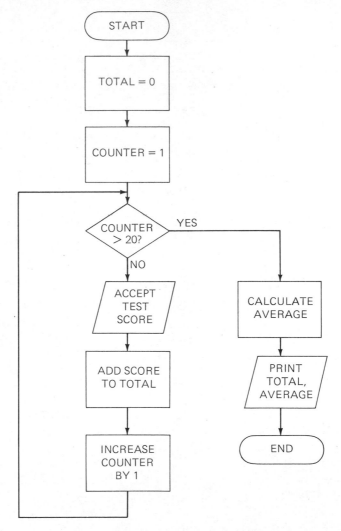

FIGURE B-8.   Flowchart of the program to total and
average twenty test scores.

A WHILE loop can be flowcharted with a decision symbol for the condition that determines whether the loop should be repeated. For example, Fig. B-9 shows a flowchart of the tuition-calculation program with a WHILE loop (see Fig. 5-11). Notice that the loop is repeated as long as the condition is true.

There is no standard way of flowcharting a FOR loop. The FOR and NEXT statements imply all of the operations necessary to control a counting loop. One approach is to show the initialization, modification, and testing of the control variable as separate steps in the flowchart. However, this can be cumbersome when many loops are involved.

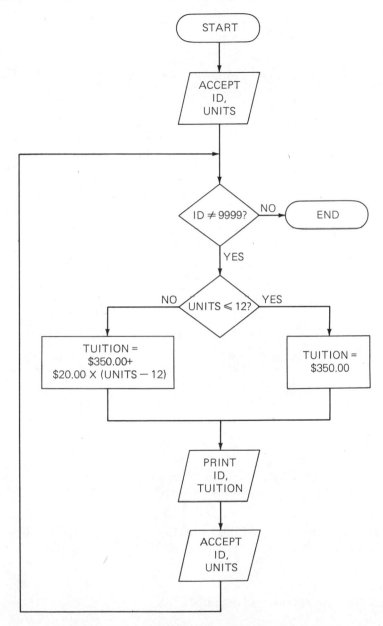

FIGURE B-9. Flowchart of the tuition calculation
program with a WHILE loop.

Another approach is shown in Fig. B–10, which is the flowchart of the
program to total and average twenty test scores using a FOR loop (see
Fig. 5–16). In this flowchart a single symbol is used for the FOR and
NEXT statements. The symbol shows the initialization of the control

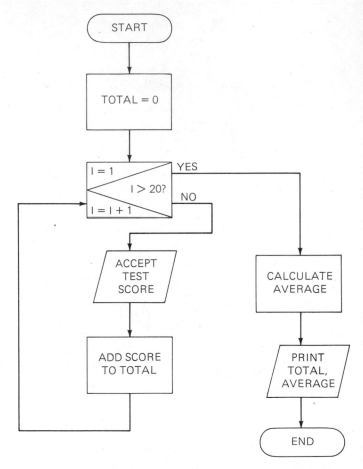

FIGURE B-10.   Flowchart of the program to total and
average twenty test scores using a FOR
loop.

variable (I=1), the testing of the variable (I>20?), and the modification
of the control variable (I=I+1). The loop is repeated until the test becomes true.

Flowcharting Advanced Programs

The flowcharts shown in this appendix illustrate basic concepts of
flowcharting. Flowcharts of more complex programs are drawn in the
same manner, but with more steps. Such complex flowcharts often
cover many pages. There are a number of good textbooks that describe
both elementary and advanced flowcharting.[†]

[†]A complete description of flowcharting can be found in Marilyn Bohl's book,
Flowcharting Techniques, published by Science Research Associates, Inc.

ANSWERS
TO SELECTED
REVIEW QUESTIONS

Chapter 1

1. electronic, internal storage, stored program

3. input

5. printer

7. central processing unit (CPU) or processor

9. Each instruction in the program is brought from the internal storage to the processor where it is analyzed by the control circuits. Then signals are sent to the other units based on what the instruction tells the computer to do.

11. magnetic disk, magnetic tape

13. In batch processing all data that is to be processed is gathered together in a batch and then processed by the computer. Weekly payroll preparation is an example of batch processing. With interactive processing, each piece of data is entered directly into the computer (usually through a terminal) and then processed before the next data is entered. In effect, a human interacts with the computer. Airline reservation processing is an example of interactive processing.

15. syntax

17. A machine language program needs no translation in order to be executed. A high-level language program must first be translated into machine language before it can be executed.

19. compilation or interpretation

Chapter 2

1. statement

3. Keywords are words that have special meanings in BASIC.

5. The LET statement performs a calculation and stores the result in a storage location.

7. the program

9. Syntax errors are discovered when the program is entered. They are usually errors in the use of the language. Execution errors are discovered during the execution of the program. Logic errors are the result of not using the correct processing method in the program.

11. understand the problem, design the program, code the program, test the program, document the program

Chapter 3

1. (a) valid
   (c) invalid

2. (a) 423000
   (c) .0000001234

3. (a) −3.8204E4
   (c) 1E7

4. (a) invalid
   (c) invalid

5. answer depends on computer being used

7. (a) X^2−2*X+3
   (c) (A−B)/(A+B)

8. (a) 3
   (c) 13

9. 50 LET M=D/G

11. The value of X is halved.

13. Two lines are printed. The first line contains five values;

the second line has one value.

15. A question mark prompt is printed on the terminal and the computer waits for input data to be entered.

17. loop

19. 123   260   46.8   213.2

Chapter 4

1. (a) greater than
   (c) not equal to

3. 50 IF X<>Y THEN 200

4. (a) false
   (c) true

5. (a) 80
   (c) 260

6. (a) A<>B
   (c) P<=Q

7. (a) 234 180 32.4   147.6
   (c) 456 144 25.92 118.08

9. nested decisions

10. (a) 1001   350
    (c) 1003   800

11. (a) 123   410
    (c) 345   350
    (e) 567   250

13. 50 ON A GO TO 100,200, 100,100,200,300

Chapter 5

1. A trailer value is an input value that is used to signal the end of the input data.

3. 9

5. 228   76

7. answer depends on version of BASIC being used

9. 10 FOR J=20 TO 2 STEP –2
   20 PRINT J
   30 END

10. (a) 10
    (c) 7

11. The control variable is modified at the end of the loop and tested at the beginning.

12. (a) input loop
    (c) uncontrolled loop
    (e) WHILE loop

Chapter 6

1. 50 PRINT "OUTPUT DATA", A,B

3. The following answers assume that each print zone is fourteen print positions. The print positions are listed across the top.

```
          11111111112222222222333333
 12345678901234567890123456789012345
```

(a)   2   3   4
(c)   2
(e)   2   DATA

5. answer depends on version of BASIC being used

7. 50 READ A,B,C
   60 DATA 2,3,4

9. 1001   410

Chapter 7

1. sequence structure, decision structure, loop structure

2. (a) decision

(c) sequence

3. Because each basic structure has a single entry point and a single exit point, any structure can be nested in any other structure and the result will have a single entry point and a single exit point.

5. case

7. With the uncontrolled use of GO TO statements, program structures other than the basic ones may be used. As a consequence, the program may be more difficult to understand.

9. The remark merely parrots the code that follows. It should not be in the program.

                 3 DATA

11.

Statement	V1	V2	V3	I
100	8	12	4	—
200	8	12	4	—
210	8	12	4	—
220	8	12	4	—
230	8	12	4	—
250	8	12	4	—
260	8	12	4	12
270	8	4	4	12
280	8	4	12	12
300	8	4	12	12
310	8	4	12	8
320	4	4	12	8
330	4	8	12	8
400	4	8	12	8

13. an algorithm

15. The following input values for X would test the program:

   100
   115
   125
   126
   150
   200

17. Coding involves writing the instructions for a program on a piece of paper. It is one step in the programming process. Programming is the whole set of activities associated with preparing a computer program.

Chapter 8

1. answer depends on version of BASIC being used

3. (a) 2
   (c) 0
   (e) 1
   (g) 1

5. 9   12   108   10

7. A random number is a number that is as likely to be produced as any other number.

9. 50 LET Y=INT(52*RND)+1

11. answer depends on game

Chapter 9

1. (a) valid
   (c) invalid
   (e) valid

2. (a) invalid
   (c) valid

3. a string with no characters in it

5. 50 INPUT A$,B$,C$
   60 PRINT C$,B$,A$

7. (a) false
   (c) false in ANS BASIC, true in most other versions
   (e) false

9. substring

10. (a) XYZ123
    (c) 123
    (e) A

11. concatenation

12. (a) ABCXYZ
    (c) ABCDEF

Chapter 10

1. (a) An array is a list of data identified by a single variable.
   (c) An array element is an individual value in an array.

3. (a) 20.5
   (c) 5.7

5. 150 FOR I=20 TO 1 STEP –1
   160   PRINT A(I)
   170 NEXT I

7. 210 LET T=0
   220 FOR I=1 TO 19 STEP 2
   230   LET T=T+A(I)
   240 NEXT I

9. (a) ITEM 1172 COST 3.75

10. (a) ITEM 1025 NOT FOUND

11. Before   After

7	7	7	7	7
10	10	6	6	6
6	6	10	4	4
4	4	4	10	10
12	12	12	12	12

I = 1   I = 2   I = 3   I = 4

Chapter 11

1. One-dimensional array: can be thought of as organized in one direction such as a column; requires one subscript to identify an element.

   Two-dimensional array: can be thought of as organized in two directions such as rows and columns; requires two subscripts to identify an element.

2. (a) 100
   (c) 96

3. 100 DIM A(5,15),B(100,2)

5. 40 LET T=0
   50 FOR I=1 TO 4
   60   FOR J=1 TO 12
   70   LET T=T+X(I,J)
   80   NEXT J
   90 NEXT I

7. 40 FOR I=10 TO 1 STEP –1
   50   FOR J=1 TO 4
   60   PRINT Z(I,J),
   70   NEXT J
   80   PRINT
   90 NEXT I

9. (a) 110 MAT A=CON
   (c) 130 MAT PRINT B
   (e) 150 MAT B=ZER

10. (a) 210 MAT F=D+E

(c) 230 MAT C=IDN
(e) 250 MAT C=E*G

Chapter 12

1. Function: single line; defined by a DEF statement; called as part of a numeric expression; placed at the beginning of the program.

   Subroutine: multiple lines ending with a RETURN statement; called by a GOSUB statement; usually placed at the end of the program.

3. 100 DEF FNA(B)=B*(1+R)^Y

5. local, global

7. 100 DEF FNZ(X,Y)
   110 IF X<Y THEN 170
   120 IF X>Y THEN 150
   130 LET FNZ=30
   140 GO TO 180
   150 LET FNZ=X–Y+20
   160 GO TO 180
   170 LET FNZ=Y–X+10
   180 FNEND

9. 50 GOSUB 500

11. 70   90   80   240   80
    85   60   75   220   73.3333

13. 1000 SUB SUMDIF(S,D,A,B)
    1010 LET S=A+B
    1020 LET D=A–B
    1030 SUBEND

    500 CALL SUMDIF(S1,D1,X,Y)

15. Top-down coding and testing involves coding and testing one part of a program at a time beginning with the main part and working down to the subroutines. This

often involves coding "dummy" subroutines (called *stubs*) that simulate but do not actually perform the functions of subroutines called by a higher part of the program.

17. menu

Chapter 13

1. programs, data

3. field

5. A key field is a field that is used to identify a record.

7. output

9. input, output

11. (a) 100 OPEN "FILEX" FOR INPUT AS FILE 1

(b) 200 INPUT #1,A,B,C,D,E

(c) 300 CLOSE 1

13. A trailer record is the last record in a sequential file. Its purpose is to indicate the end of the file.

15. sequential

17. (a) four

(b) three

(c) four

19. The value of the key field can be the record location. A table or index can be set up which contains each key field and the location of the corresponding record in the file.

INDEX